Continuous Deployment
Enable Faster Feedback, Safer Releases, and More Reliable Software

Valentina Servile
Foreword by David Farley

Beijing · Boston · Farnham · Sebastopol · Tokyo

Continuous Deployment

by Valentina Servile

Published by O'Reilly Media, Inc., 1005 Gravenstein Highway North, Sebastopol, CA 95472.

O'Reilly books may be purchased for educational, business, or sales promotional use. Online editions are also available for most titles (*http://oreilly.com*). For more information, contact our corporate/institutional sales department: 800-998-9938 or *corporate@oreilly.com*.

Acquisitions Editor: Louise Corrigan	**Indexer:** nSight, Inc.
Development Editor: Shira Evans	**Interior Designer:** David Futato
Production Editor: Jonathon Owen	**Cover Designer:** Karen Montgomery
Copyeditor: Audrey Doyle	**Illustrator:** Kate Dullea
Proofreader: Helena Stirling	

August 2024:   First Edition

Revision History for the First Edition

2024-07-24:   First Release

See *http://oreilly.com/catalog/errata.csp?isbn=9781098146726* for release details.

978-1-098-14672-6

[LSI]

Table of Contents

Part IV. After Development

Foreword

In the last couple of decades I believe that we, the software development industry, have made many significant advances, but perhaps the most important, because it is the most fundamental, is in our approach to the development process itself.

We have more firmly established the roots of our discipline: an engineering approach based on small, iterative, incremental steps, gathering feedback after each tiny step on the quality of our work. This is the process used by nearly all of the organizations that we think of as examples of excellence in software development these daysfrom SpaceX and Tesla to Google, Amazon, Facebook, and Netflix—as well as many many more in every field of software development from AAA games to medical devices. In addition to this empirical evidence for the success of this approach, we also have evidence from the most scientifically justifiable and longest-running research into the practice of software development undertaken so far: the DORA research, which predicts that with the adoption of the techniques of continuous delivery and continuous deployment, you will build better software faster.

This progress is built on a sequence of steps forward that the industry has taken, of which my work has been a part. It began with Kent Beck's extreme programming and continuous integration and progressed through my work and others' on the practices of continuous delivery and DevOps, but the logical conclusion of those steps is to take them all the way to production. Continuous delivery does that but leaves the decision to actually release less clearly defined, which leaves the option for this to be a manual decision.

The ultimate step is to automate that decision too. In some ways, this may seem like a small decision—after all, the definition of continuous delivery that Jez Humble and I promoted in our book says, "Work so that your software is always in a releasable state." We then proceeded to explain how to automate the determination of "releasable" that underpins that.

But when we wrote our book, frequent releases for most people meant weekly or daily. These days the organizations that push the boundaries talk about "releases per second," and even for complex software in a hardware-focused environment, the boundaries have changed. Tesla famously reconfigured the physical charging system in their Model 3 to increase the maximum charge rate from 200 kW to 250 kW, and the change took them three hours, from commit to 250-kW cars rolling off the production line!

There is a chapter in our book Continuous Delivery on the next step, continuous deployment, but we don't go into much detail. This book corrects that omission. Continuous Deployment is the proof of the pudding. It is not until our software is in the hands of users delivering value that we really know that our job is done. It is only at this point that this feedback loop of immense value is closed. It is this that enables teams to build great products more easily and more reliably.

This book explores the ideas of continuous deployment in some depth, looking at many of the nuances and complexities with examples and solutions. It explores a wide range of topics from broad deployment automation strategies like "keep your pipeline fast" through design and architectural advice like "keep things stateless where you can" and "switch to event-based architecture" to more detailed pieces of advice on topics like the invalidation of client-side Caches.

I found this book to be interesting and engaging, and as an aside to the technical content, extremely well written and easy to read. I thank the author, Valentina, for an excellent addition to the literature, and I recommend this book to you.

— *Dave Farley*

Preface

This is a book about *continuous deployment*: the practice of structuring your software pipeline so that it is completely free of manual intervention. With this methodology, every code commit that passes its quality gates is automatically deployed to production.

This topic brings to the surface an often debated tension in software engineering: getting to production quickly versus getting to production safely. On the surface, continuous deployment might look like the former, but on closer inspection, it really aligns with the latter. On even closer inspection, I would argue that we don't have to choose.

In the past couple of decades, we have seen a number of practices showcasing how speed and reliability actually go hand in hand when it comes to delivering software. DevOps, eXtreme Programming (XP), continuous integration (CI), and continuous delivery (CD): these practices have demonstrated again and again how shorter iterations improve the stability of production systems, rather than hindering it. This is because shorter iterations reduce the size of changes in each release, foster communication across roles, encourage a culture of automation, and allow for early and continuous feedback. Overall, shorter iterations and frequent deployments improve software's stability and quality.

I consider continuous deployment to be the natural next step in this line of thinking.

During my career as a software consultant, I was lucky enough to work with several companies that were already practicing continuous deployment or that adopted it shortly after I joined their team. I loved its simplicity and speed, and to this day I truly believe it was the most efficient way of developing software that I stumbled upon. However, I also noticed how not everyone was comfortable with it at first. This was especially true for junior colleagues, or new joiners who had never worked with the practice before. Understandably, code going to production within minutes can be quite the culture shock if you are used to extended phases of manual testing, long feature branches, and manual approvals. I found myself wanting to help by sharing resources on how to approach it, but I found a literature vacuum around the practice.

Therefore, the only thing I could share was how I adjusted my own workflow and how I started writing code differently once I knew the deployment to production would be almost immediate.

I found that I was repeating myself often enough, on team after team, that perhaps this was an idea worth sharing with a wider audience. I didn't know it then, but in my head I had already started writing the contents of this book.

I found that continuous deployment is an increment of continuous delivery that is significant enough to warrant its own discussion. It is significant because it brings extra benefits, has extra downsides, and requires some extra considerations to work well within a team. All of those "extras" are what we'll cover in this book, building on the foundation of continuous delivery to explore fully automated continuous deployment to production.

Who This Book Is For

I wrote this book for fellow software industry professionals, and especially for software engineers who see value in improving their code's path to production.

In particular, this book is for you if:

- You are already familiar with continuous delivery, but not with continuous deployment, and you are curious to learn more about it.
- You are familiar with continuous deployment and are wondering whether it is a viable next step for your team.
- You are already set in your decision to transition to continuous deployment, but you want to know what to expect once you remove the manual gate to production.
- You are starting a greenfield product and want to use this opportunity to try continuous deployment, but you are wondering how to set it up from scratch.
- You are in the process of joining a team that already adopts continuous deployment, and you want to understand why and how they do it.

Even though this book's primary audience is people who write code on a daily basis, the book can also be valuable to people in other roles, such as QA engineers, product owners, product managers, Scrum Masters, engineering managers, and people in a variety of technical leadership positions. If your job title is in this list, you might be particularly interested in Part I, "Continuous Deployment" which provides a more holistic view of the practice. In addition, chapters in Part II, "Before Development" and Part IV, "After Development" explain how to integrate other team roles in a workflow of automated deployments to production, which is fundamental to harnessing their full potential.

If you are a developer, you might want to especially focus on Part III, "During Development" which goes into great detail on how to break the development process into small, self-contained production deployments. You should also take a look at Part V, "Case Studies" where you'll find real-world examples of companies practicing continuous deployment and see how they structure their pipelines and tools.

What You Need to Read This Book

Because continuous deployment builds on many other concepts that originated from the Agile movement, such as DevOps, CI, and CD, you should at least have some surface-level familiarity with them if you want to get the most out of this book.

Fortunately, most companies today have at least some knowledge of those practices, and they already implement them to some degree. I will provide a thorough recap of XP, DevOps, CI, and CD in Chapter 1 so that you can go back to the "why" and refresh your memory.

However, if you and/or your team have never heard of these practices before, you might want to look into them before you consider adopting continuous deployment, and leave this book for later.

What This Book Will Cover

The book consists of five parts, which are organized as follows:

Part I, "Continuous Deployment"
> This part of the book contains all the theory and explains all you need to know about continuous deployment as a practice. Chapter 1 provides an introduction and historical context for it, Chapter 2 explains its benefits, Chapter 3 focuses on its consequences and main "gotchas," Chapter 4 explains the prerequisites needed to adopt it, and Chapter 5 focuses on its challenges.

Part II, "Before Development"
> This is where things start to get more practical. This part of the book focuses on all the activities that support continuous deployment before the team starts writing code, and it is where I introduce the example that will be used throughout the rest of the book. In particular, Chapter 6 explains how to best slice your product backlog to leverage frequent deployments, while Chapter 7 focuses on how to bundle cross-functional requirements to make each increment production-ready.

Part III, "During Development"
> In this part of the book, we get into the details that can make or break continuous deployment: how to perform day-to-day development as a sequence of small and safe production increments. Following the example introduced in Part II, this part also introduces thorough code samples. The samples are written in three

technologies that I chose due to their popularity in the industry: JavaScript with React.js, Java with SpringBoot, and SQL. Even if you have never used them before, they're so popular that you probably know them well enough that you can read the code even if you work in different stacks. Chapter 8 showcases the addition of a new feature deployment by deployment, and Chapter 9 focuses on how to incrementally refactor complex functionality that is already live. Finally, Chapter 10 focuses on the intricacies of refactoring data stores with automated deployments.

Part IV, "After Development"
Part IV is where you'll learn about all the activities that happen after development, where continuous deployment really comes to fruition. Chapter 11 covers how to safely perform exploratory testing in production, and Chapter 12 covers all flavors of releases and A/B tests.

Part V, "Case Studies"
Finally, Part V consists of a number of case studies written by fellow industry professionals. It contains the firsthand experiences of companies that use continuous deployment "in the wild," including the history of how they got there, which challenges they faced, and how they structure their products' path to production.

Conventions Used in This Book

The following typographical conventions are used in this book:

Italic
Indicates new terms, URLs, email addresses, filenames, and file extensions.

`Constant width`
Used for program listings, as well as within paragraphs to refer to program elements such as variable or function names, databases, data types, environment variables, statements, and keywords.

This element signifies a general note.

This element indicates a warning or caution.

O'Reilly Online Learning

O'REILLY® For more than 40 years, *O'Reilly Media* has provided technology and business training, knowledge, and insight to help companies succeed.

Our unique network of experts and innovators share their knowledge and expertise through books, articles, and our online learning platform. O'Reilly's online learning platform gives you on-demand access to live training courses, in-depth learning paths, interactive coding environments, and a vast collection of text and video from O'Reilly and 200+ other publishers. For more information, visit *https://oreilly.com*.

How to Contact Us

Please address comments and questions concerning this book to the publisher:

O'Reilly Media, Inc.
1005 Gravenstein Highway North
Sebastopol, CA 95472
800-889-8969 (in the United States or Canada)
707-827-7019 (international or local)
707-829-0104 (fax)
support@oreilly.com
https://www.oreilly.com/about/contact.html

We have a web page for this book, where we list errata, examples, and any additional information. You can access this page at *https://oreil.ly/continuous-deployment*.

For news and information about our books and courses, visit *https://oreilly.com*.

Find us on LinkedIn: *https://linkedin.com/company/oreilly-media*

Watch us on YouTube: *https://youtube.com/oreillymedia*

Acknowledgments

When people say "this book would not have been possible without…," I find that it's usually an exaggeration. In my case, however, it's really true. This book would definitely not exist had I not received the support I did from two colleagues at Thoughtworks: Chris Ford and Andrew-Harmel Law, who encouraged me throughout the process and offered thoughtful technical review and input (some of which became a core part of this book). The same is true for several people in my personal life, but particularly Fergus Orbach, who provided all sorts of technical back-and-forth and fueled my passion for this topic; and Daniel Forsberg, who offered his expertise to help me finish the very last chapters. Thank you both for supporting me through the year while I was writing this book. For the same reason, I want to thank my good friends Rares Musina, Emma Baddeley, Anthony Scatchell, Giulia Mercurio, Glenn Wolfschoon, Nicolò Gardoni, Francesco Guatieri, and Davide Orsucci.

I want to also express my gratitude to the people at O'Reilly who made this project a reality, especially my editors, Shira Evans and Louise Corrigan. You have been a pleasure to work with. I would add to this list all my colleagues at Thoughtworks who helped me find time to dedicate to this book, gather the case studies, and promote the book, but there are too many of you to mention. Instead, I will express my thanks to Thoughtworks as a whole for making this happen: I received an incredible amount of support for this project, proving that Thoughtworks keeps being a fantastic place for growing thought leadership and aspiring writers.

Speaking of case studies, I want to sincerely thank all the companies and individuals who contributed to this book with their firsthand experiences: Maarten Ackermans, Julian Austin, Ilias Bartolini, Alberto Ramírez Fernández, Atte Huhtakangas, Lloyd Jones, Simon Mittermüller, Roberto Mosca, Alison Rosewarne, Javier Tejero, Thiago Vacare, and Tom Vollerthun.

Continuous Deployment

Part I offers an overview of the theory behind continuous deployment. It starts with an introduction and historical background and then discusses its benefits and the shift in mindset required to accommodate automated deployments. It also addresses challenges, downsides, and critical aspects to be aware of. Finally, it covers the technical and organizational prerequisites needed to adopt this practice.

CHAPTER 1

Continuous Deployment

For as long as software engineering has been a discipline, a great deal of care and attention have been given to application code and its architecture. All manner of paradigms, programming languages, and architectural patterns have originated to ensure that code is both well-organized in developers' editors and running efficiently later in production. It took more than half a century to collectively realize that we hadn't given enough thought to what happens in between.

Deploying Every Few Months or Years

Before the early 2000s, the average software product's path to production was an error-prone and clunky journey full of repetitive manual tasks. On this journey, changes from individual contributors were often integrated with delays, artifacts were built by hand, configurations and dependencies were tweaked outside of version control, poorly documented deployment steps were executed in meticulous sequences... and let's not forget testing, which was performed painstakingly by hand for every new version. As a result, release life cycles could span months or even *years*. Figure 1-1 is a fact-based depiction of those times.

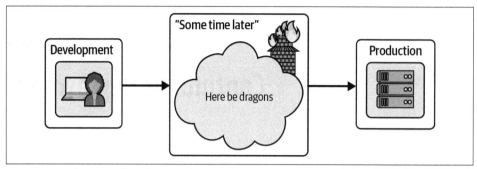

Figure 1-1. The typical path to production before the early 2000s

Such a lengthy path to production meant that all the up-front engineering investment in software design would not pay off until much later. Often, by the time new code finally found its way to users (if it ever did), the original requirements would have already changed—or, sadly, the market would have moved on, thus making the code irrelevant.

Fortunately, that has changed. Over the past two decades, businesses and organizations have become increasingly accustomed to shipping software rapidly in order to drive their operations without sacrificing reliability. Even in a (highly) hypothetical scenario where a company can brag about a flawless codebase and excellent product, a big-bang release every year or two is no longer a sustainable strategy for keeping up with market demands. That is why, in the past couple of decades, we have seen increasing attention being given to shortening the journey from "code committed" to "code running in front of users." The focus is no longer just on writing good-quality code, but also on ensuring that it is swiftly and painlessly released to production. After all, production is the only environment where code can repay the debt it has incurred from having been written in the first place.

Deploying Every Few Days

Companies have already been making their software delivery life cycles shorter and shorter, and they have achieved this mainly through the use of automation. The rationale behind automation's benefit is no mystery. Any human task or human decision represents a bottleneck in the fast-paced world of software development. Both our typing and thinking are several orders of magnitude slower than the pace at which code is executed—and both are vastly more error-prone. Therefore, major components of the path to production that used to be performed manually, such as building artifacts, testing, and deployment, have instead been automated through various tools over time (see Figure 1-2).

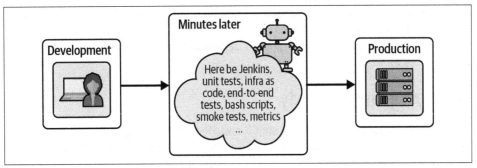

Figure 1-2. The typical path to production today

However, reducing the takeover of automation to merely "some tooling" would be doing a disservice to my readers, as the tooling is just one tangible result of something much more interesting: a set of schools of thought that changed the paradigm from writing code to *delivering software*. Practices such as eXtreme Programming (XP), DevOps, continuous integration (CI), and continuous delivery (CD), all now widely adopted, championed this shift in focus. If you haven't heard of them, I encourage you to familiarize yourself with them a bit more before diving into this book.[1] Continuous deployment stands on the shoulders of giants after all, and those are the giants' names.

XP, DevOps, CI, and CD introduced automation and repeatability into the path to production, from the moment code is checked in to the moment it is deployed, reducing manual intervention to a minimum. This automation provided the much-needed technical baseline to achieve speed without compromising safety. What followed was also a challenge for software engineers to cultivate an even broader set of skills around scripting and infrastructure, and to take ownership of their work on a level that far exceeds seeing their code run on a laptop. This mindset shift isn't constrained to only technical folks: these practices have also challenged organizations to rethink their overall culture (and structure) around the manufacture of custom software. Before them, huge batches of work were handed over from one segregated department to the next, with little to no communication between them. After them, we started seeing the emergence of cross-functional teams that are able to take care of their products from end to end.

---

1 Paul M. Duvall, *Continuous Integration: Improving Software Quality and Reducing Risk* (Boston: Addison-Wesley, 2007). Jez Humble and David Farley, *Continuous Delivery: Reliable Software Releases through Build, Test, and Deployment Automation* (Boston: Addison-Wesley, 2010). Kent Beck, *Extreme Programming Explained: Embrace Change* (Boston: Addison-Wesley, 2004). Gene Kim et al., *The DevOps Handbook: How to Create World-Class Agility, Reliability, & Security in Technology Organizations* (Portland, OR: IT Revolution Press, 2016).

These movements have already produced results that used to be unthinkable: making software release cycles more reliable and dramatically faster. As a result, more than two-thirds of companies are now able to deploy to production *between once per day and once per month*.[2]

Deploying Continuously

Continuous deployment is another step forward along the progression of engineering excellence that has seen automation taking over software's path to production. In a sense, continuous deployment represents its logical culmination. While its predecessors automated some or even *most* of the code's journey to users, continuous deployment automates it all. Even the decision to perform the final production deployment is made by a pipeline agent, not by a person.

In a nutshell, continuous deployment means that a commit being pushed or merged into the main branch always results in a production deployment (provided all quality gates are green). For the first time, the journey from "code committed" to "code running in front of users" encounters no manual intervention whatsoever, and it is completed at the granularity of every commit. By removing even the very last human bottleneck, continuous deployment further reduces the software feedback loop from days or hours to mere minutes.

Such a dramatic acceleration has important consequences for engineers, who work with the knowledge that the tiniest increment of code will be subjected to full production-quality feedback practically immediately. With continuous deployment, tasks are no longer "dev-done, pending production deployment is successful later"; they are actually and demonstrably done. Production deployments themselves become trivial in virtue of their frequency, since the delta of changes is just a few lines as opposed to days' or weeks' worth of accumulated changes, greatly reducing the risks associated with each deployment. (I will throw more light on the relationship between deployment size and deployment frequency in Chapter 2.)

But as is the case with most engineering practices, the real paradigm shift in continuous deployment is best evaluated from the point of view of the businesses that adopt it. If production code increments can be maximally granular and lightning fast, product increments can be too. Small (or big) product decisions can be made and reversed much more easily, and made at the last possible moment—which is also the most

---

2 See *https://oreil.ly/ZJS1G* to read the DORA "Accelerate State of DevOps Report 2023" in full.

responsible way to make such decisions.[3] Sudden surprises in user behavior or requirements can be addressed immediately, with no pending deployments clogging the path to production and complicating last-minute changes. Ordinary releases themselves are broken down into slices so small that it is possible to experiment and gauge user behavior with precision, if that is what one wishes to do. Such a process takes the "responding to change" value of Agile to the extreme, and offers the narrowest possible feedback loops within the paradigm of iterative development.

In my professional experience, continuous deployment has resulted in an improvement to all the metrics that mattered to my teams when delivering software: the time it took to deliver any given change, the number of changes we could deliver overall, the rate of defects, and the speed at which we recovered from them. In this book, I want to share that experience because I believe the conversation about the journey from "code committed" to "code running in production" is still very much ongoing. I hope this book will represent a positive contribution to this: placing continuous deployment on par with all those other well-beloved practices.

So how exactly does continuous deployment work? What else does it contribute to code's path to production that hasn't been achieved already? How does it differ from its very close relative, continuous delivery? And why does that difference matter?

To answer these questions, we need to go back to the origins of this automation movement and spend some time understanding the practices that came before it. Only by understanding the principles guiding its predecessors can we appreciate how continuous deployment builds on them.

Let's start chronologically: with the introduction of *eXtreme Programming*.

eXtreme Programming

Tasks such as testing, reviewing, integrating, and deploying are central to code's path to production, but they can also be painful and awkward to execute. As a result, they used to be relegated to the very end of long iterations, completed infrequently, and completed mostly by hand.

The change in discourse around these tasks picked up between the late 1990s and early 2000s with the popularization of eXtreme Programming (XP), which brought these noncoding activities at the margins of software development to the center of the conversation. XP is an Agile software methodology that emphasizes doing the most important parts of software development (which are not necessarily *writing* software)

---

3 The last responsible moment (LRM) is the strategy of delaying a decision until the moment when the cost of not making the decision is greater than the cost of making it, as explained by Mary and Tom Poppendieck in their book *Lean Software Development: An Agile Toolkit* (Addison-Wesley, 2003). This strategy helps you make decisions only when the maximum amount of information is available.

as often as possible. As Kent Beck writes in *Extreme Programming Explained*, "Take everything valuable about software engineering and turn the dials to 10."[4] This process involves practices such as pair programming, where two programmers work together at one workstation (thus reviewing code continuously); test-driven development, which involves writing tests before the code (testing continuously); and continuous integration, where code changes are integrated in the main branch as frequently as possible (this one even has "continuous" in the name).

XP was among the first movements to challenge the old-fashioned behavior of delaying painful steps, and it suggested instead that increasing the frequency of these tasks (doing them continuously) will in turn reduce their difficulty. It might seem counterintuitive, but the motto of XP was the first principle that enabled the automation of code's journey to production: "If it hurts, do it more often."

If It Hurts, Do It More Often

When I started out, I thought that if reviewing, integrating, testing, and deploying were painful, we would surely want to put them off as much as possible. Why on earth would we want to do them more often than we needed to? We could write our code in our little walled gardens (or feature branches) for weeks and weeks, and when the merge-and-release hell could not be postponed any longer, we could put our heads down for a few days and just get them over with. Then we could forget all about the ordeal and return to the peace and quiet of our personal code gardens. That is, until somebody asked our team to show another working version of the software, including all the new features we had been working on individually. Then, we would have to start all over again. *If only those annoying stakeholders stopped interrupting us with their demos and releases*, I thought. *Then, we developers could get the* real *work done around here!*

I started to grasp what "If it hurts, do it more often" really meant only after working in teams where we had to integrate and release on different schedules. Curiously, the shorter the cadence was, the less work our team had to do in order to get our software ready, and the less rework came back to our desks. "If it hurts, do it more often" is not about feeling more pain from integration and deployments but about how increasing their frequency enables us to feel *less* pain. And not just less pain in each release, but less pain overall.

Smaller, less-painful batches

Doing the most-painful activities, such as merging, testing, and deploying, more often means that smaller and smaller amounts of code need to go through that

---

4 Beck, *Extreme Programming Explained*, p. 127.

activity. That is because commits don't get a chance to accumulate while they wait to be processed. The more often we integrate, test, and deploy our software, the less software we need to integrate, test, and deploy each time.

By integrating often, change deltas get small enough to make merges straightforward. By deploying often, bugs that could have taken days of investigation can, within hours, be traced back to the change that introduced them; after all, the lines of code to sift through are so much fewer.

Incentive for automation

Doing things more often (and in smaller batches) is also a strong incentive for developers to streamline repetitive and risky processes. Automating a task—however nightmarish—that used to happen once every blue moon didn't make much sense before short iterations became the norm. But automating a daily sequence of error-prone steps certainly did. And so automation started to take over, and now we have pipelines automatically polling our latest code changes from version control, building artifacts from it, running all sorts of automated tests, and even performing deployments all on their own. We tend to automate these tasks when doing them more often highlights slowness and inefficiencies and frankly makes them just a lot of work. One of the best virtues of us programmers is our laziness.

As a result, the integrate, test, and release phases that we used to dread have become much less painful—basically, routine for a lot of companies. This didn't happen *despite* markets demanding we do these things more often, but *because* companies started doing these things more often.

Reduced pain and increased frequency have also allowed our businesses to gather feedback on new initiatives much earlier and helps reduce the ultimate waste: building things that users don't want or need.

Applying this idea of "doing painful things more often, in smaller batches, and automating as much as possible" has radically simplified the most painful parts of shipping software. But as we discussed, these improvements didn't happen all at once. Different practices took over from XP's early good instincts to play a big role in the following years. Following the "If it hurts, do it more often" principle, software's path to production was later automated one chunk at a time: starting from building artifacts and ending up at deployments to production.

For example, it could be said that the well-known practices of CI and CD are respectively rooted in the pain of integrating our code with other people's and the even worse pain of delivering production-ready software. Some might even say that the practice of DevOps is rooted in the pain of miscommunication and friction between traditional Dev and Ops departments.

Few people might quote XP nowadays, but the mindset that it sowed continues to guide teams and organizations as they shrink their feedback loops and go to market more and more quickly. Let's go through a bit more history to understand what happened following its introduction.

DevOps

DevOps is not a job title (sorry, recruiters), but the name of a movement that emerged as a response to the dysfunctional separation between the activities of writing and running software. It emerged between 2007 and 2008, and in 2009 Patrick Debois founded the first DevOpsDays conference.[5] The movement continued with the publishing of two key pieces of literature: *The Phoenix Project*[6] and later, *The DevOps Handbook*.[7]

DevOps aims to break down the traditional barrier between software development and IT operations, which used to be distinct and siloed departments. In other words, developers used to be focused solely on writing code, while operations was responsible for deploying it and maintaining it in production.

The DevOps movement sought to change that, as it identified that separation as the culprit for much of the pain associated with releasing and operating software at the time. Instead, it encouraged a culture of collaboration and integration between the two functions, with the aim of establishing a path of continuous learning from each other. On a technical level, this also encouraged continuous learning in terms of lessons learned in production being fed back into the development process.

Let's take a deeper look at those dysfunctions to understand why.

The Barrier Between Dev and Ops

Before DevOps, most development and operations teams worked in isolation from each other—sometimes physical isolation, with departments on different floors or even in different buildings. This would quickly lead to a lack of understanding of each other's work and priorities, and difficult handovers between departments. Of course, miscommunication would only get worse when the latest deployment wouldn't work as expected (which was often), leading to a lot of finger-pointing and a general "throwing stuff over the wall" attitude.

---

5 Steve Mezak, "The Origin of DevOps: What's in a Name?", DevOps.com, *https://oreil.ly/TCzso*.

6 Gene Kim et al., *The Phoenix Project: A Novel About IT, DevOps, and Helping Your Business Win* (Portland, OR: IT Revolution Press, 2014).

7 Kim et al., *The DevOps Handbook*.

The separation also led to *knowledge silos*, which hindered the ability to address problems effectively (especially the ones that sat at the boundary between application code and infrastructure). Devs had limited visibility into how their code performed in production, while Ops had limited insight into the codebase and its dependencies and configuration. This lack of visibility made it much harder to diagnose issues, resulting in longer resolution times and overall increased downtime. It also made software more likely to develop those issues in the first place, since it wasn't written with production conditions or operability in mind.

However, and even more importantly, this "handover" process between departments was a major culprit in the slower delivery cycles at the time. A code handoff between departments for the purposes of deployment would, of course, lead to lengthier deployment times. Lengthier deployment times would then cause delays in releasing new features and an inability to quickly respond to changing requirements or feedback.

Addressing all of these dysfunctions would only be possible by removing the organizational problem at the heart of them: the separation between departments.

Joining Dev and Ops

Because of these issues, the DevOps movement advocates bridging the gap between the two functions. It should be no surprise that the primary tenet of the movement is focused on communication, collaboration, and a fundamental organizational reshuffling.

DevOps is all about avoiding handovers and ensuring shared ownership of the code, its deployment process, and its permanence in production. Nowadays, a "true DevOps team" is cross-functional. It is a team that makes both code and infrastructure changes, deploys them, and supports the resultant systems in production; as Amazon CTO Werner Vogels famously said, "You build it, you run it." And it doesn't stop at infrastructure. DevOps advocates for all functions required to evolve and maintain a product to be embedded into the team (e.g., quality assurance, security). This doesn't mean that specialized engineers are a thing of the past, of course. It means that each team can, and should, take accountability of its application's tech stack from top to bottom. To quote from *The DevOps Handbook*:

> Imagine a world where product owners, Development, QA, IT Operations, and Infosec work together, not only to help each other, but also to ensure that the overall organization succeeds. By working toward a common goal, they enable the fast flow of planned work into production (e.g., performing tens, hundreds, or even thousands of code deploys per day), while achieving world-class stability, reliability, availability, and security. In this world, cross-functional teams rigorously test their hypotheses of which features will most delight users and advance the organizational goals. They care not just about implementing user features, but also actively ensure their work flows smoothly and frequently through the entire value stream without causing chaos and disruption to IT Operations or any other internal or external customer. [...] By adding the

expertise of QA, IT Operations, and Infosec into delivery teams and automated self-service tools and platforms, teams are able to use that expertise in their daily work without being dependent on other teams.[8]

This shift from siloed departments to cross-functional teams was fundamental. Collaboration early and often in the software life cycle improves the quality of the software itself because all the necessary perspectives are considered early in the development phase, reducing issues and rework later on. For example, software becomes more operable in production because developers finally benefit (or suffer) from the operability consequences of the decisions they make. I consider this to be a perfect example of the "It hurts [communication between Dev and Ops], so we do it more often" principle in practice.

Collaboration and cross-functional teams are also what unlocked the automation of software's path to production, which is the second tenet of the DevOps movement and the focus of this chapter. After all, automation of the path to production would not have been possible if its ownership had been scattered across multiple departments.

Automation, Automation, Automation

The other core tenet of the DevOps movement is indeed its explicit focus on automation. Automating repetitive and manual tasks such as infrastructure provisioning, configuration management, testing, and deployment has been a key interest of DevOps for all the reasons we already discussed: it is faster, reduces risk, and allows teams to streamline otherwise clunky and error-prone processes.

While automation had been popular before, DevOps is the movement that has put the most emphasis on it, elevating it to a core principle and a first-class citizen instead of a pleasant side effect of other practices.

The rise of cloud computing was also conveniently timed around the emergence of DevOps, and it made for an excellent technical baseline to support this principle.

Cloud computing gave developers a much-needed abstraction layer on top of physical infrastructure, and it diminished the need for in-depth expertise in the areas of server and network maintenance. It also allowed teams to quickly tear down and rebuild infrastructure, which has tended to make it more immutable and predictable. To understand why, I will rely on a popular distinction in the DevOps community: the one between "pet" and "cattle" servers. Servers in on-premises data centers are often treated as "pets," whereas servers in the cloud are more analogous to "cattle." Pets are heavily customized servers that cannot be turned off (and like real pets, they usually belong to *someone*, which goes against the shared ownership principle). On the other

---

8 Kim et al., *The DevOps Handbook*, Introduction.

hand, cattle servers are disposable: they can be deleted and rebuilt from scratch in case of failures, losing any customization in the process. This means immutability becomes a requirement and one-off manual changes become an antipattern, which is a great baseline for automation.

The abstraction layer given by cloud computing has since evolved even further, with *infrastructure as code* (IaC) tooling becoming widespread. IaC has allowed teams to represent the infrastructure required to run their software as version-controlled "executable" files. This has allowed for even further automation, and it has made infrastructure just as easily versionable and self-documenting as application code, not to mention more easily manageable by developers.

The ability to both abstract away the physical infrastructure and represent it within its own codebase is what unlocked deployment capabilities for automated pipelines, which are fundamental to the practice of continuous integration and continuous delivery. Those are the practices we will talk about next.

Continuous Integration

The next fundamental practice for the automation of software delivery was *continuous integration* (CI), which radically changed the initial steps of the path to production. It was popularized in 2007 by Paul Duvall in *Continuous Integration*. Actually, continuous integration was already described as a practice by XP, but since the supporting practices that surround it took a while to develop and the Duvall book is the most complete account of it, I'm inserting it into our story here. Since then, CI tools have proliferated and have become mainstream.

Due to the abundance of tools and their popularity, continuous integration has suffered from semantic diffusion[9] and has become synonymous with automated pipeline tools over the years. But at its core, CI is not an installation of Jenkins, CodeShip, or Travis. It is the practice of integrating developer changes as frequently as possible in the same version-controlled branch.

Integrating big chunks of changes is painful and error-prone (it hurts), so it can be improved by doing it continuously (we do it more often). In short, CI is about ensuring that the amount of code to be merged and verified is reduced to a minimum.

CI can be achieved by adding code changes to "trunk" (master, or main) as often as possible. *Trunk* is where the latest version of everyone's code resides, so it's the only place where true *integration* can happen. In practice, this is best achieved with *trunk-based development* (TBD), where code is always pushed directly into the main

---

9 Semantic diffusion is the phenomenon in which a term is coined with a very specific definition, but then gets spread through the wider community in a way that weakens that definition.

branch. TBD means forsaking feature branches, which are the very definition of "walled gardens" of code, where commits can pile up and integration can be endlessly
delayed.

So, is it impossible to do CI with branches? We will explore this topic in more depth
in Chapter 3, but for now I can say this: it's not strictly *impossible*, but it is certainly
much more difficult. Some teams do achieve successful continuous integration by
using short-lived branches and/or pull requests (PRs), but they do so by still integrating into trunk as often as possible—ideally, at least once a day.[10] So, while it is possible, branches and PRs make it difficult to do the right thing (remembering to
integrate often) and easy to do the wrong thing (adding "just" another commit
without integrating). TBD does the opposite.

Now that we have talked about integration, let's talk about the better-known aspect of
the CI methodology: the automated build pipeline. You can see it in Figure 1-3. This
is how it works: once code is merged or committed to trunk, a centralized server
shared by the whole team will detect a change in the version control system. When it
notices the change, it builds the code into an artifact. An *artifact* is the final "bundle"
containing all the code, dependencies, and configuration necessary for the new application version to work. For example, an artifact could be a compiled binary, an
archive, a *.jar* or *.war* file, or even better, a container image. Once that artifact is created, the pipeline verifies its correctness through automated tests and code inspection
tools. The shared build pipeline then gives feedback to the team through information
radiators, and notifies them whenever any of the checks have failed.

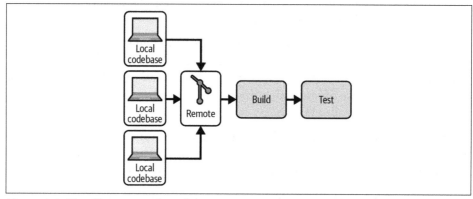

Figure 1-3. The CI automated pipeline

This automation around the pipeline, coupled with integrating early and often, highly
improves the granularity of the building and testing phases. Whereas before they

---

10 Martin Fowler writes about continuous integration at *https://oreil.ly/SqElv*.

were performed once in a while, now they are triggered for every commit, shortening the integrate-build-test feedback loop and making defects much easier to spot.

The automated build pipeline is indeed a powerful concept, but CI is more than a tool. It's a set of practices and mutual agreements that operate within a team. Integrating often and keeping the shared pipeline green are the crucial principles of CI, as the pipeline state represents the fundamental ability to have a proven working version of the software. If we have a proven, latest working version of our code, being ready to deploy it on short notice isn't much of a stretch anymore.

If the pipeline is red, or if we haven't merged in a long time, there is no latest artifact and nothing new to deploy: it's as if the new code were not there at all and the team hadn't made any progress since the latest green build. As David Farley said to me while reviewing this book, "That's because in practical terms, they haven't!"

Having this centralized source of truth and validation has radically changed developers' ways of working, shifting the definition of *done* from "Well, it works on my machine" to "It works once it's integrated, built, and *proven* to work." Merging, building, and testing were previously painful tasks that have now become an ordinary occurrence, removing the need for any last-minute scrambling to get something ready. And stakeholders couldn't be more thankful for it.

As I mentioned at the beginning of the chapter, before the concept of CI came along, there was little engineering around the process for code to reach its users once it had been written. Continuous integration was the first practice to change that, and the concept of a centralized pipeline has been the basis of all automation that followed.

Continuous Delivery

Shortly after continuous integration came the concept of *continuous delivery* (CD), which can be seen as the obvious next step in the automation of the path to production. It was made popular in 2010 by Jez Humble and David Farley in *Continuous Delivery*, and since then it has enjoyed a similar level of popularity as continuous integration. It has become the latest de facto standard for engineering practices and the one most companies strive to implement today. This is made evident by the fact that most popular automated pipeline tools now feature all the capabilities required to perform CD as well as CI.

Indeed, the technical baseline for this practice requires extending the functionality of the automated pipeline (Figure 1-4). The pipeline itself still builds and validates the latest version of the code, but CD also states that it should be able to deploy to any environment in an automated fashion—at any time. This can be achieved through IaC and provisioning tools (another gift of the DevOps movement), which guarantee the automation and repeatability of deployments.

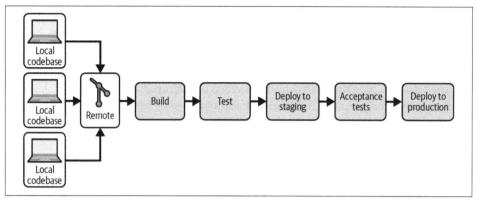

Figure 1-4. The CD automated pipeline

In the most common implementation of CD, every build will be automatically promoted and deployed to a staging or UAT environment, or even several of them. Once deployments are automated, sophisticated automated tests can then be run against those prod-like environments. As a result, each code increment that makes it to the end of the pipeline has such a high likelihood of correctness that it can be considered a release candidate. The deployment to production of this release candidate can then be triggered on demand, usually through the same pipeline tool.

With CD, the automated pipeline owned by the development team becomes the tool that covers the application's entire path to production. In doing so, it finally bridges the gap between traditional Dev and Ops functions, allowing one team to fully own both development and deployments.

However, just like CI, CD doesn't represent only a tool. First and foremost, it represents a collection of ways of working to leverage the tool successfully. In the case of CD, those ways of working are centered on one simple concept: ensuring that the codebase is always in a deployable state (treat every commit as a release candidate) so that the automated pipeline can be leveraged to deploy to production at any moment. This allows teams to dramatically increase their deployment frequency. A higher deployment frequency leads to fewer and fewer lines of code between one deployment and the next, which lowers the average deployment risk. Once again, this is the "If it hurts, do it more often" principle in action.

The shorter feedback loops introduced by this practice also bring to the table something else that is far more valuable than reducing the annoyance of deployments. With CD, showing the latest version of our software to stakeholders isn't nearly as much of an inconvenience as it was before. The most recent version of the software is likely sitting on a freshly deployed pre-prod instance at all times, having been delivered there by the latest pipeline run. In most cases, all we have to do is open a new tab in our browser to get a working demo in a real environment. This used to be unthinkable in the days of manual deployments, especially with the added communication overhead due to having separate Dev and Ops teams.

With CD, stakeholders can see the software quickly, and releasing it to end users is just another step away. Deploying to production doesn't have to be scheduled months in advance; it can be easily done several times a week. Requirements can be validated much more quickly than before, by testers, stakeholders, and most importantly, the market. It turns out that when we deploy more often, we enable our organization to get feedback—and adjust to the market more often too. In many cases, this results in building less software, as early feedback causes product owners to realize a feature or an entire system got to "good enough" earlier than expected.

If continuous delivery has established anything, it's that "the real work around here" for us developers was never to produce endless code in a walled garden, but to release working software early and often. In only this way can we bring value to users as quickly as possible.

In short, the evolution from CI to CD can be framed in terms of what is being automated: CI automates the determination of "Does my change look safe and self-contained?" while CD automates the determination of "Is my change deployable?" Later, we will see how CD automates the question, "Shall I deploy *now*?"

A Final Gate to Production

Most companies implement continuous delivery in such a way that deployments happen without human intervention in at least some preproduction environments for every build. However, the same automation does not carry changes all the way to production. To cover that last step, a human still has to press a button in the pipeline tool to deploy the release candidate (Figure 1-5). The presence of that manual "button" is the main differentiator between continuous delivery and continuous deployment.

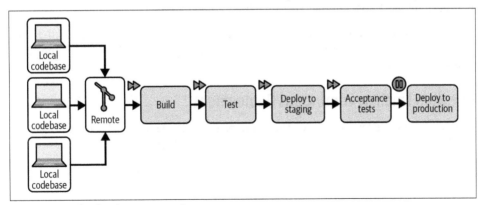

Figure 1-5. The final gate to production

Even with a final manual gate, many more phases of the path to production are streamlined: deployments to preproduction and tests at higher levels of abstraction can be executed for every increment of code rather than for weeks' worth of accumulated changes. Ninety-nine percent of the path to production is completely automated. It is close to perfect.

However, this implementation of continuous delivery still has one remaining bottleneck in the overall process of getting code in front of users: the last human's manual approval to perform that final deployment. This 1% might look insignificant, but it does make a difference.

Teams might handle production deployments in different ways, ranging from ad hoc deployments when there are enough substantial changes, to sophisticated schedules where deployments happen on a fixed cadence. By the time manual intervention happens, however, a batch of commits might have accumulated in preproduction, and they will usually be deployed all at once—increasing deployment risk, delaying feedback, and slowing down debugging if (when) something goes wrong.

The bigger the deployment is, the more oversight is required, and the more potential defects lurk in the growing number of lines of code waiting to be rolled out. Also, the more changes that are made at once, the more code we must dig through to diagnose the cause of post-deployment issues.

If the process of deploying to production requires lengthy manual verification (e.g., extensive manual testing in staging or UAT), it is not really a continuous process, and so it might not even strictly qualify as continuous delivery. Manual intervention defers the point of release even further and exacerbates this problem, making each deployment bigger and more complex.

In addition, just like with TBD versus branches, a gated production environment makes it difficult to do the right thing (deploy as often as possible) and easy to do the wrong thing (add "just another commit" before deployment).

Even though most companies are enjoying great benefits from continuous delivery, they are still not deploying to production as often as they could; that is, with the granularity of every commit.[11]

One Step Further: Continuous Deployment

Now that we have learned about the principles of XP, DevOps, CI, and CD, we can finally understand the thinking behind continuous deployment.

---

11 Aficionados of Lean manufacturing will know this as "one-piece flow." See Chapter 2 for more details.

A couple of decades after the discourse around the path to production started changing, the DORA State of DevOps research program, led by Nicole Forsgren, came along to validate XP's earlier instincts about doing the most painful parts of software frequently.[12] This program is the longest-running academic investigation into software delivery practices so far. Through six years of research, it has confirmed that a shorter lead time for changes and a higher frequency of production deployments are reliable predictors of high performance in software development teams (and their organizations). It is also worth mentioning, from a selfish point of view, that the DORA research has found a strong correlation between those metrics and better quality of life for engineers, with overall higher job satisfaction and less burnout. These findings apply to both commercial and noncommercial organizations.

Encouraged by the DORA findings, teams that already follow the values of XP, DevOps, CI, and CD are now trying to make their deployments happen more and more frequently and with less and less gatekeeping. Engineering practices that enable deploying to production as often as possible have become a key focus of organizations looking to reduce their time to market and their ability to respond to change.

Therefore, it is only natural that some teams might be thinking of going one step further with continuous delivery and removing the final manual barrier to production: automating the last step of their automated pipeline, and therefore enabling continuous deployment (shown in Figure 1-6).

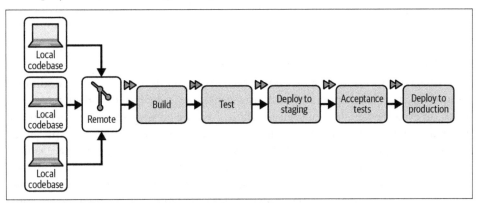

Figure 1-6. The continuous deployment automated pipeline

The term *continuous deployment* was coined by Timothy Fitz in his 2009 article (*https://oreil.ly/gBltB*) of the same name. The concept hasn't been included in a lot of literature since then, but it has gained traction and has been successfully adopted by companies such as Facebook (*https://oreil.ly/dS1qF*), Google (*https://oreil.ly/l4GGL*),

---

12 You can download the DORA "Accelerate State of DevOps Report 2023" at *https://oreil.ly/epiI8*.

and many more. Because continuous deployment is still relatively undocumented, there is no official data showing exactly how many companies have adopted it overall (most studies focus more generally on continuous *delivery*, not specifically on continuous *deployment*). That is why I have collected several case studies in this book: so that you can have an idea of how a good sample of companies make it work in their day-to-day in all sorts of industries: from retail to banking to automotive and more.

Continuous deployment can be understood as a specific implementation of continuous delivery, acting within its framework of ensuring that every code increment is production ready. Indeed, continuous deployment takes the "production-ready" principle quite literally. Its defining characteristic is that the decision to deploy code to production is fully automated by the pipeline, with no manual intervention required.

Every commit going through the pipeline not only will be *considered* deployable to production, but will actually *be* deployed to production.

This means no more waiting around in a UAT or staging environment for manual exploratory testing, and no more human intervention to decide whether to send the changes live. The pipeline does it all, and humans can finally sit back and watch the automation do its job until the end.

We have already talked about how the "If it hurts, do it more often" principle of XP is reflected in the practices of DevOps, CI, and CD. All these years later, I consider the same principle to be the main motivation behind adopting continuous deployment to production as well. Perhaps continuous deployment is the practice that takes this concept to its very limit.

What has *ever* been more painful for any software team than deploying to production? Integration with the live versions of third-party services, high-traffic conditions, unforeseen user behaviors, and real user-generated data has historically wreaked havoc on even the best-laid-out release plans. And the consequences have been much worse than a bad merge day or a disappointing demo. Real users have been presented with broken applications, unusable features, and even the loss of their data. Deploying to production has led to business outages lasting hours or days for countless teams. As we will see in later chapters, the production environment is full of quirks that are hard or impossible to replicate on developer laptops. Even the fanciest, most sophisticated preproduction setups often aren't quite production-like enough to catch all those quirks.

Deploying to production is a scary ordeal, and when it goes wrong it can disappoint a lot of people. I have a hard time thinking of anything more painful for a software team than deploying to production after days or weeks of hard work, only to realize that their code had an unforeseen defect that is now being paraded in front of users and stakeholders. Most experienced developers know how mortifying that can be. Or even worse, they might know the disappointment of working long hours to get the Big New Feature over the finish line, only to find out users are happily ignoring it.

Deploying to production can definitely hurt. Therefore (in true XP fashion), we should do it as often as possible; ideally, at every commit that is proven worthy by our best automated tests. Only then will it be possible to ease that pain and actually look forward to deploying multiple times a day instead of dreading it once a month. That's what continuous deployment is, and in a nutshell, that's what this book is about.

In my view, continuous deployment represents the culmination of the decades-long automation journey I have described in this chapter. With it, automation can finally cover the entire path to production from end to end and leave no manual work in the value stream of software.

With immediate deployments, the code commit life cycle goes into lockstep with the deployment life cycle. Each code increment in the codebase corresponds to an almost immediate code increment in production, so every commit must be production ready from its inception. Developers work within the narrowest possible feedback loop every day, and even every hour.

Indeed, every developer might easily oversee multiple production deployments while creating code for a single task. This makes them intimately familiar with the production environment and all its quirks, interdependencies, and performance constraints. Continuous deployment fully empowers developers to take responsibility for both the value *and* the destructive potential of their changes. Overall, this framework promotes production to a first-class citizen in the day-to-day cognitive effort of writing code. It already should be, but it is easy to forget about it when deployments happen "sometime later" or are overseen by someone else.

With a 1:1 correspondence between commits and deployments, the state of the codebase and its relationship to the state of production becomes straightforward: they are always one and the same. There is no need to switch to an older version of the code to debug live issues, no question about which version is out at the moment, and no need to revert undeployed changes if an urgent fix has to be rushed through. The tiniest of experiments can (and should) go live in a trivial amount of time: ideally measured in minutes—whether it is a new log line for debugging, or changing the color of a button under a feature toggle.

Overall, working in this fashion reduces the risk of production unpredictability by managing it in the smallest possible increments: within the granularity of every commit.

Implementation

The implementation of continuous deployment itself can be quite simple. Adapting an existing continuous delivery pipeline to support continuous deployment usually only requires a reconfiguration of the production deployment step.

If your software respects all of the following conditions:

- It is version controlled.
- It has automated test coverage.
- It has an automated pipeline.
- The automated pipeline runs on every new commit on trunk (the main branch).
- The automated pipeline is responsible for the entire path to production, from commit, to tests, to deploying to any environment (including production).
- The "trunk" version of the software is deployed to your main preproduction environments and, of course, to production.
- The automated pipeline runs in a reasonable amount of time (say, all steps combined should take less than one hour, discounting any pauses for manual checks).

After these conditions are satisfied, all you need to do is ensure the following: once a commit is pushed (or merged) to trunk and all quality gates have passed, the deployment to production happens immediately. There should be no manual steps, and no buttons waiting to be clicked by a carbon-based life form. If you have already adopted continuous delivery, this usually means deleting a "pause" instruction before production deployment in your pipeline tool of choice.

If there are any other required change approvers, or any earlier manual gates in between a push and a production deployment, they should also be automated. When any push or merge event to the main branch is able to trigger its own production deployment, that's when you know you are done.

How do you know when your automated quality gates and infrastructure are good enough to make this switch? If you are looking for an indication of when you might be "ready," you might enjoy reading Chapter 3.

Continuous Deployment to…Staging?

Some companies refer to their release process as continuous deployment, but with the caveat that it is only *continuous* until staging or UAT. After that, somebody needs to give a go-ahead to go to production, because it is deemed "too risky" to let it happen by automation only. I would suggest that continuously deploying to a preproduction environment is a natural part of practicing continuous delivery, but it is not really continuous deployment. On this topic, I rather agree with the words of David Farley and Jez Humble, who began to explore the topic back in 2010:

> Of course it's not just continuous deployment (I can continuously deploy to UAT all I like: no big deal). The crucial point is that it is continuous deployment *to production*.
>
> —Farley and Humble, *Continuous Delivery*, p. 266

With continuous deployment, according to the original definition, *all* manual gates are removed from the automated CD pipeline. Each step triggers the next step in an automated fashion, and the culmination of all those steps is a production deployment. Any code change pushed to the main branch is a fully fledged release candidate. If proven correct by the automation, it *will* make it all the way to the users.

And that's it. There will be no more pipeline implementation details in this book, because this is really all there is to "implementing" continuous deployment.

A continuous deployment pipeline is certainly not laborious to build. To switch from continuous delivery to continuous deployment, Very Senior Developers don't have to spend weeks coding complicated scripts full of deployment steps, configuration of cloud permissions, infrastructure as code, and elaborate testing setups. In most cases, all they need to do is remove a step from their existing pipeline. Implementing continuous delivery from scratch might take months or years, while switching to continuous deployment often just requires a one-line change. As most teams these days have already invested in a continuous delivery process, it certainly looks like the switch might not be that hard for most companies.

So, what are we going to talk about in the rest of the book, then?

Implications

Continuous deployment could be dismissed as a trivial subcategory within continuous delivery, but this underestimates the radical simplicity of an automated pipeline that goes straight through from push to production.

The challenges of continuous deployment do not lie in its deceptively simple implementation. Rather, they lie in the adoption of all the practices that it depends on and the ones that it unlocks. It might be a one-line change, but it is a one-line change that (in my experience) represents a complete reimagining of the day-to-day software development process.

For example, these are just some of the questions that we'll address in the rest of this book, and that emerged for my teams only *after* the switch to continuous deployment:

- How do we hide unfinished code if we are deploying every commit?

- How do we ensure that *every single* commit is backward compatible?
- How do we avoid breaking contracts with other production services?
- How do we separate a deployment and a feature release?
- What is the effect of very frequent deployments on the stability of infrastructure?
- How does this change how the team works and its definition of "done"?
- What happens with preproduction environments?
- Is anything ever "dev-done" anymore if everything is in production?
- How can manual exploratory testing still be done when deployments are immediate?

A continuous deployment workflow is radically different from a traditional continuous delivery workflow with a gate to production. So, because we have already talked about how to "implement" continuous deployment, the rest of this book will cover its ramifications and the implementation of all of its supporting practices.

Is It Dangerous?

If your heart skipped a beat when you read about manual production approvals being removed, don't worry. You are far from alone.

When teams practice good continuous integration and use of short-lived feature branches or, even better, trunk-based development, they send multiple changes through the pipeline every day. Some teams might even send multiple changes every hour, all of which will end up in production one after the other. This streamlines the engineers' workflow considerably, but it is also a responsibility not to be taken lightly.

Each commit ending up in production requires developers to be extremely disciplined with all the principles introduced by continuous delivery. The pipeline, preproduction environments, and automated tests must be maintained to impeccable shape so that they can accurately discard bad changesets. For developers, treating every code increment as a potential deployment candidate also becomes mandatory. After all, each commit will become an actual deployment: they are not just "candidates" anymore.

Indeed, one might argue that the production readiness offered by continuous delivery is only theoretical without continuous deployment.

But as cool and shiny as this practice is, it does present some risks: because each change developers make goes immediately to production, it has the potential to affect a complex web of services. A lot has changed since the early days of XP and "continuous anything": organizations have moved away from "simple" monolithic applications and embraced distributed and service-oriented architectures. These services depend on each other in often intricate ways, and interdependencies in distributed systems are among the hardest things to test. If continuous deployment is not done carefully and responsibly, one poorly thought commit has the potential to bring production down.

Continuous delivery practices are a necessary baseline, but some more precautions are needed to perform safe continuous deployment to production, which I already hinted at in "Implications" on page 23. Extra safety nets need to be put in place to guarantee the lowest possible risk of regressions, which have emerged in the years since continuous delivery became popular. Quality gates need to be restructured around the novel proximity of the production environment, and the team's ways of working need to be adjusted to take immediate deployments into account.

Yet, doing continuous deployment responsibly is possible. Yes, even when not all team members are senior. Teams are doing it every day and enjoying great benefits and incredibly fast feedback from it. In this book, you will find out more about what those benefits are and how they do it. You will learn a framework to perform safe incremental releases during everyday development work that is structured exclusively around the challenges of continuous deployment in nontrivial, distributed systems.

Summary

In this chapter, we introduced continuous deployment: the methodology that will be the focus of this book. In continuous deployment, the entirety of the path to production of code is fully automated—even the final decision to deploy to production.

We then recapped the practices that focused on code's path to production over recent years: starting from XP's "If it hurts, do it more often" motto, to DevOps tearing down the barrier between development and operations, to continuous integration introducing automation until an artifact build, continuous delivery extending that to high-level testing and deployments, and finally, continuous deployment removing all human factors from the automated pipeline.

We discussed how continuous deployment has profound ramifications for engineers' workflow, which needs to be adapted to account for continuous production deployments. We talked about how this results in more granular feedback and more responsibility to implement sturdy quality gates. Commits and deployments need to be planned carefully to keep production in a working and performant state.

In the next chapter, we will see what makes this investment worthwhile.

CHAPTER 2

Benefits

Adopting continuous deployment is a significant cultural undertaking for any team, even those that have a mature engineering culture and are already comfortable with continuous delivery. For continuous deployment to work well, it requires a comprehensive safety net of practices and buy-in at all levels, from management to newly hired junior developers. This might seem daunting, but the payoff has been high for the many companies that have achieved it and are doing it successfully.

In this chapter, we will focus on those payoffs: why continuous deployment is worth the effort and why we should bother with the cultural and technical changes required to send every commit to production. By reading this chapter you will know more about these benefits, and by reading the rest of the book you'll find out how to realize them.

We can summarize the benefits of continuous deployment as follows:

- Improves the efficiency of the software value stream by reducing waste and rework (minimization of batches and queues of inventory)
- Reduces time from customer order to change applied in production (lead time and cycle time)
- Dramatically increases deployment frequency, which is a core indicator of engineering health
- Reduces the rate of faulty changes applied to production
- Reduces the mean time to recover from faulty changes
- Moves quality control earlier in the development process, improving collaboration between roles

- Increases engineering ownership, which prevents handovers of work in progress and loss of context

You might have already recognized that this list includes several familiar concepts in software engineering, particularly the fundamental principles of *Lean manufacturing*, DORA metrics, and the shift-left principle. These concepts have already proven their effectiveness in helping product teams cocreate value with customers more quickly and more reliably, ultimately leading to improved business performance. Throughout this chapter, we'll explore how continuous deployment aligns with these concepts and amplifies their impact.

Let's kick things off by talking about Lean manufacturing and the flow of inventory.

One-Piece Flow and Lean Manufacturing

Some of the greatest benefits of continuous deployment are how it improves responsiveness to customer demand and market changes and minimizes wasteful work in the delivery pipeline. It achieves this by closely embodying the core tenet of Lean manufacturing: a one-piece, continuous flow of inventory. This means it can fully leverage all the benefits introduced by the Lean thought process and its heuristics for managing batching, queues, and bottlenecks. In the next section, we will see why continuous deployment gets closer to a one-piece flow than any other methodology. Some readers might not be familiar with Lean principles, so before we dive in, I will provide a condensed recap. However, if you are already well-versed in the topic, feel free to skip ahead.

Origins of Lean Manufacturing

Lean manufacturing is a systematic approach to production that aims to eliminate waste, optimize efficiency, and deliver high-quality products. Its roots go back to the 1940s, when Toyota revolutionized the automotive industry with its Toyota Production System (TPS) and Kanban system.

At the time, the demand for cars in Japan was smaller than in the United States. Because of this, Toyota felt it could not copy the mass-production model used by Ford and General Motors, where the goal was to produce as much inventory of the same item as possible, which would eventually be sold. Instead, Toyota had to figure out how to make a smaller quantity of different vehicles based only on customer demand, all on the same assembly line.

To achieve this much more streamlined production line, the company focused on reducing work-in-progress costs, shortening the time from customer order to item delivered, and reducing waste in the overall process. In doing this, it realized that making as many parts as possible (maximizing inventory) was not a good strategy at all; instead, the company opted to produce at the exact rate of customer demand, which would later become the concept of just-in-time production and one-piece flow.

In Figure 2-1, you can see the difference between the classic batch and queue production model and Toyota's one-piece flow system, whose goal is to have the bare minimum inventory between processes.

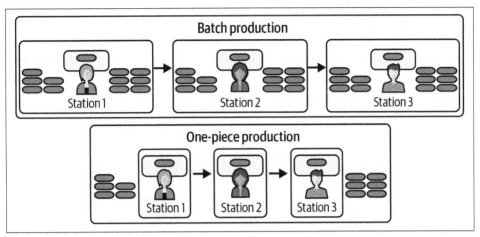

Figure 2-1. Batch and queue versus one-piece flow

Notice in the figure how in batch production there is a buildup of inventory between workstations, but in one-piece production one item at a time is processed, minimizing the inventory accumulating through the value stream. Let's spend some more time comparing the two.

Batch production

At the top of Figure 2-1, we can observe how the traditional batch and queue production system is characterized by a significant amount of inventory between stages. Large batches are produced based on forecasted demand, and they move through the line from one workstation to the next, or into storage.

An interesting aspect here is that items are produced at individual workstations regardless of the actual pace of work in the subsequent process. This localized optimization can potentially lead to bottlenecks and local overproduction, rather than considering the global optimization of the entire system.

The accumulation of inventory in this process incurs various costs, including obvious ones such as storage and handling costs, as well as more subtle (but very disruptive) inefficiencies. These inefficiencies, as opposed to the "physical costs" of inventory, are what make the introduction of Lean worthwhile.

In particular, excessive inventory masks quality issues, making it difficult to address defects. That is because any defects won't be noticed until well after the production of an entire batch, and perhaps many more. Large batches also amplify the *impact* of defects, as a higher volume of faulty items may need to be scrapped or reworked.

In addition, and worst of all, large batches result in overall longer timelines from the start to the completion of an individual product. Queues form within the value stream, where inventory waits and sits idle until it can be processed. This extended timeline means less responsiveness to customer demands and delays in delivery times. It also introduces variability and unpredictability into the system, increasing the risk of disruptions.

Jeffrey Liker, author of *The Toyota Way*, writes about big batches:

> The problem is that big buffers (inventory between processes) lead to other suboptimal behavior, like reducing your motivation to continuously improve your operations. Why worry about preventive maintenance on equipment when shutdowns do not immediately affect final assembly anyway? Why get overly concerned about a few quality errors when you can just toss out defective parts? Because by the time a defective piece works its way to the later operation where an operator tries to assemble that piece, there may be weeks of bad parts in process and sitting in buffers. [...] Local efficiencies were emphasized at the cost of slowing down the value stream by creating large amounts of in-process and finished-goods inventory and taking a long time to identify problems (defects) that reduced quality. As a result, the plant was not flexible to changes in customer demand.[1]

One-piece flow

The concept of one-piece flow involves working on only one item at a time in an ideal system, without accumulating batches between workstations. This approach has two significant effects.

First, it reduces waste by eliminating inventory buildup. Idle inventory does not generate value; instead, it adds unnecessary costs and can lead to suboptimal systemic behaviors, as discussed in the previous section.

More importantly, however, one-piece flow reduces the time spent by individual items in queues within the system. This principle, known as the *Batch Size Queueing Principle*, was illustrated by Donald G. Reinertsen in his book *The Principles of Product Development Flow: Second Generation Lean Product Development* (Celeritas Publishing, 2009). This effect is clearly observed in the cumulative flow diagram shown in Figure 2-2, which represents a system with a single workstation/process, and how

---

1 Jeffrey Liker, *The Toyota Way: 14 Management Principles from the World's Greatest Manufacturer* (New York: McGraw Hill, 2004), p. 30.

work is processed relative to batch size. The diagram illustrates three states of items: arrivals, in queue, and processed.

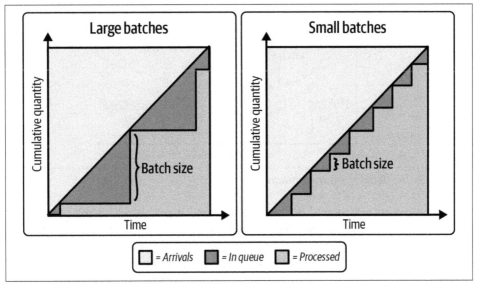

Figure 2-2. The Batch Size Queuing Principle

It is important to note how smaller processing batches result in less time spent in the queue, as well as reduced variability and unpredictability. With shorter queue times between individual processes, the overall cycle time from the beginning to the end of the flow is also reduced.

This increased efficiency allows for more granularity in the end result, facilitates quicker experimentation, and enables true just-in-time delivery. This is the goal of Lean manufacturing. Overall, and contrary to the popular concept of "economies of scale," small batches are what guarantee predictable and fast delivery.

Reducing batch sizes. However, simply reducing batch sizes is not a straightforward task. It requires careful consideration of other factors to avoid unintended consequences. This is especially true when the time taken to process each batch is significant. Figure 2-3 illustrates how achieving optimal batch size is a balancing act between the holding cost of inventory and the processing cost for each transaction.

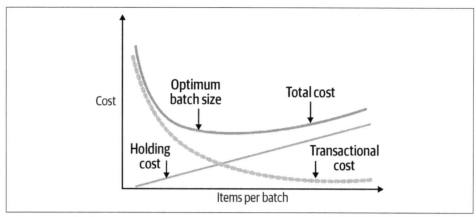

Figure 2-3. The batch size optimization problem

The holding cost (represented by the solid line) encompasses various expenses incurred when inventory remains idle. Storage costs are the most apparent, but as explained in the preceding section, the holding cost also includes the overall inefficiency of accumulated inventory. On the other hand, the transaction cost (depicted by the dotted line) encompasses all the activities involved in processing a batch. When the transaction cost is high, splitting work into smaller batches becomes inefficient because it means incurring the high cost repeatedly. Therefore, the key factor enabling small batches is the reduction of the transaction cost per batch.

Lowering transaction costs. Although transaction costs are often considered fixed and unchangeable, that is not always the case. More often than not, transaction costs are anything but fixed. Toyota, for instance, challenged this notion by addressing the long changeover times in its die stamping machines that were preventing the company from processing smaller batches. By implementing single minute exchange of dies (SMED), Toyota successfully reduced the changeover time from 24 hours to less than 10 minutes. This significant reduction, amounting to more than two orders of magnitude, completely transformed the company's economies of batch size, allowing for substantial reductions of batch sizes without increasing transaction costs.

So far, we have covered inventory, batches, and transaction costs. To summarize, the goal of Lean manufacturing is to enable just-in-time delivery, which is done by keeping the overall system cycle time as low as possible. Low cycle time is made possible by minimizing queues within the system, which means processing smaller batches of inventory (one-piece flow). Reducing the batch size can be enabled by lowering the transaction cost per batch. This, in a nutshell, is the relationship between inventory and efficiency, and it's represented in Figure 2-4.

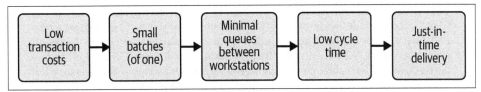

Figure 2-4. The principles of Lean manufacturing

You might be wondering what this has to do with software development. To find out, we must understand what the similarities are between custom software manufacturing and physical manufacturing. That's what we are going to talk about in the next section.

Lean and Software Development

The core principles of Lean have influenced various fields beyond manufacturing. One such field is, of course, software development. Agile methodologies, which emphasize short iterations and fast feedback, align well with the principles of Lean that we discussed in the previous section. As a result, when the Agile movement picked up momentum, the Lean thought process swiftly followed.

The idea of kinship between Lean and Agile gained traction with the publication of material such as *Lean Software Development: An Agile Toolkit*[2] in 2003. This book introduced the application of Lean principles specifically tailored to software products, such as minimizing waste, optimizing flow, and promoting continuous improvement. Since then, Lean software development has been embraced by organizations worldwide, leading to effective software delivery and experimentation.

Inventory in software

Although many companies are striving to adopt Lean principles, the parallel between producing physical goods and producing custom software is not always easy to keep at the forefront of one's mind. Thinking about the various artifacts involved in software in terms of inventory doesn't come naturally. However, it is fundamental if we want to improve our operations. In *The Principles of Product Development Flow*, Reinertsen does a great job explaining why that is the case:

> In manufacturing, we are keenly aware of our inventory. We see it every time we walk the factory floor. Our chief financial officer (CFO) can report the exact amount of work-in-process inventory (WIP) by simply reading it off the balance sheet. If we cut WIP by $10 million, the CFO is overjoyed because we just freed up $10 million in cash.

---

2 Mary Poppendieck and Tom Poppendieck, *Lean Software Development: An Agile Toolkit* (Boston: Addison-Wesley, 2003).

Unfortunately, our situation is quite different in product development. If we ask our CFO, "How much design-in-process (DIP) inventory do we have?" we will get a puzzled look and the reply, "There is nothing on our balance sheet called design-in-process inventory. We have no inventory in product development." If we don't believe the CFO, we can walk through the engineering department and look for inventory. But since the inventory in a product development process is not physical objects but information, it is virtually invisible. Inventory could double overnight in an engineering department, and we would see no change in the physical appearance of that department.

One engineering manager from Hewlett-Packard (HP) remarked, "Our inventory is bits on a disk drive, and we have very big disk drives here at HP!" Inventory in product development is both physically and financially invisible.

But just because this inventory is invisible doesn't mean it doesn't exist. Product development inventory is observable through its effects: increased cycle time, delayed feedback, constantly shifting priorities, and status reporting. Unfortunately, all of these effects hurt economic performance.

[...]

Product development queues [of inventory] do much more damage than manufacturing queues for two reasons. First, product development queues tend to be much bigger than manufacturing queues. It takes orders of magnitude more time for work products to flow through the product development pipeline compared to the manufacturing pipeline. Even worse, because these queues are invisible, there are no natural predators keeping them under control. Companies do not measure queues, they do not manage queues, and most don't even realize that queues are a problem. Ironically, some companies are even proud of their queues, boasting of the size of their product development pipeline.[3]

Since inventory in software development is both especially dangerous and especially *invisible*, we should make it a point to hunt it down and reduce it to the bare minimum that should flow within the system.

Wherever intellectual artifacts are produced along software's path to production, that's inventory. Feature discovery boards are inventory, user experience (UX) mockups are inventory, architectural vision diagrams are inventory, user stories in our backlog are inventory, code in feature branches is inventory, undeployed artifacts are inventory, and even features that are in production but under an OFF feature flag are inventory. Everything that is not in front of users, generating value, is inventory and, therefore, waste in the system.

In this book, we will mostly focus on technical forms of inventory along software's path to production: the ones generated between the engineers writing software and the users triggering its execution. In other words, the main form of inventory we will

---

3 Donald Reinertsen, *The Principles of Product Development Flow* (Redondo Beach, CA: Celeritas Publishing, 2009), pp. 47–48.

concern ourselves with is *code*. We will talk about how code inventory moves through several "workstations" in the form of integration, analysis, testing, and deployments.

However, that is not to say that continuous deployment doesn't help to reduce other forms of inventory too. When deployments are frequent, that means designs, user stories, and other intellectual artifacts are also dispatched quickly.

Batches in software

Now that we have discussed inventory in software, it is essential to establish an understanding of what we mean by "batches" in this context. After all, the reduction of batch size is a fundamental principle of Lean, and it is also what we should strive for in software development. Therefore, we need a vocabulary that relates directly to software and enables concrete discussions on this topic. But how do we define batches when it comes to code? A batch, by definition, is a group of units. Can we even define what a "unit" of code is?

Code is hard to quantify. Defining a unit as an individual instruction or a line is insufficient, because those concepts do not provide standalone value. Instead, I find that for us developers, the most intuitive understanding of a unit of software is a code commit.

A *commit*, when done properly, represents a single atomic change to the codebase that is self-contained and demonstrable. It is the smallest possible unit by which we are able to review software, build it in our pipelines, and ultimately deploy it. Therefore, that's the definition I am going to use throughout the rest of the book.

By considering one commit as a "unit" of code, we can define batches of code inventory as the accumulation of code commits at any stage along the path to production.

When commits (units) accumulate, code changes begin to form batches. This can happen in long-lived feature branches that go unmerged for an extended period, or even in local copies of the main branch if we follow trunk-based development (TBD) and forget to push for a while. Commits can pile up when they are stuck behind red builds, or when more and more changes land in preproduction where they wait for manual testing before a scheduled deployment to prod. Any bottleneck in the path to production presents an opportunity for commits to accumulate and form a batch.

Of course, exceptionally large individual commits might also be considered big batches of inventory on their own. But I like to think that working in such a way is recognized as an antipattern widely enough that we don't need to address this edge case—or at the very least, we can resolve it by saying "Just don't do that, it's not nice."

Larger batches of software inventory, just like physical inventory, have a negative impact on overall delivery speed, and they can obscure unforeseen defects, leading to inefficiencies and rework in later stages. Instead of relying on traditional batch and queue processes such as waterfall, the Lean approach promotes minimizing lead times by reducing the amount of undeployed code.

What follows is that, *just like Lean strives to ideally have only one piece of inventory flowing through the system (one-piece flow), the ideal number of commits flowing through the path to production is one.* This is the most efficient way to minimize queues and overall cycle time.

Lowering transaction cost in software

Just like in physical manufacturing, we must first lower our transaction cost if we want to reduce our batch size to one commit. Now that we have established a vocabulary to discuss inventory, units, and batches in code, we can delve into the topic of reducing the time it takes for our path to production to process one commit (transaction cost).

In the realm of software development, the primary approach to decreasing transaction costs has always been through automation. For example, if a QA department takes two days to manually conduct regression tests for each release, the transaction cost associated with each release will be high. In such a scenario, the natural reaction of most companies will tend toward cramming as much as possible in each release (optimizing costs by making bigger batches). That makes sense from an economic optimization perspective, but it introduces inefficiency in the overall process of releasing. Instead, we must take the opposite approach. To reduce the batch size of releases in this scenario, it would be necessary to first lower the transaction cost by replacing manual tests with automated ones. A similar analogy can be made for lengthy and manual deployment processes. The automation of manual tasks and decisions is the main enabler for streamlining the path to production so that it can process more frequent and smaller batches.

In Chapter 1, I described how the guiding principle of "If it hurts, do it more often" in eXtreme Programming (XP) emphasizes the importance of handling smaller amounts of code in the various activities of the path to production, which eventually results in the automation of those activities. Now we can see that this relationship is not coincidental; in fact, it is closely aligned with Lean's observations about the relationship between small batch sizes and low transaction costs. Lean thinking provides insights into why small batches of code and efficient automation are closely intertwined.

By reducing the size of our batches of changes through automation, we can reduce not only the number of idle waits before individual "workstations," but also the overall time it takes for inventory to travel from a developer's workstation all the way to production. By maintaining short lead times, changes in production can be produced swiftly and in direct response to customer orders. This allows for maximum efficiency and no waste, and it is the concept of one-piece flow fully applied to software's path to production.

Given our focus on automation as a catalyst for achieving smaller batch sizes, let's reexamine the key practices that introduced automation throughout the path to production: continuous integration, continuous delivery, and continuous deployment. In particular, let's highlight how these practices influence the dynamics of batches and queues.

One commit = one artifact with continuous integration. Let's start with continuous integration (CI). Before it came along to automate the test and build phases, changes would pile up very early in development (literally on developers' laptops or long-lived branches) and remain there for a long time. Code inventory would already have formed painful batches once it made it to the very first stages of the path to production, complicating integration, testing, and releasing. A developer's laptop used to be the very first workstation of an old-fashioned batch and queue process, as shown in Figure 2-5.

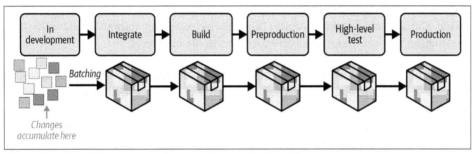

Figure 2-5. Batching in the path to production before CI

Working in a walled "code garden" might feel very productive for developers, whether it is locally or on a branch. I have heard many colleagues over the years say that long stretches of uninterrupted work make them feel like they are "in the zone." However, just like in traditional batch and queue manufacturing, this is only a local optimization, and it comes at the expense of slowing down the global value stream.

With the automation introduced by CI, code increments are integrated, verified, and built one commit at a time instead of all at once. If all developers respect the "integrate early and often" principle, the automated pipeline lets them achieve a "one commit = one artifact" workflow that makes the integration, build, and test phases straightforward. One commit corresponding to one artifact closely resembles the one-piece workflow introduced by Lean manufacturing, instead of a batch and queue workflow. CI applies the one-piece flow principle to the first steps of the path to production, as you can see in Figure 2-6.

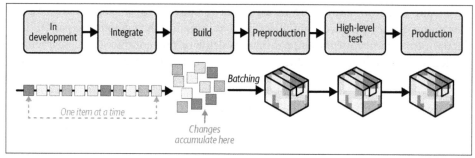

Figure 2-6. Batching in the path to production after CI

With continuous integration only, however, changes are still allowed to pile up after the artifact build phase. Once in the repository, successful changes wait in a queue until they travel the rest of the way to production in batches again (with newer artifacts containing more commits). Continuous integration offered development teams a first glimpse into working more efficiently by replacing human bottlenecks with automation, but continuous delivery took this to the next level.

One commit = one preproduction deployment with continuous delivery. As we discussed in Chapter 1, the most common implementation of continuous delivery (CD) sees the automated pipeline making decisions autonomously until preproduction, elevating builds to the status of release candidates if they pass all the checks. The more granular, one-piece flow of code started by continuous integration is extended all the way to automated high-level tests and preproduction: just one step away from production itself. This is shown in Figure 2-7.

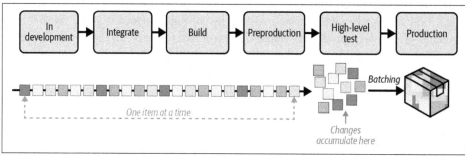

Figure 2-7. Batching in the path to production with CD and a manual gate to production

Many more phases are automated. Because of this, deployments to preproduction and tests operating at higher levels of abstraction can be executed for individual commits rather than for weeks' worth of accumulated batches. Continuous delivery achieves a "one commit = one preproduction deployment" workflow.

However, having a last manual approval process in the pipeline still represents a bottleneck, which means that changes to production still tend to be rolled out in batches, instead of enjoying the granularity of verification at every commit that all the preceding phases do. The whole value stream adheres *almost* perfectly to the one-piece flow, except for one last nonautomated decision standing in the way.

With inventory accumulating in preproduction for days or even weeks, the identification of defects is delayed, resulting in many unpleasant side effects once the deployment to production occurs. These can include difficulties in debugging, loss of context on what is going live, and a much higher likelihood that the deployment will contain problematic changes.

One commit = one production deployment with continuous deployment. Continuous deployment, as a specialized implementation of continuous delivery, eliminates even the final manual action in the path to production, which is the very last bottleneck for commits.

This has a significant impact on the inventory flow within the system. Any human involvement in an otherwise automated delivery process creates a bottleneck, resulting in a buildup of unfinished work in progress: a batching point and a queue. With continuous deployment, each human task is replaced by faster computation, where one step triggers the next. This enables development teams to achieve a true "one commit = one production deploy" approach, as depicted in Figure 2-8.

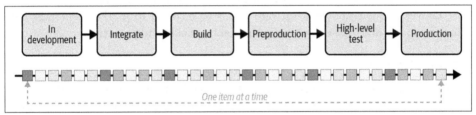

Figure 2-8. Batching in the path to production after continuous deployment

Figure 2-8 illustrates how continuous deployment eliminates batching and queues in the path to production. By adopting this approach, the code's journey closely aligns with the end-to-end one-piece flow principle advocated by Lean manufacturing. This full realization of a one-piece flow is the primary advantage of continuous deployment, allowing it to unlock all the benefits of Lean observed in physical manufacturing. Figure 2-9 provides a visual representation of the parallel between the two.

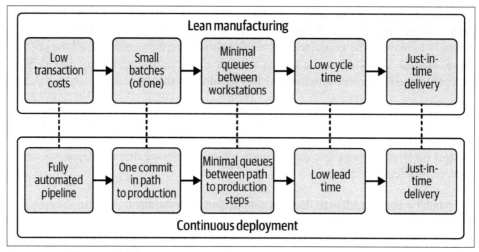

Figure 2-9. The parallel between Lean and continuous deployment

In conclusion, the adoption of continuous deployment has far-reaching implications for efficiency and responsiveness to change. Implementing a fully automated pipeline without manual gates enables an uninterrupted flow of code that eradicates queues and batching from the software value stream. By embracing continuous deployment, organizations can closely mirror the principles of Lean manufacturing and just-in-time delivery. This empowers software teams to respond to market demands, customer feedback, and ever-evolving requirements quickly and proactively.

Continuous flow ratio

Because the goal of Lean is to eliminate batching and queues at all steps of the path to production, it follows that the definition of continuous deployment should not just be tied to the central pipeline having no human tasks in it. Keeping changes small and integrating frequently before the pipeline has a chance to step in is just as crucial.

When a team wants to evaluate how close it is to a one-piece flow (or one-commit flow), it should measure the ratio of changes as seen from both ends of the path to production:

Number of production deployments / Total number of commits

where the number of total commits should be measured from any source control branch. When this ratio is close to 1:1, it implies that commits aren't piling up in the most common bottlenecks, such as in long-lived branches, in manual reviews, behind red builds, or at any other congestion point.

This allows the definition of continuous deployment to stretch so that it can also accommodate scenarios in which teams have no choice but to temporarily close the gate to production. Sometimes it's just not possible to rely on automated regression tests to verify some changes, and manual intervention is unfortunately required. Temporarily closing the gate to production has been necessary from time to time in the teams I have worked with. This happened, for example, when we were about to push particularly risky and hard-to-test changes, such as moving critical infrastructure around. To keep close to the 1:1 ratio, however, this should be a very rare exception, and the rest of the team members should refrain from adding more code on top of a paused pipeline.

With continuous integration, a red pipeline prompts the team to stop whatever it is doing and collectively focus on making the pipeline green again. Similarly, for continuous deployment, a pipeline that is paused before production should prompt the team to stop whatever it is doing and focus on removing the bottleneck so that it can restore the continuous flow of code to production as quickly as possible.

If this ratio is treated as a service-level objective (SLO), teams can organize their work around an "error budget" and keep an eye on their current performance with continuous deployment. Dropping this metric might highlight issues, such as lots of failed builds or the team's low confidence in its current work (which might lead to behavior such as hoarding commits in long branches).

DORA Metrics

Lean manufacturing is an excellent framework for managing inventory and optimizing a value stream, but it can also be a very theoretical subject. In this section, we'll look at something more concrete: how continuous deployment affects the four key metrics of software delivery.

The DORA State of DevOps research program (*https://oreil.ly/SIFwg*) has analyzed years of research data from tens of thousands of IT professionals worldwide. It is the longest-running academic investigation into software delivery practices, and year after year it has shown a clear correlation between high deployment frequency and IT performance. With software being a key differentiator for companies in most industry domains, IT performance should in turn be a key concern for companies that want to remain competitive and delight their customers. The following quotation explains this relationship well:

> In order to measure organizational performance, survey respondents were asked to rate their organization's relative performance across several dimensions: profitability, market share, and productivity. [...] Analysis over several years shows that high-performing organizations were consistently twice as likely to exceed these goals as low

performers. This demonstrates that your organization's software delivery capability can in fact provide a competitive advantage to your business.[4]

DORA researchers measure IT performance through the lens of two groups of metrics: throughput and stability. Throughput is measured as lead time for code changes (the time it takes for a code commit to reach production) and deployment frequency. Stability is measured as the time it takes to restore service after a bad deployment and the change failure rate (the occurrence of incidents and bad deployments). You can see a summary of all four metrics in Figure 2-10. Organizations that perform well in these metrics report significantly less time spent on rework, less time dedicated to unplanned work, higher productivity, higher profitability, and last but not least, a much improved quality of life for engineers.

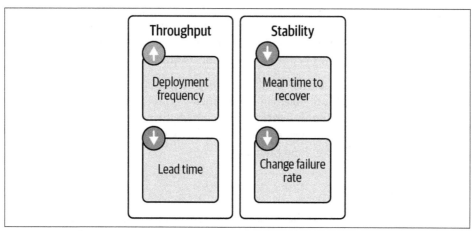

Figure 2-10. The DORA metrics

Continuous deployment is a practice that significantly alters the day-to-day software development life cycle, and in doing so, it also beneficially affects these metrics.

The remainder of this section offers a detailed explanation of the impact this practice has had on each of the four key metrics in the teams I worked with that adopted continuous deployment, and our understanding as to why we perceived each change. We don't have academic research that is specific to continuous deployment at our disposal to judge its full impact yet, although I hope we will soon. Instead, this section includes qualitative considerations that originate from working with continuous deployment across multiple organizations—with vastly different scales and business models—and from exchanges with fellow industry professionals who have had similar experiences.

---

4 Nicole Forsgren et al., *Accelerate: Building and Scaling High Performing Technology Organizations* (Portland, OR: IT Revolution Press, 2018), p. 58.

Throughput Metrics

Throughput refers to the rate at which a development team delivers new features and updates. High team throughput means that a team is able to deliver new features and updates more quickly, while low team throughput means that a team is less efficient and takes longer to deliver new features or iterate. Several factors can affect throughput, including the team's skill level, the quality of its tools and processes, and the level of collaboration and communication within the team.

Continuous deployment is primarily a process optimization, and its most immediately noticeable effect is an improvement in two throughput metrics: deployment frequency and lead time.

Deployment frequency

Deployment frequency refers to the number of new code updates rolled out to production within a given period. It can be easily measured by counting the number of deployments within that time; for example, deployments to production within a 24-hour period (Figure 2-11).

One important thing to note when measuring deployment frequency is that a deployment (code update) does not necessarily equal a release (new functionality visible to users). We will explore this in depth in Chapter 3. For now, let's just focus on the fact that not all code updates have the goal of changing the external behavior of the system, and not all releases require a code update (e.g., when using runtime feature flags).

For this reason, the number of releases is naturally much smaller than the number of deployments. Releases also follow a completely different schedule, which is dictated by product needs rather than engineering and maintenance needs (although a higher number of deployments can certainly *enable* a higher number of releases).

From now on, when I talk about deployment frequency I am referring to the frequency of code deployments only, not the frequency of feature releases.

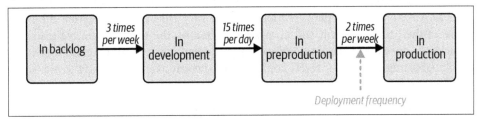

Figure 2-11. Deployment frequency

Perhaps unsurprisingly, continuous deployment dramatically increases deployment frequency. Before continuous deployment, a manual gate before production meant that several changes could pile up in preproduction, waiting to be manually released in batches. Once this gate to production is removed, a single commit will (in most cases) correspond to a single code deployment. This leads to an increase in deployment rate, which rises to match the organization's code commit rate.

Considering how many code commits developers can check in on a daily basis, this might seem like a daunting number of deployments overall. However, a high number of daily deployments is an increasingly common phenomenon these days and shouldn't be feared, mainly because reducing batch sizes decreases the risk of each deployment (as we will see in "Change failure rate" on page 49). Research from as early as 2016 shows how teams in high-performing organizations deploy their services to production multiple times per day, with companies such as Amazon and Netflix reaching astonishing aggregated numbers of thousands of deployments per day (over the hundreds of services that comprise their production environments). This is mentioned in the DORA "Accelerate State of DevOps Report 2016":

> This year, high performers reported that they are routinely deploying on demand, performing multiple deployments per day. Low performers, by comparison, reported deploying between once per month and once every six months. We normalized these ranges to 1,460 deploys per year (four deploys per day x 365 days) for high performers and seven deploys per year for low performers (average of two deploys and 12 deploys). These figures show that high performers deploy code 200 times more frequently than their low-performing peers. It's worth noting that four deploys per day is conservative with respect to companies like Etsy, which reports deploying 80 times per day, or to companies like Amazon and Netflix that deploy thousands of times per day.[5]

Organizational size can make for really large numbers in aggregate. But while aggregated metrics can be impressive, I encourage you, the reader, to focus on deployment frequency at the team level. When services are sufficiently decoupled, teams can deploy independently, and each team performing continuous deployment will see its deployment frequency match its code throughput, as seen in Figure 2-12. A team's code throughput tends to remain stable regardless of organization size. This means the average team deployment frequency can be measured in the same order of magnitude, regardless of whether that team belongs to a startup or to a massive company such as Amazon. Deployment frequency might vary based on the current life-cycle phase of the product, but it will always be limited by the team's cognitive load and capacity. In my experience, a typical continuously deploying product team (four to 10 developers) might push 10 to 30 commits per day on average, leading to the same number of deployments.

Of course, deployments should not be performed for deployments' sake, and on their own they are not what drives good organizational performance. After all, one could

---

5 DORA "Accelerate State of DevOps Report 2016," p. 16. You can read the full report at *https://oreil.ly/rw8BS*.

log in to their favorite pipeline tool and re-trigger the deployment button several times in production, thereby deploying zero lines and adding zero value.

Instead, it is the number of deployments closely matching the number of code changes that enables individual teams to move quickly. When each change can be rolled out independently, teams greatly improve their flexibility, as they are able to adapt to changing conditions with maximal speed and granularity.

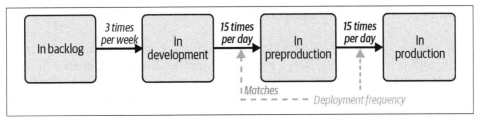

Figure 2-12. Deployment frequency matching code commit frequency

Frequent deployments are akin to a healthy heartbeat in terms of indicating that the team is integrating frequently and is smoothly deploying what it integrates. With continuous deployment, deployments to production are practiced so often that they become a nonevent: just as routine as pushing a code commit to a git remote (quite literally, since that is the trigger for any deployment). The process for defining a code change in version control becomes the same as the process for applying a code change to production, or at least they happen close enough together that they are hard to distinguish. This makes deployments boring for developers and stakeholders alike, as they become a natural side effect of writing code every day. Boring deployments allow everyone to stop treating production with fear, and to experiment quickly and fluidly instead.

Lead time for changes

Lead time refers to the time it takes to deliver a new update to production. DORA's approach to measuring lead time is to start the clock when a change is shared to the git remote of the source control system, in any branch, and to track how long it takes for it to make its way to production. Some competing definitions start measuring lead time earlier, and they add the time it takes for the new increment to be fully developed. For the purposes of this chapter, we can focus on what happens after a code check-in (Figure 2-13).

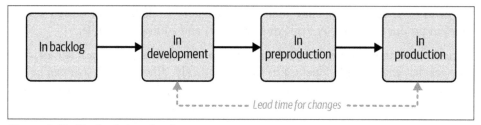

Figure 2-13. The lead time for changes

How long does it take for changes to make it to production when the team practices continuous delivery but still keeps a gate to production? In my experience, it takes from at least a few hours to a few days. Changes arrive as a steady stream of rollouts in preproduction environments, but they get promoted to production quickly only if there's a strong incentive to do so, such as an active incident or an urgent bug fix. Deployments to production might be forgotten for a while unless they are planned on a schedule. And even on a schedule, they will still accumulate and wait for at least a few hours.

However, top-performing organizations reported (*https://oreil.ly/VSAkq*) lead times of less than one hour in 2021. This is a significant improvement from even a few years ago, when lead time was still measured in days, and is proof that the industry is moving more and more quickly.

With an approval gate, specific deployments can *potentially* still go to production very quickly (provided they don't have to be untangled from other unrelated changes first), but such a short lead time requires the availability and attention of a developer to review and manually promote the deployments. In practice, this is sustainable only for high-priority fixes and leads to a two-track process in which the expedited path is exercised only during times of stress—which leads to mistakes. Achieving a stable average lead time of less than one hour is impractical without continuous deployment. Any human review process that could operate fast enough to support hourly deployments would arguably be better expressed in automation, especially given how repetitive the review step would become when a team deploys so many times a day.

When replacing the review process with full automation, lead time depends not on the time it takes for the pipeline to finish *and* the time it takes a human to make a decision and then act on it. Rather, lead time is measured by the speed of the automation only, which is much more stable and predictable (and obviously much faster). Therefore, the removal of human interaction from the code's path to production lowers and stabilizes lead time for changes significantly.

The incredibly short lead time brought on by continuous deployment brings both simplicity and predictability. A fast, continuous flow of changes is very simple to reason about, as the codebase won't have time to diverge far away from production and one change will correspond to exactly one deployment. There is no confusion as to when the last deployment to production occurred, whether a change is live, how many changes it contains since the last one, and whether the deployment step is still working at all since the last time it was triggered.

Most importantly, a short lead time generates insights quickly for developers and testers, who will get feedback for new code changes as quickly as they can develop them. Sometimes engineers and stakeholders need to see a change in production before they can decide what they have to do next, especially when running experiments. Getting changes in front of stakeholders and customers more quickly allows for validating product decisions and making incremental changes without being slowed down by process, whether that means rethinking a whole feature or just tweaking some details. In short, it reduces waste.

For end users, short lead time can provide a better user experience, as they have access to new features and improvements more quickly and more predictably. It can also help improve the overall stability of the software, as developers are able to quickly fix bugs and other issues. Overall, short lead time can help improve the speed, cost, and quality of software development. And the removal of manual steps encouraged by continuous deployment can shrink lead time in such a way that changes feel almost instantaneous.

Stability Metrics

Stability refers to the ability of a software system to function reliably and without unexpected behavior or errors. Stable software can be trusted to work reliably, even when undergoing frequent updates.

In the past, delivery speed and software stability were thought of as opposites, where one must be traded off against the other. However, the DORA research has since proved that for most high-performing organizations, quite the opposite is true: speed (throughput) and stability actually go hand in hand, each enabling the other in a virtuous cycle of engineering excellence.

This virtuous cycle is also reflected in the impact of continuous deployment. While its most obvious side effect is increased throughput, it also has a positive effect on stability metrics. Let's have a look at the impact on those metrics, starting with mean time to recover.

Mean time to recover

Mean time to recover (MTTR) refers to the average amount of time it takes for a software system to recover from a failure or disruption. In other words, it is a measure of the resilience of the application and its ability to quickly bounce back from unexpected issues.

MTTR is a broad metric. It includes failures and disruptions that can be automatically corrected by infrastructure orchestration and automation, or by tweaking an application's configuration at runtime (e.g., turning a toggle off). However, it also includes a vast range of issues whose only possible fix is to roll out a code or configuration change. In this section, we will focus on the latter type, shown in Figure 2-14.

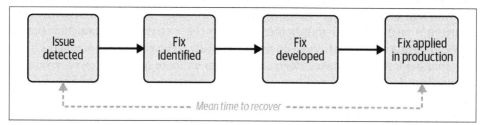

Figure 2-14. The mean time to recover with code changes required

Perhaps the most obvious example of how speed has the pleasant side effect of enabling stability is continuous deployment's positive influence on the average MTTR. The resolution to many active incidents requires code tweaks to make it through the whole path to production, as you can see in Figure 2-15; sometimes even multiple times when incidents are nontrivial and some trial and error is involved.

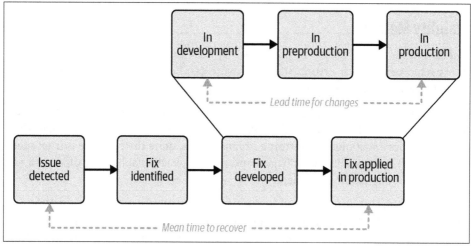

Figure 2-15. The mean time to recover including lead time for changes

When the lead time for an application is as short as it can possibly be, the time it takes to release an urgent fix is also as short as it can possibly be. It is not surprising that the MTTR measured (*https://oreil.ly/uxFxA*) in 2021 closely resembles the lead time measured the same year: less than one hour for top-performing organizations.

Some cans of worms only open up under production conditions, and that's when a short lead time and no manual gate to production enables developers to quickly deploy debugging mechanisms and remediations. Instead of being limited to a fixed number of deployments per day or having to chase approvers around during emergencies, developers can implement as many changes as they need to effectively put out the fire and are only limited by the speed of their own pipeline.

To further accelerate fixes, continuous deployment also ensures that the latest version of the code is always in a deployable state. The top of the main branch is always self-contained and deployable by definition. Indeed, when a developer checks in a fix, chances are that the previous commit is already in production. That means the only change the developer needs to consider is the fix itself, which is incredibly helpful under stressful situations where the cognitive load is high. Continuous deployment forces developers to be very disciplined with each code increment, and one of the biggest payoffs is the guaranteed deployability of the codebase at any given time. There is never an undeployable mess of tangled changes that have diverged very far from the current production version, so any urgent fix can go to production without waiting for half-finished, undeployed code to be put aside first.

Additionally, continuous deployment makes production issues caused by new rollouts trivial to debug. When change deltas are as small as one commit, the lines of code to investigate become very few. Cause and effect are far clearer. In my experience, it often takes less than one hour to determine the root cause of an issue. In many cases, even just a few minutes of looking at the source diff has been enough. And when the root cause cannot be determined (or the degradation is so serious that a team can't wait to debug and produce a fix), each increment is so small that it can be rolled back with minimal impact. Rolling back won't undo unrelated functionality that happened to be bundled with the problematic change but that might be very urgent to someone else. This decouples code changes from one another in production and allows for fine-grained control over which lines of code are live at any given moment.

Change failure rate

Change failure rate refers to the percentage of changes made to a system that result in errors or other disruptive behavior for users (Figure 2-16). It is a measure of the safety of the changes and can indicate the overall reliability of the software delivery process. To calculate change failure rate, development teams typically track the number of changes applied to production and the number of those changes that result in downtime, regressions, or other issues. The change failure rate is then calculated by dividing the number of changes that result in failure by the total number of changes.

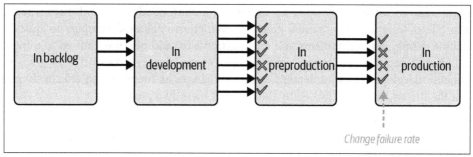

Figure 2-16. The change failure rate

Continuous deployment lowering the rate of failures might sound counterintuitive. After all, wouldn't a stream of manually unverified changes reaching production multiple times a day be a guarantee that something will go wrong far more often?

Quite the opposite is true, and it is true for the same reason that integrating code more often makes integration easier: deploying in big batches is much riskier than deploying multiple smaller changes, one at a time.

If we want to be pessimistic, each line of code that is changed can be thought of as a potential source of a new bug or unexpected error that will appear after rollout. Things are not usually *that* bad, but you don't need to be very pessimistic to see that the odds of each rollout being successful are inversely proportional to the number of lines of code changed within it. Changes that address completely unrelated functionality can be especially tricky, making testing overwhelming.

Continuous deployment brings the change delta from one deployment to the next down to a very low number of lines of code: one commit's worth. Shrinking the number of changes batched together in this way reduces the change failure rate because good changes are not contaminated by bad ones. In Figure 2-17, we can see this effect in more detail.

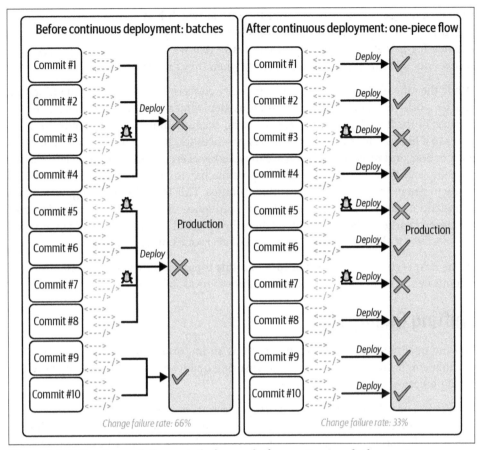

Figure 2-17. The change failure rate before and after continuous deployment

As you can see in the figure, the sample of commits for both scenarios is identical: the same three commits out of 10 contain a bad change. However, with batches, faulty commits get bundled with healthy commits, polluting the whole batch. More frequent and granular deployments decrease the overall change failure percentage in production, even when the same number of defects are being produced.

Some people might object that this is just improving how the metric looks, and the actual rate at which the team is producing bad code remains identical. That is true, but there are other factors that need to be taken into consideration. For instance, reverting a production deployment in the situation on the right doesn't force us to revert other good changes bundled within it, which is what happens in the situation on the left. Also, on the right, the diagnosis of each issue can be much simpler and more granular. Finally, notice how in the drawing on the left, two unrelated issues are being deployed together, complicating debugging even further (in my experience, this situation is very common without continuous deployment).

I would even go so far as to say that the rate at which bad commits are being produced is not a hugely important factor. One of my biggest takeaways from software engineering is that we should *expect* failures so that we can optimize our processes to recover our systems quickly and gracefully when they inevitably happen.

While the rate of bad commits is not a primary concern here, it is also something that can be positively impacted by continuous deployment. In my experience, that is because immediate deployments can act as an accountability tool that holds the engineers to a high standard. All of the team's practices for good-quality production code, automation, and regression testing are thoroughly exercised every time a code change is made, and they all have the highest possible bar to clear: generating code that is ready to run in front of real users within minutes. This tends to make engineers more conscientious and thorough, and it is a big influence on the positive feedback loop I mentioned earlier: where stability enables the speed of continuous deployments, but the speed itself also keeps stability in front of everyone's minds.

In the next section, I will delve deeper into this topic and describe in detail how continuous deployment can influence the culture around software quality.

Shifting Quality Left

Shifting quality left, or building quality in, is an important principle of quality strategy that emphasizes the importance of ensuring quality at early stages of the development process.

Quality is a broad term that refers mostly to testing, but also to verifying aspects such as performance, security, and other *cross-functional requirements* (CFRs). By implementing all testing and quality gates early on, developers and QA engineers can uncover potential problems before they turn into major issues or become expensive to fix.

This shift-left principle can be observed both from the perspective of the team's workflow (e.g., their board) and from the perspective of the code's path to production, as shown in Figure 2-18.

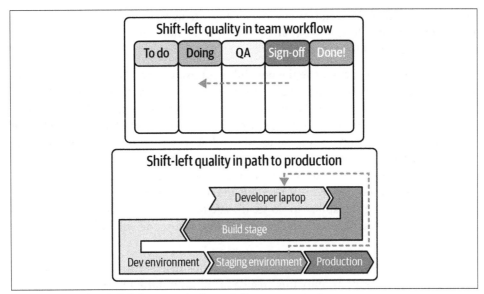

Figure 2-18. The shift-left principle from different perspectives

Building quality and testing early can save time and resources and can ultimately result in a better product, as has been confirmed by DORA research in several State of DevOps reports.[6]

How Continuous Deployments Force a Quality Shift to the Left

By sending every code change to production, continuous deployment is an enormous influence for the entire team to shift quality and production readiness considerations to the very beginning of each task.

Before continuous deployment, it was not easy for a developer to oversee their code all the way to production: stories changed hands soon after development, when they were tested or deployed by someone else. And as a task changes hands, the responsibility for it does too. This makes it easy to "throw code over the fence" (in fact, it encourages it), and it becomes easy to be superficial about the code and tests one is producing, relying on a false sense of safety given by the knowledge that someone else will have a second look later on. Handover can also lead to a loss of knowledge, as key information may not be adequately transferred from one team member to another.

But with continuous deployment, production deployments become a routine part of the in-progress phase of any task and are overseen by the same developers who

---

6 See *https://oreil.ly/ksQGT* to read the DORA "Accelerate State of DevOps Report 2016" in full. See *https://oreil.ly/K9--m* to read the DORA "Accelerate State of DevOps Report 2018" in full.

author the changes. This end-to-end ownership encourages engineers to write more thorough automated tests and pay attention to production worthiness, and it discourages making changes lightheartedly.

Immediate deployments remove the possibility for excuses and "I'll do it later" thinking that would otherwise be offered by the code temporarily resting in preproduction, allowing for late manual tests. Many times I have seen tasks having to do with performance, security, and observability be relegated to the very end of a feature, where at best they are much more expensive to add and at worst are deprioritized by stakeholders in a hurry to release. I have vivid memories of the panic on developers' faces when they realized that a teammate just deployed the system earlier than they expected. Continuous deployment prevents the temptation to cheat at "shifting quality left" by removing the ability to do so. It's safe to say that it's much harder to defer testing and good practices with the awareness that your code will be live in less than one hour.

In the first team where we moved from continuous delivery to continuous deployment, the sense of responsibility this created for us only started hitting us a day or so after the gate to production had been opened. Suddenly, as we were about to check in new changes, we were reminded that the lines we were about to check in would be in front of the users just 30 minutes later. Never before had we felt the potential impact of our mistakes so strongly.

But that responsibility we were feeling wasn't new at all: our code was *always* going to end up in production sooner or later, with the same potential for errors and mistakes. It just happened to do so long after we had forgotten we had written it. And by that point, we had stopped feeling personally responsible for it. Our code reaching production used to be out of our direct line of sight, but now it was right in front of us as the direct consequence of a "git push" command.

That feeling of immediate accountability made us care much earlier for our tests, and for cross-functional aspects of our code. It made us take test-driven development more seriously, have more thorough story kickoffs, and spike our changes out before starting a user story to make sure we would send things to production in the right order when dealing with interdependent systems. It also made us introduce safety mechanisms to hide our work in progress much earlier than we would have done otherwise (we'll talk about those in Chapter 3). In short, it increased quality.

And yes, all of these tasks should be done even without continuous deployment, but it was continuous deployment that forced us to do them as early (as left) as possible.

The Effects of Automating Quality Gates

Automating and shifting quality gates is usually great news for QA engineers. With developers having to write thorough automated quality gates during implementation, repetitive and detailed manual regression checks by QAs become a thing of the past (as it should be, given that computers are much better at following checklists, and they don't have souls that get crushed by endless repetition). This frees people to do more valuable and rewarding work, such as helping their team reflect on their overall quality strategy, exploratory testing on new features, or outlining the quality requirements for whole products and programs: all things computers cannot do.

Taking care of testing and other cross-functional aspects of the code[7] as early as the implementation phase also has the secondary effect of bringing all roles closer together so that they can collaborate on each in-progress item. By working together, developers, QA engineers, and designers can ensure that each code change is well-written, well-tested, and ready for deployment. Every role bringing their unique perspective early in development helps to create a more well-rounded and robust product.

Summary

Continuous deployment can represent many improvements for teams willing to try it. Most importantly, it is the methodology that most closely resembles the one-piece flow of inventory that is core to Lean manufacturing. In addition, it positively affects the four key metrics for IT performance introduced by the DORA research: it increases deployment frequency and drastically lowers lead times, which implies lower mean times to recover, and it results in smaller change deltas that in turn lower the change failure rate. It also represents a very literal interpretation of the shift-left principle: ensuring that all the activities that make code production ready and well-tested are taken care of in the development phase rather than "later on" in the path to production.

---

7 Criteria that measure characteristics of a system that are not related to specific behaviors or functions.

CHAPTER 3

The Mindset Shift

As I mentioned in Chapter 1, initiating continuous deployment requires only a small change for a team that already has a good continuous delivery pipeline. Usually, this change amounts to one line: removing manual approval from production deployments.

The real challenge with this practice does not lie in its implementation, but in the fact that as soon as it *is* implemented, developers have to start thinking differently about how they write code. In particular, they need to author every commit while keeping in mind their immediate proximity to production.

Planning development with immediate production deployments in mind is a big difference in workflow, and one that might take some time getting used to. This has certainly been my experience, and for a time it has caused a sense of uncertainty in my teams when touching our codebase. Back then, I wished there were more resources to explain how to adapt our day-to-day work to this paradigm, which is also one of the reasons I started to write about it. Although it seemed a bit intimidating at the beginning and we made some mistakes along the way, over time we noticed how our gradual shift in mindset made a positive impact on the speed and quality of our work.

Therefore, the aim of this chapter is to collect the main "gotchas" of continuous deployment to help you fast-track the same learning process that we had to figure out from scratch and harvest its benefits earlier. I hope this will help reduce the initial cognitive load on teams that are trying continuous deployment for the first time and will provide some useful key concepts they otherwise would need to figure out on their own.

Let's dive right in with the first of these gotchas: the difference between defining and applying changes.

Defining a Change Versus Applying a Change

With a gate to production (i.e., sans continuous deployment), two distinct actions will occur for every change: defining it and then applying it to the production system. *Defining* a change means specifying how the running code in production *should* look at some unspecified time in the future, and committing that specification to a version control system. *Applying* the change is the deliberate act of selecting an existing change definition (a commit or a build) and making the production system conform to it. In other words, it is the actual deployment. These two distinct manual actions are illustrated in Figure 3-1.

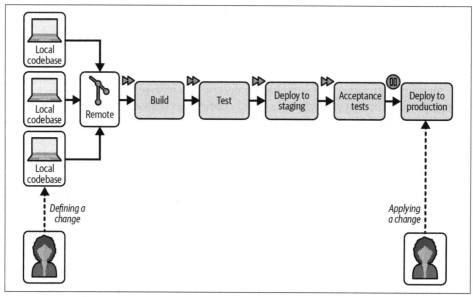

Figure 3-1. Defining a change and applying a change with a gate to production

The fact that these are disconnected manual steps has a strong impact on the team's way of working and gives a (perhaps false) sense of security to developers while they are writing code. They are aware at all times that further manual intervention is required to actually apply what they are writing to the production system, usually by another set of eyes. This means that it is not as crucial that every increment is correct or self-contained the first time. Every code change will receive at least a second look after being written, acting as a kind of "Are you sure?" dialogue for deployment. Of course, this second look will often happen in less than ideal circumstances: usually in a rush to get a release going, after the context for that code has faded from everyone's mind, by another person with less knowledge of it, or all of the above.

This sense of security, misguided or not, definitely ends with the introduction of continuous deployment. With it, the action required to specify a change (committing code to trunk in version control) is effectively the same action that applies the change to production. Sure, no pipeline is instantaneous, but the delay is insignificant compared to when the time between deployments used to be measured in days or weeks. The absence of further manual intervention makes it so that defining and applying a change to production becomes the same decision.

Therefore, under continuous deployment, changes are made to both version control *and* production in one step, as shown in Figure 3-2.

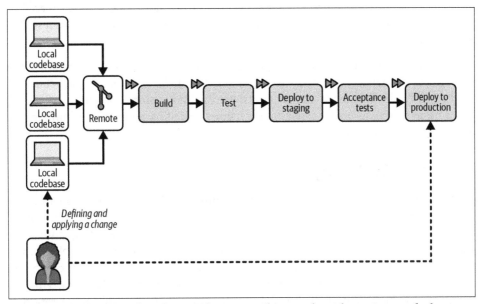

Figure 3-2. Defining and applying a change simultaneously with continuous deployment

In my experience, the absence of this distinction makes the act of writing code feel markedly different. To draw an analogy, it's like the difference between an electrician designing cabling for a new building to be installed from scratch and being on-site to maintain an existing system without causing disruptions to its users. For example, imagine an electrician doing work in a large office building that is in use. In the latter scenario, extra precautions must be taken, such as isolating the subsystem that requires work, implementing temporary redundancies or diversions to ensure uninterrupted service, and only integrating work in progress with the larger system when it is ready.

One could argue that teams not using continuous deployment still manage live systems, and therefore they should *already* be striving to make changes as nondisruptive as possible. However, developers often fail to consider this when they have only a vague knowledge of when or how those changes will be deployed in the future. Typically, most developers are working in scenarios resembling the second mindset (on-site maintenance), but with a manual delay that puts them in the mindset of the first scenario (architects or designers who are creating abstract projects). I believe this effect is one of the reasons why so many deployments end up with unintended consequences. The biggest benefit of continuous deployment might just be this: how it brings the reality of altering production systems to the forefront.

To address this reality, it is important to get ahead of production issues by ensuring that all quality assurance steps are completed during the development process. After all, there is no "after development": there is only production. That will be covered in Chapter 4, where I will outline practices such as continuous code reviews, test-first automation, and code scanning tools that can help achieve that.

In the following sections, however, I will explain not so much how to guarantee the correctness of changes, but rather which changes to make and *how*. In particular, I'll try to help you think more like an electrician making changes on-site: performing precautionary actions such as making diversions, installing temporary redundancies, and isolating subsystems.

Hiding Work in Progress

As discussed in the preceding section, any commit that developers send to trunk will end up being applied to production soon after. With the practice of continuous integration, we are also told that commits on trunk should happen very frequently; ideally many times a day, especially with trunk-based development. How developers are able to achieve this without exposing users to broken, "in progress" code is one of the first questions I always receive whenever I mention continuous deployment. This is a great question because it highlights that this practice involves careful consideration of the development work itself. You don't get successful continuous deployment by coding like you always have and pushing straight to production.

With code, "in progress" is usually synonymous with "unfinished," which, in turn, is almost always synonymous with "broken." Clearly, nobody wants to expose their users to broken changes. However, the association between "in progress" and "broken" is not necessarily true. In this section, we will discuss how we can keep unfinished changes hidden from users, keeping the codebase and production in *both* an unfinished *and* thriving state.

Version Control Branches

Even without continuous deployment, all teams have to deploy to production once in a while, and when they do, they normally have in-progress features they are working on at the same time that they aren't ready to send live. The problem of hiding work in progress during either the development of a big feature or refactoring is not unique to continuous deployment. It is present in any team with semi-frequent deployments to production.

To solve the issue of work in progress, teams have historically kept the code hidden away in version control branches for long periods of time until they were confident it could be released, as shown in Figure 3-3.

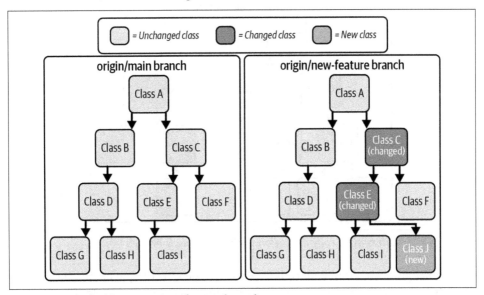

Figure 3-3. Code divergence in a feature branch

But continuous integration tells us that long-lived feature branches are to be avoided, as they cause painful merges and allow lots of unverified work to pile up. In Chapter 2, we talked extensively about the evils of batches of inventory (commits) piling up. Many teams that live by this principle either keep their branches short lived or perform trunk-based development. Their features might not be ready, and yet they will be routinely deployed to production, even in that state. So how do *they* do it?

Execution Branches

In recent years, two techniques in particular have gained popularity; they allow developers to hide away their changes, even when committing them to trunk. These techniques are *feature toggles* (or *feature flags*) and *expand and contract* (or *parallel change*).

Both techniques rely on segregating in-progress code in different *code execution branches* rather than in *version control branches*; see Figure 3-4. This means that instead of changing code directly, developers have to group all the code changes in an alternative code path that is not invoked by any caller until it's complete. Dave Farley and Jez Humble call this pattern "branch by abstraction."

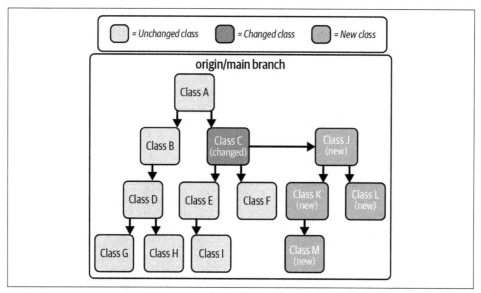

Figure 3-4. An alternative code execution path in the main branch

The branch by abstraction pattern is a very convenient technique because using your programming language to hide work in progress gives you more tools and more expressive power than relying on just the textual manipulation that your version control system is able to do. For example, your version control system might limit enabling and disabling of features to actions such as merge and revert (and sometimes cherry-pick), while code can represent complex conditions under which a feature might be visible or not. These conditions might be as simple as an ON/OFF switch or as complicated as limiting to specific test users or locations.

Feature toggles and expand and contract rely on storing code in separate execution branches. The main difference between them is how they allow switching to the newly created execution branch. Feature flags allow us to configure that at *runtime*, while expand and contract requires modifications at *compile time*.

Both techniques allow the entire team to work on trunk and integrate their code frequently, while still having a safe place to keep work in progress hidden from users' eyes. With continuous deployment, it's crucial that the whole team is comfortable using these two practices, as deployments to production happen all the time, and even a green test suite won't guarantee that a feature is actually ready to be seen by users. I will provide concrete examples of how to use these practices to perform common code modifications in Part III of this book, but for now we'll focus on the theory.

Feature toggles

Feature toggles (also known as feature flags) allow switching between different code execution paths at runtime. In short, they allow you to turn a feature on or off without deploying new code. They enable gradual feature rollouts, A/B testing, and controlling access to features for different user groups. They do so with the use of the following:

- Decision points in the code that evaluate the toggle state and decide whether to invoke the old or new flow based on its value.

- A persistence layer that stores the state of the toggle: ON, OFF, or something more complicated. Some teams avoid this by using the application configuration to store whether the toggle is active, making the feature flag effectively static (more on this later).

- An interface to change the toggle value so that developers and stakeholders have convenient access to the external persistence layer and can change the toggle state at runtime.

Implementation. In practice, the implementation of a feature toggle is usually as simple as a typical `if` statement:

```
const useNewAlgorithm = ... // <- retrieve toggle state
if (useNewAlgorithm) { // <- toggling behavior
  return newWayOfCalculatingResult();
} else {
  return oldWayOfCalculatingResult();
}
```

Both branches of the code (with the toggle ON and OFF) will of course need to be maintained and tested until the toggle is removed. This might add a little burden to the maintenance of quality gates, and in particular, duplicate some parts of the test coverage. In my view, it is a small price to pay for the flexibility the toggle offers, and this effort is quite easy to manage for simple, short-lived toggles.

The engine storing the toggle state and how to access it, however, can get quite a bit more complicated than an `if` statement, as it typically requires storage outside the application runtime, an administrator role, and a related interface. You can see an example of such an interface in Figure 3-5.

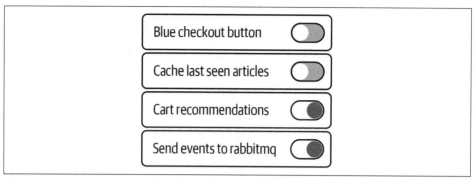

Figure 3-5. An example interface for a feature toggle system

Fortunately, this is a one-time investment, and you don't even have to build it yourself. There are a number of advanced feature toggle frameworks out there for all the major tech stacks, with the option to use different persistence engines, such as relational and nonrelational databases and file storage services. You might also want to consider an external, dedicated feature toggle platform that multiple services can use, such as Unleash (*https://www.getunleash.io*). If you'd rather not spend the time to build or install anything (which is often the best choice), you might want to consider feature flags as a service instead, offered by companies such as LaunchDarkly (*https://launchdarkly.com*).

Most feature toggle frameworks and services allow for advanced configuration options beyond a simple "ON or OFF for everyone." They often allow activating the toggle based on the user performing the request, their cookies, headers, a percentage of users, geolocation data, or even based on whether the user satisfies an arbitrary condition.

Back when continuous integration and continuous delivery were becoming popular, many teams questioned the up-front cost of creating an automated build pipeline when starting up a new project. However, nowadays it is widely accepted as a necessary investment to deliver safely, and it routinely gets set up within iteration 0 of any new product. In my view, feature toggle infrastructure should be held in the same regard. It is a necessary precondition to guarantee that the codebase can stay releasable and testable at any given time. Let's talk more about why.

Benefits. With a feature toggle in place, it is possible to develop an entire feature safely in a new code execution path. As long as the value of the toggle is OFF, the work in progress is invisible, so it is possible to commit incomplete code provided that it doesn't affect any other functionality. More advanced toggling strategies can then be activated to allow stakeholders to perform manual exploratory testing, and to later release the feature in a highly controlled way, gathering invaluable insights from it.

To achieve all of this, the same feature toggle can be reconfigured throughout its life cycle to serve those different purposes. While in development, it can start with a simple ON/OFF configuration to hide new features that are still in construction. During the QA phase, it can be set to activate by user or request to allow for testing in higher environments, especially production. Finally, it can be configured for randomized A/B experiments or incremental ramp-up during the release phase, letting stakeholders control how the new functionality should be seen by users.

What follows is that a toggle protects the entire team throughout all phases of a feature's life cycle: it protects developers from exposing unfinished code, QAs from performing unreliable tests, and product owners from releasing features that users don't like. This change is illustrated in Figure 3-6.

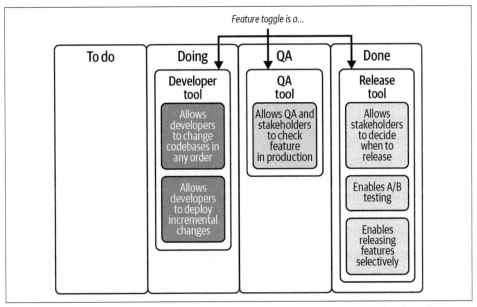

Figure 3-6. The nature of a feature toggle in different phases of a feature's life cycle

This fine-grained control over whether work in progress is visible (and to whom) makes feature toggles a must-have tool for teams continuously deploying their code straight to production.

A famous article (*https://oreil.ly/ykL2s*) by Martin Fowler makes a similar distinction between release toggles, experiment toggles, and ops toggles. While the nature of a toggle can be very different depending on what the team is trying to achieve, I believe that in practice this transformation can happen within the life cycle of the toggle itself, rather than requiring different, explicit toggles for every phase. For example, in my experience, we rarely used a different toggle for controlling release and performing A/B experiments. With most toggle frameworks, we could reuse the same one and just change its configuration.

Exploring how to manage toggles and how to leverage their capabilities will be the focus of Part IV of this book.

What about static feature toggles?.   There are a few reasons why teams might not appreciate a runtime feature toggle evaluation. For one, it usually introduces another network request in the application's flow, with all the latency that comes with it. Even more importantly, when most requests need to evaluate toggles, the toggle platform itself becomes a new single point of failure for the application.

For these reasons, some teams might prefer to keep the toggle state as a build-time variable: it will be part of the application configuration and/or its code, and it will be bundled into the deployment of the new version.

This measure, of course, removes a lot of flexibility. To turn a feature ON or OFF, a new code change and deployment is needed, which is not nearly as fast as a runtime change. To make releases safe with this method, teams require a very fast pipeline. Other activation strategies, such as traffic percentage and A/B testing, will also be mostly unavailable, as there is no centralized engine to "remember" which users fell into which toggle group.

But all is not lost. With some tweaks, static feature toggles can at least still allow for manual testing in production. If the team enriches them with ways to override the toggle based on runtime parameters (e.g., a special header or a cookie), then the toggle can remain static while still allowing a per-request override—all with no traffic leaving the application instance.

Overall, I would always recommend a full runtime feature toggle platform due to its flexibility, revert speed, and power to enable product experimentation. But static toggles can still be a good compromise in network-intensive applications.

Coincidentally, static feature toggles somewhat resemble the next alternative code execution path strategy I want to showcase, which also operates at build time: expand and contract.

Expand and contract

Expand and contract (or parallel change) is a coding technique that allows developers to switch between alternative code execution paths incrementally. It consists of implementing an alternative code branch in parallel to the old one (potentially with a different interface) and then migrating all callers to the new flow, one at a time. This granularity means the codebase can stay in a green and deployable state during the execution of this pattern.

The changes consist of three distinct phases: expand, migrate, and contract, as shown in Figure 3-7.

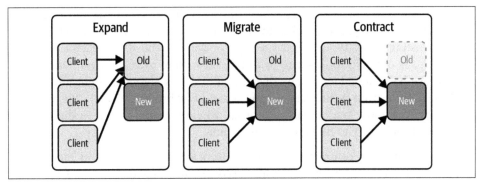

Figure 3-7. The expand, migrate, and contract phases

Implementation. In the expand phase, the alternative implementation can be built from the ground up. It should not be invoked yet, so the work in progress can be committed safely without affecting existing functionality.

Once the new execution branch is complete, the migrate phase starts. Each client of the old code will be updated to call the new code instead. Committing safely while some clients are not migrated is also possible during this phase, as the execution paths should be equivalent to each other.

Once all clients are calling the new code and the old execution branch is unused, then the contract phase can happen, where the old branch is safely deleted.

In more concrete terms, let's imagine we want to refactor a very long and complex function that is heavily coupled to the rest of the codebase in ways we are not quite sure of. We'll call that nightmare function `calculateResult`. If we wanted to refactor it safely with expand and contract, we would first rewrite that code and its tests from the ground up (expand), perhaps with a new name such as `calculateResultNew`. Keep in mind that `calculateResultNew` is still never called, so we have ample time to test it for correctness. Once it is thoroughly tested, we can hunt down every part of the codebase that invokes `calculateResult` and update it so that it calls `calculate ResultNew` instead (migrate). Once all callers are updated, we can finally delete the now unused original `calculateResult` (contract). The codebase has remained deployable throughout these steps, which might not have been the case if we had made several complicated changes to the original `calculateResult` all at once.

Benefits. Expand and contract is especially useful for refactoring because it allows developers to keep the codebase in a working state as opposed to making disruptive changes scattered all around the code. This works great in tandem with small and continuous deployments to production.

Often, expand and contract makes refactoring even easier because (as most developers know) it can be much quicker to implement something from scratch than to rework existing code. We can build a copy of what we need to refactor from the ground up, as opposed to tinkering with the old version over and over. During this process, we have the added bonus that the old code is always in sight and readily available to learn from (which lets us copy-paste useful bits and pieces). This wouldn't be as easy with more traditional refactoring, where we would need to dig through version control history to find our starting point.

Overall, expand and contract is a great pattern for making safe and incremental changes during refactoring, and it should become part of the daily toolbox for teams that use continuous deployment. Without manual gates, this pattern is one of the safest ways to perform most nontrivial refactoring actions.

Feature toggles versus expand and contract by type of change

The attentive reader might have noticed that feature toggles could *also* be used to hide work in progress during refactoring. This is certainly possible, and in some situations I would even encourage it (e.g., when the refactoring is really risky).

However, when refactoring, the features under change are already live. Developers can duplicate the code and introduce a new toggle, but that brings all the overhead of managing a new toggle's life cycle without offering any release experimentation benefits (the release process for that feature already happened, after all). It can quickly become inconvenient to introduce a toggle for all refactoring changes; for example, to change the signature of an existing function.

Toggles for refactoring can offer other relevant benefits (e.g., runtime rollback, testing the new path in production, slow ramp-up of traffic), but they are not my default choice due to their high overhead. Even when the change is big, feeling the need for a toggle could actually be a signal that the refactoring could be broken down into smaller, safer, and more incremental steps.

And vice versa: the expand and contract pattern can also be used for releasing new features. We could hide the unfinished feature code in an alternative execution branch, and require deploying a line of code as a "release" of the new feature instead of controlling it with a runtime flag. Again, this is certainly possible. In fact, it even resembles the static/build-time feature flags approach I mentioned earlier. However, it means forgoing all the fast feedback that could be gathered by a runtime approach, such as canary releases with a subset of traffic and the possibility to perform randomized A/B testing.

Ultimately, which technique to use for hiding work in progress is up to preference, but in Table 3-1 you can find my personal heuristic.

Table 3-1. Feature flags versus expand and contract by type of change

	Release/revert speed	Overhead	Type of change: Introducing new feature	Type of change: Refactoring live functionality
Feature flag	Very fast: Happens at runtime	High: Requires managing state, configuration, incremental release, and life cycle of the toggle	Use by default	Use when the new execution branch is big and/or likely to impact cross-functional requirements (CFRs) such as performance, resilience, etc.
Expand and contract	Slow: Requires new commit traveling along the path to production	Low: Managed in code only	Use when new feature doesn't need experimentation and is very safe to release	Use by default

Based on my day-to-day work maintaining and growing codebases and production, I find this approach to be the most pragmatic, as it considers the speed and overhead trade-off in the context of different types of changes. In Chapters 8 and 9, I will provide practical examples of how to apply feature toggles and expand and contract in this fashion.

A conclusion on hiding work in progress

With the use of either the feature toggles or expand and contract pattern, it is safe to implement new features or perform a lengthy refactoring while keeping the codebase green and deployable while we work on it. For teams that are used to hiding code in feature branches, these patterns might take a while to get used to. Developers won't be able to implement changes only where the old behavior happens to be, which is where it might feel most natural. Rather, they will have to look at the overall application beforehand and decide how to best group all of their changes in an alternative code path. This means resisting the temptation to change the existing code in place. In addition, if the behavior to change is scattered throughout the codebase, introducing a clean branching point might require some preparatory refactoring.

However, using these two techniques extensively results in a codebase that is virtually always in a stable and deployable state during development. Being more thoughtful of how we introduce our changes seems like a small price to pay in comparison.

This is a perfect example of how continuous deployment encourages us engineers to rethink our mindset during our day-to-day coding. Rather than following our gut feeling and starting to change things as soon as we find the relevant lines, we have to take a step back and plan how our changes will fit into the upcoming deployments and impact the running application first.

Hiding code in execution branches has many benefits over using version control branches, but that code still represents undelivered inventory.

Changes piling up in an expand phase or under a feature flag can also start to form batches. Just like with version control branches, letting changes accumulate can be dangerous if we forget about them, don't test them in production, and leave them to rot for a long time.

That is why it is still important to release changes to real users in a timely manner, independent of the strategy we use to hide work in progress. Not doing so means forgoing the main benefit of continuous deployment, which is fast iteration. But more importantly, it jeopardizes the safety of our releases.

Distributed Systems

Another one of the pervasive mindset shifts we adopted in our workflow was recognizing that in most teams, continuous deployment doesn't deal with just one deployable unit of software. Rather, most teams are dealing with a network of distributed subsystems, all deployed continuously and independently.

For example, a single microservice owned by our team could consist of different distributed units, such as a persistence layer, an application layer, and a UI. In its orbit, we could usually find even more distributed units, typically infrastructure pieces such as external caches, queues, and lambda functions. All of those components have separate deployments, even when they live within the same codebase, which complicates the management of contracts between them.

In the rest of this section, I will explain how to manage contracts with continuous deployment affecting several distributed components. In the process, you will see how this practice might actually lead to better contract management.

Contracts Between Systems

When talking about the complexities of distributed systems, the main topic is almost always their integration: in other words, the contracts between them.

This topic has been explored in depth in other literature, which has resulted in concepts such as contract testing (*https://oreil.ly/9ZX7_*), consumer-driven contracts (*https://oreil.ly/dshFP*) (CDCs), and a myriad of tools to put them in practice. I find that with all of these practices, the conversation's focus has mostly been on contracts that exist between a team's systems and "outside world" systems. Outside world systems might be maintained, for example, by other teams or third-party vendors. However, there is another situation that is under-discussed and which I already hinted at earlier. This is when a team maintains a service that has distributed subcomponents (i.e., within the same logical microservice) that also form contracts with each other—although usually the contracts are less formal. This is especially relevant to the successful application of continuous deployment within a team, so let's understand it better by elaborating on the example I gave earlier.

Formal contracts

Let's imagine a service maintained by a hypothetical team A. As you can see in Figure 3-8, its API (consumer) might rely on a third-party system to perform some task (provider), or vice versa. Every time a change request pops up, team A's developers will need to interact with the people responsible for the outside systems and update the affected contracts accordingly.

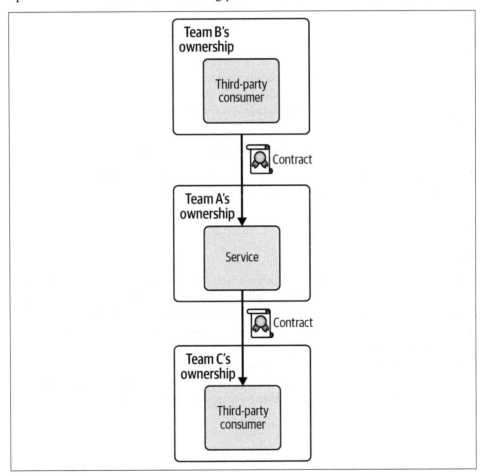

Figure 3-8. An example service collaborating with external systems

Most organizations already have processes in place to deal with this scenario. For example, they might have scheduled coordination meetings to ensure backward-compatible changes between teams A, B, and C. If team A is diligent, it might manage these contracts as CDCs and automate its verification with some kind of contract testing tool. Even if team A uses continuous deployment, it is both constrained and protected by other teams making compatible changes and has to follow an agreed-upon schedule.

Contract Compatibility Beyond Data Shape

It should also be noted that the considerations about contract compatibility can span way beyond data shape. For example, aspects such as response times and security could (and should) be part of the contract of a provider system, especially when it is externally facing.

Often, even client expectations that were never agreed upon can become part of a contract. It is possible for any change to an operation's internal implementation to break consumers, as long as the change has an observable side effect (e.g., becoming faster, changing the way data is ordered), even if the aspect in question was never agreed upon.

Hyrum's Law (*https://www.hyrumslaw.com*) summarizes this concept best:

> With a sufficient number of users of an API, it does not matter what you promise in the contract: all observable behaviors of your system will be depended on by somebody.

Informal contracts

Formal contracts with outside systems are a well-studied area and are not particularly affected by continuous deployment. But now let's zoom into team A's ownership boundaries; see Figure 3-9. A typical system such as that owned by team A tends to have lots of distributed bits and pieces. In this example, it is split into three deployable units: its persistence layer, API, and UI all talk to each other over the network. And contracts certainly need to be managed between them too: the UI consumes the API and expects it to respond in a certain way. Also, the API can be seen as the consumer of the persistence layer, as it relies on a specific schema being available.

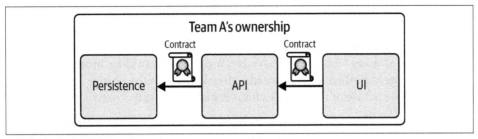

Figure 3-9. Distributed components owned by team A

While it was expected to think of team A's integration with team B in terms of formal contracts, we wouldn't think explicitly about contracts between those independent units deployed by team A only. For example, I have rarely seen teams putting contract testing tools between their backend and frontend, and I have seen exactly *zero* teams putting formal contracts between their backend and database schema. This is for good reason: when all changes are managed by the same team, the overhead of practices such as CDCs and contract testing would introduce rigidity and would slow development unnecessarily. In most cases, those contracts remain informal, and their management is left to the common sense of the team.

This is markedly different from a situation with formal contracts, whose changes require outward-facing communication. At least, there are certainly no formal vendor/customer meetings to make sure changes are backward compatible and sequenced correctly between provider and consumer.

And yet, those services are separate executables in production that have to communicate with each other. As such, they *do* have contracts between them, whether formal or informal. And if we are not paying attention to how we deploy those components, those contracts (and production) can break.

We have to take care of both types of contracts while developing and deploying, but we should be especially careful around the informal type.

We have distributed components and informal contracts the very moment any sort of interprocess communication happens. This can happen over the network, or through the filesystem, pipes, sockets, and so on. Most nontrivial systems respect this definition.

We have distributed subcomponents (and we risk breaking production contracts), even in the most monolithic-looking deployments. Think, for example, of a backend system's code and its database schema evolutions: they are usually versioned together, and changes to both are applied in quick succession during deployment. However, the database and application are different executables, usually even in different machines. A change that isn't backward compatible can break the contract between them for a few seconds, or even minutes. Another type of monolithic-looking deployment is that of a JavaScript UI and an API residing in the same repository, possibly even served by the same application (i.e., with server-side rendering). We might think that changing both sides of the contract of an HTTP call won't result in any disruption. Yet, for users who already have JavaScript loaded in their browser when the backend change is applied, communication breaks down if the change isn't backward compatible. The nature of most applications is distributed at its core.

These are just basic examples, and it only gets more complicated with domain-rich systems that include such things as message queues, event buses, NoSQL databases, file storage, and external caches.

By now you might be thinking, "Right, but how is this especially related to continuous deployment?" It turns out that the answer is "A lot more than one would expect."

Contracts Between Paths to Production

When we have distributed subcomponents (i.e., separate executables), we almost always have separate paths to production for them as well. Even when they don't have separate pipelines, different steps within the same pipeline are required to deploy them. If we have systems that depend on each other in production, then their deployments have dependencies too.

As we know, continuous deployment dramatically alters the way we must think of the concept of "the path to production," transforming it from asynchronous to synchronous. That is why interdependent paths to production between different executables deserve to be at the center of the conversation.

Any given task a developer picks up can span multiple distributed subcomponents, with informal contracts between them. Take, for example, frontend and backend. If the team has split its user stories into valuable increments, developers will deliver features end to end *by design*.

In the rest of this section, we will explore the relationship (or contract) between the path to production of a consumer system and a provider system, such as a frontend and a backend, an example of which is shown in Figure 3-10. We will see how changes made under continuous deployment can affect the production environment, especially when there aren't (and there shouldn't be) any formal contracts.

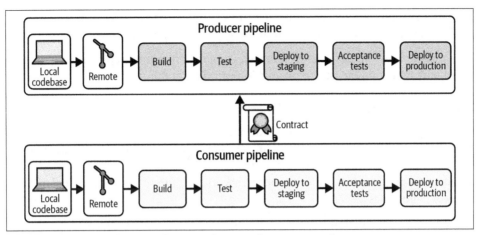

Figure 3-10. The paths to production of a provider system and a consumer system

The interdependencies between paths to production for consumer and provider systems can be described along two main axes: the order and timing of their deployments. Order is important when consumers rely on providers (providers need to be updated first), and timing is important when both depend on each other (e.g., requiring a simultaneous update). In Table 3-2, you can find a summary of how these factors are impacted by different styles of paths to production (i.e., with and without continuous deployment).

Table 3-2. Order and timing of deployments with and without a manual gate

	Order of deployments	Timing of deployments
Path to production with a manual gate (traditional continuous delivery)	Changes go live in the order in which the components are manually deployed (order of deployment).	Changes go live only when the components are manually deployed (timing of deployment).
Path to production without a manual gate (continuous deployment)	Changes go live in the order in which they are developed (order of development).	Changes go live as soon as they are developed (timing of development).

Let's see how this impacts the two main activities around software products: adding new features and refactoring live functionality. We'll start with the former.

Adding New Features: When Order Matters

Adding new features almost always requires making changes to several systems bound by informal contracts, and it is the most common example of paths to production showing a dependency on each other.

When adding new features that require changes in both a provider and a consumer, the changes need to be applied to the production system in a certain order: first on the provider and then on the consumer. If the underlying provider API is not ready, the consumer will be left broken and unusable from the point of view of users.

Let's explore how this contract is managed *without* continuous deployment to understand how removing the gate to production can disrupt this process.

With a gate to production: Order of deployment

When deployment to production is not happening on every commit, dependencies between providers and consumers can be manually managed at deployment time. Usually, this is done by deploying systems in the correct order: providers first, consumers second. This is a common occurrence with more conservative implementations of continuous delivery.

Remember the distinction between defining a change and applying a change that we talked about at the beginning of this chapter? This means that anyone who picks up a task can start defining changes on whichever component they wish, and in any order. Those changes will wait in preproduction to be applied in the correct order later on, at deployment time.

Or, we can say that code changes go live in their *order of deployment*.

In Figure 3-11, you can see an example of a change spanning two codebases owned by the same team: a provider system and a consumer system. You can see that the order of development (to the left) doesn't affect the order of deployment (to the right).

With a gate to production, it doesn't matter which codebase developers start working on first. Even if the consumer codebase will not do anything useful without the corresponding changes in the provider, the consumer changes can be committed first.

The gate to production in this case is allowing the team to not think about interdependencies between distributed components at development time, and to defer those decisions to deployment time.

Even though this can be done, it doesn't mean it should be done. Relying on waiting in preproduction to keep production stable means that we cannot release any other urgent change if the necessity arises. Accumulating work in progress in preproduction is also contrary to the principles of continuous delivery (keeping everything releasable), but it is hardly enforced without continuous deployment.

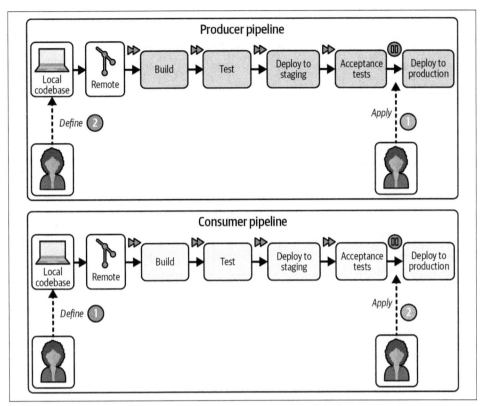

Figure 3-11. Changes going to production in their order of deployment

Without a gate to production: Order of development

Continuing with the previous example, imagine that the gate to production, and the human guarding it, have been removed, as implied by continuous deployment. Suddenly, interdependent changes won't pause in some staging environment. They will be immediately deployed.

If providers and consumers are updated out of order, the production environment will break—at least until the corresponding change to the provider is also committed, as shown in Figure 3-12. Users might see an error on their page, or a partly built feature that they shouldn't see.

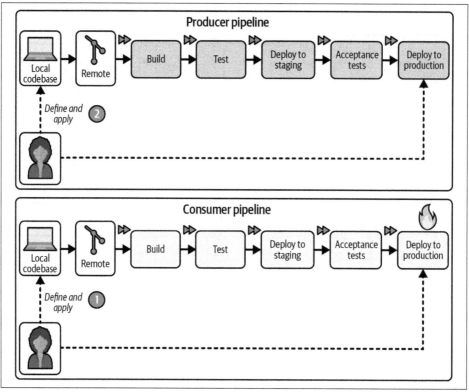

Figure 3-12. Incorrect order of development

The same developers deciding to start from one place or another would now release a breaking change, even if they didn't do anything differently and made the exact same changes in the exact same order.

The gotcha with continuous deployment is that changes go live in their *order of development*, not in their *order of deployment*. Therefore, engineers must adapt their daily workflow to respect the interdependencies between distributed components. They need to ensure that the order in which they make changes in their repositories respects the direction of provider–consumer relationships in their systems, as shown in Figure 3-13.

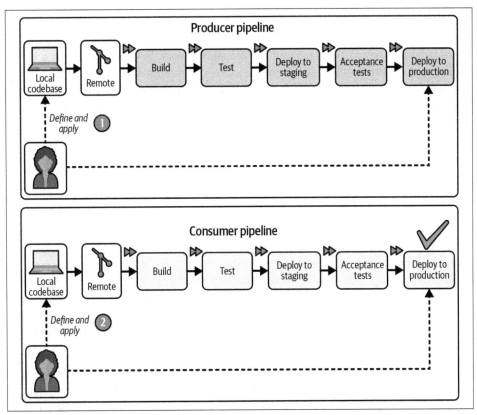

Figure 3-13. The correct order of development

This is a substantial change: with a gate to production, there were no serious consequences if developers picked a new task from their backlog and just started *somewhere*, maybe on the codebase they were most familiar with or with the first change that came to mind. With continuous deployment, it's not enough to know which component needs changing and how, and it's not even enough to perform those changes perfectly and without defects. There must be conscious planning of the order of code changes going live, at the granularity of individual commits. Being diligent with continuous delivery could be treated as optional before, but it becomes mandatory now.

If this is not taken seriously, things can get out of hand and can prevent teams that should be moving rapidly and independently from doing so. Fortunately, there are some tools at our disposal to lessen this cognitive load and to let continuous deployment allow some room for mistakes.

Feature toggles

When I talked about feature toggles in "Hiding Work in Progress" on page 60, I explained how they are a great tool for managing work in progress within a single codebase. As it turns out, they also come in very handy for avoiding system interdependence issues that are caused by code going live immediately after it is committed. They are an efficient way to relieve the pain of planning every commit, and they can be used to give developers some breathing room.

 Although feature toggles should be used with continuous delivery for the same purpose, they become a necessity when dealing with continuous deployment across interdependent systems.

Let's see how we can use them in the paths to production of our provider and consumer systems. A feature toggle placed on the consumer as a first step makes it possible to deploy (and therefore work on) the two codebases in any order. The broken feature on the consumer side is incomplete without the provider; however, this is not an issue. Anything broken is safely tucked under the OFF toggle, at least long enough for the team to complete the provider changes. As shown in Figure 3-14, the team can now work in the original order again.

In teams on which I have practiced continuous deployment, we have relied on feature toggles extensively to decouple our changes in this way and avoid problems originating from the order of development. With such a setup, our developers were empowered to work freely on any codebase on the condition that the code commit containing the feature toggle would always come first and would always be on the outermost consumer system (closest to the users)—and, of course, on the implicit condition that all tests and checks had to be green.

We will look at a very extensive example of how to use feature toggles to add new features in a live distributed system in Chapter 10.

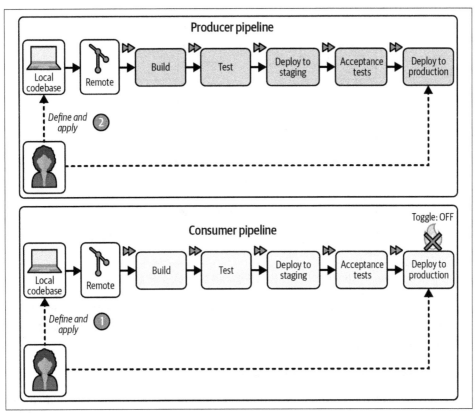

Figure 3-14. The incorrect order between provider and consumer hidden behind a feature toggle

Refactoring: When Timing Matters

There is another common scenario where paths to production of different systems depend on each other. Interdependence doesn't only happen when adding new features; it also happens when teams rearchitect existing, live functionality across multiple components. Refactoring contracts and changing their shape introduces a new challenge.

Think, for example, of a change spanning two services, A and B. Service A calls an endpoint on service B, or sends a message through a queue to it. We want to change the type of a parameter exchanged between the two from type X to type Y. There is no right order to deploy A's and B's changes. Whichever one is upgraded first will immediately be incompatible with the other and start generating errors, as shown in Figure 3-15.

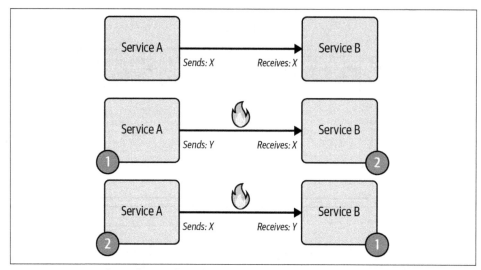

Figure 3-15. Interdependence when changing an existing contract

This makes the changes on providers and consumers interdependent in another way, one that can't be addressed with "correct" ordering. Both need to be updated to version $N + 1$ to be compatible again.

With a gate to production: Timing of deployment

Although this situation seems tricky, most teams practicing manual deployments to production (traditional continuous delivery) address it routinely, and often without even noticing. With a gate to production, provider and consumer systems can be kept compatible by upgrading them to version $N + 1$ "simultaneously," as shown in Figure 3-16. This might come for free when all systems are waiting for the "weekly deployment o'clock," or by manually clicking on the "deploy" button in close sequence. With set deployment windows, teams often deploy everything all at once anyway, so they don't have to address tight interdependencies explicitly.

Even so, this type of deployment still introduces a short window of application errors, as it is impossible to enforce multiple deployments at the same *exact* moment. Many find this short window tolerable in noncritical systems, and others might not even notice it. In my experience, the incompatibility delta with simultaneous deployments can range from a few seconds to a minute or so, so it's easy to miss or to ignore.

The key takeaway here is that with a gate to production, we have explicit control over the *timing of deployments* (e.g., making them happen simultaneously) as well as the order. This can reduce incompatibility issues between versions N and $N + 1$ to that short deployment window.

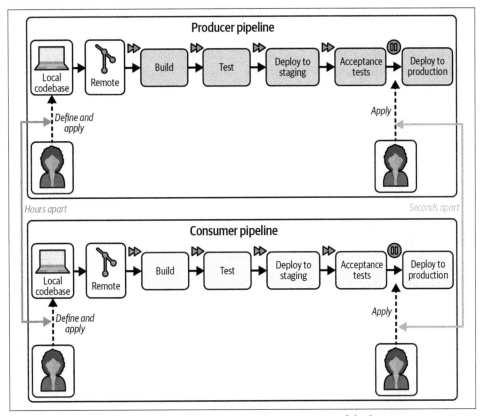

Figure 3-16. Changes going to production according to timing of deployment

Although using a gate to production to resolve interdependency issues in this fashion might seem tempting, I want to discourage this approach. I don't recommend it, for several reasons. First of all, it still *does* leave a short window of errors, which has the potential to break user trust, and it encourages developers tolerating strange behavior during a deployment. This is an open invitation for worse issues going undetected. For example, I have seen many teams where "weekly deployment time" was associated with a short burst of application 500s, and this was an accepted fact that nobody really questioned too much, treating it as a deployment glitch.

Most of all, however, I avoid simultaneous deployments because they once again encourage batching code in preproduction as a quick fix. They discourage thinking of how our components depend on each other, and how to safely upgrade them from version N to $N + 1$, which makes contracts even more implicit.

Without a gate to production: Timing of development

With no gate to production, the "simultaneous deployments" approach is not a concern, because it's completely off the table. As a thought exercise, let's see what would happen if developers applied changes the same way, but under continuous deployment instead.

As changes are developed and applied simultaneously, any delay in development on different codebases corresponds to an equal delay between deployments. It is not possible to perform deployments simultaneously. As shown in Figure 3-17, this would cause hours of errors, which is obviously not acceptable in most production systems.

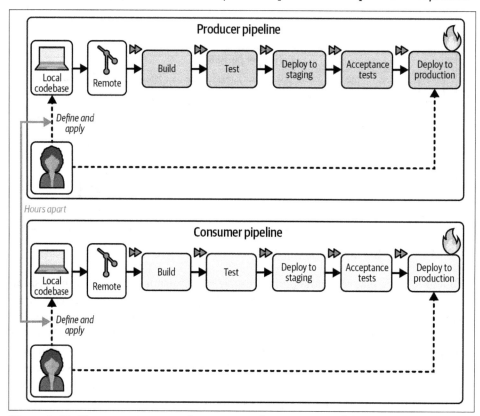

Figure 3-17. Changes going to production according to timing of development

Changes are applied to production with the *timing of development*, as there is no explicit time set aside for deployment. This removes any wiggle room that lets us have manual control of interdependent deployments, and changes to production adopt the same rhythm as the developers' code commits.

Because of this loss of manual control, it might be tempting to try to synchronize interdependent deployments to production with means other than the deploy button. Let's see why that is not likely to produce good results.

Antipattern: Delaying integration.   A workaround that might come to mind to synchronize deployments, even when the pipeline is performing them automatically, is to define the changes first and then wait to merge them into trunk until all codebases are ready. This, however, is not only impractical for developers but also not very effective. Even with simultaneous code pushes, we cannot guarantee that the automated pipeline for each codebase will take roughly the same time to finish. And we haven't even mentioned what would happen if one of those pipelines were to fail (which is very likely because healthy, frequent integration has been interrupted).

Antipattern: Pausing pipelines.   Because delaying integration is not very effective, we might try to resolve this by pausing the pipelines so that they stop in preproduction, and then deploy to production manually when we are sure everything is ready. This can force an almost simultaneous production deployment, but at the cost of interrupting the continuous flow of changes we worked so hard to set up. Since this type of interdependent change can come up fairly often, paused pipelines would get in the way of continuous deployment on a frequent basis.

The problem should be addressed at the root instead. Attempting to synchronize deployments is not a great solution, even without continuous deployment, and it becomes even more impractical *with* it. The real solution to tight interdependency issues between $N + 1$ versions is to not have those tight interdependencies in the first place. We should structure changes so that every version $N + 1$ of any system is always compatible with production version N of any other system. Let's see how to do that.

Expand and contract

Expand and contract is another pattern to hide work in progress that we discussed in detail earlier and that can be used very effectively to prevent broken integration between systems. It removes the interdependency of changes from the start, and it is also my go-to recommendation to approach types of refactoring that imply changing contracts.

By using this pattern in our continuous deployment workflow, we can leverage the intermediate phases of expand and migrate to prevent the natural timing of development from interfering with the functionality of the live system, as shown in Figure 3-18.

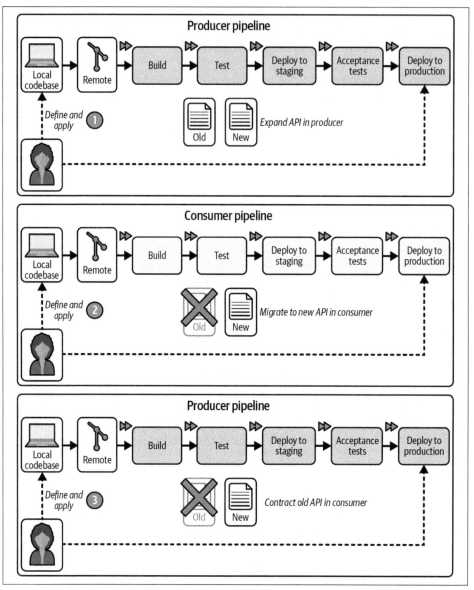

Figure 3-18. The expand and contract pattern applied across a provider and consumer system

As you can see in the three steps in the figure, the provider API will be expanded to support the new contract as well as the old (expand phase), which is a change that can go to production independently. After that change is applied, we can define another change in the consumer system to start relying on the new contract (migrate phase). Finally, the provider system can be updated again to do away with the old code.

Notice how this pattern removes the interdependency between changes completely, as each new version of the provider ($N + 1$) and the consumer is compatible with the current production version of the other (N). With this pattern, production can keep running in an intermediate and incomplete state without degradation of functionality.

This approach relies on coordinating (but not synchronizing) changes, where the different phases must be implemented in sequence. It can get more complex when there are multiple layers of providers and consumers impacted by the same change, but the payoff is huge: all systems remain compatible with one another at all times, and their path to production is free of obstacles when we need to make unrelated changes. This is another example of how the workflow enforced by continuous deployment has a beneficial impact on stability. We will see a thorough example of how to apply this pattern with multiple layers of providers and consumers in Chapter 9, and how to use it to refactor around databases without data consistency issues in Chapter 10.

A Deployment Is Not a Release

As we have discussed in this chapter, continuous deployment implies the absence of a distinction between declaring and applying code changes. This means that development teams have to rely heavily on techniques to keep changes hidden and keep contracts compatible, such as the expand and contract pattern and feature flags.

Incorporating those techniques into day-to-day work is already a mindset shift in and of itself, but their pervasiveness also brings another topic to the forefront of the conversation: the distinction between a production deployment and a production release.

Releases

We can define a *release* as a change that involves altering the observable behavior of the system as experienced by end users. This is not the case for most ungated deployments to production. After all, most types of deployments don't "release" anything new with continuous deployment: work in progress on new features is usually hidden under OFF feature flags or in separate execution branches, making deployments unnoticeable from the end users' perspective. A release also doesn't necessarily *require* a production deployment; for example, when it's hidden under a feature flag that can be enabled at runtime.

In short, with continuous deployment, not every deployment is a release, and a release doesn't require a deployment.

An actual release (e.g., turning a feature flag ON at runtime) changes the visible behavior of the system, so it carries implications for business metrics (think of conversion rates, user engagement, etc.) and the stakeholders who are invested in how the product is performing. Visible additions are naturally surrounded by a lot of process and coordination, even beyond the team. Success depends on positive reception of the feature, so the process normally involves tracking user behavior to understand how users are experiencing it, coordinating an A/B testing window to compare it with the old behavior, and deciding whether the new functionality is there to stay or should be turned off. A release is all about improving the *external quality* of the system, as experienced by its end users.

Deployments

A production deployment, on the other hand, will most often contain either new code hidden in a separate execution path, or other invisible changes such as refactoring, improvements to CFRs, and updating of test coverage. Ultimately, a deployment improves the *internal quality* of the system first and foremost, which can include adding new capabilities to it that can be released later.

Under continuous deployment, a production deployment should not be perceptible to external users, and therefore, it can be treated as a purely technical event. As such, it can be fully managed by engineers within the team, and it can be driven fully by technical needs, such as the need to improve the system's maintainability or to keep the code delta small between trunk and production. Of course, this means that any unplanned change in observable behavior resulting from a deployment should be considered a regression.

Differences

In Table 3-3, you can see a condensed version of the differences between production deployments and releases. These differences can also apply to continuous delivery, but they become much more pronounced with continuous deployment.

To summarize, we can consider production deployments as a technical means for engineers to keep the systems healthy and enable the business side to perform releases as frequently or infrequently as necessary. In an ideal continuous deployment scenario, the process and frequency of deployments to production is a decision owned by the engineers within the team. The process and frequency of releases, on the other hand, can be a decision fully owned by the product function. If both sides are doing their job well, the product function shouldn't need to interfere with deployments to production, and vice versa.

Table 3-3. Deployments versus releases

	Production deployment	Release
Visibility	No perceptible changes in the behavior of the system	Visible change in the behavior of the system
Motivation	Driven by technical needs	Driven by product requirements
Quality assurance	Does not require extensive manual testing; automated tests can catch regressions	Requires manual exploratory testing to ensure that requirements are met, and A/B testing to ensure that users react positively
Who is involved	Self-managed by engineers; does not usually need other stakeholders involved	Requires coordination with product owners and other stakeholders
Which metrics are impacted	No impact expected on business metrics, but might have an impact on technical metrics	Implies an impact on business metrics such as user engagement
When to revert	Reverting means something went wrong with the change (regression).	Reverting means a product hypothesis didn't yield good enough results.
Frequency	Performed routinely, multiple times a day	Performed when there is something substantial and self-contained to release, in coordination with other departments

For example, a product owner should never be in a situation where they have to ask developers to hold off on a deployment because another experiment is in progress (all new deployments should be undetectable, after all). At the same time, a developer should never be in a situation where they have to ask a product owner to delay a release because their deployment pipeline is stuck (the code for the feature should have been deployed well before release time).

Overall, the number of releases performed by a product team will normally be much smaller than their number of production deployments, perhaps by several orders of magnitude.

Overlap

A production deployment is often not a release, and a release is not a production deployment. But in some cases, the two will overlap; for example, when exposing visible behavior through the expand and contract pattern or a static feature toggle (both of which require code updates). Sometimes teams implement visible changes that are so small they don't require a feature flag, such as bug fixes and tiny layout improvements. In Figure 3-19, you can see a representation of this overlap, along with some examples.

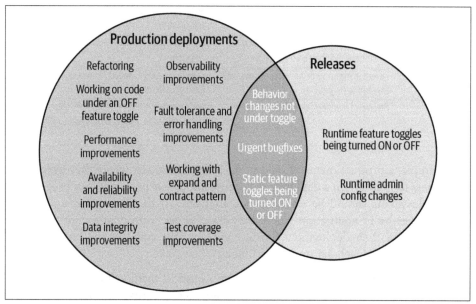

Figure 3-19. Production deployments versus releases

Overall, *deployments* and *releases* have been almost synonymous for a very long time, but it is especially empowering to separate them when operating under continuous deployment, as deployments can become daily occurrences while allowing releases to remain unaffected.

By deliberately separating them in our vocabulary, we can also separate the processes that we put in place around them. Different processes and people involved help ensure that developers keep the independence to perform any necessary deployments, while stakeholders have full control over releases that affect the product's impact on its market.

Continuous deployment doesn't mean continuous (and uncontrolled) releases, although it does enable releases to be more frequent.

End-to-End Delivery Life Cycle

In the preceding section, you saw how deployments to production happen routinely throughout development and are independent of releases. One of the least mentioned gotchas of continuous deployment is how that change, in turn, radically simplifies a team's day-to-day workflow. In the first team in which we used continuous deployment, this newfound simplicity was something that really surprised us. In retrospect, I now consider it one of the biggest improvements offered by this practice.

To understand what happens to teams moving from continuous delivery to full continuous deployment, let's compare what a typical team workflow would look like before and after opening the gate to production. Personally, I find the most useful and concrete visualization of a team's workflow to be its daily board, so I will use that as a basis for our comparison.

Without Continuous Deployment

Let's consider how a team's tasks might flow on the team's board with a gate to production. In my experience working in teams without continuous deployment, Figure 3-20 shows what an abstracted team board usually looks like and how items progress within it.

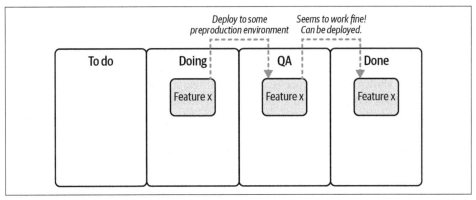

Figure 3-20. A team board without continuous deployment

Each column in the board can be roughly mapped to an environment for the code to run in, and also to different people who poke and prod it to check that it behaves as expected. In particular, the tasks in the "Doing" column are checked on a developer's workstation, while the ones in the "QA" column are looked at by testers, who mainly work in preproduction. This mapping is shown in Figure 3-21.

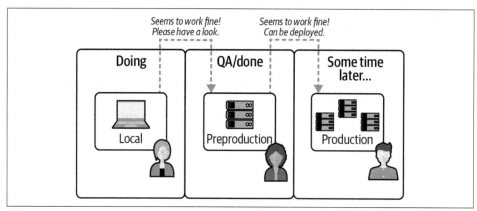

Figure 3-21. A workflow and environments without continuous deployment

Here is a more detailed description of what usually happens in every stage shown in Figure 3-20, which might ring familiar to most readers.

Doing

The bulk of developers' work is focused on the "Doing" (or "in progress") column, where they test their changes locally and might deploy them to a preproduction environment for further manual verification. Once developers believe the functionality is complete, they move the task to the QA stage.

QA

The QA stage shown in the figure is very simplified, and in reality it could comprise several steps. Each company and each team approaches QA a little bit differently, but for the purposes of this explanation, let's bundle that together in a generic "QA" step. It might involve testers trying to break the feature, a thorough session with a product owner and other stakeholders, a demo, deployments to other environments, or all of the above. The core of the QA work usually consists of manual acceptance and regression checks. Those checks tend to happen in preproduction environments, and not in production. Once all the relevant eyes have seen the functionality working in preproduction, tasks that are deemed fulfilling of their acceptance criteria are marked as releasable, or "done," which is the next and final step.

Done

In the "Done" column, items are considered ready to be deployed to production and subsequently released. The next deployment to production will bundle up all changesets that have been finished since the last deployment. It might be performed on a schedule, on demand, or whenever someone on the team considers the changes consistent enough to be rolled out.

Implications

On the surface, this workflow looks very simple (and it might be familiar to a lot of readers). However, the most interesting aspect of this very common process is that for a task to be considered done, it doesn't have to be seen working in production at all. In fact, none of the development or even the QA phase considers "working in production" as a bar to clear (and I would argue that is the most important bar to clear of all).

 If code isn't proven to be working under production conditions, as far as I'm concerned it is not proven to work. Calling such changes "done" dangerously lets everyone lower their guard before the actual deployments to production happen, which often turns out to be the riskiest step.

The definition of done without continuous deployment often more closely resembles what some people might call "dev done" instead, which is a concept that in my time spent working in Agile teams I have come to recognize as an antipattern. The actual work of deploying to production happens invisibly and is tracked outside the team's main working process visualization, as shown in Figure 3-22, even though it is the true last step for all work in progress.

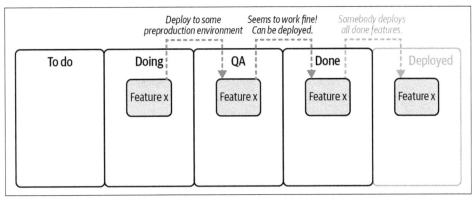

Figure 3-22. An invisible deployment step

Some companies, to their credit, do attempt to track the code's journey all the way to production. As a result, they might try to closely catalog all the deployment and verification steps needed, and they find themselves with a lot of columns with confusing names such as "Waiting for deployment," "Scheduled for next deployment," "Deployed in production," or "Tested in production and it actually works there too" (OK, those last few might not be actual names, but I do stand by the concept and I have seen some boards get really out of control).

Regardless of how teams track their production deployments, the key takeaway is that deployments happen at the very end of the workflow. And when they do take place, that's when (unpleasant) surprises happen too. As we will discuss in detail in Chapter 11, preproduction environments are by their nature imperfect, and very often defects slip through the cracks. This is especially true in medium to large companies, where the production environment is under heavy stress, contains lots of old data, and integrates with services belonging to many other teams as well as with a variety of third-party systems. All of these factors make production conditions extremely difficult to replicate despite our best efforts to create the Perfect Staging Environment.

Therefore, however simple this workflow might look on the surface, it quickly degenerates into chaos when production deployments will inevitably reveal unforeseen defects that were not caught by the QA phase, as shown in Figure 3-23.

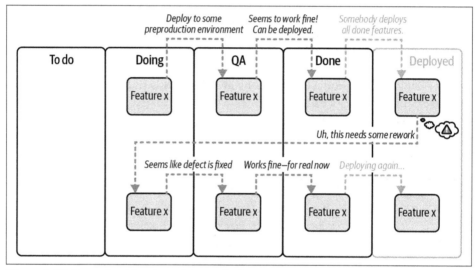

Figure 3-23. Rework without continuous deployment

Features needing rework will suddenly reappear in development to be investigated and fixed, long after the original engineers have moved on to new tasks. Developers have to context-switch to fix the problematic feature, pausing whatever they were doing before. This causes the actual number of items that are marked as "work in progress" to start exceeding the number of developers who are available to work on them, leading to an accumulation of even more unfinished inventory. Paused items could be left in a waiting or blocked state for a long time, with their code half-finished and already starting to rot. In my experience, all of this is very disruptive to developers' focus and lowers the visibility of which items are actively being worked on.

After an issue is considered fixed, the original feature it belongs to will need to go through the whole QA and handover dance all over again, increasing the cognitive load for the rest of the team too. The team will have to remember what it tested the first time around, what it needs to retest, and what was broken, as well as juggling brand-new items coming from other streams.

Overall, the feedback loop for developers in this scenario is very long, and it's not easy to experiment and debug issues quickly unless entire phases of the process are completely bypassed. This can lead to either a "two-track system" for urgent issues, or repeated and frustratingly long iterations that send items back and forth between production and then again into development several times. Figure 3-24 illustrates this repetition.

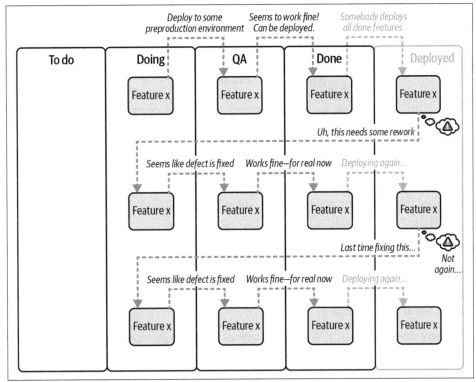

Figure 3-24. Repeated rework without continuous deployment

With Continuous Deployment

With continuous deployment, a team's board might look quite similar, but the meaning of each step and the activities within them change. Columns on the board no longer map directly to running environments: "in progress" for the developer's laptop, "QA" for staging, and so on and so forth. Instead, any code commit is promoted through all environments and reaches production at least once during the "in progress" phase alone; see Figure 3-25.

All of the necessary deployments are clustered around one phase of the workflow, and collaboration of different roles usually follows. It is not uncommon to see QA engineers and designers working side by side with developers.

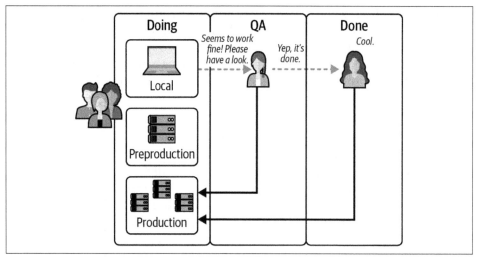

Figure 3-25. Workflow and environments with continuous deployment

Let's look at each individual stage again, only this time assuming the team is continuously deploying code to production. I will share what the different phases can look like based on what my colleagues and I have experienced.

Doing

When work is in progress, code is already being deployed to production routinely. As team members work on small commits and integrate on trunk frequently, this might mean several deployments per day.

As I mentioned in "Hiding Work in Progress" on page 60, techniques such as feature flags and expand and contract are heavily used at this stage. These techniques allow engineers to deploy the codebase even as they are in the middle of working on it, and to peek at their changes in production through toggles and monitoring without disturbing users.

Any integration issue that would otherwise have only been caught after the developer has marked a task as "done" will already emerge here, which is when a developer or pair of developers have the maximum amount of context that is required to fix it; see Figure 3-26.

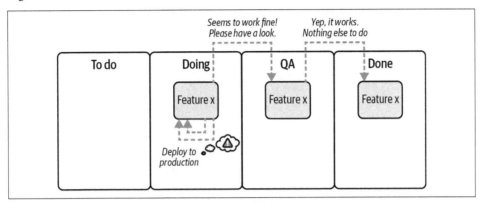

Figure 3-26. The team board with continuous deployment

QA

The QA phase often consists of different people peeking at the feature in production, usually under a feature toggle, to check that it is usable and functionally complete. This will be covered in detail in Chapter 11. At this point, there is already high confidence that if the changes are proven to be complete and working, there will be no unexpected surprises later on. When production-only defects are found in the QA phase, the overall feedback loop will be much shorter: tasks are not considered "done" prematurely and therefore they don't traverse the whole board several times. Rather, they only bounce back and forth between QA and development, as shown in Figure 3-27. Short feedback loops such as these help keep the context fresh for developers and testers, without long delays between deploying fixes and getting feedback.

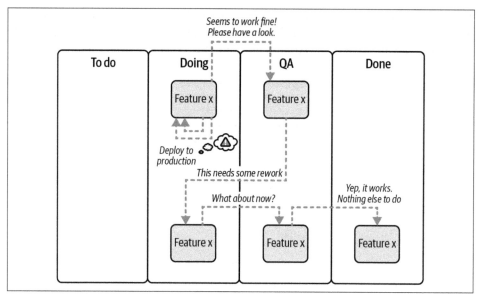

Figure 3-27. Rework with continuous deployment

Some teams might decide to go even further and completely merge the in-progress and QA phases, having developers, testers, and stakeholders work very closely on each item being developed. Some teams even go so far as to forgo the tester role altogether as they realize that the automated tests are good enough for their needs.

Done

When a task is moved to "Done," its code has been in production for quite some time already and there is truly nothing else for developers to do. After all, the required deployments have already happened. Code is proven to work because it can be safely run in the most "prod-like" environment of all: production itself. Once a task is in the "Done" column, it very rarely comes back due to later production issues. At this stage, stakeholders and product owners can stop worrying about whether implementation will survive production conditions and instead can focus on product decisions such as when and how to release the feature to all users; for example, by running a canary release or by doing an A/B test (which we will explore in Part III of this book).

Implications

With deployments to production shifting from a high-attention event to boring developer tasks that happen almost hourly, the team's workflow stops being centered on deployments in this or that environment. Instead, it reflects more interesting tasks and decisions around the product.

The team's board stops being tightly coupled to infrastructure (and to code physically running in certain machines), and instead it becomes purely a reflection of human activities. Human tasks such as exploratory testing, making release decisions, and evaluating usability become orthogonal to technical decisions such as when and how to deploy code.

Summary

In this chapter, we saw how continuous deployment removes the distinction between the definition of a change and the application of a change. This presents teams with a stronger requirement to hide work in progress in production, which they can do through techniques relying on hidden execution branches, such as feature toggles and expand and contract.

Changes being simultaneously defined and applied also introduces new challenges for teams maintaining distributed systems. As there are hidden interdependencies between providers and consumers, developing (and therefore applying) changes in the wrong order or at the wrong time might expose the production system to broken functionality. These interdependencies also require the heavy use of alternative code execution branches to keep compatibility between subsystems.

This new workflow brings a much more pronounced separation between simple deployments (which now happen routinely at development time) and actual releases. The whole team's workflow (and its board) can be restructured around the decoupling of technical activities and product activities.

These concepts represent the main differences when working with and without a gate to production. Getting more comfortable with this different way of working will be the focus of Parts II, III, and IV of this book.

CHAPTER 4

You Must Be This Tall

The phrase "You must be this tall to ride" commonly appears on signs at amusement parks and carnivals to let people know the minimum height requirement for certain rides. The signs are not meant for gatekeeping, but for safety. Martin Fowler used this metaphor in his article (*https://oreil.ly/NFbbH*) about prerequisites for microservices architecture. In the same fashion, you can think of this chapter as the "you must be this tall" sign that can help you figure out whether it's safe for your team to get on the very fast ride of continuous deployment. In particular, I will describe a list of safety-focused practices that teams should implement before switching to a fully automated pipeline.

Sending each commit to production without manual intervention has the potential to break things, of course. Critical defects slipping past inadequate quality gates can cost businesses some serious money and scare stakeholders right back into overcomplicating the release process (and into putting heavy gatekeeping on production). That's why it is our responsibility as software professionals to carefully evaluate whether our teams are ready, and if they aren't, to place continuous deployment within the context of a bigger journey of continuous delivery maturity. The goal of this journey should be to build up a technical and organizational foundation that allows people of all levels of experience to participate in a fast-paced deployment life cycle.

The purpose of this chapter is not to explain how to prevent developer error. We should accept that developers are human beings who will have bad days and that mistakes *will* happen. Our focus should be on catching errors early and fixing them quickly rather than trying to achieve absolute developer perfection, which is an unmeetable (and unfair) standard. We can strive instead to build a safety net of practices and automation that makes it OK to fail and easy to recover. That's why we will talk about continuous feedback tools such as frequent integration, thorough testing, code scanning, and observability. Proficiency with these safety-focused practices is what we should be judging our teams' performance by, instead of the occasional mistake.

Now that I have put forward this disclaimer, let's take a closer look at the practices themselves. Most of them are well-established practices of continuous delivery for which we'll just do a small refresher, while others have emerged more recently and are especially relevant for continuous deployment. This list will inevitably be incomplete, and new innovative techniques might pop up after this book is released. Nevertheless, let's use it as a start.

Cross-Functional, Autonomous Teams

Siloed teams are typically organized around specific roles or disciplines, such as development, testing, or design. A cross-functional team, on the other hand, consists of members with a range of skills and should include all the roles that are required to deliver the product as a whole (see Figure 4-1). This could include infrastructure skills, frontend skills, and backend skills, but also testing, security, design, and project management.

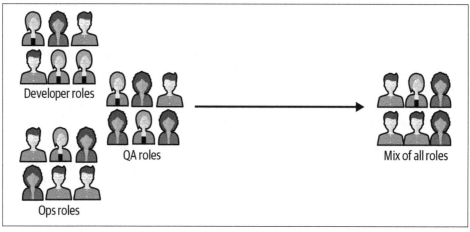

Figure 4-1. Siloed teams (left) versus cross-functional teams (right)

Cross-functional teams have several benefits compared to teams that are siloed, with closer collaboration between roles, increased speed, and less organizational friction being the main ones. When a product team is truly cross-functional, it also has several qualities that enable continuous deployment.

Fast Decision Making

The biggest enabler for fast-paced delivery is that cross-functional teams can act spontaneously and be flexible, without the need to involve others in their decisions. Their decision-making process is self-contained, so they can quickly adapt to changing requirements without having to reach across team boundaries to implement a change.

A team continuously deploying small increments to production needs to be equipped to handle the rapid pace of changes that comes up with a very short feedback loop. With continuous deployment, new code updates are released to users on a daily basis, or even multiple times per day. This requires a high level of adaptability in which the team must be able to react quickly to changing direction and potential fixes.

A team that depends on outside support or approval can quickly find itself overwhelming (or annoying) its external collaborators if it starts to deploy many times a day. The more the team succeeds in its goal to release frequently, the more it will upset the outsiders, which is not what the team wants.

Implementation Autonomy

A truly cross-functional team should contain all the engineering skills required to build and deploy the application. Continuous deployment (or even continuous delivery) doesn't do well with backend-only, frontend-only, or infrastructure-only teams, because deploying often can surface the complex interdependence between all these software components. Changes to one part of the system often require corresponding changes to another part in order to roll out safely, and vice versa. And when small changes are applied individually to production it is essential to avoid constant blockers introduced by team boundaries, which would cause large amounts of work in progress to get stuck.

Feature flags and expand and contract, for example, are especially common coding techniques with continuous deployment, and they require that developers update provider and consumer systems in quick succession so that they can guarantee the stability of the production environment. If teams were siloed based on tech stack or specific parts of the system, the coordination of these changes would become difficult: teams naturally have different backlogs with different priorities, and they would often be stuck waiting for each other rather than working on features.

Overall, the ideal team practicing continuous deployment is one that contains all the roles and technical skills necessary to take care of a vertical slice of the business: a product team. This works especially well in microservices-oriented architectures where products are technically as well as organizationally isolated from each other.

Having cross-functional teams does not mean every team should look the same, or that there is no room for specialized teams anymore. In fact, in their book *Team Topologies*,[1] Matthew Skelton and Manuel Pais recognize four categories of teams, some of which are *highly* specialized:

---

1 Matthew Skelton and Manuel Pais, *Team Topologies: Organizing Business and Technology Teams for Fast Flow* (Portland, OR: IT Revolution Press, 2019).

Stream-aligned team

As the name suggests, a stream-aligned team is aligned with a particular stream of work (or domain). This type of team is responsible for delivering value to customers quickly through new user-facing features and improvements.

Enabling team

An enabling team supports stream-aligned teams by providing specialized expertise and tools. For example, it may help other teams adopt new practices or technologies, or solve complex problems.

Complicated-subsystem team

This type of team works on complex subsystems that require deep technical knowledge; for example, ones that require expertise in calculation or mathematics.

Platform team

A platform team creates and maintains a set of internal products and tools that other teams can use to accelerate their work, usually ones that can be used in a self-service fashion.

Each of these teams will have a certain specialization, whether that is a business domain, a particular technology, or a complex type of problem. And all of them could maintain their own products too, whether they are externally facing or internally facing. Those products are all potential candidates for continuous deployment. The requirement for practicing continuous deployment on those products, however, is that within that team's specialization (whichever it may be), there are all the capabilities required to develop them and deploy them. This means full autonomy and mastery of the chosen software stack, from end to end.

For example, in one of this book's case studies, Tom Vollerthun from OTTO describes in detail how his company transitioned the QA role from being held by one gatekeeping team to letting individual QA engineers be members of product teams. This was a key enabler for the adoption of continuous deployment at OTTO, and I encourage you to read his case study to understand how the company achieved it.

Frequent Integration

As I discussed in Chapters 1 and 2, integrating code frequently is the backbone of continuous integration, and it is a baseline for continuous delivery and deployment too. In practice, it means adding our code changes to the team's shared, mainline branch at least once a day (or multiple times a day). Frequent integration keeps change deltas small and manageable, which is a principle that becomes imperative to follow when there is no manual verification in a preproduction environment.

Hoarding thousands of changed lines on our development machines or in a branch, only to send them to production all at once, can generate chaos and disrupt users, stakeholders, and the rest of the team. Therefore, it is fundamental that all team members are aligned on a code commit etiquette that keeps changes small and integrates them frequently into main.

A good commit etiquette with continuous deployment should also include tools to make the version history easy to understand: squashing interdependent commits together, rebasing frequently to allow for fast-forward merges, and meaningful commit messages with a task identifier and coauthors. All of these small actions allow the team to keep clarity on which code changes are bundled with which production deployment.

The main tool to improve our understanding of what is deployed, however, is frequent integration, first and foremost. There are two main ways in which modern software teams achieve this: (very) short-lived branches and trunk-based development (TBD). Both are compatible with a continuous deployment strategy, although TBD is definitely a favorite due to its simplicity.

Short-lived branches

With short-lived branches, a developer can simply create a new branch off of main, make their changes, and then submit a pull request (PR) to directly merge the changes back when they feel their work is self-contained enough. Once the changes have been reviewed and approved, they can be merged into the main branch and go to production. This offers an optional checkpoint to perform code reviews. It is important to note that for a branch to be called "short-lived," the development of a big feature should normally outlast the shelf life of an open branch, and developers will need to merge back into main multiple times during development. This is why short-lived branches should still be used in conjunction with other techniques for hiding work in progress that don't rely on version control, such as feature toggles.

Not all branches are created equal. It's important to remember that short-lived branches are intended to be used for small, focused tasks and should not be used for long-term development efforts or whole features. Ideally, they shouldn't live for more than a day. Short-lived branches are in direct contrast with feature branches, for example, although the two might look the same in our version control systems.

Short-lived branches versus feature branches

Long-lived feature branches are an antipattern in continuous integration. They are typical of development workflows such as Gitflow, which aims to segregate the changes of entire initiatives until they are ready to go to production. Such workflows introduce a tight coupling between the release process and the functionality of the version control system, and they discourage the use of more modern techniques like feature flags.

It must be acknowledged that models like Gitflow work remarkably well for open source projects on collaboration platforms such as GitHub, where developers collaborate over longer periods and communication is asynchronous by nature. However, in a cohesive team with real-time communication channels, long feature branches bring more overhead than value. In fact, they are actively disruptive. They encourage code drifting significantly from production and let it accumulate into big, painful batches that lead to messy merges and tricky releases.

Many teams successfully use short-lived feature branches with continuous deployment, but this requires a great deal of discipline and continuous integration maturity in order to not degenerate into long-lived feature branches. All it takes is for one developer to succumb to inertia and forget to integrate for a day or two, and a branch will accumulate enough changes that it cannot be called "short-lived" anymore.

Using branches as part of everyday coding in the team makes it easy to do the wrong thing (accidentally hoard changes), and makes it hard to do the right thing (consciously integrate often). That is why many teams that look to encourage good practices use a different paradigm: *trunk-based development*.

Trunk-based development

TBD is a methodology in which all developers work on a single branch, typically known as *trunk* or *main*. This approach is in contrast to other models relying on separate branches, where developers keep their changes away from main and merge them periodically.

In TBD, developers are encouraged to commit small, incremental changes that keep the codebase green and deployable at all times. This allows for an even shorter feedback loop, as changes are available to all other developers as soon as they are committed. With continuous deployment, they will also be available to users minutes later.

Another key benefit of TBD is that it reduces the complexity of the team's version control. With branches of any kind, it can be difficult to track changes and merge them back into main due to conflicts and delays. By working on a single branch, developers can avoid these issues and focus on building new things.

TBD is still controversial in some communities, but it is practiced successfully by many teams, including most of the ones I have been lucky enough to work with. This is what the DORA researchers shared about it in 2018:

> Our research also found that developing off trunk/master rather than on long-lived feature branches was correlated with higher delivery performance. Teams that did well had fewer than three active branches at any time, their branches had very short lifetimes (less than a day) before being merged into trunk and never had "code freeze" or stabilization periods. It's worth re-emphasizing that these results are independent of team size, organization size, or industry.

Even after finding that Trunk-based Development practices contribute to better software delivery performance, some developers who are used to the "GitHub Flow" workflow remain skeptical. This workflow relies heavily on developing with branches and only periodically merging to trunk.[2]

Notwithstanding this, there are some challenges to using TBD. The whole team adding to the same branch can make it more difficult to work on multiple tasks concurrently and to coordinate activities among multiple developers. Also, the burden of ensuring that developers won't step on one another's toes (or one another's lines of code) needs to be addressed during the planning of day-to-day work. But this is not necessarily a negative: when working with branches, developers still risk making overlapping changes; they just wouldn't notice these changes until merge time, when context is stale and the contested lines might have diverged even more significantly. One could say that TBD helps merging issues surface earlier, when they are easier to fix.

When practiced together with continuous deployment, TBD means every single code commit will be immediately deployed to production. This makes for the most straightforward implementation of a one-piece, continuous flow of changes. As discussed in Chapter 1, this concept from Lean manufacturing is what makes continuous deployment so powerful: it eliminates waste and batching from the path to production. I would argue that for this reason, the combination with TBD is the purest implementation of continuous deployment, although the use of very short-lived branches remains a good compromise where this is not an option.

In the case study on digital bank N26 in Part V, you can read about such a situation: unable to do TBD due to regulation constraints, N26 engineers use microbranches and PRs to provide proof of peer review and to ensure that no arbitrary changes are made to the system by single developers. However, they couple this process with pair programming and mob programming so that the code review happens live and integration into main can be expedited.

This brings us to the next topic: reviewing code.

Frequent Code Reviews

Code reviews are essential, as they provide a crucial point of human feedback for the design, correctness, and completeness of the code. Under continuous deployment, this human channel of feedback is also the *only* human form of feedback in the entire path to production. This makes code reviews especially meaningful, as they become the only tool that ensures that every line of code is checked by more than one set of eyes before production.

---

2 Nicole Forsgren et al., *Accelerate: Building and Scaling High Performing Technology Organizations* (Portland, OR: IT Revolution Press, 2018), p. 91.

No matter how well tested a piece of functionality is, if the developer who wrote it has misunderstood the requirements, they will write incorrect tests to go along with an equally incorrect implementation. No matter how many elaborate code scanning tools we have, only a human can detect whether code respects functional requirements and whether it respects team agreements regarding design and structure. There are many such code design principles that go beyond trivial linting rules, and books upon books have been written about them. For example, code needs to be well partitioned, be unsurprising to read, belong to the right level of abstraction, and be conceptually aligned to its architecture. After all, if we were writing code only to be understood by machines and not by other people, we might as well ditch all of our design books and highly abstracted programming languages and go back to the ancient assembly spaghetti that our grandmothers[3] had to deal with.

Putting such an emphasis on code reviews might seem at odds with the other messaging in this book so far. As we discussed in Chapter 1, we are striving to completely remove manual bottlenecks from the path to production. Aren't code reviews an example of a manual bottleneck where changes might accumulate and get stuck? And didn't we just look in the preceding section at the benefits of TBD over long feature branches and PRs? How are we supposed to perform code reviews without PRs?

Pull requests

It is worth mentioning that by keeping their branches small, a lot of teams also create very tiny PRs, which lead to quick code reviews that don't disrupt the continuous flow of code to production all that much. In those teams, all developers need to be very engaged with the code review process so that they can minimize the time spent waiting by their colleagues who want to integrate. A lot of engineers work this way, and they manage to keep their wait times reasonably low and achieve a somewhat smooth workflow.

Still, I think we can do even better than that.

Something I noticed is that over the years we have come to collectively associate the review of an open PR with the only time and place for code to be reviewed. I would like to challenge this concept. There is another practice in the eXtreme Programming toolbox that offers an alternative to PRs as the engine for code reviews: pair programming.

Pair programming

Pair programming is a very old practice; almost as old as programming itself:

---

3 Although this is not well-known, programming used to be a job held by women. In fact, the first programmers in the early 19th century were female. To learn more, visit *https://oreil.ly/cQb11*.

Betty Snyder and I, from the beginning, were a pair. And I believe that the best programs and designs are done by pairs, because you can criticize each other, and find each other's errors, and use the best ideas.

—Jean Bartik, one of the very first programmers[4]

Pair programming regained popularity in the early days of Agile, although it seems to have sadly fallen out of fashion, as many companies have forgotten to make it part of their "Agile transformation." But as practices like TBD and continuous deployment become increasingly popular, pair programming is worth reevaluating, as it can offer more safety than ordinary code reviews through PRs.

With pair programming, all production code is developed by a pair of developers sharing a keyboard and screen; virtual ones in the case of remote pairing. As the pair work through a task, they switch roles between typing and reasoning about the code design. As each member of the pair has to verbalize their assumptions and design ideas, they continuously debate the implementation and the requirements, therefore performing a *continuous* code review.

A second set of eyes is on the code before and during the writing process, not just after the fact. This can be more helpful than a review at PR time because it offers a much bigger (and earlier) window of opportunity to amend design errors or clarify misunderstandings of the requirements. It also happens to avoid the social awkwardness of requesting big changes after a colleague has done a lot of work on a PR, which is a further barrier to code quality (and, sadly, one that I have seen get in the way many times).

Pair programming can also speed up the implementation of features and the resolution of bugs because more than one brain is available to tackle problems as they come up. It also speeds up integration because it removes the bottleneck of having to find available reviewers, who might need to context-switch in order to unblock their colleagues. Due to this continuous and more engaging code review process, the final design of the code is usually of higher quality and requires less rework, saving a lot of time.

The main objection to pair programming is usually along the lines of "it takes twice the work hours to implement the same thing!" But I find that to be inaccurate in most cases, because it fails to consider all the time it has saved. Even if that objection was accurate and it really *was* that much more expensive to have a continuous code review process, I would argue it is still an investment worth considering. We are deploying every commit to production, after all, and we aim to keep a high level of safety from human error in the process. Speed and agility always require an investment.

---

4 "Jean Bartik, ENIAC's Programmers," Computer History Museum, 2011, video, *https://oreil.ly/4S38P*.

Personally, I have used pair programming as a code review tool in almost all of my teams, and most developers I worked with found it to be a great help in delivering products, onboarding new team members, and maintaining a shared sense of code ownership.

Psychological safety

Regardless of whether your team uses PRs or pair programming, you should ensure that code reviews are a detailed and frequent process if you plan to adopt continuous deployment. It is the responsibility of all senior team members to create a space where all colleagues, especially junior ones, feel empowered to give honest feedback and ask difficult questions. The definition of "good code" can be personal, but it doesn't mean it shouldn't be debated and negotiated by the team every day. Briefly upsetting someone's feelings is never pleasant, but it is better than the alternative: a circle of ruinous empathy where everyone is patting one another on the back at the expense of the product's stability in production.

Automated Code Analysis

We have talked about the importance of more than one set of eyes looking at code, but that doesn't mean that catching common oversights and mistakes cannot be automated. This is where code analysis tools can play an important role, also enhancing the safety of continuous deployment. With the help of automation, developers and their pairs (or PR reviewers) can stop worrying about finding low-level issues that might easily be overlooked, and instead can focus on the bigger picture: for example, how the changes fit in with the existing architecture, how they should be released, and whether they satisfy requirements.

Static code analysis tools can analyze code without actually executing it, and they are usually quite fast, so they can be integrated as an early step of the pipeline to catch common mistakes, or even in IDEs and pre-commit hooks. They can be used to identify all sorts of common issues, such as bugs, security vulnerabilities, and resource utilization issues, as well as enforcing coding standards early.

Many open source code analysis tools are available that support a wide variety of programming languages. There might be some up-front setup and configuration to be done, but most of them are fairly straightforward to keep using afterward. I find that in the vast majority of cases, the reasons to include them outweigh the reasons not to.

In short, static code analysis tools are excellent at preventing bugs that originate from inattention and common programming mistakes. However, there are two features that I want to especially call out as useful in a continuous deployment scenario: security vulnerability scanning and performance analysis.

Some of the human errors with the direst consequences for popular applications are related to security and performance. They are also among the hardest to spot, as automated tests usually look for regressions in behavior rather than in the cross-functional characteristics of the software. As developers work in small increments, it is quite easy to be forgetful and introduce a resource leakage that will only cause problems in an environment experiencing heavy load, such as production. It can be equally easy to forget to sanitize our inputs correctly in every commit, opening the system up for yet another problem that will only be evident once it is in front of unknown, untrusted users. Automated code scanning alleviates those concerns and can give peace of mind to developers and stakeholders alike when considering everything that could go wrong with a constant stream of changes.

Test Automation

As this is the 21st century, it should go without saying that test automation is preferable to manual regression testing before each deployment. It is faster, more efficient, more consistent, and cheaper. Automated tests can be run quickly and repeatedly, without the need for human intervention, so they are not subject to human error or variation in the way that manual tests are. Software testing of every commit is the textbook example of a repetitive and exact task that is perfectly suited to the endless patience of a computer, and it has no business being performed by human hands. Human creativity and attention should be reserved for challenging assumptions and pushing the system in unexpected ways, not repeatedly verifying the same features over and over.

Automating any regression tests that used to be manual is something that should be at the top of the to-do list of any company by now, but it should be taken especially seriously by teams looking to adopt continuous deployment.

We shouldn't continuously deploy code that doesn't have good test coverage. As Michael Feathers writes in *Working Effectively with Legacy Code*, code without tests is just as bad as (and can be considered) legacy code:

> To me, legacy code is simply code without tests. [...] Code without tests is bad code. It doesn't matter how well written it is; it doesn't matter how pretty or object-oriented or well-encapsulated it is. With tests, we can change the behavior of our code quickly and verifiably. Without them, we really don't know if our code is getting better or worse.[5]

Indeed, it doesn't matter how pretty our code looks: without a pipeline backed by thorough automated tests, we can't stop regressions from being deployed to production. Absent or neglected test coverage might have been somewhat more tolerable with changes stopping in preproduction to be manually verified, but it becomes

---

5 Michael Feathers, *Working Effectively with Legacy Code* (Boston: Pearson, 2004), p. 16.

reckless when the gate to production is wide open and no manual verification is possible. Later in his book, Feathers goes on to say that there are two ways to make changes in a software system: "Cover [with tests] and Modify," or "Edit and Pray." It shouldn't need saying that if we are using continuous deployment with the Edit and Pray approach, we are going to have to pray extra hard.

Now that we have that disclaimer out of the way, we can talk about what kinds of tests are necessary. After all, there are many types of automated tests in a developer's toolbox, and they come with all sorts of levels of abstraction and granularity: unit tests, integration tests, acceptance tests, component tests, visual regression tests, contract tests, journey tests…just to name a few (I couldn't possibly cover them all in this section, or it would become its own book). Beyond unit tests, which are generally well understood, the terminology has been historically fuzzy throughout the industry, with competing definitions for several types of tests. If you lock two developers in a room and show them the same test code, you will probably get three different names for it.

However, after working in a few teams, I started to realize terminology doesn't really matter as long as the whole team agrees to and sticks to the same definition. Each team member should be aware of the types of tests used in their team, their level of abstraction, when and where they are appropriate, and the boundaries of their system under test. The team should periodically update its testing strategy and renegotiate which coverage is needed as its product grows.

The layers of tests to use will vary from application to application and from tech stack to tech stack. Which types of tests to add, and how many, is a matter of opinion and might be unique to each team, but I find that the most helpful rule of thumb is to follow the well-known *testing pyramid* model.

The testing pyramid model

The testing pyramid is a visual metaphor that describes the different categories of testing that should be performed on a system. It is a pyramid shape because the idea is that there should be lots of low-level tests, such as unit tests, and much fewer high-level tests, such as end-to-end tests. The tests at the bottom of the pyramid can be numerous, as they have a high granularity (individual classes or functions), run very quickly, and are easy to write. On the other hand, the tests at the top of the pyramid are comprehensive and valuable, but they also run a lot more slowly and require elaborate setups, so we should use them only to validate the most valuable behavior of the system rather than all of its details.

In Figure 4-2, you can see some examples of what a testing pyramid might look like for two different types of applications: a REST API and a one-page application frontend.

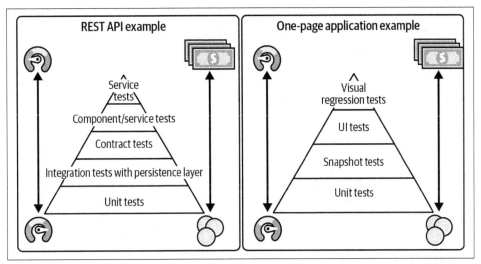

Figure 4-2. Two examples of testing pyramids

In the past, only the unit tests at the bottom of the pyramid were written during the implementation phase by the developers themselves. The laborious task of writing high-level coverage has been historically left to QA roles as a productivity optimization of the manual testing work they would have been doing anyway. This would usually happen after the development phase.

As we discussed in Chapter 2, this approach to test automation is not sustainable in modern teams using continuous deployment. When code never sits waiting in an artifact repository or in preproduction, the time window for adding high-level tests "later" is lost. Therefore, it is imperative that the team shifts testing to the left and that each layer of the testing pyramid is updated during the development phase itself.

Working with automated tests at each level of the testing pyramid is something that every team member who writes code should feel comfortable doing, regardless of their seniority. Only when this is true can each change go to production safely, no matter who produced it. With immediate production deployments, writing good tests might even be more important than writing good code.

The Swiss cheese model

Another good model for test coverage that can complement the classic testing pyramid is the *Swiss cheese model*. This model was first proposed (*https://oreil.ly/fYhYZ*) by James T. Reason, and while it was originally applied to domains such as aviation safety, engineering, and healthcare, it is excellent at representing software testing as well.

In this model, all layers of the testing pyramid can be thought of as different slices of Swiss cheese. The holes in each slice represent different weaknesses or missed coverage in the testing layers. A defect might pass through one or two layers, but it can later be caught by another one with slightly different coverage, as shown in Figure 4-3. The bugs that make it all the way through the slices of cheese are the ones that the users get to experience in production.

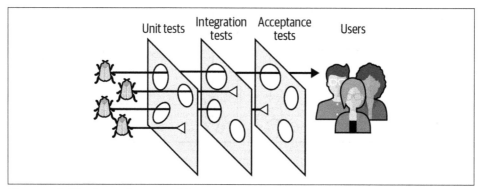

Figure 4-3. The Swiss cheese model

By examining the characteristics of each layer (e.g., speed, flakiness), we can reason about what is the appropriate amount of coverage. For example, tests that are appropriate to write in the first, more detailed layer might be way too granular for slower and more expensive layers, and would be redundant as well.

The Swiss cheese model can also be helpful for making decisions about areas where there is an unavoidable overlap between the layers. More overlap means more protection in case the coverage is changed incorrectly in one of the other layers, but it also means a higher cost of maintenance, as changing the functionality will require updating more layers of testing.

Test-first

Continuous deployment requires writing tests during the implementation phase of code, but that in itself is not a new concept. Unit tests have been integrated into the development life cycle for a while, especially with the introduction of the "test-first" principle and test-driven development (TDD). You can read about TDD in much more depth in *Test Driven Development: By Example*,[6] but for now I'll summarize how it works.

---

6 Kent Beck, *Test Driven Development: By Example* (Boston: Addison-Wesley, 2002).

As shown in Figure 4-4, TDD consists of three phases: writing a failing test, writing the minimum amount of code required to make that test pass, and finally refactoring the code once you are protected by the test.

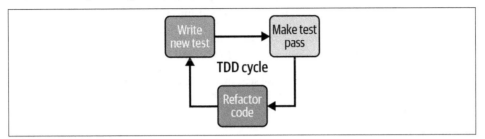

Figure 4-4. The TDD life cycle

Practicing TDD is another one of my default recommendations whenever a team is considering automated deployments. The reasoning is simple. Writing failing tests before writing the code to turn them green is a reliable way to make sure that tests actually get written and coverage remains sturdy. This might seem obvious due to the rules specifically forbidding writing any production code without a corresponding test, but there is another, more subtle advantage to test-first over test-after that acts as a positive influence on test coverage.

By writing the tests before the code, the tests act as the very first consumer of the code's API. This forces developers to think deeply about the contracts of their classes and functions and the way they interact with one another, before they even think of their implementation. As a result, code that is written test-first is inherently testable and modular. On the other hand, writing tests after implementation is finished doesn't always work well: a developer might find that they have a hard time injecting the necessary mocks or setting up the system for the test to execute when they didn't design their code with testability in mind. They might have produced code that is very dense, which leads to complicated tests that need to perform a lot of assertions or setup. This added difficulty might discourage developers from writing tests after the fact, or it might lead to not covering the functionality as thoroughly as needed. Though it might seem counterintuitive, writing tests first is easier than writing them afterward.

With continuous deployment, all work in progress should be hidden under feature toggles or the expand and contract pattern so that we can commit it at any point as long as it compiles and passes the tests. With the addition of the quick TDD loop, what follows is that the codebase should always be, at most, one failing test away from being committable, and therefore deployable to production.

Outside-in

TDD is a very useful practice for designing software with unit tests leading the way, but it covers just the "unit" layer of the testing pyramid, or the Swiss cheese. You might be wondering, where do higher-level tests fit into this process?

It turns out that it is easy to also incorporate higher-level tests in a test-first workflow. This process was described in *Growing Object-Oriented Software, Guided by Tests*:

> When we're implementing a feature, we start by writing an acceptance test, which exercises the functionality we want to build. While it's failing, an acceptance test demonstrates that the system does not yet implement that feature; when it passes, we're done. When working on a feature, we use its acceptance test to guide us as to whether we actually need the code we're about to write—we only write code that's directly relevant. Underneath the acceptance test, we follow the unit level test/implement/refactor cycle to develop the feature.[7]

Figure 4-5 illustrates the process.

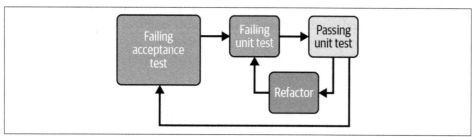

Figure 4-5. Outside-in TDD

Failing high-level tests that are written before implementation can act as a guide for developers, giving feedback on the completeness of their feature and letting them know when the code they have implemented is sufficient. However, high-level tests might stay red for a long time, sometimes much longer than what is a desirable interval between code commits. It is OK to mark them as ignored before performing a commit of in-progress work so that they won't fail the pipeline, reenabling them locally, and only checking them in once they are green. Of course, this implies that the incomplete code is well hidden and will not impact any existing functionality.

In my experience, using a combination of the test-first and outside-in principles when we worked with continuous deployment was a major part of what allowed our teams to feel confident about the test coverage of our application. Each new line of code we added was leaving behind a trail of unit and high-level tests. Similarly, every bug we fixed was first proven through a failing automated test that we could make

---

7 Steve Freeman and Nat Pryce, *Growing Object-Oriented Software, Guided by Tests* (Boston: Addison-Wesley, 2009), p. 7.

green and that would prevent the bug from popping up again. This approach was making our safety net for regressions sturdier and sturdier as our products evolved.

What about legacy?

Not every team has the luxury of working on greenfield codebases where they can progressively build up their test coverage as they build up their code. Furthermore, it is a tricky decision to make as to whether a legacy or inherited application can do well under continuous deployment, and if so, at which point in time. Also, relying only on TDD to add coverage opportunistically might not be enough, as some legacy areas of the code might remain untouched for a long time or be difficult to refactor. In scenarios such as these, test coverage often needs to be worked on up front for the system to be safely changed. When the application code is very tangled, even making openings for the sake of adding tests can impact unrelated areas that haven't yet been covered.

My rule of thumb here is to implement a high-level test suite first, which can poke and prod the system from the outside and treat it like a black box, instead of attempting any code untangling to add tests at the unit level. This should be enough to verify that any business-critical functionality is well protected and allows you to refactor some openings later on.

Such a test suite can be created even if we don't necessarily understand all the system's features, which might be buried under a mountain of convoluted code that is the result of years and years of requirement changes. With the approach that Michael Feathers describes (*https://oreil.ly/Xq2kz*) as "characterization testing," we can use the tests themselves to poke and prod the system and challenge our assumptions about how it works.

With characterization testing, we can write tests that trigger a behavior with the input we want to test, but then go on to make "dummy" assertions that we know will fail, such as asserting against null values. The failure message will reveal the actual result of the operation, which will allow us to go back and amend our test to make it green. Then we can go on to the next test, until we have exhausted all the different types of input we think the system might receive in the real world. This process leaves behind an executable specification of what the production system currently does, and can protect it from unintended changes later on (even when its behavior might be counterintuitive).

Characterization testing can be helpful in preparing a legacy application, if not for continuous deployment then at least for safe refactoring and adding features.

Zero-Downtime Deployments

Perhaps one of the most obvious items on this list, but one worth mentioning just in case, is *zero-downtime deployments*. Zero-downtime deployments are a prerequisite for teams that want to deploy very often. We definitely don't want our users to see a maintenance window message multiple times per day, which is what happens if we just tear down our infrastructure and rebuild it with the new version, as shown in Figure 4-6.

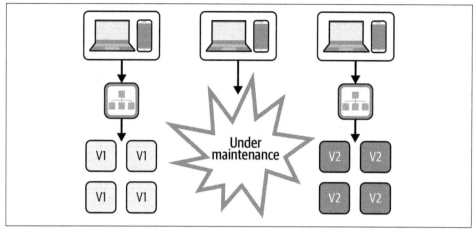

Figure 4-6. Deployment with downtime

There are several techniques to avoid a deployment window and achieve zero down-time, the most well-known being *blue/green deployments* and rolling deployments.

Blue/green deployments

Blue/green deployment is a technique that relies on using two identical production environments, referred to respectively as "blue" and "green." During a deployment, the new version of the application is initially deployed to the blue environment. Once the blue environment has been proven to work as expected and it is ready to go live, incoming traffic is rerouted and the new version is live. Both the blue and green stacks are up and running during deployment, and the traffic entry point simply switches between the two; see Figure 4-7.

Each company might implement a blue/green setup a little bit differently. Most spin up a new environment right before deployment, while others leave both environments always running for extra safety, mainly so that they are able to roll back at any time (although the double infrastructure can get quite expensive). Which stack is referred to as "blue" and which is "green" can vary as well. In some cases they have fixed names, while in others the names are swapped upon deployment. Implementation details do not matter for our purposes, though, and we can simply refer to blue/green deployment as any setup that alternates between identical fleets of production servers.

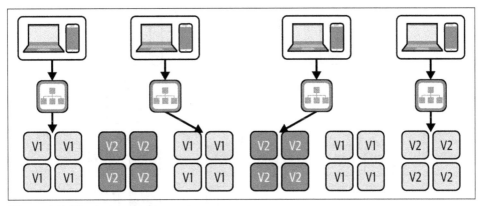

Figure 4-7. Blue/green deployment

One advantage of blue/green deployment is that it allows for rapid rollback in the event of a problem with the new version of the application. If there are issues with the green environment, traffic can simply be routed back to the blue environment, minimizing downtime and minimizing the impact on users.

A blue/green deployment relies on keeping two different versions of the application up and running, at least during a small overlap window. This guarantees there will always be at least one running version of the application available to serve traffic, which removes the downtime gap.

However, it is important to note that this overlap causes some overhead on developers. When making a change, they need to keep the codebase for each new version N of the application always able to run alongside version $N - 1$. This is especially true if we want to truly maintain the ability to roll back.

Maintaining $N - 1$ compatibility means developers need to be especially careful, for example, when applying database schema evolutions, changing the contract between backend and frontend, or changing the contract with any other external components.

Rolling deployments

Rolling deployments (or rolling updates) is a technique for deploying updates to the application cluster by replacing the current instances with fresh instances containing the latest version. As the new instances become healthy, the old ones can be gradually phased out, as shown in Figure 4-8. This technique is commonly used in setups where the application is running on a container cluster, such as ECS or Kubernetes.

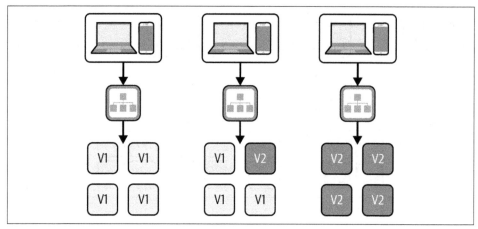

Figure 4-8. A rolling update

This approach is less expensive than blue/green deployment, as it only needs one running stack of the production infrastructure. It is most commonly used with container-based deployments, although it can be done with old-fashioned virtual machines as well.

Like blue/green deployments, this approach also suffers from the $N - 1$ compatibility problem: for a short amount of time, instances of the new version will coexist with the old, so it is important to ensure that the contract with any external systems remains compatible with both versions.

Canary deployments

Before we start describing *canary deployments*, it is worth mentioning that this is an area where terminology can get confusing: canary deployments are sometimes referred to as *canary releases* and vice versa. Deployments and releases are distinct events, especially in the case of continuous deployment, where teams routinely decouple releases and deployments through feature toggles (as I explained in Chapter 3). In this section, I will talk about canary deployments only, which means rolling out new instances with the newest version of the code and configuration. We will talk about "canary *releases*" in Chapter 12, where I will show you how to perform progressive rollouts of a visible feature (ideally at runtime and through the use of a feature flag that doesn't require a new deployment).

A canary deployment can be seen as an increment on zero-downtime deployments. Its goal goes even beyond providing zero downtime: it also allows for validating the new version of the application with a subset of traffic before rolling the update out to all users; see Figure 4-9.

This is achieved by deploying a subset of the instances with the new version (the canary), and then making the rollout to the rest of the infrastructure conditional to how well the new version performs. This comparison is automated by collecting metrics for both the new and old versions and comparing them against each other. This capability is offered by tools such as Spinnaker (*https://oreil.ly/aNR0D*).

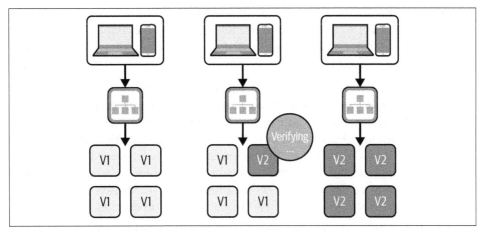

Figure 4-9. A canary deployment

This strategy gives more accurate feedback than a simple rolling or blue/green deployment, where automated checks often consist of just a simple health check or a smoke test. A canary deployment can detect things that are much more interesting, such as a significant difference in application error rate or performance issues.

Canary deployments automated around application metrics can be an extremely powerful tool to check that new versions of the code don't have an unforeseen impact on production. This kind of thorough, extensive feedback can be a prerequisite in large companies that want to adopt continuous deployment but are fearful of the impact on performance or other critical cross-functional requirements.

However, canary deployments can have some major downsides. They can be quite complicated to set up, and they require the metrics they rely on to be meaningful and stable. Additionally, collecting the necessary data for a statistical analysis to yield accurate results could take a long time, slowing down the deployment process and creating a bottleneck.

Given these issues, I would consider canary deployments to not be a "must have" for continuous deployment in most small to medium-sized organizations. Personally, I have used simpler deployment strategies in all the teams where we practiced continuous deployment. We did not feel the necessity for sophisticated canary deployments, as our test coverage, feature toggles, and observability and alarms were comprehensive enough to keep us safe.

That said, canary deployment is definitely an interesting technique that can put stakeholders at ease when new deployments are seen as high risk, and I'm excited to see them evolve and be adopted by more and more companies.

Deployment strategies and manual steps

It is worth noting that some teams perform manual steps within blue/green or rolling deployments as a QA tool and/or a feature release tool—for example, by performing only a partial deployment to production and then executing some manual verification steps before completing it.

This type of workflow fits reasonably well with continuous delivery, but it is not compatible with continuous deployment. When the rate of commits arriving to production is much greater, adding human intervention in the middle of deployments awkwardly builds up a huge queue of changes to sort through. Manual intervention also makes the new version of the application in production behave like preproduction: deployments themselves become a queuing point where we wait for testing or experimentation to be done before the "final final" deployment step. Partial deployments with manual activity around them are still a gate to production.

I would discourage such an approach, and I believe that runtime feature flags and automated testing are much better suited for verifying changes without coupling deployments to QA and product experimentation.

Antipattern example: Blue/green as a QA tool.   I have come across teams relying on manual blue/green deployments to test new versions on the blue environment. This involves accessing the temporary environment in a private URL and performing regression testing to ensure that everything works as expected. Only when the team has determined that the new version looks good will it switch to the green environment. However, this process should be automated if the team wants to switch to continuous deployment, perhaps by replacing it with automated regression testing in lower environments, automated smoke tests, or canary deployments.

Antipattern example: Partial deployments as a canary release tool.   Similarly, teams may be tempted to manually control rolling deployments as a form of A/B test to validate new features. They include the new feature in the next version of the application but only roll it out to a few instances. If the feature performs well with the exposed traffic subset, stakeholders will decide to roll it out to the rest of the infrastructure.

As I mentioned, this sort of manual and partial rollout of changes is not compatible with continuous deployments to production. The deployment should be fully automated, with the user-facing A/B testing process being replaced by feature flags. Using feature flags for user feedback allows for more fine-grained control over which users should see the feature than a partial deployment. For example, they allow selecting a subset of users by percentage of traffic or even by region, rather than an arbitrary number of requests arriving at specific instances. More importantly, if a feature doesn't perform well, there's no need to perform a rollback, and waiting for user feedback won't awkwardly hold up other code changes from being rolled out.

I would recommend to any team thinking of switching to continuous deployment to replace manual deployment steps with a combination of feature flags and automated tests before they open the gate to production. In a continuous deployment pipeline, the deployment to production should always be fully automated.

Observability and Monitoring

However sophisticated your code reviews, testing, and deployment strategies may be, production issues can still occur. Sometimes this can happen a long time after the latest deployment, as the necessary conditions for problems to surface can appear randomly.

That is why it is fundamental that developers are able to get quality information about the status of the production, and that the information is highly visible in information radiators available to the whole team.

Observability refers to the ability to monitor and understand the behavior of the deployed system by examining its outputs, such as logs, metrics, and traces. It represents the fundamental ability to ask new questions about the running system, affording an exploratory way to understand it. It also allows teams to identify and diagnose problems, as well as to get insights on how the system is functioning (or failing) under different conditions.

If you are in doubt as to what you should monitor, at least on the technical side, Google provides an excellent starting point in its SRE book (*https://oreil.ly/VnrBN*), which describes four golden signals:

- Latency, or the time it takes for the system to service a request.
- Traffic, a measure of how much demand (e.g., HTTP requests, incoming messages, transactions per second) is being placed on the system.
- Errors, or the rate of errors, especially in comparison to overall traffic.
- Saturation, or how much of your system's "capacity" is being used. This could translate to memory and CPU usage, current instances as opposed to your scaling limit, or hard drive fullness.

On the frontend side, you should also keep an eye on the evolution of the following Core Web Vital metrics (*https://oreil.ly/GhosH*) over time:

Largest contentful paint (LCP)
This is a measure of when the largest element on the page is rendered, which is an indicator of overall load speed as perceived by the user.

Cumulative layout shift (CLS)

When an element changes position from one frame to the next, that is a layout shift. Layout shifts should be kept to a minimum, as they can disrupt the user experience in many ways.

Interaction to next paint (INP)

This is a measure of latency for all click, tap, and keyboard interactions with a page, and in particular, the longest span. This is an indication of the perceived responsiveness of the page.

In addition to purely technical metrics, the team should make sure to also collect data for business-relevant metrics that reflect the application's domain; for example, the number of searches performed, conversion rates, click-through rates, and bounce rates.

The generation of outputs such as logs, metrics, and traces should be built into every increment of functionality added to the system, for two reasons: to get visibility as early as the very first deployment, and because adding it after the fact can require a redesign of the code, leading to wasteful rework.

All of this information can easily become overwhelming and noisy for developers, which is why it's also important that the most crucial signals are condensed into easy-to-read dashboards, examples of which are shown in Figures 4-10 and 4-11. It shouldn't take more than a glance for a developer who is familiar with the system to determine whether it is operating normally. If issues are detected, more detailed information such as individual logs and traces should be available to be searched for debugging purposes in separate spaces.

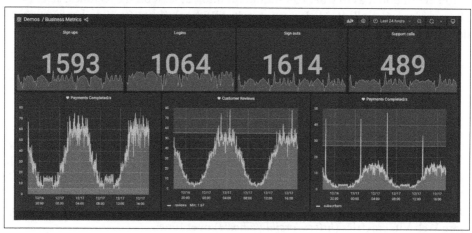

Figure 4-10. An example dashboard with business metrics

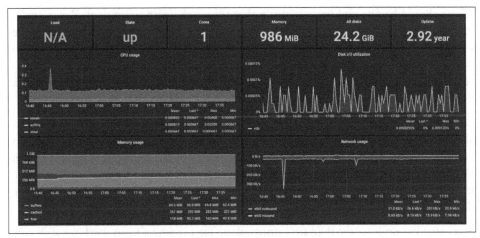

Figure 4-11. An example dashboard with technical metrics

A lot of innovation is happening in the observability space, with tools such as Data-dog (*https://www.datadoghq.com*), Splunk (*https://www.splunk.com*), Prometheus (*https://prometheus.io*), Grafana (*https://grafana.com*), and NewRelic (*https://newrelic.com*) proliferating and seeing more and more adoption in recent years.

Alerts

Keeping an eye on dashboards during day-to-day work is crucial with continuous deployment, but developers cannot be expected to keep their eyes glued to their Data-dog tab 100% of the time. That's why developers should be notified of abnormalities proactively, even if they try their best to pay attention to monitoring tools. This can be achieved through the use of alerts.

Most observability tools offer alerts that notify developers through a variety of chan-nels—Slack notifications, SMS, phone calls, carrier pigeons, and so on—when specific metrics start behaving weirdly. This is a must-have with frequent deployments.

Alerts can be based on a variety of different factors, such as the system's performance, usage patterns, or the appearance of specific log messages or errors. By configuring them on key indicators, teams can be notified of issues as soon as they occur, allowing them to take proactive steps to address the issue before it becomes critical.

Information versus noise

A lot of alerts and monitors can become overwhelming if not configured properly. When there are too many monitors, or when alerts go off constantly because they are flaky, developers can quickly learn to tune them out and lose interest, potentially ignoring critical issues.

Alerts should be few and meaningful rather than noisy and redundant. For example, on the technical side you might want to alert on only a few key metrics, such as spikes in application errors, out-of-control latency, or insufficient healthy instances. But don't disregard business-facing metrics. The sudden absence of certain types of requests, for example, can signal that users are having trouble completing a particular flow (e.g., the latest commit has somehow turned the checkout button invisible).

Some teams create new alerts for any new metric, and keep thresholds low for the alert to fire more often. That might seem like a comprehensive approach, but it is not helpful. Alerts crying wolf can be even worse than not having alerts at all. Having no alerts at least keeps the team paying attention as they are aware there is a gap of information, while bad alerts offer a false sense of security by virtue of their existence, despite being ignored most of the time.

Bad information is worse than no information. That is why a team working with continuous deployment should get into the habit of refactoring its observability and alerts with the same attention it reserves for its application code, its automated tests, and its pipeline.

The Datadog team provides a good heuristic on its blog for what constitutes "meaningful" alerts, and helps separate these alerts from noise—alerting on symptoms rather than causes, which is also covered in Google's SRE book:

> Pages [as in "paging someone"] are extremely effective for delivering information, but they can be quite disruptive if overused, or if they are linked to poorly designed alerts. In general, a page is the most appropriate kind of alert when the system you are responsible for stops doing useful work with acceptable throughput, latency, or error rates. Those are the sort of problems that you want to know about immediately.
>
> The fact that your system stopped doing useful work is a symptom—that is, it is a manifestation of an issue that may have any number of different causes. For example: if your website has been responding very slowly for the last three minutes, that is a symptom. Possible causes include high database latency, failed application servers, Memcached being down, high load, and so on. Whenever possible, build your pages around symptoms rather than causes. [...]
>
> Paging on symptoms surfaces real, oftentimes user-facing problems, rather than hypothetical or internal problems. Contrast paging on a symptom, such as slow website responses, with paging on potential causes of the symptom, such as high load on your web servers. Your users will not know or care about server load if the website is still responding quickly, and your engineers will resent being bothered for something that is only internally noticeable and that may revert to normal levels without intervention.[8]

---

8 Alexis Lê-Quôc, "Monitoring 101: Alerting on what matters," Datadog, 2016, *https://oreil.ly/M3Wzn*.

Stakeholder Trust

In this chapter, we talked a great deal about the *technical* prerequisites for working safely under continuous deployment. I think it's necessary to close the chapter with a reflection on the impact of the human factor.

Opening the gate to production to all commits is a trust exercise between stakeholders and their team. As developers who work on the system daily, we have intimate knowledge of all the safety measures we put in place in order to prevent Bad Things™ from happening to production. With continuous deployment, we are the ones who remain in control of quality gates: after all, we are implementing and configuring the automation that will act on our behalf. But our stakeholders cannot say the same. All they might see, from their perspective, is a loss of their chance to provide input and to block dangerous changes before it's too late. They have no visibility into the meticulousness of the layers and layers of automation that make their approval unnecessary, and they have to trust our word as engineers. We are effectively asking them to relinquish their only power over the path to production. Given this big ask, we should strive to be empathetic to any concern they put forward. Even if we have done an excellent job at implementing a perfect technical foundation, the cultural one might still be the trickiest after all.

Yet, enabling continuous deployment is a team effort, and our stakeholders being on board is necessary in order for them to make the most of this practice. Stakeholders being confident will also make them more patient with any teething pains as the team gets used to this new way of working. So let's talk about how to make them enthusiastic (rather than fearful) of automated deployments.

How Do We Convince the Boss?

As a consultant, I have had to do my fair share of convincing in the teams where we were close to continuous deployment, but not quite there yet. In my experience, this convincing is best done when little convincing is left to do.

None of the practices discussed in this chapter are needed exclusively by continuous deployment: each of them can be implemented independently and is a more than justifiable investment on its own. They will undoubtedly improve the quality of the application even with a manual gate to production still in place.

Therefore, I would encourage my fellow engineers to put them in place regardless of whether continuous deployment is the final goal, as they will still lead to a more robust implementation of continuous delivery.

Once the team has reached a great level of continuous delivery maturity, painstaking manual testing of every detail will start to feel redundant rather than necessary. When the team has reached that point, my experience is that even stakeholders will learn to find manual testing annoying. That is when it is easiest to suggest going one step further without triggering strong reactions. The suggestion might even be welcomed at that point, as its only consequence will be removing redundant work.

In my experience, this approach not only removes most of the "negotiating" from these conversations, but it also helps the team ensure that it is indeed ready, as it has evaluated how much it still relies on human eyes over automation. Your boss might even appreciate that continuous deployment readiness is a clear and concrete goal that the team can adopt to guide its continual improvement.

This raises the question, "So how do we know when we are ready?"

As you will see in the case studies in Part V, some bold companies such as Auto-Scout24 make the decision to adopt continuous deployment from day one, as soon as they shift to a modern production ecosystem with microservices, feature flags, and so on. However, if your company is a bit more hesitant, the next section might give you some useful pointers.

When Are We Ready?

We have covered a lot of practices here, and it might be tempting to think that each of them has to be gold-plated to perfection before even considering the removal of human steps from our pipelines. I would like to discourage my readers from that line of thinking. As we discussed in Chapter 2, one of the benefits of continuous deployment is that, once enabled, it puts any and all quality gates to a very thorough test. As code goes to production more and more often, any gaps in our processes will expose themselves rapidly, and they can be addressed by the team as they come up. If we wait for our safety nets to be absolutely perfect, we might never end up taking the leap. Doing the painful thing earlier and more often lets the practices refine themselves naturally.

Whether the time is right or not is a difficult question, and ultimately one that each team needs to answer based on the circumstances it finds itself in. That's why I will answer this question with another question—several, in fact. These are some things I would suggest that you consider so that you can come up with your own conclusions:

- Is my team aware of all the practices discussed in this chapter?

- Have we implemented each practice in this chapter? If yes, to what degree of sophistication? And if not, do we have a good reason why we don't need it?

- For each practice we have implemented, is every team member working with it confidently rather than ignoring it or circumventing it?

- If we implemented continuous deployment tomorrow, what type of code defect would worry me the most (e.g., performance impact, security vulnerability, regression on a specific feature)? What type of defect would worry *my stakeholders* the most? Is the protection against them manual or automated today?

- If we implemented continuous deployment tomorrow, is there any particular signal from the production system I would especially keep an eye on? Do we have easy-to-access metrics giving us visibility of it today? If there is a degradation, do we already have alerting for that signal?

- Is there a significant number of defects that are currently only caught by checking changes manually? If yes, what do they have in common? What kind of automation would be necessary to catch them earlier?

- Given our technical practices, does the manual gate to production feel like a life-saver today, or does it feel redundant and like an inconvenience? Does every member of the team feel the same? Do our stakeholders feel the same?

These are just some of the questions I like to ask when evaluating whether continuous deployment is the right choice at a particular point in time. Even for those who don't plan to implement it anytime soon, the process of finding the answers to these questions might lead to a more thorough understanding of the team's quality strategy and the robustness of its system.

Summary

In this chapter, we talked about some of the practices that our teams should implement before switching to continuous deployment. Some requirements are cultural and organizational, such as stakeholder trust and cross-functional, autonomous teams with a habit of frequent integration and code reviews. The majority of other requirements are technical: zero-downtime deployments, a pipeline with several layers of automated tests, observability, and alerts.

These are not investments that are valuable for continuous deployment only. Rather, they are good practices that stand on their own. This means that they can be implemented as improvements in isolation and still result in great outcomes for the team's software delivery life cycle. The decision to switch to continuous deployment can be made (or reversed) later at no loss.

This foundation of practices can ensure that removal of the final gate to production will be as painless as possible.

CHAPTER 5

Challenges

No new technology or practice is a silver bullet, and continuous deployment is no exception to this rule. In addition to requiring that the team be well-practiced in its implementation of continuous delivery, continuous deployment comes with its own set of challenges. It would be irresponsible of me not to mention these challenges in this book. Furthermore, I believe that understanding them provides a more well-rounded approach to continuous deployment itself. In case your team ends up facing these challenges, I will describe some strategies you can adopt to overcome them or mitigate them.

In this chapter, we will look at a variety of scenarios in which teams might struggle to adopt continuous deployment or require some tweaking to their processes or systems to make it work. You will learn about some of the pain points of the practice and the concrete implications that they have for real teams. Depending on the organization's context, these pain points might be inconsequential, manageable, or completely unacceptable. It will be up to you to evaluate them and discuss their impact. You will have to ultimately decide whether you can mitigate them with the strategies described in this chapter, learn to live with them, or settle for not performing continuous deployment at all.

We will also look at systems in which the speed offered by continuous deployment might be inappropriate or even technically infeasible. However, such cases are the exception and not the rule. It's important to be able to tell the difference and ask the right questions so that you can know which battles to pick and which to leave when considering whether to deploy continuously to production.

Systems That Are Sensitive to Deployments

There are many benefits to maintaining a high deployment frequency, as demonstrated by the research coming out of the DORA program. In general, as I explained in Chapter 1, frequent and small deployments are much better for system stability. However, something that is often not talked about is how, for many applications, even a single deployment can be a disruptive event. It is not uncommon to witness errors or subpar application performance during or right after a deployment, but it is a phenomenon that often gets ignored when deployments are infrequent: it's not that impactful in the grand scheme of things, and it would be hard to debug anyway.

With a high deployment frequency, however, any deployment glitch is amplified and can quickly turn into a problem. In this section, we will look at the most common ones and how to mitigate them so that many deployments per day don't affect the stability of the live fleet and the usability of the application. This is another example of the "If it hurts, do it more often" principle in action, which gives us an opportunity to improve areas that we wouldn't pay much attention to if our deployments were occurring weekly or monthly.

Interruption of Long-Running Processes

In some cases, application instances contain long-running processes that are at risk of being disrupted by deployments, such as background jobs that get triggered upon a user request. For example, a user might prompt the generation of a computationally intensive report that could not possibly be completed in time to send an HTTP response, so it is served asynchronously by the instance at a later time.

In other cases, long-running operations are completed synchronously, but they might still be time-consuming and involve complicated transactions across multiple systems. In particular, distributed write operations tend to be especially sensitive and cause pesky data consistency issues when they are interrupted.

When multiple deployments occur in quick succession, they can get in the way of these long-running processes by triggering a replacement of all instances. This is already a problem with ordinary scale-down events, but continuous deployment makes it even more likely that these interruptions will take place, especially if there is a hard timeout for draining instances before they are taken out of service in favor of a new version.

Mitigation: Switch to messaging or event-based architectures

I would argue that individual instances that are both serving traffic *and* relying on long-lived processes are an antipattern in and of themselves, even without considering continuous deployment. Instances in a horizontally scalable system should be as stateless as possible so that they can be started and decommissioned at any moment, without putting the system in an inconsistent state. After all, as I mentioned, scale-down events are always a possibility.

Any process that must be completed asynchronously or that cannot be interrupted should rely on external messaging platforms. Using queues, for example, could be a better way to guarantee that jobs won't get interrupted or lost, thereby avoiding reliance on flaky sequences of HTTP calls or lengthy background computation.

While a slightly unoptimized architecture might have been tolerable with less frequent deployments, teams that aim to deploy continuously might want to revisit this architectural choice. Opening the path for continuous deployment is just one of the many good reasons to implement appropriate asynchronous processing into a resilient, distributed model.

Instances whose job is to complete jobs.   It is worth noting, however, that not all application instances are meant to serve short-lived requests. The primary aim of some applications is exclusively to process long-running jobs (perhaps coming from a queue or an event system, as suggested in the previous section). Those types of instances are particularly inconvenient to shut down and redeploy, as they tend to stay busy for long periods.

Teams can avoid this problem by moving the job's internal state externally so that it can be easily interrupted and then resumed after deployment. However, this might make the job completion time even longer by adding network requests to store state to the already long list of tasks to complete. Even so, this is the option one of my teams took when faced with this issue. We had a system whose job was to process and transform all product data on a schedule. Originally, it was doing the whole computation in-memory, which took around 30 minutes. Because this system was difficult to redeploy, we later switched to saving intermediate states to an external database, which did lead to a significant increase in processing time. However, processing time was not crucial in our case. The possibility to gracefully redeploy and have new instances resume where the old ones left off greatly outweighed the pain of slower job completion. The state being external also made the process easier to debug, and gave us reassurance that an instance dying unexpectedly would not compromise data consistency or require a complete rerun.

If completion time is critical, teams might instead want to implement a "lock" mechanism on deployments, which is essentially a longer type of graceful shutdown. This, however, has some serious downsides of its own, as it can lead to deployments that can last for a very long time when instances are very busy or the jobs are very long, which introduces a bottleneck. This mechanism can also be quite complicated to implement, as the definitions of *idle* and *busy* are application dependent.

Due to these complications, this is an area where teams might want to carefully consider the trade-offs of continuous deployment and perhaps come to a compromise instead.

Sticky Sessions

Another problem with the combination of instance-level state and frequent deployments is the disruption of sticky sessions. *Session stickiness* (or *session persistence*) is the process by which an application load balancer keeps track of which instance was assigned to a specific client at their first request. With session stickiness, the load balancer then tries to ensure that additional requests from the same client always arrive to that instance for the duration of the session.

This mechanism is sometimes employed when the state of a (supposedly) short-lived user session is stored in the application, which is a scenario in which talking to the same instance becomes critical for the correct functioning of the user flow. For example, an instance might store shopping cart data across different page visits from the user.

Just like with long-running jobs, any application that relies on in-memory state becomes unreliable under a constant flow of deployments. Instances will very often be replaced with new instances, and any state will be lost. Storing state in-memory might lead to simpler applications, but it has the potential to severely disrupt user experience during any deployment or scaling event.

Mitigation: Keep state external

Once more, the main mitigation for state issues and frequent deployments is to store state externally. Application instances must be as stateless as possible—so much so that in-memory state should be considered a bug. Any data that needs to be persisted across requests (even for a short time) should be kept in an external data store that can remain unaffected by deployments.

Of course, this might complicate the application architecture (as in the case of external caches). However, I would argue that this case is outside the realm of a "nice-to-have" optimization: application-relevant data that is critical to the functioning of the overall system should be persisted properly in adequate, nontransient storage. Moving such state to a persistence layer is something I would always recommend, despite the additional overhead.

Invalidation of Client-Side Caches

Many applications rely on some level of caching on the client side to guarantee that things that won't change between deployments also won't be fetched every single time. This usually applies to HTML/CSS and JavaScript assets in frontend applications, which are often distributed by content delivery networks (CDNs). How-ever, client-side caches can also sneak in in more subtle ways; for example, by brows-ers doing heuristic caching on their own when there is no cache control.

With deployments happening monthly, weekly, or every few days, all of these caches on the client side can be convenient for keeping a good perception of application per-formance. However, continuous deployment takes us into the realm of 10, 20, or more deployments *per day*, where all of these new versions mean cache invalidation. Therefore, we have to expect more cache misses, which sometimes imply slower per-formance from the perspective of our users and more incoming traffic into our sys-tems. If you are like me, then caching policies might not be the first thing on your mind when developing an application. But if your caching policies are incorrect, more frequent deployments could also lead to incompatibility issues between client and server.

Mitigation: Be deliberate about your caching policies

If your application is popular enough for this to become a problem, then you might want to assert more fine-grained control over your caching policies. For example, you might want to consider carefully using Cache-Control and Expires headers in your frontend code and tweaking the configuration of your build tools. You might find that some static files, for example, do well with less aggressive caching invalidation than others due to their low likelihood of changing, even under continuous deploy-ment (think of, say, the *index.html* of a React application).

In general, you should evaluate any point at which caching could occur in between client request and server response in your specific infrastructure, how each of those caches might be invalidated by a new deployment, and the likelihood of that happen-ing. Once you have that information, not only can you configure cache expiration correctly, but you can also prepare the right components of your infrastructure for a slightly higher load after you open the gate to production.

Scaling Interruptions

Another possible effect of a high density of deployments is that, depending on your platform of choice and/or autoscaling configuration, the deployments might get in the way of scale-up or scale-down events. This problem might be more or less pro-nounced based on each team's type of deployment (e.g., blue/green, rolling deploy-ment), its infrastructure, and the metrics used for scaling. For example, depending on your setup, a new deployment and a scaling event might not be able to occur at the same time. Even when that is not the case, a new deployment might affect metrics used by the autoscaler, such as CPU utilization, memory, and incoming requests per instance.

Peak traffic times for applications are often in the middle of the business day, which also happens to be the busiest time for developers working on changes. A deployment that forces all instances to be replaced could cause responsiveness issues if it coincides with scale-up events due to heavy traffic, and it can delay the fleet's ability to reach the desired capacity. If lots of deployments are being performed continuously, they may get in the way of autoscalers and reduce the application's overall adaptability to sharp traffic changes.

It is worth investigating how this interaction works in your current platform, and ensuring that the team is aware of which processes are disrupted during a deployment and which aren't. However, there are a couple of mitigations for this problem that can be applied in almost all circumstances.

Mitigation: Keep application startup time low

The impact of deployments on autoscaling can be alleviated by keeping the application startup time low so that the time spent on creating new instances is kept to a minimum (whether for scale-up or replacement purposes). This can be achieved by minimizing the work done by the application at startup before an instance can return a green health check. Examples of such work might be ingesting data at startup, retrieving something from the persistence layer, calls to downstream services, or a mix of all of the above. Ideally, the time for an application to start should be measured in seconds, not minutes.

New instances should be able to be put in service very quickly so that each individual deployment can stay fast, even when replacing a high number of running machines or containers. Shorter deployment durations make the window between deployments much larger, giving more time for the autoscaling to do its job effectively.

In Figure 5-1, you can see the status of a production application on a timeline. Given a setup where scaling and deployments cannot happen simultaneously, notice how the same number of deployments has a drastically different impact on scaling responsiveness, based solely on their duration.

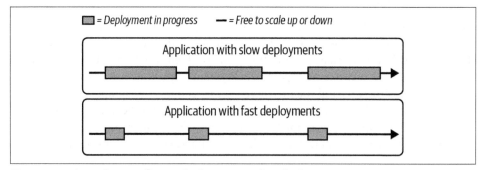

Figure 5-1. A production fleet with slow versus fast deployments

The same principle works in the opposite direction as well. When new instances can be put in service quickly, autoscaling events will be over very quickly, allowing a bigger window for new deployments to occur. Overall, keeping application startup time to a minimum always improves production responsiveness.

Mitigation: Introduce more generous scaling policies

An alternative way to deal with tricky scaling around deployments is to tweak scaling settings so that they are more generous when calculating the desired capacity and/or more aggressive when detecting traffic changes. For my teams, this meant ensuring that the base number of instances was higher than we would normally have and that smaller thresholds would activate a scale-up event.

This is an effective mitigation strategy for a short-term issue, but it can become quite expensive in terms of infrastructure cost in the long term. That is why I would only recommend it if the startup time of the application truly cannot be reduced any further, or if the engineering cost of achieving it is much higher than what would be at the bottom of the cloud provider bills—which, admittedly, is a very real possibility in some scenarios.

Mitigation: Perform pre-scaling

Another way to get out of tricky scaling issues in a pinch is to manually pre-scale the application. With enough advance knowledge of an incoming traffic peak, developers can manually set a desired capacity for the fleet ahead of the anticipated time. This allows the team and stakeholders to not worry as much about publishing changes during a sensitive time window.

Still, every time pre-scaling is needed there needs to be some coordination between development and product, so I would recommend using this strategy sparingly due to the manual effort involved.

We have found ourselves relying on pre-scaling on rare occasions, usually in preparation for very public events that would instantly flood our systems with new requests (ones where we didn't trust our systems to scale quickly enough anyway). For example, we used it when working in retail systems where the marketing team would organize limited-time sale events. I encourage other teams to do the same: focus on keeping scaling as responsive as possible and on shortening deployment times, but consider pre-scaling as another tool in your toolbox if you are dealing with planned and sharp traffic spikes.

A Constant Stream of Cold Instances

Another side effect of a constant stream of deployments is that the likelihood of any given container or instance being brand new is very high. This might cause problems for applications that perform at their best when their uptime is on the longer side, such as services that need some warm-up time to fill up caches.

As developers *and* users are often most active during the day, lots of consecutive deployments might cause caches to be cold when they are needed the most, which can increase not only the load on downstream systems but also the response times for end users.

In Figure 5-2, you can see the potential impact of frequent deployments (represented by the thin vertical lines) on application caches warming up.

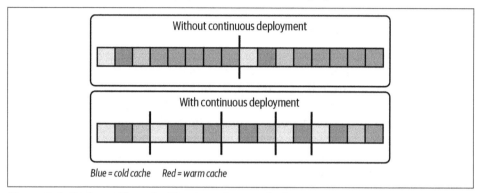

Figure 5-2. Caches with and without continuous deployment

Mitigation: Use external caches

The problem of cold caches can be managed through the use of caching systems that live outside the application runtime, such as Redis or Memcached. When new deployments replace all instances, an external caching system will not be affected and won't need to be repopulated from scratch. With an external cache, we can guarantee that application instances will respond with the same speed, regardless of whether it is after one second of uptime or one hour of uptime.

However, external caches have some downsides. First, although they are designed to be fast, they still introduce some latency, as they require network calls to be reached. This means losing precious milliseconds for each request. The fact that an in-memory cache was introduced in all likelihood means that the application had a requirement to be fast in the first place, and such a delay might be unacceptable.

External caches being separate infrastructure components also makes them more costly to maintain. They are quite literally more expensive, as they represent another item on our cloud provider's bills, but they are also costly in terms of cognitive load on the team. They are yet another piece of infrastructure that needs to be maintained, secured, and kept up-to-date.

Finally, external caching systems introduce another persistence layer. All persistence layers (even nonrelational ones) have some sort of schema or contract with the application about the shape of the data they hold. Such contracts need to be explicit and evolve as the application code changes, introducing a refactoring cost. This can be cumbersome when compared to a simpler in-memory cache, where the code managing the shape of the cache is usually very close to the application code that talks directly to it.

All of that said, external caching systems are pretty sophisticated these days, and they represent a viable option for teams that are worried about their application performance with a steady stream of fresh deployments.

User-Installed Software

Continuous deployment to production assumes that the product team has full control over the production system and what code is running within it. But what if the production system is a mobile device that is (literally) in the hands of users, a laptop sitting on their desk, or even an appliance that needs to be physically installed at a customer's location?

In such situations, the final step of the path to production is not as straightforward as an automated pipeline spawning new servers to replace old ones, or updating files for browsers to fetch at the next refresh. When the production environment physically belongs to a user, how often software gets deployed onto it is not a choice that belongs to the application's developers, but a choice that belongs to its owner. Therefore, continuous deployment in those situations can be technically impossible, or at least very impractical. The very definition of a deployment can even become blurry. When is a production deployment actually finished? Is it when the code gets installed on the first user's device or when it gets installed on the last one?

That said, if a new team is starting up with a strong commitment to continuous delivery, there are ways to retain some control over what code is running on user-controlled devices. They involve either giving some rendering control back to the server or performing updates without the user explicitly installing a new version.

Desktop Applications

Desktop applications are a primary example of an environment where developers cannot control the software's installation. Even when the application can manage its own updates without downloading a new installer, prompting users for updates every hour of every day will quickly impact usability.

Mitigation: Introduce self-applying updates

Self-applying updates seems to be the most popular way for desktop applications to guarantee that the latest version of the code is running on the user's device. A self-updating application polls an update server at regular intervals when the device is connected to the internet, allowing developers to release new versions continuously if they wish to.

The device's connectivity to the internet might seem like a problem in this case, as an offline device cannot perform updates. However, most of the issues with client-side updates being missed lie in the compatibility with the server. When the device is offline, the server cannot be reached anyway, so the affected functionality won't be available in the first place. This makes self-applying continuous updates over the internet a viable strategy that can resemble continuous deployment.

Self-updating can be achieved through native technology offered by the application's platform, such as the Windows ClickOnce (*https://oreil.ly/sBbdK*) deployment strategy, or by carefully implementing the auto-updating functionality by hand. Some multiplatform frameworks, such as Electron (*https://oreil.ly/hnfpF*), offer self-updating technology as well.

That said, whether users will react favorably to automatic updates is something that inevitably depends on the application and should be carefully considered by product teams.

Mobile Apps

In the case of mobile apps, self-updating functionality is not an option. In the most popular platforms (Android and iOS), the App Store or Play Store is in charge of managing application versions.

As well as managing all updates through the store, Google and (especially) Apple have historically acted as a manual quality gate for any new app version, effectively preventing developers from deploying continuously to production.

To complicate things even further, users might turn off automatic updates from their platform of choice, or only allow updates over WiFi. This means whenever a new version is released, it remains on some users' devices for a long time, causing issues for developers working on the backend who will need their APIs to continue supporting old app versions for months or even years. This is sometimes referred to as the *long tail problem*. With continuous deployment on the backend side, this problem is felt even more strongly, as there are more opportunities for client-side code and server-side code to drift apart.

Figure 5-3 represents this typical long tail problem, showcasing the number of users on current (N) and older ($N - 1$, $N - 2$...) app versions at any given time.

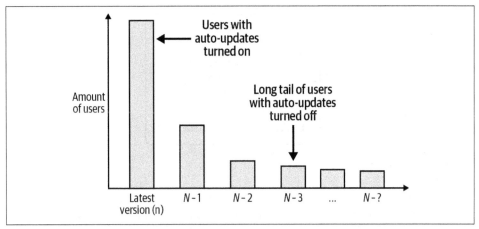

Figure 5-3. The long tail of users still on old versions

Some mobile app developers attempt to solve this issue by introducing a barrier in the UI that forces users to update when it detects that the version is too old, or the back-end returns a certain "force update" flag. Apps such as WhatsApp and Messenger even work with a rolling window of forced upgrades.

However, this strategy must be introduced very early in the product's life cycle, as all previous versions will be unaffected. It might alleviate some pain when urgent updates are needed, or cut off the tail for really ancient versions, but it is not a reasonable strategy for continuous deployment of the app code, unless we want to pester our users with endless forced update screens.

Mitigation: Shift control to the server side

To perform continuous deployment of mobile apps, the only solution lies in moving some client-side code back to the server, which is under the developers' control. This can be achieved through several means.

Options for implementing this strategy involve frameworks or features that allow for server-side code to determine most of what gets rendered on the screen. As shown in Figure 5-4, this is usually achieved by a *wrapper* application installed on the device, which acts as an empty container. The app retrieves rendering instructions from the server, much like a web browser would (in many cases, this is powered by a *literal* instance of a web browser under the hood).

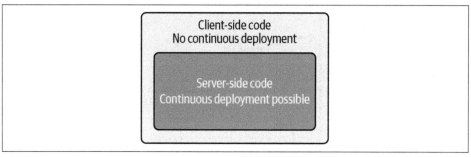

Figure 5-4. Rendering server-side content on devices

These options can approximate continuous deployment on mobile devices, but they are also very binding architectural choices that come with their own downsides (usually performance and compatibility related). As such, they are choices that need to be made very early in development and that not only affect development but might also preclude using certain device features. This makes them inaccessible to many teams that are already years into building their native apps and are not keen to do a complete rewrite.

At the time of writing this book, it is also worth noting that variations of strategy all seem to sit in a gray area within the rules of different app stores. They seem to be allowed (and indeed many companies are already relying on them), but they effectively evade oversight mechanisms on new app versions, which is something that the stores take very seriously. Therefore, caution is advised in this space.

Implementing server-side control does not free developers of the burden of releasing new versions to the stores either. As new versions of operating systems come in or the store policies change, new versions might be needed in order to update basic requirements such as the permissions that are needed on the device.

Despite these downsides, these options are certainly worth understanding, so let's go through a quick overview.

Web views. Web views in iOS and Android apps are used to display web content within the app itself. They provide a way for developers to embed web content in their native app without having to launch a separate browser.

A native application can be partially or completely composed of web views, potentially allowing teams to decide which sections of the app should be kept native for better performance and user experience.

Progressive web apps. Progressive Web Apps (*https://oreil.ly/auNF8*) (PWAs) are a type of web application that combines the features of a traditional web page with the functionality of a mobile app, effectively rendering them "installable websites." They are built using web technologies and can be accessed through a web browser on any device, but they also can be installed on a user's home screen, just like a traditional app, and they can even receive push notifications. A PWA can also be submitted to all the major app stores, either as a first-class app or wrapped in a web view (*https://oreil.ly/MzMve*) so that it can be made discoverable just like a traditional mobile app.

PWAs have several benefits, such as quick installation and fast load times. Most of all, they work on all platforms and devices, so companies don't need to create multiple product versions for each operating system. And last but not least, they allow you to continuously deploy new versions because of their model allowing (mostly) server-side control.

At the time of writing this book, however, PWAs still have serious downsides. For example, they are not able to access all of the phone's APIs in the same way that a native app does. Overall, many companies are adopting PWAs to complement their existing strategy, but a PWA-only approach doesn't seem popular just yet.

Server-driven UIs.   *Server-driven UIs* (SDUIs) are a newcomer to this space. SDUIs are a new paradigm being driven by companies such as Airbnb and Lyft that aim to allow the server to control what is displayed in the interface of their mobile apps. Unlike web views and PWAs, this is not achieved through web technologies. SDUIs rely instead on custom markup "language" (*https://oreil.ly/eXIE2*) shared by the app and the server. Instead of fetching just data, the app also fetches markup information alongside it. This allows for the code in the app to remain unchanged, even as new features are released through the server.

Even with an SDUI strategy, developers are still not completely free of app updates. The custom markup language itself will need new features or rearchitecting once in a while, as new ways of laying out data are imagined by the business.

At this time, there are no popular frameworks to quickly set up an SDUI, and implementing this paradigm from scratch might be a daunting challenge for small to medium-sized companies. However, SDUIs are worth keeping an eye on as a promising alternative to traditional native apps. While still able to leverage all of the device features (as opposed to web views and PWAs), they have the potential to greatly simplify app release cycles and can allow the continuous deployment of new features to a suitable degree.

Appliances and Other Devices

When it comes to the vast world of software made for devices that are not smartphones or personal computers, providing updates over the internet seems to be the only practical way to make new software versions available. That is, if the devices can connect to the internet at all.

The sheer range of possible applications is so vast that it is very difficult to tell how such updates should be managed, even when they are possible. For example, should they be self-applied in the background with a short polling interval, or should they be carefully executed only after receiving the explicit consent of the user through several warning screens?

The security implications are vast. Think of the difference, for example, between a self-driving car applying a software update while driving in the middle of a busy intersection and a smart toaster self-updating while preparing your breakfast. A deployment gone wrong would result in quite different scenarios: tragic loss of life or slightly burnt bread. These might sit at two extremes, but what about gray areas, such as software installed in point-of-sale systems? Some people might argue that a self-applying update will likely not result in deadly accidents, therefore deeming it completely fine. Others might be rightfully worried that an interruption of service would cause an entire chain of stores to shut down. And still others might argue yet again that such an interruption would be comparable to an ecommerce website experiencing checkout issues after a bad deployment: not pleasant, but also not an unheard-of occurrence.

These are just a few examples. Overall, due to the vastness of applications and the myriad of factors to consider in each case, this is one of the few areas where I would hesitate to recommend continuous deployment as a default option. When making software for the vast world of other devices out there, self-applying updates might be too risky, and focusing on users' consent and/or explicit update windows might be a safer default. Traditional continuous delivery with short release cycles should be the starting point, and whether continuous deployment is a sensible next step should be carefully evaluated.

Libraries and Frameworks

Any piece of software that is built to be invoked by other software, rather than being executed on its own, is another tricky scenario for applying continuous deployment. The production environment in this case can be thought of as other developers' programs, and the installation process into production is each program's build configuration, which is fully under the control of the author.

Theoretically, nothing prevents a team whose product is a library or framework from continuing to release new versions to the repository of its language of choice in a fully automated fashion. Such a process could be considered continuous deployment to (almost) production.

However, each new library or framework update would represent a version upgrade to be done on the other developer's end, which is rarely an automated process. Many new versions popping up frequently might annoy developers who already need to manage versions of *their own* software, causing some headaches even if the updates don't contain breaking changes (i.e., they are minor or patch versions).

For this reason, it might be in the interest of library or framework usability to avoid continuous deployment and to (sensibly) batch commits going into new versions instead.

Regulated Industries

Companies at the core of domains such as government, transportation, healthcare, and finance might have strong regulatory constraints around code being deployed to production. The goal of such regulations is usually to ensure that changes are being applied in a safe and high-quality manner, and at the same time to guarantee each change is auditable in case something goes wrong. These regulations are usually in place for *really* good reasons, mostly focused on protecting regular citizens. That is why it's hard to challenge their necessity, but that doesn't mean that their implementation should be immune to improvements.

Regulatory constraints often take the concrete form of more eyes needed to oversee what gets included in each new release. This often translates to several process quirks: long feature branches, a subset of chosen "admins" to act as gatekeepers, mandatory stops in staging environments, and more formalities along the path to production; in other words, all of the things that continuous deployment aims to do without. This might make it seem like regulated industries and continuous deployment are mutually exclusive, but that is not necessarily the case.

Mitigation: Isolate critical components

One of the most straightforward ways to work around constraining processes is to isolate the critical systems by splitting them into separately deployable units, giving them independent paths to production, but most of all, implementing separate change approval processes. This can allow the noncritical areas of the business (which is usually most areas) to work in a more Agile fashion and only keep heavyweight processes where they are absolutely necessary.

In one of my teams, we were working in a specific subcategory of the transportation industry that was subject to very tight scrutiny. Even so, we could negotiate a very relaxed approach to deployments because we were creating mostly internal products that would never interact with critical production infrastructure. In the rest of the company, different teams operated at various points of the spectrum between relaxed constraints and a much more formal release process.

Still, applying a lightweight process for only a few lucky teams is just a workaround, and it doesn't resolve the core issue for teams that handle more critical systems and whose health could also benefit from a more modern approach.

Mitigation: Find the source of constraints

How do we know when we *truly* are in a situation where a heavyweight change approval process cannot be avoided? Usually, when a developer joins an existing team or organization, they find themselves immersed in an engineering culture shaped by processes that are years (sometimes decades) old and that are well accepted by their peers. It is a reasonable assumption to make that if certain gatekeeping is in place, it must be for good reasons that ought not be questioned. However, sometimes this is not the case. Avoiding asking tough questions can lead to missed opportunities to slim down engineering practices, even when time, organizational changes, or technological advancements have made existing gatekeeping redundant.

In my opinion, it is always worth investigating the source of anything that is forcefully slowing down delivery. Developers and managers might find that what they assumed would be a hard requirement of their industry was actually a company-level policy rooted in someone's risk aversion; maybe someone who worked at the company years ago and has already left. Or they might find that they are building a product that is only adjacent to the critical core of their business and can actually be built under much more relaxed conditions.

Mitigation: Use leaner practices to satisfy compliance requirements

Compliance frameworks have to accommodate different scenarios. Therefore, they can actually be open to a variety of implementations.

The NIST framework (*https://oreil.ly/a3U3T*), for example, doesn't explicitly mandate "thou shalt have a GitHub org administrator approve pull requests (PRs), and only after all the relevant code is in The One Feature Branch," even if that is what a lot of managers assume. Instead, it is more broadly trying to ensure segregation of duties, where no individual should be solely responsible for both implementing and approving arbitrary changes.

The DORA "Accelerate State of DevOps Report 2019" explains how such a requirement might be satisfied in different ways, some more lightweight than others:

> Segregation of duties, which states that changes must be approved by someone other than the author, is often required by regulatory frameworks. While we agree that no individual should have end-to-end control over a process (the intent of this control), there are lightweight, secure ways to achieve this objective that don't suffer the same coordination costs as heavyweight approaches. One approach is to require every change be approved by someone else on the team as part of code review, either prior to commit to version control (as part of pair programming) or prior to merge into master. This can be combined with automated thresholds that bound changes. For example, you may implement checks to not allow developers to push a change (even with peer review) that will increase compute or storage costs over a certain threshold. This

lightweight, straightforward-to-implement process presents a clear opportunity for practitioners to improve change management.[1]

Pair programming can be used to replace merge-time code reviews as a way to demonstrate that every change has gone through separate approvals before being applied. This can remove the need for long branches and allow teams to get closer to a one-commit/one-deploy workflow. As I already mentioned, Part V includes a case study on digital bank N26 where you can see an example of this straightforward change management in action. N26 engineers use pair programming and PRs in tandem to provide proof of review with continuous deployment.

Another one of the most common requirements for regulatory regimes is to provide an audit trail of all changes to the production system. Dave Farley wrote a great article (*https://oreil.ly/8_kcB*) on continuous compliance in which he explains how this requirement can be automatically satisfied by an automated build pipeline:

> If we tie together our requirement-management systems with our Version Control System [...], then we have complete traceability. We can tell the story of any change from end-to-end.
>
> "Who captured the need for this change?"
>
> "Who wrote the tests?"
>
> "Who committed changes associated with this piece of work?"
>
> "Which tests were run?"
>
> "This change was rejected, what failed to reject the change?"
>
> "Who was involved with any manual testing?"
>
> "Who approved the release into production?"
>
> "Which version of the OS, Database, programming language, etc was deployed and used?"
>
> "Which version of the deployment script/tooling was used?"
>
> All of this information is available as a side-effect of building a Deployment Pipeline. In fact it is quite hard to imagine a Pipeline that doesn't give you access to this information. I sometimes describe one of the important properties of Deployment Pipelines as "providing a key'ed, search-space for all of the information associated with any production change." This is Gold for people working in compliance, regulation and audit.

Indeed, an automated build pipeline can actually *remove* the need for extensive documentation and bureaucracy over every individual changeset. With it, the documentation is self-generating. This is yet another example of how regulations can be satisfied by existing lightweight software good practices.

---

1 DORA, "Accelerate State of DevOps Report 2019," 48–49. You can read the full report at *https://oreil.ly/x3mqW*.

It is important to remember that the environments subject to these requirements often are the same environments where Agile has been slower to arrive, along with all of its additional tools for keeping quality consistent. In such organizations, things like very formal change approval processes and separation between Dev and Ops have often been seen as the only protection from poor-quality and rushed emergency fixes. It is worth exploring whether Agile practices that came later (such as the automated deployment pipeline, shifting testing to the left, test-driven development, infrastructure as code, and pair programming) might actually satisfy an organization's regulatory requirements to the same or an even better degree, while allowing developers to work in a leaner fashion.

Overall, slowing the pace of changes is only an unpleasant side effect of most regulatory frameworks, and it is far from being their goal. Organizations applying Agile principles can satisfy these frameworks while still deploying multiple times per day, in some cases even continuously.

At the same time, as professionals, we also have to be prepared to find answers that we do not like and to accept that some gatekeeping might indeed be unavoidable after all. Slowing us down is sometimes a fair price to pay to shield the general public from defects or malicious actors that would cause them a disproportionate amount of harm.

Cognitive Load

When the influx of commits to trunk is significant, the resulting number of production deployments can throw our team into disarray, or simply add more to think about. In this section, we will look at the more human side of things: in particular, some of the effects that automated deployments can have on the team's cognitive load and how this can be mitigated.

Overly Busy Path to Production

When a very large team or multiple teams are working on a single service, the automated pipeline is undoubtedly working hard at all times. Changes are pushed to trunk frequently, which means there are many builds queued to be tested and deployed to higher environments, sometimes in a too-quick succession. It becomes tricky at best for engineers to feel like they have full control of the situation and to know at a glance which of their many changes is currently being processed.

When automatic deployments to production are thrown into the mix, this confusion can become more dangerous. With any production deployment, the engineers must have clarity on exactly which change is being applied so that they can monitor the application's stability and react with confidence. But a pipeline rapidly applying deployment after deployment to production drastically shrinks the window of time for observing the impact of each change, which has the potential to throw a team into confusion when one bad change is interleaved in a mix of good ones.

For this reason, it would be hard to recommend continuous deployment to, say, a team of 100 developers working on a monolithic application. The sheer number of changes being worked on would cause an uninterrupted stream of constant deployments, with probably a few more always waiting in the queue. No sophisticated deployment strategy could ever make that situation pleasant to work with. Production issues in that situation will be just as hard to debug as issues after very large releases.

In the case study with startup TravelPerk (see Part V), you can read about such a situation. With a large cross-team monolith being part of its collection of services, TravelPerk was facing the issue of too many deployments happening too quickly. In this case, the company opted to make its monolith an exception to continuous deployment and batch its commits to go live every 30 minutes instead.

However, there are other actions that can be taken to address this problem at the root.

Mitigation: Break your monoliths

Breaking large, monolithic applications is the most obvious approach to this problem. Smaller applications (or microservices) are favorable not just from the perspective of fewer and more independent deployments, but for many other reasons: independent scalability, fault isolation, flexibility of choice of technology, ease of debugging, and better boundaries between teams, to name just a few.

However, breaking a monolith can be a very long-term initiative, and some compromises (such as avoiding automated deployments for a time) might be necessary in the short to medium term.

Mitigation: Rethink your teams and domains

Another scenario in which too many deployments might end up in the queue is the one where the team itself is simply too big for the product it is maintaining.

What is a "good" team size for continuous deployment? This is a question that can be explored in depth by referencing books such as *Team Topologies*,[2] which talks at great length about how to ensure that the team's cognitive load remains tolerable, which also translates to cognitive load of all the changes reaching production. However, I like to refer to an even simpler rule: the Two Pizza Team rule, introduced by Jeff

---

2 Matthew Skelton and Manuel Pais, *Team Topologies: Organizing Business and Technology Teams for Fast Flow* (Portland, OR: IT Revolution Press, 2019).

Bezos in the early days of Amazon: "Every internal team should be small enough that it can be fed by two pizzas" (i.e., usually no more than 10 people).

Luckily, embracing a microservices architecture (*https://oreil.ly/TL-g9*) and healthy DDD bounded contexts[3] can not only help to keep team size and product size reasonable, but also will make individual services independently deployable and independently scalable, further reducing the impact of frequent changes. For a medium to large organization, reasonably sized services and teams are a prerequisite to perform stress-free continuous deployment.

Keeping a close eye on product domains, microservices scope, and team sizes can help technical managers prevent the number of changes going through a single pipeline (and therefore the number of deployments) from getting out of hand.

Ultimately, however, this might be seen by some as a limitation. Companies in their startup phase, for example, often start from monolithic applications as they begin their journey and don't start splitting their services until they reach a critical number of engineers.

Inattention During Deployments

The company Etsy is famous for its continuous delivery maturity. Its engineers originated the concept of the push train, and Dan McKinley wrote about it in an article (*http://pushtrain.club*) in which he also brought forward the problem of developer inattention with fully automated deployments. He explains it in this anecdote:

> A while ago Uber yolo'd a self-driving car trial in downtown San Francisco. It ended abruptly right after a video surfaced of one rolling right through a pedestrian intersection during a red light. It's important to note that there was a human sitting in the driver's seat, but that person didn't intervene. Uber blamed that person for the incident. But that's the wrong way to look at it. The automation was capable enough that the human's attention very understandably lapsed, but not capable enough to replace the human. The human and the car are, together, the system. Things you do to automate the car affect the human. Automating deploys is often just like this.

It's hard to disagree with this point: a system advertising itself as being fully automated often makes humans feel more relaxed and lets them lower their guard. But in my opinion, this is a risk that can be mitigated and shouldn't deter us from continuous deployment to production.

It is true that the more daily deployments we have, the more opportunities there are for inattention to what the automation is doing, and the more engineers might become accustomed to seeing a production deployment as a "nonevent." However, I

---

3 Eric Evans, *Domain-Driven Design: Tackling Complexity in the Heart of Software* (Boston: Addison-Wesley, 2003).

would suggest that the requirement to keep one's eyes glued to production dashboards is a little unfair to developers, and is bound to fail due to its repetitiveness.

The way we can manage this risk most effectively, in my opinion, is to build a system whose automation is straightforward, doesn't try to be overly clever and is aware of its limits, and proactively notifies its maintainers when manual intervention is required.

Mitigation: Use good alerting

Luckily, to do this we don't have to reinvent the wheel. As we discussed in Chapter 4, observability and alerting systems have reached a great deal of maturity in recent years. A set of carefully curated alerts can notify developers if their deployments have had unintended consequences, diminishing the risk that a newly introduced production defect will be left unattended for too long.

Developers will be able to check in their code with minimal supervision, due to the confidence that they will be promptly notified of any issues and can interrupt their work if necessary.

Some colleagues even mentioned that metrics shouldn't be created to be looked at, and should just be used as a necessary means to create alerts. Although that might be more of an inspirational statement, I believe it is definitely thinking in the right direction.

Of course, as we also discussed in Chapter 4, this presupposes that alerts are actively maintained by the team. To work as intended, the team needs to be kept up-to-date with every new feature and every change to the application architecture. Alerts must be treated as first-class citizens and be part of the definition of "done" for any task. This attention to meaningful alerts also works toward the "you build it, you run it" mindset that should be core to the engineering team.

Mitigation: Keep your pipelines fast

Keeping feedback loops short is also a great way to help ensure that developers keep their attention on the changes that they are applying to production. The time between change committed and change applied ideally shouldn't be longer than half an hour, and ideally it should be shorter than that. This ensures very fast reaction times, but it also requires constant pipeline maintenance and cleanup of slow automated tests (perhaps by pushing them down the testing pyramid).

Mitigation: Shift mindset around development

However, once again continuous deployment cannot rely solely on technical means without an underlying cultural change. Developers who wish to adopt it need to consider adopting a new rhythm to their workflow as well, which includes treating each commit to trunk for what it really is: an upcoming production change.

The first time I was on a team where we adopted continuous deployment, this took a while to get used to, but once we settled into the idea of keeping an eye on production after every commit, we had remarkably few problems that went unnoticed. And the ones that did get noticed usually turned out to be very subtle, which meant they wouldn't have been noticed after a manual deployment either.

Breadth of Knowledge Required

As the attentive reader might have noticed, the "you must be this tall" discussion in Chapter 4 is quite long. It contains a few necessary organizational changes for managers to arrange, but the reality is that the brunt of the work to responsibly perform continuous deployment falls on the shoulders of the engineers. Sometimes the breadth of knowledge necessary to perform it can feel overwhelming.

Just knowing how to create clean and performant application code is no longer enough for a team to maintain and evolve products, and it hasn't been since continuous integration and delivery were popularized. Engineers in a typical product team must now also be familiar with pipeline tools, different types of testing, observability, automation and scripting tools, operating systems, networking, cloud providers, infrastructure, security, and so on. Continuous deployment makes the learning curve even steeper in a way because it pushes all of these production-readiness concerns to the granularity of every commit, which removes the possibility for a developer to add those things in later.

Not all team members have to individually master all of these topics, of course, and in a cross-functional team it is expected that communication will flow between individuals to cover most gaps. But it is undeniable that these ever-increasing knowledge requirements can affect the team's confidence and ability to welcome new engineers.

Mitigation: Introduce comprehensive training programs

Companies that want to keep a healthy continuous delivery and continuous deployment environment and minimize culture shock for new engineers should consider complementing their hiring (or rotations) with comprehensive training programs. For example, new hires should have a chance to actively learn about the company's continuous integration/continuous delivery practices to reduce the friction when they enter existing teams and to alleviate the workload for the colleagues onboarding them.

Steep Onboarding Curve

Even beyond theoretical concepts, a continuously deploying team has to keep its knowledge fresh on several artifacts that it needs in its everyday work. Writing just one truly production-ready commit requires familiarity with the team's testing strategy (possibly across several layers of the architecture), feature toggle systems, dashboards, metrics, logging systems, code scanning tools, alerts, and so on and so on.

This might result in the onboarding of new team members taking much longer, even when those new team members are already perfectly familiar with the theory of continuous deployment.

Mitigation: Use pair programming and mob programming

Even in companies where pair programming isn't commonplace, it can still be used as an onboarding tool. Pair programming can relieve some of the pressure junior and new engineers may experience by ensuring that they are not alone when making changes. At the same time, it doesn't relegate them to reading page after page of documentation before they can finally get their hands on the codebase. Starting to write code from day one (under supervision) is often the most effective way to learn and the quickest way for new joiners to build confidence.

For this reason, I would encourage companies that want to adopt continuous deployment to give pair programming a try, even if only for onboarding activities and/or supporting junior engineers.

Scheduling Development Work

Without continuous deployment, the way developers organize their schedules can be fairly relaxed. A commit represents a simple "save point" where developers can store their progress and resume later. Developers can freely self-organize their work with the knowledge that any upcoming deployments will have a dedicated time and place and can be executed with their full attention.

However, with every change going to production, the meaning of code commits changes. They are not side-effect-free save points anymore, but active changes to the production system.

That's why, in some of my teams, we engineers had to self-manage our routine and commit etiquette a little more carefully. This could span from simply not pushing our changes right before a meeting, to avoiding situations where not enough team members were present to oversee production changes. The latter, in particular, can become tricky.

Everybody has a life outside of work. Unsurprisingly, some people might want to change their working hours, move one hour here around different commitments, or occasionally work overtime. This has become especially true with the newly found popularity of remote work. Some teams that are distributed across the globe even make it a habit for team members to work completely different hours.

However, a continuously deploying team cannot always be flexible around this. For example, an engineer working solo late at night or early in the morning can increase the risk of something going wrong with production. Also, something can go wrong because there is nobody available to review code, or a freshly applied change might have unintended consequences that the original engineer doesn't have enough context to fix by themselves. A production issue might require alerting whoever is on call, disrupting other people's personal time.

Even if an engineer working solo pauses the pipeline, they will still accumulate changes on top of changes, making deployments riskier once everyone else is back online, where nobody else has the context of what new code was introduced.

Overall, an effect of automated deployments is raising the bar for how many people are required to work on the system at any given time. The majority of the team should always be available and aware of changes to the state of the main branch, because it will correspond to the newest state of the production system minutes later.

Mitigation: Core development hours

This is why in most of the teams I have worked on, we had the informal agreement that nobody should work on code by themselves early in the morning or late in the afternoon, and we should reserve active development work for core team hours only. When working with offshore colleagues, we would also set up core hours in our time zone overlap.

Engineers who need to work outside of core hours (temporarily or permanently) might need to work on tasks other than changing production code; for example, improving the quality gates and documentation.

However, this limitation can become tedious, especially if this is not done on an exceptional basis and a few people consistently keep different working hours than anyone else. That's why teams or companies considering continuous deployment should carefully set expectations around core hours. However, imposing such limitations might spark some backlash in companies where extreme flexibility around working arrangements is an important part of the culture.

Mitigation: Perform team code reviews

Another effective way to manage this problem on an exceptional basis is to perform a code review with the team when an engineer has been working alone. Checking in changes can be deferred until the majority of the team is available, by storing them on a local copy or in a temporary branch.

Once back in normal working hours, the team can walk through the changes to regain the knowledge it has missed out on. This allows everyone to be up-to-date on the latest state of the codebase, and finally perform the deployment to production that was held back with all the necessary context.

Summary

In this chapter, you saw how, depending on context, continuous deployment requires some compromises or might not be a sensible choice. In some cases, the challenges are technical, as in the case of an application that is especially sensitive to deployments, is too monolithic in architecture, or whose production environment is outside the developers' control. In other cases, they are organizational; for example, companies that operate in heavily regulated environments, or even very modern companies that place a high value on engineers being able to work solo most of the time. Even so, there are mitigations that can be used to implement continuous deployment in some of these difficult situations. Whether these mitigations are feasible (or even advisable) in your unique context is something you will have to determine for yourself, with the help of your team and your stakeholders.

Summary

Before Development

This part of the book marks the beginning of our journey into the more practical aspects of continuous deployment and is focused on setting the team up for success before coding begins. In particular, it outlines how to slice upcoming work in a manner that facilitates immediate deployments and harnesses their full potential. It also showcases how to bring cross-functional requirements into the process to guarantee built-in production readiness.

CHAPTER 6

Slicing Upcoming Work

Part II of the book takes a closer look at how the full software life cycle is affected by continuous deployment. This chapter starts at the beginning of that life cycle, focusing on what happens prior to the coding work: the construction and maintenance of a product backlog that works with continuous deployment rather than against it.

The product backlog should be the source of truth for all of the upcoming work on a product, including its desired features, enhancements, and fixes. A well-structured backlog will not only facilitate frequent deployments and allow meaningful and early testing in production, but it will also leverage the speed and granularity of continuous deployment to support frequent experimentation.

Slicing work in a product backlog is essential when dealing with initiatives (epics) that are too long to fit into a single iteration. Subdividing epics into smaller, well-thought-out pieces allows for better visibility of progress as well as incremental delivery. In this chapter, I will discuss two different ways to slice epics, highlighting in particular the one that is more effective in combination with continuous deployment. Then, I will introduce an example feature and show how it can be split into increments that can be independently deployed and/or released. This example will be used throughout the rest of the book, so pay attention!

Let's start with the theory.

Horizontal Versus Vertical Slicing

Most valuable features often extend way beyond a simple backlog task, and instead require an entire epic full of interdependent items. The way in which these epics are sliced into increments (and the order in which those increments are addressed) have many ramifications for automated deployments to production.

In this section, I will compare the two most common ways to subdivide large programs of work: *horizontal slicing* and *vertical slicing*. Both are illustrated in Figure 6-1.

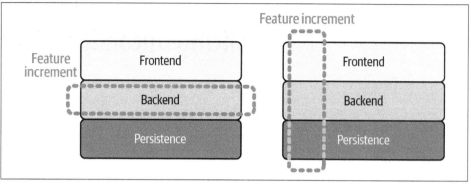

Figure 6-1. Horizontal versus vertical slicing

Horizontal Slicing

With horizontal slicing, tasks are split based on each layer of the tech stack that needs to be worked on. In a simple service, for example, these parts might comprise the backend, frontend, and database layers. This horizontal split allows developers of different specializations to work independently and only focus on one area of the architecture at a time. However, it also leads to siloed work and implementations in each layer that won't necessarily match when they are finally connected to each other. Horizontal slicing also requires that all of the functionality in every layer must be complete before the feature can be released to users.

Although most people use the term *user story* in a very lax way to refer to any backlog item, I find that talking about *tasks* is more accurate when describing the results of horizontal slicing. To explain why in a nutshell, I will quote this wise tweet from Allen Holub, which I very much agree with:

> A *user* story is the *user's* story. It describes your *user's* work, not yours (@allenholub, July 10, 2021).

A user story is meant to represent a response to a user's needs, and this cannot be represented meaningfully through technical requirements about one layer of a tech stack. Therefore, horizontal slicing is not a good methodology for generating meaningful user stories, and that is why I will refer to its output as "tasks" from now on.

Vertical Slicing

Vertical slicing aims to deliver small, visible increments that are a self-contained subset of the whole feature. Each task encompasses all the necessary architectural layers that make the increment valuable and worthwhile to build. When talking about "value" here, I'm referring to value from the user's point of view. Therefore, with this strategy, we can create actual "user stories" because they reflect the system's behavior from the user's perspective. Ideally, they do so in terms of the goal that said user is trying to accomplish.

Vertical slicing means a big program of work will be split into independent user stories that can stand on their own in production and can bring value independently. This involves more context switching for developers, as they jump from one layer of the architecture to another within each task. However, it allows them to show progress more quickly and verify that the different parts of the solution work well together from the beginning. It also makes the team more flexible in reducing scope or changing direction because the team doesn't have to wait for a feature to be 100% complete before releasing it. By releasing smaller (but still valuable) subsets of the feature first, the team can test whether users appreciate it before investing more effort into it. When product increments are granular, we gain the advantage of tailoring our platform to the precise needs of users with minimum waste instead of gambling on big programs of work with an uncertain payoff in a distant future.

Another benefit of delivering in thin, vertical slices is that the team and the business can share the same vocabulary when talking about upcoming work. The concept of "value" added by any backlog item is phrased from the user's perspective, so it means the same thing to every person in the team, and even beyond the team. This lowers cognitive load on developers (who don't have to jump back and forth from tech-speak to business-speak), improves communication flow, enables stakeholders to prioritize the backlog, and prevents the completion criteria for the work from getting lost in translation.

Vertical slicing is encouraged by most Agile frameworks,[1] especially due to Agile's emphasis on delivering value early and continuously (which makes the release delays introduced by horizontal slicing undesirable).

The most famous analogy for these two different styles is that of a layer cake, which was first introduced by Bill Wake in 2003. He writes:

> Think of a whole system as a multi-layer cake, for example, a network layer, a persistence layer, a logic layer, and a presentation layer. When we split a story, we're serving up only part of that cake. We want to give the customer the essence of the whole cake, and the best way is to slice the cake vertically through the layers. Developers often have an inclination to work on only one layer at a time (and get it "right"), but a full database layer (for example) has little value to the customer if there is no presentation layer.[2]

---

1 Scaled Agile, Inc. (*https://oreil.ly/yhwBJ*), Atlassian (*https://oreil.ly/DqNM0*), and SlideShare (*https://oreil.ly/bTrkJ*) are among those companies that encourage vertical slicing.

2 "INVEST in Good Stories, and SMART Tasks," XP123.com, August 17, 2003, *https://oreil.ly/TGNMI*.

This is the essence of vertical slicing as opposed to horizontal slicing: portioning the "feature" cake so that each slice has a meaningful representation of all layers.

With Continuous Deployment

When building a backlog for a continuously deployed product, the benefits of vertical slicing over horizontal slicing are even more pronounced. Horizontal slicing can even actively harm the system's health and the team's workflow.

Horizontal slicing with continuous deployment allows a lot of unexercised code in the deeper layers of the system to accumulate in production. It will be difficult to create higher-level automated tests for that code without an obvious entry point, especially when the part under development is far away from the user interface. The same difficulty applies to manual testing, of course. This makes it harder for developers to assess whether their changes are functioning nicely with the production environment as they accumulate more and more code. Horizontal slicing doesn't work well with the QA phase of continuous deployment at all, because it forces the team to defer exploratory testing to the very end of development, when all the layers are complete and the feature can be evaluated as a whole in production.

Many hidden code changes might have unintended consequences in the production ecosystem without anyone noticing, especially when they are interleaved with changes to existing live features or with changes to the data layer. In addition, they increase the risk of errors in the eventual release because the surface area for bugs will be much bigger on release day.

In Chapter 2, we discussed why we aim to reduce the batch size for code changes going to production, following the minimizing inventory principle of Lean manufacturing. We do that mainly to reduce deployment risk. By the same principle, we should also strive to limit the amount of code that is sitting in production but is unreleased (e.g., under a toggle): we must do that to reduce the *release* risk. Overall, when we perform continuous deployment, we deploy code with the intent that it should be used pretty soon after deployment; we're not just parking it indefinitely. That would just mean building inventory in a different place: production.

By using vertical slicing instead of horizontal slicing, we can get closer to this goal. Vertical slicing allows us to increase the granularity of our releases and bring it closer to the granularity of our deployments. This allows finer control over what is and isn't live at any given moment (e.g., with multiple feature toggles), smaller areas to debug when a go-live goes wrong, but most importantly, smaller product increments that can be measured independently.

If you are constrained to using horizontal slicing (maybe because of some organizational agreement or a peculiarity of your technology stack), I suggest you think very hard about whether continuous deployment is right for you, because you will miss out on a big part of the benefit of this style of work—and continuous deployment might even make your workflow more complex to manage.

Effective Vertical Slicing

By now, the benefits of vertical slicing should be clear, but its implementation isn't always straightforward. After all, it is not easy for a team to understand which increments can bring value to users on their own and which ones cannot. Horizontal slicing is very intuitive for developers, while vertical slicing will most definitely require assistance from product owners or other stakeholders.

Henrik Kniberg's famous illustration (*https://oreil.ly/kig2f*) on iterative value, depicted in Figure 6-2, shows how easily vertical slicing can be misunderstood and go wrong.

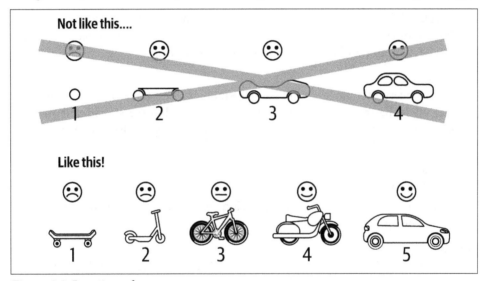

Figure 6-2. Iterative value

So let's understand the main techniques to make sure each increment we build is valuable on its own.

MVP

With vertical slicing, we have to first reduce a feature to its simplest possible form and treat every other improvement on it as an increment. Increments must then be played in a sensible order.

Figuring out this simplest possible form can be achieved by focusing on what the customer needs to achieve rather than what they ask us to implement. For example, in Figure 6-2, the customer's need is clearly to "move more quickly from A to B," so the most valuable minimum viable product (MVP) is a skateboard rather than one wheel of a hypothetical future car, which is useless on its own.

Once we have that first MVP, we can build it out in increments until we arrive at the whole feature. Of course, each increment should deliver something valuable and cohesive on its own. My personal rule of thumb when deciding whether an individual increment is cohesive enough is to ask myself the following: "If the budget for the whole initiative were pulled and I had to stop typing the second after this user story is implemented, would it bring any value to users as it is? Would I release it?" If the answer is ranging anywhere between "Meh" and "No way, I would rather revert the code," then I know I should go back to the drawing board.

INVEST

If this rule of thumb is too generic for you, you can instead use the widely known INVEST acronym as a quick reference for when a user story is well sliced. According to INVEST, a meaningful user story should be the following:

Independent
Ideally, every user story should be deliverable in complete isolation. In practice, this might be tricky for larger programs of work, but we should still strive to minimize cross-story dependencies as much as possible to disentangle the developers' day-to-day work.

Negotiable
Details in the story should be negotiable, as should the priority of the story itself. After all, the user story is an expression of value. How to achieve that value should be up to interpretation.

Valuable
As I explained earlier, the user story should bring some kind of value to users on its own. If it doesn't, or if it depends on other stories to do so, then we need to rethink it.

Estimable
If developers are exchanging puzzled looks when asked to estimate a particular user story, it means that it either is worded too vaguely, is too big, or lacks the necessary information to refine it at this point in time.

Testable
Every user story should add externally verifiable behavior to the system and express how to test it through acceptance criteria. If testing the outcome of a user story involves poking around in the innards of our system, then it is not testable.

Small Slices

Another crucial principle of effective vertical slices is that they should be as thin as possible. The duration of the implementation phase for an ideal user story is measured in hours or days, definitely not in weeks or months. As shown in Figure 6-3, we should always strive to move our stories to the left end of the "vertical slicing spectrum."

Thin vertical slicing is preferable to coarse vertical slicing for the same reason that vertical slicing is preferable to horizontal slicing in the first place: if we let a lot of code accumulate before we release, we dramatically increase release risk and we delay much-needed feedback from real users.

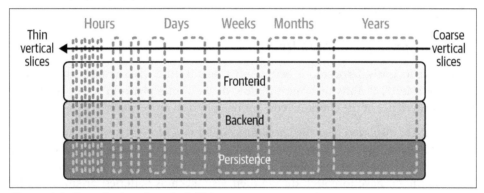

Figure 6-3. Granularity of vertical slicing

Unfortunately, in my experience, many teams nowadays still settle for slicing that is less thin than what it could be, often implementing user stories that span a whole sprint or even multiple sprints. Fortunately, and also in my experience, slicing features in a thin way while delivering value is possible, and it leads to very effective product experimentation when implemented in conjunction with continuous deployment.

As we have seen, however, effective and thin vertical slicing is more of a collection of good practices than an exact science. For that reason, it will be easier to demonstrate using an example. Keep reading to see how a real feature can be sliced into thin, independent increments that can be released independently.

Example: The Groceroo Company

In this section, we'll start to follow a fictional startup company called Groceroo. I'll be referring to this example in the rest of the book, with the goal of demonstrating how you can write code for production, test it, deploy it, and release it in an iterative manner.

Groceroo is a fictional company that provides at-home delivery services from affiliated grocery stores. Customers can access the Groceroo web application, select which store they would like to place an order from, add items to their cart, and pay for them. After the checkout process is complete, a personal shopping assistant will physically travel to the grocery store location and pick up and deliver the items at the specified time slot.

Groceroo also maintains a partner portal that store managers can access with their credentials. In this portal, store managers can import their product inventory, customize their shop logo, and update their stock information. For simplicity, let's imagine that the web application and partner portal are served by the same system. One of Groceroo's goals for the quarter is to increase its average order size, which it aims to achieve with a brand-new feature.

The Feature: "Last-Minute Items"

To achieve its goals, Groceroo is betting on a new feature: "last-minute items." With this new feature, it aims to bring the flow of its online platform closer to the in-person experience of the checkout counter in a physical grocery store.

Items that are displayed near the checkout counter at a grocery store are strategically chosen to encourage customers to make last-minute purchases while they wait in line to pay for their goods. Stores might feature seasonal items, such as sunscreen; items a customer might have forgotten during their visit, such as batteries; or small, "guilty pleasure" items such as snacks and sweet treats that are easy to buy on impulse. The checkout counter in Figure 6-4 might look familiar to most readers.

Similarly, Groceroo's product team wants to add a "last-minute items" carousel to the checkout flow. The carousel will contain products that are selected by the admin team and the stores themselves that will closely replicate the selection found at the checkout counters of their physical stores. The product hypothesis is that users will be likely to add small items they have forgotten during their visit to the website, or treat themselves to a little snack for a job well done on their digital errand.

Figure 6-4. A physical checkout counter

The User Interface

The carousel should be a scrollable selection of the store's preconfigured products, with an "Add to cart" button and a quantity selector. To maximize the visibility of popular items, the products should be "ranked" and ordered by the number of times they have been added to the carts of other users. Figure 6-5 shows a mock-up of the user interface.

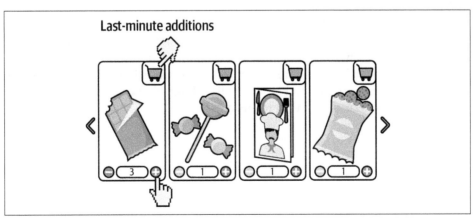

Figure 6-5. "Last-minute items" user interface design

The Admin Interface

As part of the "last-minute items" feature, a new section must be added to the shop manager portal so that each store can customize the products it wants to show just before checkout. This will be a simple form that allows for editing a list of product identifiers, as shown in Figure 6-6.

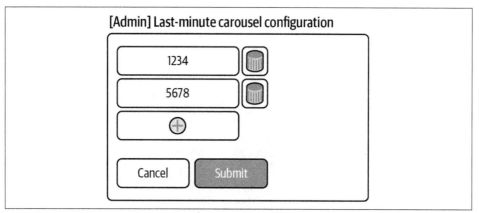

Figure 6-6. Admin interface design for the "last-minute items" feature

The Problems of Implementing with Horizontal Slicing

Let's explore what would happen if we were to slice this feature horizontally. To do this, we will consider the changes on each layer as an individual developer task.

As many teams tend to do in this situation, let's start with the database layer and work our way up.

Task 1: Persistence layer

At the database level (imagining we are in a relational world), we will need to add a new last_minute_items table to contain the data for the items to display in the carousel. Each table entry must contain a reference to the product, a reference to the store it belongs to, and a field to represent how many times it has been added to the cart through the carousel (its ranking in the list). It might also contain some validity constraints. All of these tasks are represented in Figure 6-7.

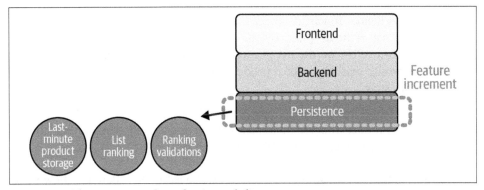

Figure 6-7. The persistence layer horizontal slice

Notice that if we were to develop these changes with continuous deployment, we would have no way to check them in production other than by connecting to the live database (which is…frowned upon, at the best of times). Even if we did verify that the change was deployed successfully, this approach only verifies an implementation detail of the overall feature (the application's internal state), which might have been shaped under misguided assumptions about the acceptance criteria or the technical implementation of the backend.

As you can imagine, at this point something subtle could have been missed; for example, a necessary index or validation might not have been added to the new tables/columns. If that happened, it might very well not be noticed until the entire feature had been completed and deployed. Fixing it that late would be much more expensive in terms of lost context.

Task 2: Backend layer

Let's move on to the backend side. To support both the user interface and the admin form, we will need to allow some basic CRUD operations on our new "last-minute items," as shown in Figure 6-8.

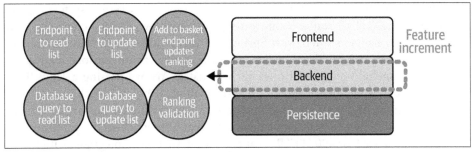

Figure 6-8. The backend layer horizontal slice

Create and modify items. In particular, we need to implement two endpoints: one GET to retrieve the list of items (used by the user's UI and to display the form), and another to perform PUT on the list (for admins only). The PUT endpoint will need validation to ensure that the selected products exist, that the list isn't empty, and that the list isn't too large.

But that is not to say that the GET endpoint won't have any logic. We probably don't want to display products that are no longer in stock or are temporarily unavailable, so some basic filtering and table joins will be required.

"Add to basket" logic. In addition, the products will need to be ordered by how many times they have been added to the cart. This means that the existing "add to cart" endpoint needs to be changed so that it can remember "from where" an item was added to the basket. This allows us to update the ranking of last-minute items independent of other unrelated "add to cart" actions.

Let's imagine the team decides to implement this with an extra payload field called `"source"`: `"last-minute-carousel"` in "add to basket" events coming from our new feature. This field will have other values, such as `product-detail-page` or `catalog-page`, for other locations that trigger an "add to basket" call. Only when the source is `last-minute-carousel` will the endpoint perform an extra database update to increment the "add to basket" counter on the `last_minute_items` table for the item being added to the cart.

This is quite a lot of work on the backend already. So how do we test these changes?

All of these endpoints will already be in production by the time we are finished, but there is no UI to call them yet. We can test them by performing the requests with Postman or curl, but once again we are limited to verifying an implementation detail of the overall feature. We are testing from an engineering perspective because we are still one layer removed from real user behavior.

It might seem common to design backend functionality in isolation, but this can lead to many oversights and therefore rework. For example, it is very easy to forget to expose the actual HTTP routes if our testing tools work by invoking controller code directly (which happens often with Spring and many other frameworks). An even easier mistake to commit is to make bad assumptions about payload or request parameters, especially nontrivial ones such as dates: Are we passing a Unix timestamp? In seconds or milliseconds? A date-formatted string? In which format? Is it time zone aware? And what about authentication headers? I can't tell you how many times we found ourselves with meticulous tests that were green in the pipeline, only to be faced with a 500 or 400 HTTP error code when we finally integrated with the UI changes.

Even if we got all of the above right, no sizable number of users are calling these endpoints yet. This means that any performance issues with our code or our database queries will also be hidden until release, which is still far away.

In addition, any misunderstood requirements within the database-level work will emerge only now that the integration with the application code has begun. If that task has been closed already, what now? Should we move it back to in-progress, or open a new one? And what about the current task? Will it remain blocked until then? As you can see, implementing a feature from one horizontal slice to the next can lead to interdependence issues. Of course, we are assuming that tasks are played sequentially here, but the same interdependency can and will happen, even while parallelizing work.

Let's look at the last slice.

Task 3: Frontend layer

On the frontend side, we have to make quite a few changes in terms of implementing the carousel and the admin interface. All of them are shown in Figure 6-9.

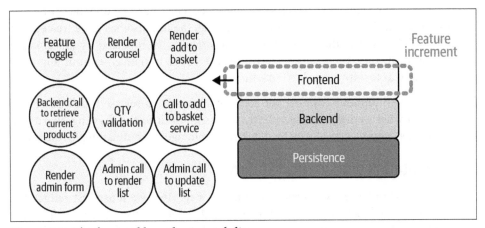

Figure 6-9. The frontend layer horizontal slice

Carousel. The carousel should make a call to the backend so that it can render the items that are relevant to the selected store, and render them as tiles. Each tile should contain a quantity selector with very basic validations, and an "Add to cart" button that makes another backend call when clicked.

Admin interface. We must also render an admin form to allow store managers to update the list from the partner portal. The form must perform a GET call to pre-populate itself with the current list, and when submitted it will trigger the authenticated PUT request to update the contents.

Feature toggle. Unless we want to release to all users right away, this is the best place to add a feature toggle. After all, we are changing the layer closest to the user. We can wrap the carousel display and the admin interface around a toggle that will be disabled for now, and will allow for manual testing in production and maybe a progressive release later.

The manual testing in production at this point can be performed from the user's perspective for the first time, with the help of the toggle. This might surface problems with the backend and database layers that weren't spotted before and are made evident by using the UI in an unforeseen way (e.g., what happens when users remove the item from their basket?). Some rework could be expected, bringing interdependency issues between layers to the forefront again. In this example, we have sliced the task in three perfect horizontal blocks and played them in order of system dependency as well. In reality, as tasks are broken down further by layer, things could become much messier. Any late requirement would wreak havoc on this workflow, as tasks across all layers would need to be reopened.

Even worse, notice how going layer by layer has pushed us to treat the feature as a monolith, and has made us code ourselves into a corner where we only have one feature toggle for it. If we are running any A/B testing, the test also has to be treated as a monolith, which means that if the feature's desirability is impacted by just a small component of it, we'll get a false negative on the entire initiative, without any clear understanding as to why users don't like it.

Working with continuous deployment actually allows us to release much more frequently than what we have just seen here, so let's go back to the drawing board and try slicing this feature vertically instead, taking advantage of granular deployments.

Implementation with Vertical Slicing

As I mentioned in "Effective Vertical Slicing" on page 163, we must first reduce the "last-minute items" carousel to its simplest possible form if we want to build on it effectively. Anything in the feature that is not fundamental to fulfilling the user's need must be stripped down, and it can be treated as an increment later. This way, we can avoid all the pitfalls of horizontal slicing, test and release in a more granular fashion, and also pivot if it looks like our carousel should go in a different direction.

Let's see an example of how that works.

User story 1: Add a simple carousel

For our "last-minute items" carousel, the simplest valuable thing we can do is to just display a carousel with the items, but without any of the frills. For example, we can do without the "Add to cart" button, the quantity selector, the ranking logic, and even the admin form in our partner portal. Those can all be considered increments in their own right. A bare-bones interface for our MVP is shown in Figure 6-10.

For our first iteration, we can simply hardcode some initial values into our table for a store or two, perhaps with the help of the marketing department (they could get the list, say, from the particular store that requested this feature). The user must then click on the item to go to its detail page and add it to the cart from there.

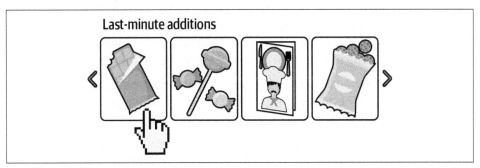

Figure 6-10. The first-iteration interface

Notice how this basic implementation already fulfills the user's main need: to be reminded of any small purchase they might have forgotten during their digital shopping trip. If the budget for the entire feature suddenly ended after only this first slice was implemented, it would still be worthwhile to have it in production; at the very least in order to get feedback from users.

We can represent this task as a proper user story by adding meaningful acceptance criteria, which can be centered on user value:

Summary

As a user

I want to see a selection of last-minute possible purchases before I complete my order

So that I can quickly add anything I might have forgotten

Acceptance criteria

Given I have items in the basket

And the current shop has last-minute purchases configured

When I go to checkout

Then I should see a carousel with some last-minute purchases for the current shop

Given I have items in the basket

And the current shop does not have any last-minute purchases configured

When I go to checkout

Then I should see the normal checkout page without any extra carousel

If we had to go live very early, we know that this basic implementation could serve as a pilot to determine whether users are interested in interacting with the carousel. If we had to stop development here because of an emergency, we could keep the feature as is: configuring items for other stores would not be very practical, but it would still be doable with the help of a developer who can manually add them to the database.

In terms of tasks, as you can see in Figure 6-11, our team would need to address all layers of the application to make it possible. However, each layer's implementation can start out as relatively simple.

We would still need a table and an endpoint to retrieve products from it, but we don't need to worry about ranking, about updating existing " add to cart" behavior, or even about endpoints for updating the items. Our frontend can also be much simpler with a feature toggle, a GET call to retrieve the products, and the rendering of a basic carousel. The initial products can be added through the same database evolution we are using to create the table.

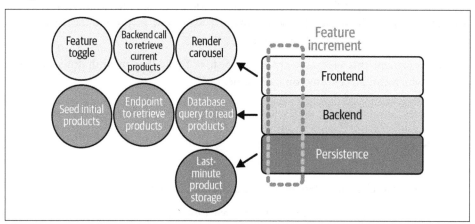

Figure 6-11. The first-iteration vertical slice

By using a feature toggle, we can already manually validate the full end-to-end behavior in production. Even better, we can already cover the feature with end-to-end tests that trigger it from the user interface, bypassing the toggle. This way, any bad assumption about the data shape or the interaction between application layers becomes apparent much earlier and can be corrected while still in development.

Although it might seem like this is slightly more work, notice that due to this iterative approach, we can already start collecting user feedback, even if we have implemented just one basic user story. If our product owner wants to run an experiment early, they can immediately enable the carousel to a small subset of users to gauge interest. Most modern feature toggle frameworks allow this. Perhaps we could even configure our toggle to only be active for one or a few pilot stores.

Experimenting early can lead to a complete pivot in how the feature will look, which can save the team time, effort, and rework. It might even turn out that users fail to respond to the feature, or that it has the unintended effect of distracting customers and reducing checkout completion, in which case we have the option of abandoning it and moving on to our next product idea.

User story 2: Make the carousel configurable

Our first iteration was helpful, but it was far from perfect. Adding more and more database changes to alter products can work as a start, but it is far from a viable long-term strategy. That is why the next slice in order of priority should be an admin interface that contains everything necessary to let partners self-manage their store's "last-minute items"; see Figure 6-12.

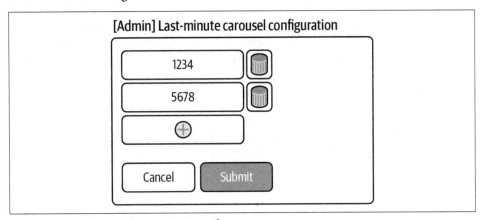

Figure 6-12. The second-iteration interface

Here is the user story:

Summary

As a store manager

I want to configure the last-minute items for my store

So that I can update them by myself, without having to wait for Groceroo's team

Acceptance criteria

Given I am logged in to the admin portal

When I view my store's dashboard

Then I should see an extra section called "last-minute items"

And it should contain a form where I can add and remove products

Given I am logged in to the admin portal

And I have added products to the last-minute items list

When I submit the last-minute items form

Then I should see those products in the checkout page for my store

Given I am logged in to the admin portal

And I have removed products from the last-minute items list

When I submit the last-minute items form

Then I should not see those products anymore in the checkout page for my store

Once again, we have to update multiple layers of the application to make this work: in this case, the backend and frontend layers, as seen in Figure 6-13. Notice how vertical slicing doesn't necessarily imply modifying *all* layers. Rather, it's a layer-agnostic approach in which we aim to make whatever changes are necessary to deliver value, regardless of where they are in the tech stack.

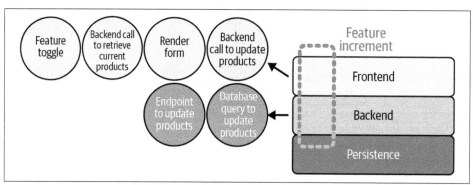

Figure 6-13. The second-iteration vertical slice

Our frontend needs to render a new tab within the partner portal, which displays a new form. The form itself can be pre-populated with the current values by performing the same GET request that serves the items to the users (i.e., the same request we implemented in the previous story). However, we will also need to implement a new PUT endpoint that will be invoked on form submission.

This interface can be displayed under the same feature toggle as the previous task, or if necessary it can also be controlled by a separate toggle. This might be required, for example, if we want to give admin access to partners early. That way, they can play around with the feature configuration for their own store before it is visible to the users at checkout.

By doing this, we can discover any problems or mistaken assumptions with the admin interface immediately. For example, it might turn out that most store managers access our application through tablets as they move around their store, instead of from a fixed workstation, and they are really inconvenienced by having to type out the items one by one on an on-screen keyboard. As a consequence, they don't use the feature as much as they could, even if it would increase orders for their store. Perhaps a lookahead search or a small catalog display would be a much easier way for them to engage with the feature.

This freedom to add separate feature flags at any point is a good example of how, with the combination of frequent deployments and small vertical slices, we can enable much more flexibility on the product side.

Of course, multiple feature flags can also be added with the horizontal slicing solution, but that is a decision that has to be made up front, usually in the design phase of all the tasks for that slice. On the other hand, with small feature increments, our stakeholders can see the feature working end to end and make these decisions in between tasks. Decisions made at the last responsible possible moment are the best-informed ones.

User story 3: One-click add to basket

For our next iteration, we can go back to the user-facing side and improve the usability of the carousel. Clicking on each item to add it to the basket from its detail page is not a great user experience, and it interrupts the user checkout flow. Our UX designer might rightfully point out that this gives users more opportunities to drop out of the checkout funnel, adding a distraction while they are just about to complete their payment.

To avoid this, the interface will start displaying a convenient "Add to basket" button, and also use its data to order the items within the list, as shown in Figure 6-14.

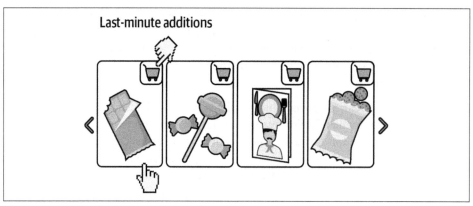

Figure 6-14. The third-iteration interface

Here is the user story for this iteration:

Summary

As a user

I want an "Add to cart" button on the last-minute items

So that I can place an order more quickly, avoiding going back and forth between checkout and article detail pages

Acceptance criteria

Given I have items in the basket

When I go to checkout

Then I should see the last-minute items have an "Add to cart" button on them

Given I am viewing the last-minute items carousel

When I click the "Add to cart" button

Then the product should be added to my cart

And I remain on the checkout page

This change requires updates to all three layers of the application; see Figure 6-15.

The frontend layer will need to render the button and call the existing "add to basket" endpoint with the new parameter source: last-minute-carousel. Other "add to basket" entry points might also need to be updated to pass a different source for the action.

The existing "add to basket" endpoint will also need to be updated to receive the new parameter. It will need to increment the ranking of items in the last-minute table only when they are added in our new flow. The GET endpoint will need to be modified as well, as the items will need to be ordered by the ranking data.

Finally, the database layer must start supporting the ranking. It needs to store the number of times a certain item has been added to the basket (in other words, its popularity), along with performing some basic data integrity validations.

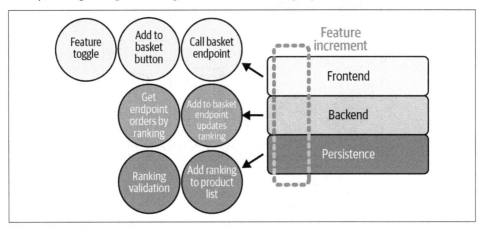

Figure 6-15. The third-iteration vertical slice

If our feature is already live, the new button can be put under another, separate feature toggle. This allows for developing the new improvement in isolation, and manually testing it in production without impacting the ongoing pilot for the rest of the feature.

Once the development is complete, we can ask stakeholders whether they want to perform a separate A/B test just for the button and/or ranking, or simply turn the toggle ON and bundle this improvement with the ongoing experiment.

Then, when we release this, we can start making performance judgments on the ranking mechanism. For example, if we were doing an A/B test between the default order of items (as input by the store managers) and the "popularity ranking" order, we might find out that the new popularity ranking we've worked so hard to implement actually performs worse. This could be due to the fact that store managers know their customer base better than our simple algorithm. For example, on specific dates, they would configure seasonal items to go first even though they haven't been bought all that often until then (think of how sunscreen suddenly becomes a popular purchase in June, even though it gets few orders throughout the winter).

User story 4: Add to basket by different quantities

Our very last addition to the feature can be the "UX sugar" of selecting the item's quantity before adding it to the basket; see Figure 6-16. This is not crucial to the user flow at all, and the same can be accomplished by incrementing the basket quantity later in the checkout process. However, this addition might still lead to a further increase in average order size.

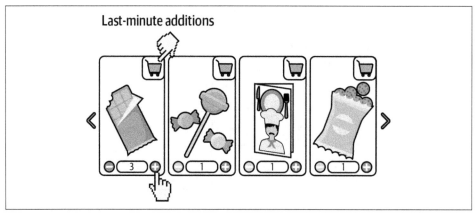

Figure 6-16. The fourth-iteration interface

Here is this iteration's user story:

Summary

As a user

I want to be able to add more than one of a last-minute item at once

So that I can place an order more quickly without clicking on the basket button multiple times

Acceptance criteria

Given I have items in the basket

When I go to checkout

Then I should see that the last-minute items have a quantity selector

And the selector allows me to modify the number in it (between 1 and 20)

Given I am viewing the last-minute items carousel

And I have not interacted with the quantity selector

When I click the "Add to cart" button

Then one unit of the product should be added to my cart

Given I am viewing the last-minute items carousel

And I have modified the quantity in the quantity selector

When I click the "Add to cart" button

Then the number of units added to cart matches the ones in the selector

And the selector resets to 1

At this point, the rest of the feature is implemented, so we only need to make minor modifications to the frontend and the backend to take the quantity into account, as shown in Figure 6-17.

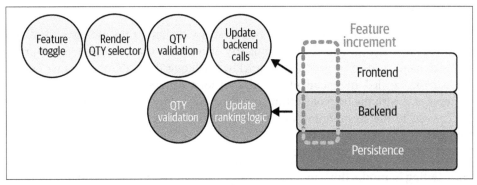

Figure 6-17. The fourth-iteration vertical slice

The biggest change will be on the frontend side, where the quantity selector will need to be rendered within each tile. The call to add to basket will also be modified to include a quantity field.

On the backend layer, the ranking logic also must be updated to consider adding more than one product to the basket (if it didn't already). This should come with sanity checks on the quantity to avoid negative numbers (or huge ones), and perhaps some validation logic around the remaining items in stock.

Once again, our stakeholders will need to decide whether this addition is safe enough to bundle with the rest of the feature or whether they would like to perform a separate experiment on it.

This user interface is more cluttered than the previous one, so there's a real chance it won't perform as well as we expect it to. If this were the case, it would be incredibly easy to remove if it was under a separate feature toggle. Changing it to OFF wouldn't even require a redeployment. This kind of change is certainly worth A/B testing, as even fractional differences in usability can lead to a big difference in orders.

The most interesting aspect of a follow-up A/B test like this would be that it doesn't just compare the performance of a "blank" status quo against the fully built feature. The benefits of having the carousel have long been proven by this point, and this A/B test can actually fine-tune different UX versions of the same strategy. This way of getting feedback is much more granular and iterative, and it lets us not only validate whether an entire program of work is worthwhile or not, but also narrowly target the best variation of said program.

This approach of building out one "valuable increment" at a time also allows the team to stop when only a portion of the work is done if the value has already been delivered, as proven by the relevant metrics. This is not possible with horizontal slicing.

Summary

As depicted in the Groceroo example, using vertical slicing for upcoming work allows us to fully leverage the speed and granularity of continuous deployment. Small product increments can go to production quickly, small questions about customer behavior can be tackled independently, and decisions can be made or reversed with extreme ease with the help of runtime feature flags. This way of working is the closest we can get to the "responding to change over following a plan" value of the Agile mindset.

Horizontal slicing, on the other hand, makes automated deployments tricky, prevents early testing in production, and fails to take advantage of rapid deployments by treating features as monoliths. It doesn't matter how frequently we can deploy code to production if what we deploy can't be released to users for weeks and weeks.

Continuous deployment is an engineering discipline first and foremost, but I hope that this chapter showed you how integrating the practice into the product development process yields real business value for the whole team. Therefore, the understanding of this practice by nontechnical functions such as product owners and business analysts is fundamental to really make the investment worthwhile. Continuous deployment is about exposing your ideas to reality as quickly as is technically possible, which is kind of a superpower when exploring something as subtle and perplexing as user behavior.

CHAPTER 7

Building for Production

In Chapter 6, we discussed the importance of preparing a backlog that makes the most of continuous deployment. In particular, you saw how narrow vertical slicing makes our changes more granular and gives us better control over incremental code updates to production.

While vertical slicing is necessary, it is not sufficient. Typically, when we talk about a vertical slice we tend to focus only on the functional changes required to implement a new feature. However, to safely deploy an increment to production you must consider a lot more than just functional changes. You also must consider the numerous cross-functional aspects of the application that are less visible.

Cross-functional requirements (CFRs)[1] are the aspects of a system that are not tied to any specific functionality but are nevertheless fundamental for the system to function correctly. Figure 7-1 shows some example CFRs and how they are transversal to different user stories.

---

1 These are sometimes called nonfunctional requirements (NFRs).

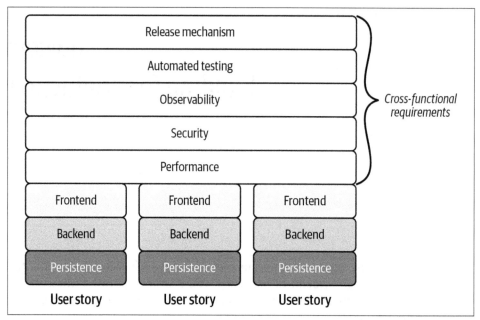

Figure 7-1. User stories and CFRs

Although CFRs are not *tied* to any given feature, they can certainly be *impacted* by any given feature. Any code change in production can affect how well a system fulfills its CFRs, so we must consider them carefully during the refinement process for new functionality. This becomes especially true in a workflow where we continuously deploy changes. Personally, I like to consider them extra layers in the "vertical slicing cake," as shown in Figure 7-2.

There is an endless list of potential CFRs, and exactly which ones are most important to your project can only be determined from your context. In this chapter, we will focus on the ones that are particularly necessary to practice safe continuous deployment: deployability, testability, observability, security, and performance. I also find that these are the ones that come up most frequently in the majority of software products.

In a pre–continuous deployment setup, it was theoretically possible (though not advisable) to delay implementing these cross-functional requirements until the end of the feature development process—as the icing on the metaphorical vertical slicing cake. Even then, however, this often led to impatient stakeholders de-prioritizing these requirements and leaving them unaddressed. In addition, adding them later was often more expensive because it required some redesign of the code.

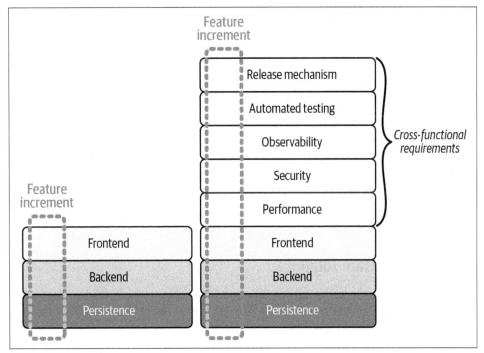

Figure 7-2. All the layers of a feature increment

With continuous deployment, this approach is no longer viable. Every increment of functionality must be production ready from the very beginning in order to go to production safely. To achieve that, the best place to start is with the refinement of the product backlog. As we prepare and refine user stories, we must give the same attention to cross-functional requirements that we give to acceptance criteria.

The main value of user stories is that they provide a structured format for communicating requirements and user needs. They are placeholders for discussions in the team. While some of the CFRs may seem highly technical, it's crucial that we leverage user stories as discussion tokens to involve stakeholders and product owners in their definition. In fact, the continuous refinement of the product backlog should already be a collaborative effort between development, QA, and product. With continuous deployment, this collaboration needs to be even closer.

In this chapter, I will give you some prompts for these discussions. I will go over the major CFRs I mentioned and provide examples of how they should be discussed before the start of the implementation phase. I hope this will lead to more comprehensive conversations within your team, and therefore more comprehensive user stories and implementation. After all, a production system is only as healthy as its product backlog.

Deployability Requirements

Perhaps unsurprisingly, given the focus of this book, the first cross-functional requirement that I will cover is deployability of the system. No matter how wonderful new code is, when working under continuous deployment, developers may struggle to integrate the code to trunk if they are unsure of the plan to roll it out. By adding deployability requirements, developers can plan their changes accordingly, starting from the very first lines of code, and always keep the system in a deployable state.

For instance, when using feature toggles or the expand and contract pattern, it's crucial to carefully plan how to bundle all code changes into a separate execution branch. This needs to be addressed in the very first commit.

Following are some strategies for how to plan for deployability depending on the task.

Hiding with Feature Toggles

Feature toggles are one of the most commonly used tools for safely deploying work in progress, but they are also a product release tool, so some extra considerations need to be considered when we use them.

New top-level toggle

A new top-level feature toggle can be introduced in the first user story that is part of a large feature. We would choose this strategy when the feature has a visible impact on the application behavior and it is independent of all other features. Our first user story should also specify on which layer of the application the toggle should be added. Toggles should ideally be placed only once: in the outermost application layer, where the behavior starts to diverge, requiring a new execution path. This helps avoid littering the rest of the code with `if` statements.

All changes under a new top-level toggle will be hidden by the toggle being OFF at first, and they can be tested in production. However, this is also a great time to discuss whether the feature can be released after the user story is completed, or whether we should wait.

Because the life cycle of a toggle can span beyond the individual user story, it should be managed and cleaned up after the feature is fully live. Therefore, if releasing is not part of the current user story, we need to create extra tasks in our backlog to remove the old toggle (or include it in the last story of the epic). Alternatively, some teams solve this problem with an extra "cleanup" column on their boards.

Because of this overhead, it is best to use toggles when we want to hide behavior from users, but not for day-to-day refactoring activities that could be managed more simply. That said, if we are rearchitecting a large part of the codebase and we are worried about things like performance, then choosing toggles as a release strategy can give us more control and safety and therefore can be justified. Another "refactoring" scenario where our teams would use toggles was when we would replace existing infrastructure components with new ones (e.g., changing from Kafka to SQS).

New nested toggle

Nested toggles are commonly used for user stories that are increments of an existing feature. Sometimes our stakeholders prefer to release the base feature and its increments separately. That is when we can add a nested toggle underneath the main one, which will only affect the current increment. If the main toggle is OFF, the whole feature will be hidden, including everything under the nested toggle (regardless of its ON/OFF status).

This adds flexibility to release all parts independently, but also some complexity: nested toggles can litter the codebase and become confusing, especially when there are multiple nesting layers. It's easy to introduce bugs in between different toggle combinations, if we are not careful. In addition, there will be a release overhead where the product function in our team will need to run multiple experiments for all the parts.

Nested toggles can be very powerful for independent microreleases, but they should be used with care. I suggest never creating more than one level of nesting, for example, and always covering all the ON/OFF combinations with thorough automated tests.

If this rule is respected, however, the life cycle of nested toggles can match the life cycle of the parent toggle. Once the feature and all the increments are live, all the toggles can be cleaned up at the same time.

Under existing toggle

Another option for increments of an existing feature is to simply add changes under an existing toggle.

This is a simple strategy, but it also tightly couples the release of the base feature with the release of this new increment: the go-live needs to wait until all the code under the main toggle is stable and proven to work in production. This might cause delays if the increment becomes more laborious than expected, and it might force the team to revert changes if a decision is made later to go live with the work that's already been done. All of these trade-offs should be discussed at refinement time.

This strategy is best used when the new increment doesn't really need to be released or A/B-tested in isolation, or if it is so small that it shouldn't have major implications for the overall feature. Because there is no new toggle, this option also doesn't require extra cleanup.

Overall, these three options for feature toggles are all viable at different times, and the choice depends on how much coupling between releases is desirable (or undesirable), as shown in Figure 7-3.

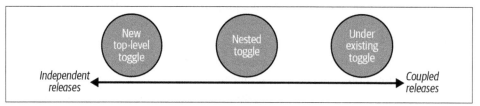

Figure 7-3. The relationship between toggle approaches and release coupling

Hiding with Expand and Contract

Expand and contract (mentioned in Chapter 3) is an excellent pattern for keeping the codebase deployable during development, and I like to use it especially for large refactoring activities. Often, these activities end up as tasks in a product backlog, so they definitely need a mention here.

When refactoring, we often don't need all of the flexibility and complexity offered by feature toggles: the behavior doesn't need to be "tested by users" again, because it is already live. That's why we can use this strategy instead for large, planned refactoring tickets, especially if they encompass multiple systems. With expand and contract, we can refactor incrementally and without forcing the developers to create a large batch of changes.

As I described in Chapter 3, this pattern consists of temporarily duplicating the functionality of a provider system that we want to refactor (instead of refactoring the functionality in place). This is so that its consumers can migrate incrementally from the old version to the new one. That duplication represents a temporary "expansion" of the provider's interface, and it can be done in different ways depending on the depth of the refactoring.

The main ways for a provider to expand its interface are to create an alternative provider system; to provide an equivalent API operation as an alternative to the deprecated one; to provide an alternative field within an API operation; or to generify a field type so that it supports multiple formats.

I will cover these main strategies in more detail in the following subsections because they should be discussed and agreed upon by the team before embarking on a long refactoring effort. I will focus on separate systems in particular, but keep in mind that all of these strategies can also be applied to code-level refactoring within the same system, if necessary: just replace "system" with "function" or "class."

Alternative system

Providing an alternative system is the broadest of the expansion strategies. It consists of essentially duplicating the whole provider: keeping the two systems up and running until all clients have migrated from the old to the new. This is the most common strategy for legacy decommissioning, where it is cheaper to rewrite a whole service from scratch than to refactor an existing one. It is also encountered when swapping competing third-party vendors or equivalent infrastructure pieces (e.g., two different types of queues).

This strategy offers the cleanest migration from old to new, as there is little chance of impacting existing behavior, because we are creating a brand-new component and not touching existing code. However, as you can imagine, it is also the one with the highest implementation cost, so it is rarely used.

The high implementation cost doesn't only come from replacing a whole system. There are also data synchronization concerns. If the current provider system stores data, it has to synchronize it with the new system behind the scenes until all clients have migrated. Alternatively, clients have to implement some temporary migration code to copy their own data across the two systems as they switch.

Alternative operation

With this strategy we are working *within* the existing provider system, where we offer a brand-new operation as an alternative to the old one. This could mean a new HTTP endpoint with a different name, a new database table, a new type of event or message in a queue, a new entity in an XML feed, and so on.

This strategy also has little chance of impacting existing behavior, because the entry point for the operation that we want to refactor is completely duplicated, so we can rewrite its implementation from scratch if we wish. However, there might still be points at which we want to reuse existing code, especially for common operations such as database access. Some implementation overlap is expected, so we should be careful not to impact the old operation as we proceed.

This strategy is very commonly used due to its simplicity, but it has a catch: it could lead to a clunky renaming process between the old and new APIs. For example, if the strategy is applied to an HTTP endpoint, that endpoint might have to be renamed more than once. Imagine, for example, a GET /product endpoint being duplicated as GET /product-new, which then has to become GET /product again. The same could happen to event names and message names. This problem can be mitigated by introducing versioning, where applicable. However, versioning in turn could encourage other bad practices, such as supporting old versions for a very long time, which can make the codebase hard to work with.

Alternative field

With an alternative field, the provider system expands its interface by either *accepting* or *producing* another field within the same operation. For example, this could mean adding a new field in a JSON response payload, a new column in a table, a new field in an event or message body, or a new attribute in an XML tag.

In the case of the provider system *accepting* a new field from the client (a write operation), we have to account for that field's absence at first because clients won't send it until the migration happens. That means either tolerating a null value or being able to calculate the value from existing data that either gets passed in or is already stored.

On the other hand, the case of the provider *producing* a new field for the client (a read operation) is more straightforward. We just need to ensure that the consumer can gracefully ignore any new, unknown field at first.

Like the alternative operation strategy, this strategy is usually simple and has a low implementation cost. It does have some important differences, though. On the positive side, it avoids the renaming issues mentioned previously, because the same API is modified in-place. However, for the same reason, it presents a higher risk of entanglement with existing code.

Generify field type

When we generify a field type, we expand the contract of a provider system to temporarily accept different types of data within the *same field* of the *same operation*. This can be done by using more generic types in the signature; for example, using a string to receive different date formats (formatted date or Unix timestamp), or using decimals to accept numbers that should be either decimals or integers (prices in dollars or in cents).

With a generified field, the provider system has to maintain its original processing while also supporting the new type of value, for both writes (e.g., accepting different types of dates in a record) and reads (e.g., being able to retrieve a record by different types of IDs). This implies implementing some temporary logic to detect which type is being passed, and performing a conversion internally. Once all clients are using the new field type, the type constraint we had temporarily relaxed can be made strict again (e.g., by using date objects instead of strings).

This strategy has a very small implementation footprint because no changes need to be made to the shape of the contract. However, it also presents a high risk of bugs (e.g., failing to detect whether data belongs to the new or old format; clients accidentally depending on the old type), and it makes code hard to understand.

Overall, this is a good example to showcase the following rule about expansion strategies: the more guarantees we want that the refactoring won't impact existing functionality, the bigger the surface area we must duplicate in our system. At the same time, the lowest effort we want to put into our change, the riskier it will become. This is represented in Figure 7-4.

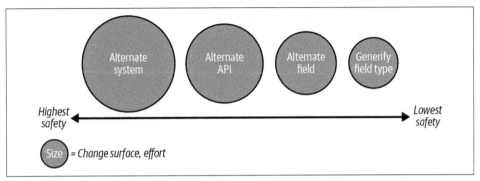

Figure 7-4. The relationship between surface area and safety of expand and contract

In my day-to-day, I have refactored contracts most often with the strategies in the middle of this spectrum: namely, alternative operation and alternative field. However, I have also found myself involved in programs of work dedicated to rewriting whole legacy systems, and therefore adopting the alternative system approach. Other times, I have relied on the simplicity of generifying a field type, knowing it was a temporary measure and the simplest way to avoid stepping on other developers' toes. Like everything else, this choice too is based on trade-offs.

Hiding in Version Control Branch

Some tasks are too pervasive to split into chunks, and they might be impossible to perform with alternative execution branches unless we want to duplicate our entire codebase. An example of this is updating foundational libraries or frameworks that are used throughout our application (I'm looking at you, new versions of frontend frameworks…).

Because we might end up changing a large proportion of our files, this is one of the few situations where we might need to rely on a longer-lived branch. After all, the changes will be testable (and deployable) only once they are complete. Sometimes the application won't even compile or build until all the affected files have been updated. This means that, because commits are likely piling up in the new branch until it's green, this strategy should be seen as a temporary suspension of continuous deployment to production.

Fortunately, this scenario occurs very rarely. However, when it does happen, I would argue that such a complex task warrants stopping all other work on the same codebase to prevent nightmarish integration issues. This should be reflected on the team board and in our expectations of velocity for the iteration.

Unhidden

Some user stories might not be worth a feature toggle at all, even if they are visible to users. This is the case with minor visual changes, for example. Bug fixes are also often released without a toggle.

This is the simplest deployment strategy, but also the riskiest. Pushing unhidden changes means that their deployment will imply their release, and if they don't work out as expected, the team will need to perform a rollback and/or a revert. This process takes much longer than turning off a runtime toggle, so we have to be sure the impact of this change is very limited to account for the worst-case scenario.

In addition, using this strategy with continuous deployment means we must make all changes in a single commit (or a single merge), which might not be ideal if the changeset has the potential to grow quite big. Such a scenario can quickly make the system *undeployable*.

Pausing the Pipeline

Some changes affect such tricky parts of the application that they cannot be thoroughly covered by automated tests or feature toggles and must be manually verified in another environment before production. Changing underlying application infrastructure is one of the main examples of this. Imagine, say, changing autoscaling parameters, database configurations, and so on.

When this happens, the only way to deploy safely might be to not deploy automatically to production, and to ensure that the pipeline stops in preproduction for manual verification instead. Like a long-lived branch, this is another instance where our continuous deployment of code is suspended, so it should be discussed with the team well before work begins.

As we discussed at the beginning of this book, we want to keep our commit to deployment ratio as close to 1:1 as possible to reduce risk. Therefore, when we resort to this release strategy we should have a clear path back to promptly unpausing the pipeline, including what constitutes a successful manual test in preproduction.

Just like changes that require longer-lived branches, however, this type of task occurs very rarely. It is surprising how often in our team we thought we were in this situation, but later found out we could break the activity down into smaller, lower-risk pieces. For example, we once had to completely change our entire persistence layer from in-memory to an external Redis instance. This change was so pervasive in our codebase that, at first, we thought we had no choice but to change all the code and infrastructure at once. That would have meant pausing the pipeline, testing extra carefully in preproduction to see if it worked, and then performing a big-bang deployment.

However, after some consideration, we noticed that we could have both in-memory storage and Redis up and running at the same time, and flip between them through the use of a feature toggle instead. This allowed us to keep doing automated deployments and build up the new code connecting to Redis little by little, under the protection of the toggle. This was especially useful not only because it spared us having to do a big-bang deployment, but also because we could test the reads and writes to Redis in production itself, turning the toggle on for one QA user only. This is a good example of why I always encourage my teams to exhaust all other lines of thinking before resorting to pausing the pipeline.

Testability Requirements

Writing and refining user stories is an excellent occasion to involve the QA function of our team early in the delivery work. This is especially true with continuous deployment because there is little to no window for extra test automation to be added after development.

As I explained in Chapter 4, cross-functional teams are an organizational prerequisite to continuous deployment. That means that the QA function should be fully embedded in the team, as opposed to all QA engineers in the company being bundled in a squad of external gatekeepers. Even then, your team might not yet be fully cross-functional, even if the team includes QAs but they act as a "subteam" that only worries about curating end-to-end tests. These two setups don't work with continuous deployment, because test coverage has to be introduced atomically with functionality instead of "after the fact."

In a fully cross-functional team, QA roles can work alongside developers and product owners. They help advise on how testing a new task will fit into the existing quality strategy, help developers create and maintain existing tests, and provide helpful insights into what types of higher-level automation should be involved in the refinement process.

High-Level Automated Tests

The most obvious example of an area where QAs have a lot of input is in automated, higher-level tests for the feature: namely, acceptance tests, component tests, contract tests, end-to-end tests, or however many layers the team maintains above the usual unit tests.

QAs can point out any layer that will be especially good for the upcoming task, or even whether the user story requires introducing a brand-new one.

They can also help highlight whether any part of the testing infrastructure needs updating with the new story. For example, we might need to introduce a new stub for our component tests whenever we add calls to new external systems. Or we might need to seed some new test data if we are introducing a brand-new feature.

All of these are notes that can be included in the user story, and they can help the developers write the right kinds of tests to guide their implementation, especially if they work in an outside-in test-driven development fashion. Of course, QAs should bring guidance and support, rather than writing predefined tests all by themselves.

Manual Exploratory Testing

Finally, features will end up being tested by humans one way or another, either locally or in production—or, hopefully, both. Therefore, it can be helpful to note how to trigger the desired behavior, any needed setup (e.g., can we create test data?), and what the observable effects on the system should be.

Any exploratory testing should follow the acceptance criteria of the story really closely, and reflecting on how to execute it at this stage can also validate whether we have split the user stories in a meaningful way. For example, being unable to verify the behavior by manually testing in production could highlight that the current user story doesn't deliver any value on its own.

Observability Requirements

As discussed in Chapter 4, observability and alerts should be considered first-class citizens and be kept up-to-date as the codebase evolves. Including their maintenance in user stories is a great way to ensure that they don't fall behind the application code.

Maintaining Logs and Metrics

The first question we need to answer is whether new functionality requires new logging and metrics, or whether it changes the meaning of existing ones. Existing logs and metrics (e.g., counters and timers) might even become obsolete as a result of our changes.

By adding these details to user stories, we can reflect, for example, on whether certain edge cases are best represented by WARNs or ERRORs. This leads to more meaningful discussion around the meaning of those edge cases, which improves the quality of the user story overall.

Another positive effect of establishing this up front is that the developers can write their functions and classes with observability as a first-class concern, and they won't need to shoehorn logs and metrics in later. This helps keep a good division of responsibilities throughout the code and avoids awkward or poorly tested logging or metrics added at the last second.

Finally, adding logs and metrics to each user story means we have many more tools to observe the functionality's behavior when we are testing it in production, whether by hand or through a canary release.

Maintaining Dashboards and Alerts

Wherever logs and metrics go, dashboards and alerts closely follow. It is easy to forget about them: they are farther away from the application code and are not embedded within it. Making a habit of including their maintenance in the definition of "done" for all user stories is a big driver in keeping them up-to-date.

Depending on the user story, the feature might require only minor updates to dashboards and alerts, no update at all, or a complete restructuring of how we observe the production system. Whatever the case, we must ensure that as the changes go live little by little, we have the means to watch the effects of our deployments to production. In fact, part of the testing in production should include looking at dashboards. This ensures not only that the feature works from the user's perspective, but also that it leaves the correct logs and metrics when it is triggered so that we can be notified if (when) it breaks later on.

Security Requirements

Securing code only after deploying it to production is the equivalent of going back to lock your house after you have been away for hours already. It is better than not locking it at all, but it is a gamble nonetheless.

Therefore, security is another aspect that has to be shifted left during development— and even more so with automated deployments. Even with the best code scanning tools in place, thinking about the security implications during the definition of a user story can save a lot of headaches and reduce the risk of something going very wrong.

During backlog refinement, we can introduce discussions around the few "usual suspects" when it comes to security, so we can maximize our chances that every deployment will be secure from its inception and won't need rework at a later stage. I will cover some of these usual suspects in the following subsections.

New User Input

An upcoming task might foresee introducing a new channel for user input to make its way into the system, or for existing user-generated data to be displayed. Any type of user input can be a new vector for attacks if not sanitized properly, so the team should discuss what type of sanitization is necessary and where in the application it should happen. As a simple example, a user story to provide a new form requires at least a mention of injection attacks.

Storing New Data

When dealing with user-generated data, accepting it and displaying it are not the only issues we need to worry about. Data is vulnerable in our storage system too, both at rest and in transit. When our upcoming work requires storing new user-generated data that wasn't in the system before, we must ask at least a few important questions about it.

First of all, is this data more or less sensitive than whatever was in our storage prior to today? If we are suddenly storing personally identifiable information (PII) and we were not doing that before, for example, we might want to reconsider our storage implementation. Introducing sensitive data might require us to do some prep work to better secure our storage mechanism; for instance, introducing encryption at rest and in transit.

In the case of PII, there are considerations, such as ensuring that some data (e.g., email addresses, names, surnames) doesn't accidentally get logged. We must also ensure that we are compliant with regulations such as CCPA and GDPR, which demand that data can be easily found and deleted upon user request.

Yet another factor to consider is availability: will our system be the source of truth of this data in the company, or do we just aim to provide a different view of data that is primarily managed somewhere else? In a microservices architecture, some data duplication is expected and even encouraged. If our system is supposed to be the primary source of truth for the new data we are storing, then the team might want to consider whether it has taken the necessary precautions to ensure its availability—for example, through redundancy in the storage mechanism and regular backups.

In some cases, these problems present even when the storage mechanism already exists. Think, for example, of onboarding customers from a new country onto an existing feature. Different countries have different laws and regulations in regard to securing customer data, and we might need to modify how (or where) we store it if we want to release a feature to a new market, even if functionality-wise it can be rolled out as is.

New Dependencies

Another way incoming user stories might affect the security landscape is by bringing in new frameworks or libraries. Any code developed by third parties can be the object of newly found exploits at any given time. The team should take the time to discuss any new dependencies and ensure that they are trustworthy before it brings them in. I cannot count the number of times when we seemed to find a promising library that did exactly what we wanted, and only later, after a closer look, it turned out that said library hadn't been patched in the past decade. Considering that we were building systems for enterprise clients with millions of transactions per day, including such a dependency would have been far from ideal. Taking the time to explore this aspect before getting started on our user stories saved us from embarrassingly introducing someone's abandoned pet project as a production code dependency.

Even when libraries are well-maintained and have an active community behind them, they can still bring a huge network of transitive dependencies into our build system (I'm looking at you, npm ecosystem). Any new transitive dependency can also be a source of new vulnerabilities, and it's easy for things to get out of hand when we try to patch and override their versions. All of this introduces a lot of overhead for teams, which have to play catch-up and mix and match versions of different libraries. In our case, the long-term cost of keeping dependencies up-to-date was often much bigger than if we had just implemented the code ourselves.

New Infrastructure

Occasionally, a new user story might require deploying new infrastructure into our cloud provider of choice. I still remember an acquaintance of mine setting up a new EC2 instance for a quick spike and leaving the access for it a bit too open. Within minutes, a crawler found it and turned it into a Bitcoin miner.

It's all too easy to misconfigure infrastructure and storage while playing around with cloud services, exposing valuable company assets in the process. Some up-front research on permissions is always warranted when provisioning anything new, and it can save us from having embarrassing conversations like the one my friend had to have with the InfoSec department.

Performance Requirements

Performance is tricky. Not only is a performant system difficult to implement in the first place, but most performance issues only show up under production conditions, which also makes them difficult to test for (and replicate).

However, just like with security, I believe we can at least round up a list of usual suspects and make a note when they are involved in our upcoming work. That way, we can get ahead of the most obvious issues and minimize time spent rearchitecting.

New Network Requests

One of the usual suspects for affecting performance is when our task requires adding extra outbound network requests. Obviously, a synchronous network request will hold up our application and increase response times. The team should be proficient with the parallelization constructs of its language of choice to ensure that any work that can happen in parallel *does* happen in parallel and that request threads don't wait longer than they have to. Sometimes this requires a restructuring of the application code.

But parallelizing requests is just the tip of the iceberg. We might need to consider resource limitations such as thread-pool sizes and the maximum number of open files or network sockets. Network-intensive applications can become very unstable, as their resource utilization depends more and more on the response times of applications' downstream systems. It is important to know what kinds of response times to expect from the new system we are calling, especially if ours is receiving a lot of traffic in the first place. We might want to protect our system with a cache, or switch to a protocol other than HTTP if its performance is unacceptable.

At the same time, we must also consider different failure modes: what happens if this new downstream system is experiencing downtime or becomes very slow? We might want to protect ourselves by setting aggressive timeouts and doing good error handling, and we must also consider how to protect downstream systems from being overloaded with traffic as they try to get up again. This area is where resilience patterns such as circuit breakers and bulkheads should be considered.

Caches are another pattern we often used to mitigate the stress of outgoing network calls. However, they come with their own considerations. When implementing a new feature, there might be implications on the caches themselves. For example, the feature could change the ratio of hits and misses, or it could require invalidating the cache more frequently. This also needs to be considered while planning new work.

Data Size

Another source of pain when dealing with network calls is the amount of data that needs to be transported in the first place. When response size gets out of control, even the most performant applications will hit a bottleneck.

For example, when encountering a new user story it is important to determine whether it will entail transmitting large collections of resources over the network. This can inform us on which limits we need to implement and which pattern, such as pagination or lazy loading, is best.

This might not be an obvious question at all. New data in the system might start small, but then grow out of control later and need pagination. It is impossible to predict the future, and I am definitely skeptical about premature optimizations. But at the same time, I have also experienced the pain of being overly optimistic about the size of data sets and seeing users complain about long loading times years later, when the feature was much harder to change. For example, in a retail business, it is a reasonable expectation for order data to keep growing and for product categories data to stay at a reasonable size. But what about comments under a specific product? Should they be paginated because we expect our ecommerce to be wildly popular, or do we not expect our users to care about reviews all that much?

Finding these answers can be difficult, so I recommend involving product owners in this discussion. They can best understand how data is expected to grow (or stay stable) over time and help us strike a balance between under-optimizing and over-optimizing.

Persistence Layer

Another big culprit when dealing with slow applications is the persistence layer, which is a microcosm of possible performance considerations in and of itself.

A new user story might introduce a new table or collection, or include new queries or updates to an existing one. The team should have a basic understanding of how much that collection will grow, how it will be queried, and the proportion between reads and writes. In the case of changes to existing data, the same questions apply. This allows us to preemptively make simple performance optimizations such as creating indexes, or more complicated ones such as denormalizing the data. Some teams even go so far as to separate read stores from write stores up front.

Finally, some new features are so impactful that they might even impact the shape of the data store itself. For example, the team might want to introduce sharding and/or increase the number of replicas.

A (More) Complete User Story Template

As I mentioned in this chapter's introduction, user stories are to be used as placeholders for discussions in the team. That's why I usually rely on a user story template that includes not only traditional acceptance criteria, but also the key cross-functional requirements we talked about. This expands our baseline for discussion, prompting all the conversations that help us continuously deploy safely. Most user stories won't need an in-depth discussion of all CFRs, but even going through the list and explicitly acknowledging that something is not relevant can do wonders for our peace of mind.

I have been using variations of the following template in most teams I have worked on, and I can say it has helped us uncover difficult discussions early in the backlog refinement process, which in turn has allowed us to perform continuous deployments to production more confidently:

Summary

As a <user>

I want to <do thing>

So that I <achieve objective>

Acceptance Criteria

Given <precondition>

When <action>

Then <outcome>

Deployability

<feature toggle/expand and contract/other?>

Testability

<notes on automated tests>

<how can we manually test this in production?>

Observability

<notes on logs and metrics needed>

<effects on dashboards and alerts>

Security

<any new user input in or out? any new data?>

<are we introducing any new dependencies?>

Performance

<any new queries or updates? what about size for any new data?>

<any new network requests?>

By using this or a similar blueprint for our user stories, we can create a product backlog of features that not only meet the functional requirements but also are testable, efficient, and secure from their earliest deployments.

Example: Adding CFRs to Groceroo User Stories

Continuing with the example from Chapter 6, let's see how we might follow the preceding template and add CFR information to the user stories belonging to the "last-minute items" feature of the Groceroo app. If you missed the Groceroo example, have a quick look at Chapter 6, or feel free to skip this section if you are only interested in the theory.

In the following subsections, you will find considerations on deployability, testability, observability, performance, and security for all of the example user stories we created in Chapter 6. Even though they might look very simple on the surface, you will see how more and more details pop up once one gets into the weeds of testing, securing, and releasing them. By "shifting left" this entire discussion, we can ensure that developers will have all of these aspects in mind from their very first deployments to production, which will indeed happen very early.

User Story 1: Add Simple Carousel

As a reminder from Chapter 6, the first user story is a minimum viable product (MVP) of the feature. It includes just a scrollable carousel with a hardcoded selection of items for a test store (see Figure 7-5).

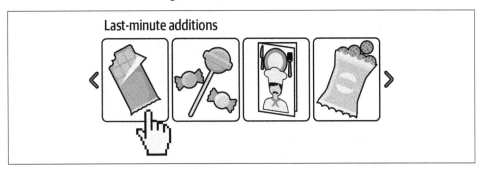

Figure 7-5. The first-iteration interface

Deployability requirements

Because this user story introduces a brand-new feature, the most appropriate deployment strategy is to introduce all changes under a new top-level feature toggle. The toggle allows us to deploy safely and test the feature in production. If necessary, the product function can also use it to run an early release and A/B test.

Testability requirements

Given that the new interface will be added within the existing checkout flow, QAs should recommend how to expand tests to cover the carousel. This should cover how to guarantee that both states with toggle OFF and toggle ON are tested. Additionally, there should be a discussion around existing visual regression tests, and perhaps screenshot tests, which should be updated to accommodate the new layout.

There will also need to be a new API test to cover the endpoint serving the carousel. We are introducing new data in the system to represent the "last-minute" items, which means that any database used by the tests, whether real or stubbed, needs to be seeded with some data so that the carousel under test isn't empty. QAs should advise on a good example data set, perhaps with some interesting edge-case values.

In terms of exploratory testing in production, some example data should be created for one shop at least; that way, any of our developers or QAs can enable the toggle for themselves and verify they can see the feature as expected. The team should make a note of cleaning up this data later.

Observability requirements

We need to introduce new metrics to go along with the new carousel; for example, the response time of the endpoint serving the items, and the endpoint's error rates (e.g., 2XX response codes, 4XX and 5XX error codes).

However, there might be a need for some discussion around what constitutes an error and what is a valid response. For example, it is pretty straightforward to flag any 5XX status and most 4XXs, but a 404 might represent a very common scenario. For example, the endpoint would return 404 when no items are found for the current shop. This conversation might even lead us to reevaluate when each status code should be returned (e.g., we might decide to return a 200 instead, even when no items are found).

These are just technical metrics, which can help us check whether the feature behaves nicely in production and keep an eye on its performance later on. However, we also need to consider adding some important business-facing ones.

On the backend, we could introduce a metric for how many items get returned on each request. This allows us to create interesting graphs showing the ratio of empty carousels displayed versus populated ones, and also to calculate what is the average size carousel the users are seeing. This can come in handy later for UX/UI considerations. On the frontend, we probably want to measure engagement through click-through rates. Most importantly, we should ensure that we can track last-minute items that end up in actual orders so that our stakeholders can indeed measure whether the average order size is affected by this feature, which was the motivation for introducing the carousel in the first place.

All of these metrics should bubble up into our dashboard tool of choice. The team needs to decide whether it wants to add new graphs and charts to an existing dashboard or create a brand-new one dedicated to this feature. It will be a trade-off between reducing noise on existing dashboards and making sure the feature's monitoring is visible to the team.

The majority of these metrics should also come with alerts. We can start with straightforward ones such as sudden spikes in errors or in latency. However, we should also consider alerting on other meaningful things, such as a high percentage of carousels returned being empty, or views and clicks dropping to zero—which can tell us something odd is going on with the feature. These last ones might be tricky. For example, they might fire immediately while the toggle is still OFF and nobody is interacting with the feature yet. The team needs to decide whether to include them early or postpone them.

Security requirements

This user story is just rendering the carousel, so no user input is required and all requests are read-only. It should be safe from most attack vectors. That said, it is likely that developers won't want to implement a traditional carousel component from scratch and use an existing library instead, to avoid reinventing the wheel.

We can highlight a few sensible choices in our user story details, or alternatively specify which criteria must be used for selection, such as open vulnerabilities, update frequency, number of maintainers, and documentation. We should also specify how this library will be updated in our delivery life cycle, and have a look at whether it brings lots of transitive dependencies (and whether those have open vulnerabilities themselves).

Performance requirements

Groceroo has about 500,000 active users, 1,000 requests per minute, and 20 orders per minute. It is not a huge platform by any means, but it is big enough that any performance issues could result in significant disruption and losses.

The new last-minute carousel appears during the checkout flow, which is arguably the most critical part of the whole application. In our first user story, we need to ensure that rendering the carousel is asynchronous in respect to the rest of the page so that we won't increase the overall page load times and accidentally drive customers away from the funnel.

However, asynchronous loading can cause the layout to shift, which in turn worsens our page performance metrics (particularly Cumulative Layout Shift [CLS]). We can fix that by adding a requirement to put a placeholder on the page during loading.

As for the performance of the carousel endpoint, there are a couple of usual suspects we must discuss: the database query to fetch them and the size of the payload being returned. If the query is too slow, we can add indexes or de-normalize some of the data to reduce the number of joins. We should also set a sensible default limit to the number of items returned by the query, which can go a long way toward protecting us from misconfigurations accidentally returning hundreds of products. This limit can be inferred by the page size of the carousel on most screens, plus the estimated likelihood that customers will scroll to new pages of it.

Optionally, we could also cache the products by store to keep response times low. Since we don't expect the shop managers to change the configuration very often, cache entries for each shop could have a relatively high time to live (TTL). However, we also know that the following user stories deal with out-of-stock logic and also introduce ordering items by their popularity. This means that the cache logic might get more and more complicated, so it would be wise to postpone this decision until we have proof that a cache is necessary.

User Story 2: Admin Area

In this second user story, we are adding the ability for shop managers to edit their own list of last-minute recommended purchases (as opposed to the list being hardcoded by devs). We are creating a new tab in the admin area to perform basic CRUD operations on the list, as shown in Figure 7-6.

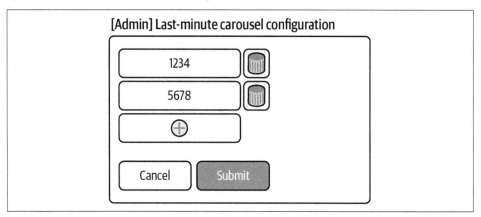

Figure 7-6. The second-iteration interface

Deployability requirements

For the admin form, we might be tempted to use the "add under existing toggle" strategy. After all, we are building an increment on an existing feature.

However, there is a catch: the group of users that should see the carousel in the shop is *not* the same group of users that want to change the shop configuration. If we put them under the same toggle, the releases will be coupled, so shop managers won't have the chance to preview and preconfigure the items before the users see them. If we discuss release strategy, and in particular this toggle coupling during refinement, our product owner might rightfully point out that letting shop managers preconfigure is a hard requirement. Because of this, we should use another top-level toggle, which can be activated just for the shop managers at the right time.

This is a good example of how thinner slicing and thinking of releases early can help us spot interdependencies and make us think of how our toggles relate to different groups of users.

Testability requirements

For shop managers, we are dealing with a brand-new user flow rather than an addition to something that already exists. Therefore, we probably need to introduce brand-new tests (journey/acceptance tests, visual regression tests), instead of plugging our changes into existing ones.

For exploratory testing, the team should discuss whether the test data it created in the previous user story is sufficient to cover the admin side as well.

Observability requirements

The new endpoints for CRUD operations will need error and latency metrics similar to the ones in the last user story. However, since it is only meant to be used by shop managers, we can be a bit more relaxed when measuring things like page performance. We also probably won't need to track engagement metrics, because the interface is only exposed to a handful of well-known users.

It can be helpful, however, to track business metrics such as the overall total of the last-minute items configured across the system, as well as the number of shops that have configured the carousel overall, which can be compared to the total number of shops in a graph. This can be used to track the interest of the shop managers in this feature. All of these values can be fetched from the database and reported periodically.

Security requirements

The admin interface is a major source of user input in this new feature. Even though it is restricted to shop managers, we shouldn't assume they are trusted users, so we should be wary of exposing new attack vectors. In this user story, we should add thorough notes about sanitizing all input against injection attacks and performing validations on the frontend, backend, and database layers.

We should also make a note to double-check the integration with the existing authentication and authorization for the admin area. As you saw in Chapter 6, the GET endpoint to retrieve the current products is public anyway and can be reused as is, but the POST endpoint to update them should be restricted to admins.

Performance requirements

With the admin interface, we don't need to be overly concerned about performance. This is for two reasons: the amount of traffic going to this part of the application is very low, and it is only used by semi-internal staff.

However, we should still keep an eye on the write performance for the last-minute items and ensure that updates don't disrupt the reads. In addition, in the last story, we introduced a limitation on the number of items retrieved by the GET endpoint. We can introduce a similar limit on the POST endpoint for creation. This will also help avoid long queries.

User Story 3: "Add to Basket" Button

For our third user story, we are adding an "Add to basket" button on the carousel items, as shown in Figure 7-7.

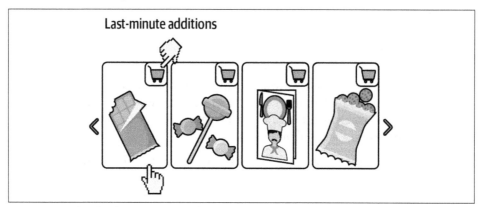

Figure 7-7. The third-iteration interface

Deployability requirements

We can choose between two release strategies: either we add the button under the feature toggle introduced in the first story or we create a nested toggle just for the button. Which one we choose will depend on a few factors. For example, we will need a nested toggle if the main carousel toggle is already supporting a live A/B test that we don't want to disturb. However, if the carousel is not live yet and our product owner isn't keen to go live before the button is there, we can just add it under the existing toggle and delay the overall release. This requires some confidence that the button is such a safe addition that it won't require a separate experiment in the future.

As you can see, a lot of these factors won't be known until it's almost time to implement the user story, or they are very likely to change at the last minute. That's why it is important to perform this type of in-depth refinement "just in time," and not over-refine the product backlog to an unnecessary depth just for the sake of filling our meetings.

Testability requirements

As all of the testing groundwork has been laid in the previous two stories, adding a button to existing testing flows should be trivial. The only aspect to discuss is possible test duplication: since the "add to basket" functionality is being reused from elsewhere in the shop, it is most likely thoroughly tested in other places. Any test covering the carousel button should be careful to not repeat existing coverage.

Observability requirements

The main metrics, dashboards, and alerts for the carousel are already in place, so we only need to add on to them by tracking the usage of the "Add to basket" button as well.

Most importantly, we need to ensure that we can track which "add to basket" events are arriving from the carousel and which ones come from other sources in the user flow. To do that, we need to figure out how the existing "add to basket" behavior is tracked before we can start on this user story, and potentially change the existing tracking to account for multiple sources.

Security requirements

The addition of the "Add to basket" button can have a much more lightweight approach in terms of security. Because it relies on existing functionality, we only need to ensure that the integration doesn't introduce new attack vectors.

Performance requirements

With the "Add to basket" button, we are introducing another source for "add to basket" events. As the endpoint for the button already exists, this user story should focus on ensuring that it can endure the additional load generated by the new carousel. We should also plan for a decrease in traffic on the item detail pages of these products, because now they can be added to the basket without opening the page.

Also, the basket data will be added to the items table and used for ordering. This implies new database queries (inserting and updating the ranking) and a modification to an existing one (retrieving items in a specific order). We should ensure that any modifications to the persistence layer take this into account and don't slow down the "add to basket" process or the read process for the items.

User Story 4: Quantity Selector

For our last user story, we are adding more capabilities to the "add to basket" functionality by introducing a quantity selector, shown in Figure 7-8.

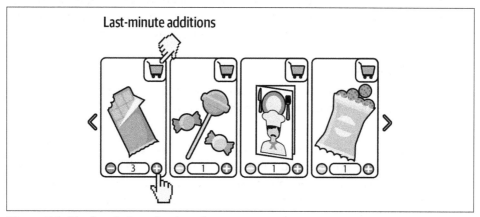

Figure 7-8. The fourth-iteration interface

Deployability

This user story deals with customizing the quantity to be added to the basket. Once again, we can choose between the "under existing toggle" and "nested toggle" strategies. Since this feature significantly clutters the user interface (and the codebase), I would personally recommend a nested toggle so that we can run a separate experiment on it and see if the users actually appreciate the new UX.

I am not a product owner or a designer, and I assume that most of you aren't either. But it is important that as engineers, we are able to also voice these kinds of product considerations so that we can explain the consequences of both release strategies (e.g., coupled releases/experiments) and allow the relevant people to make an informed decision.

For example, A/B-testing each microchange of functionality can cause the team to slow down as it struggles to support a high number of toggle combinations and execution branches. Running experiments also need to be scheduled so that they don't conflict, which delays toggle cleanup, sometimes for weeks or months.

On the other hand, product owners might not realize they have more options when it comes to A/B testing and releases, and it's on us engineers to provide context on what our release process can do. Getting granular user feedback early can help us save time if users don't like a certain addition in the first place.

Testability

While the behavior of other user stories was fairly straightforward, the quantity selector makes things a bit more complicated from a testing perspective. If you are a QA engineer reading this book, you might have already spotted a myriad of edge cases to test. For example: What happens if the user somehow submits a quantity below zero? What if they select a quantity, click "Add to basket," and then repeat the action? What should the counter display if that item is already in the basket? A conversation is certainly in order about what is the most appropriate testing layer on the pyramid to cover all of these edge cases.

These are conversations worth having early, and they might even make the acceptance criteria in the user story more comprehensive. Introducing the QA function early in refinement often improves the quality of our user stories beyond the testability aspect; for example, by helping to highlight the edge cases we just discussed, which is a skill most of our QA colleagues have been trained in, and that they can share with us during backlog grooming.

Observability

Adding the quantity selector introduces a lot of complex user behavior, so the observability impact on this story will mostly be about tracking user behavior. We will need to change how we measure engagement by taking interactions on the quantity selector into account. We also need to discuss with our product owner how to configure metrics in a way that helps us tell the difference between the overall engagement with the carousel versus with this specific feature. That is because this feature is under a separate A/B test, so we want to prove its value independently. In case the "add to basket" behavior did not support quantity before, we will probably want new metrics and graphs showing the average size, max size, and so on.

Security

When introducing the quantity selector, we are once again dealing with user input, only this time it is in a public-facing part of the application. We should again make a note to add sanitization at all layers—frontend, backend, and database—with even more attention to edge cases and improbable exploits.

Performance

Our last user story shouldn't require many extra performance considerations. After all, we have already taken care of the main pain points: writes, reads, and adding to the basket.

Summary

In this chapter, we discussed how there are many layers above the traditional "vertical slicing cake" that we must also include when preparing our product backlog for continuous deployment. These additional layers are all of the cross-functional requirements we used to relegate to the end of software delivery: security, testability, deployability, observability, and performance. With a pipeline continuously deploying changes to production from the very beginning, these aspects need to be addressed much earlier in development, even before the first commit is pushed to trunk.

I provided an extended user story template (with examples) that I have used in my teams to help us ensure that we had given enough thought to all of these requirements before starting development. I recommend using it (or a variation of it) in combination with continuous deployment to ensure that quality stays embedded in the delivery life cycle.

This might seem like a lot of work, but from my experience, most of the time these conversations are pretty short and straightforward during story refinement. When they aren't, it usually means some fundamental discussion about a critical aspect of the feature is missing, and we would have paid the price for it during development—or worse, after release.

During Development

Part III examines technical details that are critical to the success of continuous deployment, particularly how to manage daily development as a series of small, safe production increments. The chapters in this part of the book showcase the deployment of a new feature incrementally, discuss the process of refactoring complex existing functionality in stages, and address how to evolve data stores safely when deployments are automated. This will be guided by practical examples.

CHAPTER 8

Adding New Features

Now that we have discussed all of the nuances of preparing a product backlog that is suitable for continuous deployment, it is time to finally get our hands dirty with implementation. In this chapter, we will keep following the Groceroo example to learn the ins and outs of developing features with the granularity of small, continuous deployments.

My recommended workflow when picking up new user stories under continuous deployment has a 1:1 correspondence to the structure of this chapter. First, we will have a thorough look at the user story and all of its acceptance criteria, ensuring that we can point to the area where the changes should be made. Then, we will dive into the existing code surrounding that area, to form a mental image of the status quo and the existing application architecture. Finally, we will form another mental image: that of the target state of our codebase, or our intended design for the new feature. What would the codebase look like after this feature is finished and released? How is the existing architecture impacted? Are today's abstractions adequate, or do they need to be challenged?

Once we have a status quo and a target state that we can compare, that's when the interesting work happens, and we can capitalize on the techniques discussed in earlier chapters. We need to plan out small and continuous deployments of our incomplete code to get from status quo to target state smoothly, leaving production unaffected.

During implementation, we will focus on keeping the build green and the new code isolated, which is perhaps the main skill required for continuous deployment. We want to deploy to production starting from the first few lines of code, and then proceed safely, both often and in small increments. If we let a lot of undeployed code accumulate, not only will we lose most of the benefits of the practice (one-piece flow), but we will also increase the uncertainty around the work's deployability.

All of this planning might seem like extra work that is exclusive to continuous deployment. It might be tempting to think that this would be unnecessary had we used a more conservative implementation of continuous delivery. However, the orchestration needed to make production deployments safe and consistent *always* has to happen, as long as there is a production environment and we want to deploy new software on it. In our case, it is just brought to the forefront instead of being relegated to the end of development. I hope the extra payoffs will be evident by the end of this chapter.

So, let's dive right in and consider our example user story based on the fictional company Groceroo.

Our User Story

We will use the very first story from Groceroo's "last-minute items" feature as our example. As a reminder, Groceroo is a fictional company that arranges for groceries to be delivered to customers' homes. The "last-minute items" feature is about adding a carousel of last-minute recommended products to its checkout page. If you want to know more about the company or why this user story is sliced this way, I recommend you go back and have a quick look at Chapter 6. However, you should be able to follow along even with the short summary I just provided. Here are the description and acceptance criteria:

Summary

As a user

I want to see a selection of last-minute possible purchases before I complete my order

So that I can quickly add anything I might have forgotten

Acceptance criteria

Given I have items in the basket

And the current shop has last-minute purchases configured

When I navigate to the checkout page

Then I should see a carousel with some last-minute purchases for the current shop

Given I have items in the basket

And the current shop does not have any last-minute purchases configured

When I navigate to the checkout page

Then I should see the normal checkout page without any extra carousel

---

To remind ourselves of what we need to implement, Figure 8-1 shows a mockup of how the new carousel will look.

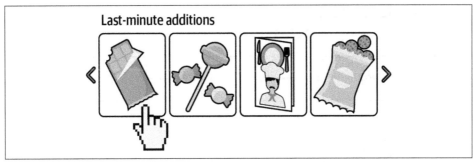

Figure 8-1. A mockup of the "last-minute items" feature

We spoke at length about cross-functional requirements (CFRs) in Chapter 7, so for the sake of brevity, we will not cover them in this chapter. The purpose of this example implementation will be to showcase how to deliver small code increments into production, so augmenting all individual deployments with concerns such as logging, monitoring, and security will be left as an exercise for the reader.

The Groceroo Application

We talked about Groceroo as a company, but we haven't said much about its actual tech stack. We will need some more insight into that before we get started with our code examples, so let's fix that now.

We will assume that the Groceroo platform is web based and has a simple layered architecture, which might look very familiar to most developers. You can find a representation of it in Figure 8-2. It has a persistence layer (a relational database, for our example), a backend that provides an API, and a single-page application (SPA) frontend. Also, we will assume the backend collaborates with third-party systems, both as a consumer and as a provider.

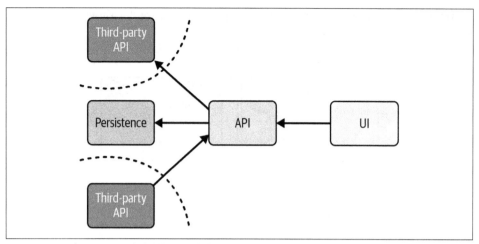

Figure 8-2. The Groceroo application's layered architecture

Once again in the interest of simplicity, we will assume the tech stack is composed of very popular choices in the industry: PostgreSQL for our relational database, Java and SpringBoot for the API, and React.js for the frontend. Most readers might be familiar with these frameworks and languages, but don't worry if you aren't. The examples should still be readable if you work in adjacent tech stacks.

The source code for the Groceroo web platform is split into two source control repositories, as shown in Figure 8-3. The first contains the backend code and the database evolutions, plus the infrastructure code to deploy them. In the second, we will find all the JavaScript code for our one-page application, and again its own infrastructure code.

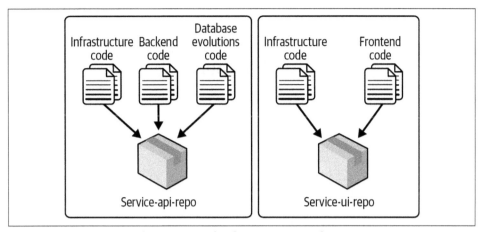

Figure 8-3. Source control repositories for the Groceroo application

Each repository has its own independent pipeline that runs all the tests and, in true continuous deployment fashion, automatically deploys to production. As explained in Chapter 7, we will also assume that this application is already live and is being enjoyed by hundreds of thousands of users whom we don't want to disturb as we make our changes.

Current State

To start development, we need to have a look at the current state: in particular, the existing checkout functionality in our frontend. Let's try to find the correct spot for our new feature in the interface, as well as in the code. What we know so far is that the new carousel will reside in the middle of the first checkout step page.

The existing checkout (in Figure 8-4) is divided into three steps: delivery, payment, and review. According to the UX designer on our team, the carousel must be added in the middle of the first step, after the order summary but before the shipping address. Due to the layout of the Groceroo checkout page, it must be positioned this way so that it is easy to compare what's already in the order with additional items that the user might have forgotten.

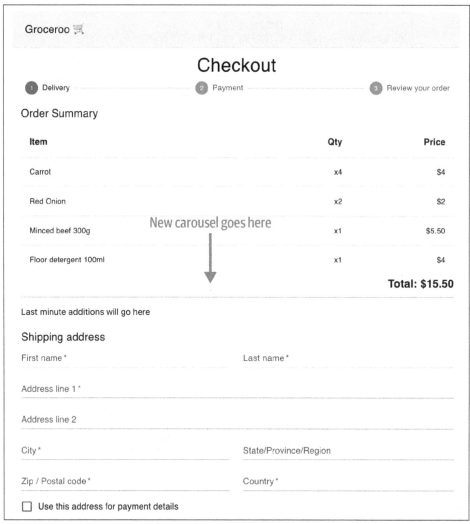

Figure 8-4. The existing checkout page

If we have a look at the following React code, we can see that this interface is provided by a CheckoutPage component ❶:

```
                                          Persistence < API < UI
export const CheckoutPage ❶ = () => {

    const cartItems = useContext(ShoppingCartContext);
    const [addressInfo, setAddressInfo] = useState({})

    return <>
        <AppHeader/>
        <PageContainer>
```

```
        <PageTitle>Checkout</PageTitle>

        <OrderSummary ❷ cartItems={cartItems}/>
        <AddressForm ❸
            addressInfo={addressInfo}
            onChange={setAddressInfo}
        />
      </PageContainer>
    </>;
  }
```

Our new carousel component should be inserted between the existing `OrderSummary` ❷ component and the `AddressForm` ❸ component.

We don't need to look at the backend codebase yet, because all of the endpoints we need to create to support the carousel will be brand new.

Now we have everything we need to get started. Let's move on to the target state to see which changes are needed to implement this feature.

Target State

In this section, we will try to imagine how the code should look when we are done and the feature is released as a stable part of the application. We can keep this new design in our head, write it on sticky notes, or even (my favorite) create throwaway code to give us a feel for the implementation. We will follow this last approach here for illustrative purposes.

This does not mean we will implement the feature exactly as shown here. After all, we have continuous deployments to consider, and that will force us to change several things along the way. I like to think of this phase as a spike, where we can quickly make a draft of our changes, without tests and even with pseudocode that won't compile. Nothing here is permanent, but it will help us plan our code rollouts to production and avoid surprises by figuring out which parts of the codebase are affected and whether existing abstractions feel right.

Frontend

On the frontend side, we will need, at the very least, a new component to represent the carousel. We can call it `LastMinuteItemsCarousel` ❶. As I mentioned, it should go between the order summary and the address form. This component will also need the information of the currently selected shop because the last-minute items might vary accordingly, so we need to retrieve that information from the broader context ❷. Here is what it could look like:

Persistence < API < **UI**

```
export const CheckoutPage = () => {
  const cartItems = useContext(ShoppingCartContext)
```

```
const currentShop = useContext(CurrentShopContext) ❷
const [addressInfo, setAddressInfo] = useState({})

return <>
    <AppHeader/>
    <PageContainer>
        <PageTitle>Checkout</PageTitle>

        <OrderSummary cartItems={cartItems}/>
        <LastMinuteItemsCarousel ❶ currentShop={currentShop} />
        <AddressForm
            addressInfo={addressInfo}
            onChange={setAddressInfo}
        />
    </PageContainer>
</>;
}
```

The implementation of the carousel should be pretty straightforward:

```
                                              Persistence < API < UI
const LastMinuteItemsCarousel = (currentShop) => {
    const [lastMinuteItems, setLastMinuteItems] =
        useState({loaded: false, response: null});

    useEffect(() => {
        fetchLastMinuteItems(currentShop.id) ❶
            .then(data => {
                setLastMinuteItems({loaded: true, response: data})

            })
    }, [currentShop])

* return lastMinuteItems.loaded ?
        <Carousel ❷
            itemComponent={CarouselItem}
            items={lastMinuteItems.response}
        /> :
        <CarouselPlaceholder /> ❸
};
```

The LastMinuteItemsCarousel component needs to fetch the existing last-minute items based on the shop data ❶, and then render them as carousel images with titles and links ❷. If fetching fails for any reason, then we can render a placeholder instead ❸. We won't go into the detail of the Carousel, CarouselItem, and CarouselPlaceholder components here, as they contain lots of UI implementation details that are not relevant to our discussion about continuous deployment. Let's assume they contain pretty much what we would expect: a generic way to display a collection of horizontally scrollable tiles, with all the necessary animations, buttons, and whatnot.

Backend

As I already hinted at, our frontend needs a GET endpoint where it can fetch the data of the last-minute items. Our backend is a SpringBoot application, so we will need a new controller for the endpoint. Our new `LastMinuteItemsController` could look like this:

Persistence < **API** < UI

```
@RestController
public class LastMinuteItemsController {
    private final LastMinuteItemsRepository repository;

    public LastMinuteItemsController(LastMinuteItemsRepository repository) {
        this.repository = repository;
    }

    @GetMapping("/shop/{id}/last-minute-items")
    @ResponseBody
    public List<Product> index(@PathVariable("id") String shopId) {
        return repository.lastMinuteItemsFor(shopId); ❶
    }
}
```

The only thing this endpoint should do is retrieve the `shopId` from the request path and forward it to a repository for fetching ❶. Keep in mind that this application's architecture is very simplified, so much so that the controller is talking directly to a repository here. Real-world applications may (and should) have more layers in between.

Next, let's see a possible implementation for the repository layer. The following code example shows how we could create a brand-new `LastMinuteItemsRepository` to go with our controller:

Persistence < **API** < UI

```
@Repository
public class LastMinuteItemsRepository {

    private final JdbcTemplate jdbcTemplate;

    @Autowired
    public LastMinuteItemsRepository(JdbcTemplate jdbcTemplate) {
        this.jdbcTemplate = jdbcTemplate;
    }
    public List<Product> lastMinuteItemsFor(String shopId) {
        String query ❶ =  "SELECT p.PRODUCT_ID, p.NAME " +
                "FROM LAST_MINUTE_ITEMS l " +
                "LEFT JOIN PRODUCTS p " +
                "ON l.PRODUCT_ID = p.PRODUCT_ID " +
                "WHERE l.SHOP_ID = ?";
        return jdbcTemplate.queryForStream(
                query ,
```

```
        new ProductMapper(),
        UUID.fromString(shopId)
    ).toList();
}

private static class ProductMapper implements RowMapper<Product> {...}
}
```

As you can see, the repository should use a brand-new table, LAST_MINUTE_ITEMS, and join it with the existing PRODUCTS table so that it can retrieve the product data to display in the carousel ❶. The query should of course be based on the shopId that was passed by the controller.

Persistence

In the persistence layer, we will need a new last_minute_items table, with some basic columns we can already guess at: at least a reference to the product ❶ and the shop ❷. The table definition could look like this:

Persistence < API < UI

```
groceroo=# \d last_minute_items;
            Table "public.last_minute_items"
   Column      | Type | Collation | Nullable | Default
---------------+------+-----------+----------+---------
 product_id ❶| uuid |           | not null |
 shop_id ❷   | uuid |           | not null |
Foreign-key constraints:
    "fk_product" FOREIGN KEY (product_id) REFERENCES products(product_id)
    "fk_shop" FOREIGN KEY (shop_id) REFERENCES shops(shop_id)
```

And it can easily be created by adding a new database evolution, like this one:

Persistence < API < UI

```
CREATE TABLE LAST_MINUTE_ITEMS (
    PRODUCT_ID UUID NOT NULL,
    SHOP_ID UUID NOT NULL,
    CONSTRAINT FK_PRODUCT
        FOREIGN KEY (PRODUCT_ID)
            REFERENCES PRODUCTS(PRODUCT_ID),
    CONSTRAINT FK_SHOP
        FOREIGN KEY (SHOP_ID)
            REFERENCES SHOPS(SHOP_ID)
);
```

How Do We Get There?

Without continuous deployment, we might simply have started adding code to any of these three components (backend, frontend, or persistence layer) in any particular order. We might have started with the one we were most comfortable with, the one that required the most changes at a glance, or the one we preferred for any other reason. But as you saw in Chapter 5, now that all code is going to production immediately, we need to pay a bit more attention. The order in which changes are made needs a certain structure because the distinction between "defining" a change to production and "applying" a change to production is gone.

If we wanted to implement the code we described in "Target State" on page 219 and avoid exposing broken functionality, we would at the very least need to start with the innermost provider system and gradually move up to the interface. This order is shown in Figure 8-5.

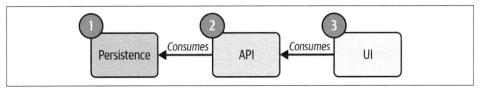

Figure 8-5. The order of implementation from providers to consumers

A developer or a pair working in this order would prevent exposing in-progress code to the users: every consumer can be released only when it can fully rely on the provider underneath it, with the UI eventually being released on top of a fully working system, ready for users to see the carousel.

This approach certainly *works*, but it has several issues. First of all, we would only know whether all of our changes work at the very end, when we deploy the UI. Also, starting deployments from the persistence layer and moving outward doesn't really give us a lot of opportunities for testing in production, which makes the likelihood of something going wrong in our final UI deployment even more likely. And finally, and maybe worst of all, this approach would couple the final UI deployment with the release of the feature, which is something we should avoid if we want to fully harness the flexibility of continuous deployment. Releases should be product concerns, and deployments should be engineering concerns.

So let's have a look at a tool we discussed in Chapter 3: feature toggles. Using a feature toggle will allow us to decouple our deployments from the release of this user story, and it will also let us apply changes to our system in any order, without worrying about provider–consumer relationships.

Feature toggles

I have mentioned feature toggles plenty of times by now, so it's time to put what you've learned into practice.

When there is no gate to production, we can use feature flags to decouple the order of changes needed to not break contracts from the order in which we want to develop. We can also use them to hide any half-baked feature from the users, even if its code is fully rolled out in production. Most importantly, they will also decouple a feature's deployments from the feature's release, maintaining the separation of concerns between engineering and product timelines.

Under continuous deployment, most new features should be under a feature toggle—unless they are small and harmless enough that the overhead of a toggle is greater than the value provided by it. Hiding new code under a toggle is a sensible practice with any implementation of continuous delivery (because it guarantees deployability of the main branch at any given time, which is one of CD's core tenets), but it becomes mandatory when there is no gate to production acting as a "last resort" to stop a change from going live.

Multiple layers: Outside in

Feature toggles allow us to adopt a more effective sequencing of changes when jumping from codebase to codebase during development. In particular, many developers prefer to approach the application from the outside in when developing something new (Figure 8-6). This is true especially if they are practicing outside-in test-driven development (TDD), which follows the path of a failing end-to-end or acceptance test (I mentioned this workflow in Chapter 4).

We are able to follow this more effective order because we don't have to worry about provider–consumer compatibility anymore. Any temporary incompatibility will be hidden away by the feature flag.

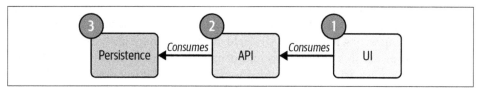

Figure 8-6. The order of implementation from consumers to providers

It is beyond the scope of this chapter to explain all of the benefits of outside-in ordering in depth, but here is a summary:

- Starting with the layers visible to the user allows for early validation of the business requirements. If it is unclear what the visible effects of the feature should be, the beginning of development will reveal this confusion immediately. Starting development becomes the latest responsible moment for challenging badly written user stories.

- The API of each layer is directly driven by its consumer (the layer above it), which makes designing the inner layers simpler and less speculative. This reduces the risk of having to rework components because we did not foresee how they would be called, or to add functionality that will end up not being used.

- An outside-in order works really well with the "mockist" or London style[1] of TDD, which is to implement one component at a time surrounded by mocks. When proceeding from the outside in, we can mock collaborators in the layers below us as we go, along with external dependencies invoked by the current application layer (e.g., backend endpoints when we are in the frontend, and database calls when we are in the backend).

- The outer layers of a system are the most visible ones to users, but they are the most visible to our tests as well. This means that by starting changes from the UI (under the toggle), we are able to perform exploratory testing in production for every single increment of code we deploy. This enables a very powerful workflow that allows developers to have a high confidence in their changes.

Due to all of these benefits, developing in an outside-in order with the support of a feature flag is my recommended approach when adding new features with continuous deployment. The flexibility and the ability to test incrementally in production are the main advantages of this way of working, which I will showcase in the implementation phase of our example. So, let's see how we can apply this workflow, bringing the system from the status quo to its target state with small and incremental deployments.

Implementing with a Feature Toggle

Let's imagine that Groceroo already has a good framework for runtime feature toggles, and their current value (ON or OFF, true or false) can be retrieved from the frontend and backend alike.

There are multiple ways in which we can hide our feature under a toggle. We can add new code under an existing toggle, add a new top-level toggle, or add a nested toggle (another toggle *under* the top-level one). As you might remember, we discussed the best release strategy for this user story in Chapter 7, and our conclusion was to add a brand-new top-level toggle. That was based on the fact that this is the first user story of the entire initiative, and there are no dependencies on other features. This toggle will be the main release mechanism for "last-minute items" going forward.

Deployment 1: Introducing the toggle

Whenever we add code that alters application behavior, the only obligatory step is to introduce the toggle at the very first commit. This already invites a question: Where should the toggle logic live? In only one layer? In all layers?

---

[1] The London style of TDD advocates starting from the outside of the application and working in toward the lower layers, relying heavily on test doubles such as mocks and stubs.

One of the tricks I learned when using feature toggles is that we should minimize the number of times they are evaluated. We don't want if statements littering our code everywhere: that's going to make removing the toggle a nightmare, and our testing brittle. To solve this, we should place only one if statement, and it should be in the outermost layer where the behavior must change. That way, we can hide all of the new code in a separate execution branch. If we manage to pick the correct place, it shouldn't be necessary to put any more if statements lower on the invocation tree, or even in downstream systems.

In the case of our user story, the placement of our toggle is pretty straightforward. The main behavioral change we need to see also happens to be in the layer closest to users: the UI layer.

We can implement the first and only evaluation of our toggle in the checkout page code, as shown here:

Persistence < API < **UI**

```
export const CheckoutPage = () => {
  const cartItems = useContext(ShoppingCartContext)
  const currentShop = useContext(CurrentShopContext)
  const featureToggles = useContext(FeatureTogglesContext) ❶
  const [addressInfo, setAddressInfo] = useState({})


  const LastMinuteItemsCarousel = () => <>last minute items will go here</>


  return <>
    <AppHeader/>
    <PageContainer>
      <PageTitle>Checkout</PageTitle>

      <OrderSummary cartItems={cartItems}/>
      {
        featureToggles.LAST_MINUTE_ITEMS ❷ &&
          <LastMinuteItemsCarousel
            currentShop={currentShop}
          />
      }
      <AddressForm
        addressInfo={addressInfo}
        onChange={setAddressInfo}
      />
    </PageContainer>
  </>;
}
```

As you can see, this *almost* looks like the code from our target state, but it has a few differences to account for the continuous deployment of code. We need to pass the toggle state, which in this example is stored in a global application context ❶, and evaluate that state at rendering time ❷. These differences are temporary, and will only last until the release is complete. After that, the extra toggle code can be cleaned up.

The introduction of this toggle is the only necessary step in our first commit. After that, we are free to deploy to production even if the `LastMinuteItemsCarousel` component is only a stub for now, or is incomplete. Under toggle, anything is fair game as long as the tests pass.

Our first push and production deployment can be as small as this handful of lines of code. We can even see our stub component in production already: all we need to do is turn the toggle ON so that only we can see it. The result could look like Figure 8-7.

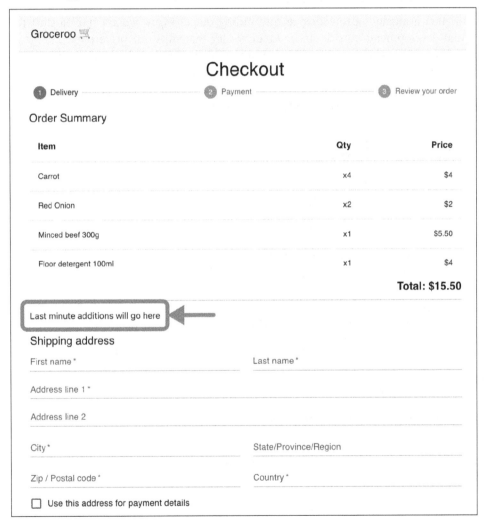

Figure 8-7. The UI with the carousel placeholder

This is an ideal time to ensure that the component is well-placed in the UI and our boilerplate code works as expected. Such a fast feedback loop is what makes it an absolute joy to develop under continuous deployment. We have added the simplest few lines of code, and we are able to manually test them in production in about 30 minutes, or however long the pipeline takes to run.

This is obviously very far from the days of waterfall, but it is an incredible step forward, even if we just consider traditional continuous delivery, where it might take days before we can see our changes in production.

Deployment 2: Adding code in the UI layer

Now that a toggle is protecting us and hiding our changes, we are free to start the actual development: outside in, or in any order that suits our preference. Let's start with completing the rest of the UI. We can implement it layer by layer, starting from the Carousel component and stubbing the layers below as we go, until we have implemented all the "leaf components" of our component subtree. Here is a first implementation of the Carousel ❶, with stubs ❷❸❹❺:

```
                                                       Persistence < API < UI
const Carousel ❺ = props => null; //some code goes here
const CarouselItem ❹ = props => null; //some code goes here

const fetchLastMinuteItems ❸ = () => {
    return Promise.resolve([]) //api call goes here
}
const CarouselPlaceholder ❷ = () => <></> //some code goes here

const LastMinuteItemsCarousel ❶ = ({currentShop}) => {
    const [lastMinuteItems, setLastMinuteItems] =
        useState({loaded: false, response: null});

    useEffect(() => {
        fetchLastMinuteItems(currentShop.id)
            .then(data => {
                setLastMinuteItems({loaded: true, response: data})

            })
    }, [currentShop])

    return lastMinuteItems.loaded ?
        <Carousel
            itemComponent={CarouselItem}
            items={lastMinuteItems.response}
        /> :
        <CarouselPlaceholder />
};
```

Keep in mind that even if the code is incomplete and full of stubs, we can still push it and deploy it to production at any time with no negative consequences. We can do so whenever we want to interrupt our work, push our in-progress code to trunk, and resume later, or even if we want to test some intermediate state of completeness of the UI directly in production. The latter is especially interesting for incremental development, so let's explore it a bit further.

As an example, for our carousel user story, we could push an in-progress version of some components so that we can verify their styles:

Persistence < API < **UI**

```
const Carousel = ({itemComponent, items}) =>
    <Box sx={{display: "flex", flexDirection: "row"}}>
        {items.map(item => itemComponent({item}))}
    </Box>

const CarouselItem = ({item}) => //stub
    <Box sx={{backgroundColor: "red", height: 100, width: 100, margin: 2}}>
        {item.name}
    </Box>;

const fetchLastMinuteItems = () => {
    //api call goes here, it is stubbed for now
    return Promise.resolve([
        {name: "test 1"},
        {name: "test 2"},
        {name: "test 3"}
    ])
}
```

Deploying this code to production allows us to see this intermediate state in the context of the real page (Figure 8-8), getting immediate feedback on whether it plays nicely when surrounded by other production components.

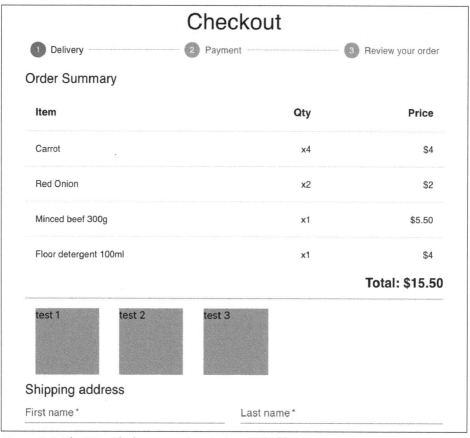

Figure 8-8. The UI with the carousel and tile placeholders

We can also get early feedback on concerns such as overall layout spacing and responsiveness by sitting together with QAs, designers, or our product owner, which allows us to stay true to the "shift-left" principle of quality and collaboration.

Pushing such small increments to production allows us to see our UI evolve in the same way that our users will eventually see it: surrounded by real components, and by all the parts of the frontend that are managed by other teams or third-party vendors (think analytics, for example). In reality, although the title of this section is "Deployment 2," we can really break these changes into as many tiny chunks as we like, and see them all deployed to production one at a time.

When we are reasonably confident that the UI looks good, we can remove any stubs for the backend that we created along the way, and deploy the final code that performs the real backend call—which of course we know will return a 404. This will most likely render an empty carousel or an error message. Even so, if we wanted to test the call itself with some stub data, we might be able to do it with any developer tool or extension that is able to intercept browser calls to the backend, such as mitm-proxy (*https://oreil.ly/Ck7vs*) or intercept (*https://oreil.ly/aOv8L*), so we can replace the response with a 200 status code and some real products.

We can now move on to the backend.

Deployment 3: Adding code in the backend layer

The code in the backend layer can be added incrementally and following the same principle: one layer at a time. Once again, we are free to deploy to production at any time while the toggle state is OFF in the frontend.

We can start with the controller, by implementing exactly the same code we imagined in our target state:

```
                                                Persistence < API < UI
@RestController
public class LastMinuteItemsController {
    private final LastMinuteItemsRepository repository;

    public LastMinuteItemsController(LastMinuteItemsRepository repository) {
        this.repository = repository;
    }

    @GetMapping("/shop/{id}/last-minute-items")
    @ResponseBody
    public List<Product> index(@PathVariable("id") String shopId) {❶
        return repository.lastMinuteItemsFor(shopId);
    }
}
```

In this case, I didn't put a toggle guard around the endpoint ❶, which means it will be visible to anyone with knowledge of the API once it is deployed to production, although it is not invoked yet.

Some people might prefer to add the toggle here too for extra security. They can wrap the outermost controller code in a toggle evaluation, which ensures that a 404 is returned until the feature is released.

This ensures that the API stays hidden, and malicious actors cannot go poking around and trigger anything that might return a 500 while it is incomplete. My personal opinion is that this slightly overcomplicates development, and instead we can use other security measures in production, such as avoiding verbose 500 error messages. That said, I recognize it is up to preference and context whether adding toggles to that list of precautions is warranted or redundant.

Regardless of whether we have a toggle around the endpoint or not, we can proceed incrementally and work our way down to the repository layer.

At the end of development, here is what the repository code should look like:

Persistence < **API** < UI

```java
@Repository
public class LastMinuteItemsRepository {

    private final JdbcTemplate jdbcTemplate;

    @Autowired
    public LastMinuteItemsRepository(JdbcTemplate jdbcTemplate) {
        this.jdbcTemplate = jdbcTemplate;
    }
    public List<Product> lastMinuteItemsFor(String shopId) {
        String query =  "SELECT p.PRODUCT_ID, p.NAME " +
                "FROM LAST_MINUTE_ITEMS l " +
                "LEFT JOIN PRODUCTS p " +
                "ON l.PRODUCT_ID = p.PRODUCT_ID " +
                "WHERE l.SHOP_ID = ?";
        return jdbcTemplate.queryForStream(
                query,
                new ProductMapper(),
                UUID.fromString(shopId)
            ).toList();
    }

    private static class ProductMapper implements RowMapper<Product> {...}
}
```

Again, the title of this section implies that this is one deployment, but in reality we can split the backend work into as many small deployments as we like; we are still protected by the feature toggle. For example, our first push could be an in-progress, stubbed version of the controller that always returns hardcoded products. This would be especially useful to verify the integration between backend and frontend in production.

Once the code in the backend is complete, we can move on to the very last layer: persistence. Our repository implementation will not work in production without a database table, after all.

Deployment 4: Adding code in the persistence layer

As our final step, let's add a database evolution with the new table to store last-minute items, which will tie the whole feature together. The code can look exactly as we imagined it in our target state:

Persistence < API < UI

```
CREATE TABLE LAST_MINUTE_ITEMS (
    PRODUCT_ID UUID NOT NULL,
    SHOP_ID UUID NOT NULL,
    CONSTRAINT FK_PRODUCT
        FOREIGN KEY (PRODUCT_ID)
            REFERENCES PRODUCTS(PRODUCT_ID),
    CONSTRAINT FK_SHOP
        FOREIGN KEY (SHOP_ID)
            REFERENCES SHOPS(SHOP_ID)
);
```

With this addition, the feature should now be working. Any high-level end-to-end test we might have added at the beginning should officially be green now. We can permanently add it to our coverage, and do some exploratory testing of the complete feature in production.

For this last step, we don't really have anything in the production database table. When I find myself in this type of situation, I usually add some test data to the production database through the evolution itself (you can also do it manually, if you feel rebellious, and open a console to the prod database directly).

With test data, we can see the complete feature end to end and without stubs, as shown in Figure 8-9.

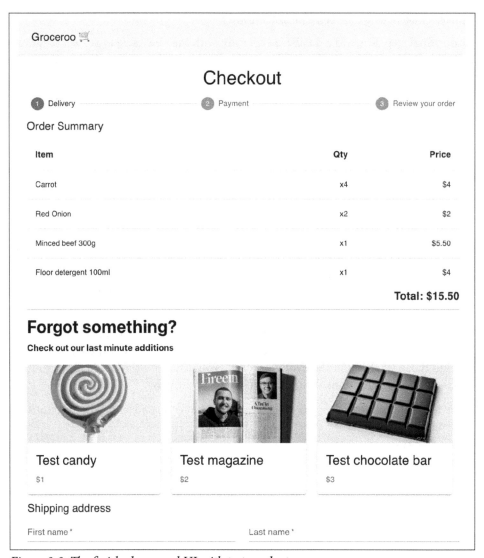

Figure 8-9. The finished carousel UI with test products

That kind of test data can be hidden through several means (e.g., enabled or disabled with another feature toggle), or simply be removed through another evolution just before the release. In Chapter 11, I will address how to perform thorough exploratory testing in production for new features, including different strategies to ensure that this kind of test data is well managed and won't impact users.

An alternative to test data is to add real, but hardcoded, data for one or two pilot stores, which will ready our MVP for release and make for more realistic testing.

Release

After thorough manual testing of the feature in production, we can perform the release. With a runtime feature toggle like ours, no new deployment is necessary. After all, no code changes are required. All we need to do is enable the toggle through the interface of our framework of choice.

This step shouldn't be frightening at all. The feature has been seen and tested in production several times by now, all throughout development. Overall, there is a *very* low likelihood for this release to go wrong.

Nevertheless, a straightforward go-live won't guarantee that users actually like our new addition to the checkout flow. That's why we can leverage our feature toggle framework to slowly ramp up the number of users seeing the feature (which can also help catch performance problems), or perform an A/B test.

Deployment 5: Toggle cleanup

On some occasions, the idea of being able to turn a feature on and off long term might seem appealing to stakeholders, tempting us to leave feature toggles indefinitely. For example, we might receive requests to enable or disable product recommendation functionality around the availability of the products themselves.

However, my recommendation is that in such a scenario, the configurability of the feature should not be left as a simple toggle. It should be implemented as first-class business logic instead, perhaps with a simple admin area where our stakeholders can fully self-manage those changes. Toggles, in my opinion, are mostly an engineering and release concern, and they are not rich enough to evolve with new requirements for the configuration of interesting applications. Making the system configurable through a toggle framework is doing a disservice to the expressive potential of its domain language, even if that framework is really powerful. By using feature flags for long-term administration, all capabilities of the system are reduced and locked into a boolean ON/OFF state, making it impossible to explore more interesting options. In addition, developers can find it hard to distinguish which toggles are meant to be long-lived and which ones are for development purposes. After all, they are expressed with the same code and with the same tool.

All of this is to say that, after the feature has been live for a while, we need to remember to remove the feature toggle. Personally, I like to wait for a week or two just in case there's any late issue with the feature (the superstitious among you might think removing a toggle too early is jinxing the release).

Since this happens later and shouldn't block the user story from being considered complete, I like to create new tasks in the backlog to take care of toggle cleanup, but others might prefer using tech debt items or even an extra column in the board.

To remove the toggle in our frontend code, we can simply remove the conditional rendering of the carousel ❶:

Persistence < API < **UI**

```
export const CheckoutPage = () => {
    const cartItems = useContext(ShoppingCartContext);
    const currentShop = useContext(CurrentShopContext) //new!
    const [currentStep, setCurrentStep] = useState(0);
    const [addressInfo, setAddressInfo] = useState({})

    return <>
        <AppHeader/>
        <PageContainer>
            <PageTitle>Checkout</PageTitle>
            <CheckoutSteps
                currentStep={currentStep}
                setCurrentStep={setCurrentStep}
            />

            <OrderSummary cartItems={cartItems}/>
            <LastMinuteItemsCarousel ❶ currentShop={currentShop} /> {/*new!*/}
            <AddressForm
                addressInfo={addressInfo}
                onChange={setAddressInfo}
            />
        </PageContainer>
    </>;
}
```

This change should be extremely simple to implement: modern IDEs make feature toggle removal even easier if you've managed to contain the toggle condition in one or two places. Delete the `if` statement, and the IDE grays out the unreachable execution paths left behind by the toggle's removal and offers you safe deletion of the now-unused code.

This means that our codebase has finally fully reached the target state we imagined at the beginning. Hooray!

Reaching this target state incrementally can also be done without continuous deployment, of course, but automated deployments ensure that we take incremental steps in the most granular way possible. None of the code we produced has stopped in any staging environment, and yet we were able to manually verify our feature throughout development—and in the most prod-like test environment of all. Furthermore, each code addition to production has never been bigger than a handful of lines at a time, greatly improving our odds of diagnosing problems quickly if something goes wrong. This would not have been practical with a manual gate to production.

Summary

In this chapter, we walked through our first real-world example of how to implement a feature incrementally under continuous deployment. Our example was simple enough: a monolithic system with three distributed components—a frontend, backend, and database layer—but the same principles can be applied with any type of distributed system.

You saw how we should look at the current state of the codebase and compare it against our desired design or target state before we start any task in a continuously deployed application. Once we know which changes we need to introduce, we can start planning a journey of incremental deployments to take us to the target state.

In particular, when adding new features in distributed systems, we should almost always leverage feature toggles to isolate our changes and work in tiny increments from the outside in. All we need to do is ensure that a toggle gets added in the outermost layer of the outermost system affected by our changes, and then we can work free of dependencies, and even test in production throughout development.

Through this example feature, you also saw how feature toggles act as a development and QA tool while we are working, but then evolve into a release and experimentation tool once the feature is complete.

In the next chapter, we will explore another type of change in which feature toggles are not as useful, and instead a different approach to planning deployments is required: refactoring live functionality.

CHAPTER 9

Refactoring Live Features

In Chapter 8, you saw how we can leverage feature toggles to deploy features to production little by little, even across different components of distributed systems. When we change features that are already live, however, we can't rely on the behavior being hidden under a toggle, yet to be seen by anyone. The stakes are much higher when the code we are working on is already being enjoyed by many users, who don't want any disruptions to their routine. That is why, when rearchitecting under continuous deployment, it is fundamental to deploy small and backward-compatible changes at all times.

Most refactoring tasks are relatively simple, usually involving only one or two codebases. I am sure that you can manage those simple backward-compatible changes on your own, without further help from this book. Therefore, in this chapter we will explore more interesting scenarios.

At least once in the life cycle of most products we are faced with changes that are so complex that they pull the metaphorical rug out from under the feet of our domain and require changing a great portion of our codebase. In such situations, it can be tempting to be afraid of continuous deployment and take the "safer" route of making a big ball of changes, parking it in preproduction for manual testing, and then deploying it all at once.

That is why I will showcase a complex refactoring example (from our Groceroo application, of course). This will allow you to see for yourself how even pervasive and "risky" changes can be deployed safely with the help of this methodology. Hopefully this will give you a comprehensive framework to approach rearchitecting and refactoring, and it will make continuous deployment a much more achievable goal for your team.

Let's dive right into the example.

Our Task

Groceroo might seem like a shiny new company, but it is in fact a bit older than people would expect. At the very beginning, it was just one local chain of grocery stores that built its own website for offering home delivery.

The home delivery model became so successful that the company split, and the portion operating the website became the Groceroo we know today. It quickly started expanding its services and onboarding many new stores as partners into its delivery network.

You might wonder: what does the company history have to do with the codebase? As is often the case with complex IT systems, which for years have been exposed to the elements of corporate politics, human inertia, and entropy, it turns out that the answer is "a lot."

The Product Identifier System

The fact that Groceroo is pretty old means that significant parts of the codebase reflect the information systems of the original store chain. One such system is the product identifier numbering system.

Before the original chain had a digital platform, products in the stores were identified with incremental numbers. Each product was represented by a six-digit number, with the first digit signifying which department it came from. For example, the fruits and vegetables section had product identifiers starting with 1, so the IDs for produce could range from 100000 to 199999. Similarly, the bathroom products section had product identifiers starting with 2, so any soap or detergent could be assigned an ID from 200000 to 299999, and so on.

This numbering system was deeply embedded into the company's IT infrastructure and, of course, the logic mapping the ID's first digit to a product category leaked everywhere into the Groceroo platform. The six-digit product number is the primary product identifier (and database pkey) to this day. When a new product gets added, its ID is generated based on this rule. As a result of this being so pervasive, hardcoded translations from first digit to product categories can be found littering the codebase.

The Problem

This might seem like little more than a curious archeological find as far as technical debt goes, but it is far from innocuous. Groceroo as a company has started growing rapidly in terms of traffic, users, and orders as well as partner stores. With each new store being onboarded, tens of thousands of new products are also being onboarded onto the system every month.

The original identifiers for each category only cover six-digit ranges; for example, from 100000 to 199999. This means only 99,999 product IDs for each category are allowed. As you might have guessed, departments are quickly running out of IDs. This system is not scalable at all, and it might be tempting to wonder what the engineers were thinking. But remember, the original system was designed with only a small chain in mind, and such a huge number of products was considered unreachable back then.

Nevertheless, as Groceroo rushes to expand, we are getting dangerously close to the ends of these number ranges. This means that once the grocery product IDs reach 199999, for example, the next grocery item added to the system will be treated as a bathroom product. Stakeholders are putting pressure on the engineering team to fix this while they regrettably tell sales and marketing to back off on forming partnerships with new stores.

It is clear that we must migrate the current product identifier and category system to a more modern, scalable one. It should also go without saying that this rearchitecting must be completely undetectable to users, so *zero* interruption of service is the standard we are aiming for.

Because of this, using a minimally disruptive hack to increase the number range is tempting, but it won't do. Stretching out the number range would only postpone the problem rather than solving it for good. Even more importantly, it would perpetuate the legacy of a counterintuitive system that increases the cognitive load on all the engineering teams. We should make the fix future-proof and bring the system closer to modern best practices rather than further away from them.

The Solution

After consulting with technical leads across the company, everyone agrees that the current numerical identifier should be replaced by two fields: a UUID for the product and a separate category field. This solution is intuitive, will scale indefinitely, and will solve the bizarre problem of restricted ID spaces at the root.

But how do we go about doing this? After all, products are the very core of the domain of our system, which means product identifiers are used in almost every single existing feature. Most people would think that rearchitecting this system would be complex even *without* throwing a practice like continuous deployment into the mix.

This is the point where some engineers might get spooked and close the gate to production, led by the instinct to do as much manual testing as possible in preproduction. However, as we discussed in Chapter 2, big changes in preproduction followed by big-bang deployments are actually riskier by virtue of their complexity.

In the rest of this example, I will illustrate how continuous deployment actually makes such a pervasive refactoring *easier*, because it keeps us locked into the good practice of making small and incremental changes. Where a gate to production might have tempted us to change most of the code all at once and then deploy and pray, continuous deployment forces us instead to rely on a framework of trivial increments. Let's see how.

Current State

As we did in the previous chapter, let's look at the current state of affairs in our codebase to get an idea of how pervasive the change is. We are looking for all occurrences of the old product IDs, and also for their translations to and from categories.

Frontend

As we discussed, all our codebases are littered with mappings from the old product ID to their category. The frontend is our first example affected by this problem, as you can see in the productCategoryFromId ❶ function:

Persistence < API < **UI**

```
const digitToCategoryMap = {
    "1": FRUIT_AND_VEGETABLES,
    "2": BATHROOM_PRODUCTS,
    "3": BAKERY,
    "4": DELI,
    "5": FISH,
    "6": MEAT,
    "7": PREPARED_FOODS,
    "8": PHARMACY,
    "9": FROZEN_FOODS,
}
export const productCategoryFromId ❶ = (productId) => {
    const firstDigit = productId.toString().charAt(0);
    return digitToCategoryMap[firstDigit];
}
```

This function is used in many places throughout the component tree, and it is invoked whenever the product category is displayed, such as in each product detail page. Figure 9-1 shows a breadcrumb containing the category being displayed at the top of the detail page.

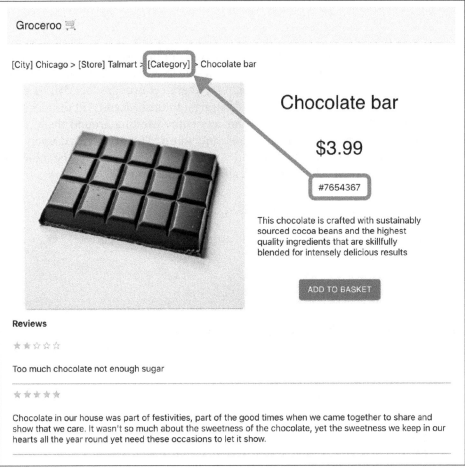

Figure 9-1. The product detail page with a category and an old product ID

As you can see in the following code, the correct category displayed in Figure 9-1 is calculated with the function that relies on the hardcoded mapping ❶:

Persistence < API < **UI**

```
export const ProductDetailPage = ({product}) => {
   const store = useContext(StoreContext)

   return <>
      <AppHeader/>
      <PageContainer>
         <Box className="breadcrumb">
      [City] {store.city} >
      [Store] {store.storeName} >
      [Category] {productCategoryFromId(product.id) ❶} >
      {product.name}
```

```
    </Box>
```

...

But the hardcoding of the category data is not even our biggest problem yet. We must replace the old product ID format with the new one in every single feature that relies on it. Unsurprisingly, the old ID is used everywhere because product data is at the very core of Groceroo's domain. It is passed straight to the backend API for most read and write operations on products, and for any entity orbiting around them: users' baskets, orders, reviews, recommendations, and so on. This ID is relied upon very heavily in contracts between the backend and frontend. For example, the following code shows the backend call made to add an item to the basket ❶:

Persistence < API < **UI**
```
const addToBasket = async (product) => {

    const response = await fetch(`${API.baseUrl}/basket/${product.id}` ❶, {
        method: "POST",
        //...
    });
    return response.json();
};
```

As another example, when fetching product details to populate the product detail page, we also do so by product ID ❶, as shown in the following code:

Persistence < API < **UI**
```
const getProduct = async (id) => {
    const response = await fetch(`${API.baseUrl}/products/${id}` ❶, {
        method: "GET"
        //...
    });
    return response.json();
}
```

However, the ID is not used only for cross-system communication. It is also displayed in many places for users themselves to reference, and these places will also need to be migrated. One such place in the UI is the product creation page for store managers, shown in Figure 9-2.

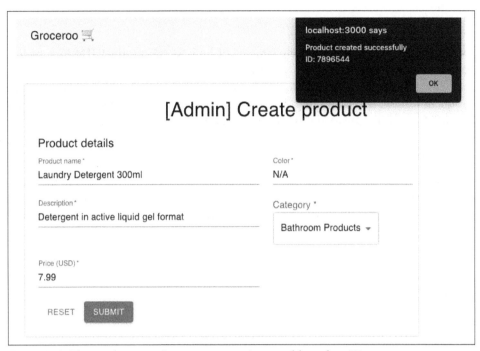

Figure 9-2. The product creation page generating an old product ID

The following example shows the relevant frontend code handling the product creation form ❶ and displaying the resulting ID ❷:

```
                                                   Persistence < API < UI
export const CreateProductPage = () => {
   const store = useContext(StoreContext)

   const createProduct = async (productData, store) => {
      const response = await fetch(`${API.baseUrl}/products`, {
         method: "POST",
         body: JSON.stringify({...productData, ...store})
         //...
      });
      alert(`Product created successfully ID: ${response}`) ❷
   };

   return <>
      <AppHeader/>
      <PageContainer>
         <PageTitle>[Admin] Create product</PageTitle>
         <CreateProductForm ❶
            onSubmit={(data) => createProduct(data, store)}
         />
      </PageContainer>;
```

```
        </>
    }
```

Of course, there are many more examples of how to use product IDs in a typical ecommerce-like application such as Groceroo. Out of simplicity, let's keep our refactoring in this chapter confined to the three I just showcased: adding to the basket, product creation, and displaying the category in product detail pages. The principles you will learn will apply to any other functionality in exactly the same way.

Backend

Similarly to the frontend, categories are not considered first-class citizens in the backend. Instead of being stored in a database table of their own, they are hardcoded in an enum, shown in the following code snippet, which is used to translate to and from the first digit of the product ID:

Persistence < **API** < UI

```
public enum Category {

FRUIT_AND_VEGETABLES("Fruit and vegetables", 1),
BATHROOM_PRODUCTS("Bathroom products", 2),
BAKERY("Bakery", 3),
DELI("Deli", 4),
FISH("Fish", 5),
MEAT("Meat", 6),
PREPARED_FOODS("Prepared foods", 7),
PHARMACY("Pharmacy", 8),
FROZEN_FOODS("Frozen food", 9);

private final String displayName;
private final Integer digit;

Category(String displayName, Integer digit) {
    this.displayName = displayName;
    this.digit = digit;
}
}
```

As you saw in "Frontend" on page 242, all API operations on products and related entities are managed by the six-digit integer ID that we need to replace. You can see the first examples of it ❶❷ in the following code, which shows the existing Product Controller:

Persistence < **API** < UI

```
@RestController
public class ProductController {

    private final ProductRepository repository;

    public ProductController(ProductRepository repository) {
        this.repository = repository;
```

```
    }

    @GetMapping("/products/{id}")
    @ResponseBody
    public Product getProduct(@PathVariable("id") Integer id) {
        return repository.getProduct(id); ❶
    }

    @PostMapping("/products")
    @ResponseBody
    public Integer createProduct(@RequestBody CreateProductPayload payload) {
        return repository.createProduct(payload).id(); ❷
    }
}
```

Even more interesting is the repository layer for products, shown in the next code example. In addition to the usual read and write operations by ID, it also offers us a glimpse of the product creation logic ❶. Whenever a new product gets onboarded by a shop manager, the ID is generated based on the selected category ❷. The repository relies on different database sequences to ensure uniqueness within each category ❸. There is one sequence starting at 100000 for fruits and vegetables, another starting at 200000 for bathroom products, and so on:

```
                                              Persistence < API < UI
@Repository
public class ProductRepository {

    private final JdbcTemplate jdbcTemplate;

    @Autowired
    public ProductRepository(JdbcTemplate jdbcTemplate) {
        this.jdbcTemplate = jdbcTemplate;
    }

    public Product createProduct ❶(CreateProductPayload createProductPayload) {
        String insert =  "INSERT INTO " +
            "PRODUCTS(PRODUCT_ID, SHOP_ID, NAME) " +
            "VALUES (?, ?, ?) " +
            "RETURNING *";

        Integer productId = productIdByCategory(
            createProductPayload.category()
        ); ❷

        return jdbcTemplate.queryForObject(
            insert,
            new ProductMapper(),
            productId,
            createProductPayload.shopId(),
            createProductPayload.name()
        );
```

```
    }

    public Product getProduct(Integer id) {
        String select =  "SELECT * FROM PRODUCTS WHERE product_id = ?";

        return jdbcTemplate.queryForObject(select, new ProductMapper(), id);
    }
    private Integer productIdByCategory(Integer category) {

        Category productCategory = Category.values()[category];

        String sequenceName = productCategory.name();

        String productIdQuery =
            String.format("SELECT nextval('%s');", sequenceName); ❸

        SqlRowSet sqlRowSet = jdbcTemplate.queryForRowSet(productIdQuery);
        sqlRowSet.next();
        return sqlRowSet.getInt(1);
    }

}
```

As I mentioned, the code relying on product IDs spans far beyond creating and managing products: any connected entities are also affected. For example, following is the BasketController class, also operating by product ID ❶:

Persistence < **API** < UI

```
@RestController
public class BasketController {

    private final BasketRepository repository;

    public BasketController(BasketRepository repository) {
        this.repository = repository;
    }

    @PostMapping("/basket/{id}")
    public void createProduct(
        @RequestBody AddToBasketPayload payload,
        @PathVariable("id") Integer productId ❶
    ) {
        repository.addToBasket(payload, productId);
    }
}
```

Here is the code for the related BasketRepository:

Persistence < **API** < UI

```
@Repository
public class BasketRepository {

    private final JdbcTemplate jdbcTemplate;
```

```
  public BasketRepository(JdbcTemplate jdbcTemplate) {
    this.jdbcTemplate = jdbcTemplate;
  }

  public void addToBasket(AddToBasketPayload payload, Integer productId) {
    String insert = "INSERT INTO BASKET AS original " +
                    "(product_id, user_id, quantity) " +
                    "VALUES (?, ?, ?) " +
                    "ON CONFLICT ON CONSTRAINT PKEY DO UPDATE " +
                    "SET quantity = " +
                    "original.quantity + excluded.quantity;";

    jdbcTemplate.update(insert, productId, payload.userId(), payload.quan
tity());
  }
}
```

Persistence

In the persistence layer, we can of course find our main product table, which has the
unwanted ID as its primary key ❶. The following example shows its structure:

Persistence < API < UI

```
groceroo=# \d products
                Table "public.products"
    Column     |  Type   | Collation | Nullable | Default
---------------+---------+-----------+----------+---------
 product_id ❶| integer |           | not null |
 shop_id       | uuid    |           | not null |
 name          | text    |           |          |
 ...
```

The ID is referenced through foreign keys ❶ by other tables, such as the basket table
shown next. In the basket table, the product ID is even part of a composite primary
key ❷—one basket entry is uniquely identified by its user ID and product ID:

Persistence < API < UI

```
groceroo=# \d basket
                Table "public.basket"
   Column     |  Type   | Collation | Nullable | Default
--------------+---------+-----------+----------+---------
 user_id      | uuid    |           | not null |
 product_id   | integer |           | not null |
 quantity     | integer |           | not null |
Indexes:
    "pkey" PRIMARY KEY, btree (user_id, product_id) ❷
Foreign-key constraints:
    "fk_product" FOREIGN KEY (product_id) REFERENCES products(product_id) ❶
    "fk_user" FOREIGN KEY (user_id) REFERENCES users(user_id)

...
```

In the following table, we can observe the sequences responsible for generating new IDs by category, which are used by the repository we saw on the backend. Notice how each of them has a different starting point:

```
+----------------+---------------------+---------+-----------+---------+
|sequence_catalog|sequence_name        |data_type|start_value|increment|
+----------------+---------------------+---------+-----------+---------+
|groceroo        |fruit_and_vegetables |bigint   |100000     |1        |
|groceroo        |bathroom_products    |bigint   |200000     |1        |
|groceroo        |bakery               |bigint   |300000     |1        |
|groceroo        |deli                 |bigint   |400000     |1        |
|groceroo        |prepared_foods       |bigint   |500000     |1        |
|groceroo        |meat                 |bigint   |600000     |1        |
|groceroo        |fish                 |bigint   |700000     |1        |
|groceroo        |pharmacy             |bigint   |800000     |1        |
|groceroo        |frozen_foods         |bigint   |900000     |1        |
+----------------+---------------------+---------+-----------+---------+
```

These sequences, along with the old ID column, should become obsolete after our replacement.

Target State

If we had to imagine an ideal target state for the codebase after this refactoring, the legacy product IDs would disappear in favor of a new UUID field. Moreover, category data should be a first-class citizen, stored in a database table with a proper relationship to the product table. Let's see what the target state should look like.

Frontend

In the frontend, we should have category information displayed without any translation. The category field will come directly from the product instead ❶, as shown in the following code:

```
...

return <>
  <AppHeader/>
  <PageContainer>
      <Box className="breadcrumb">
    [City] {store.city} >
    [Store] {store.storeName} >
    [Category] {product.category ❶} >
    {product.name}
      </Box>

...
```

Likewise, the new ID field should be used for all operations—first for product retrieval ❶:

```
const getProduct = async (uuid) => {
    const response = await fetch(`${API.baseUrl}/products/${uuid}` ❶, {
        method: "GET",
        //...
    });
    return response.json();
}
```

then for adding to the basket ❶:

```
const addToBasket = async (product) => {

    const response = await fetch(`${API.baseUrl}/basket/${product.uuid}` ❶, {
        method: "POST"
        //...
    });
    return response.json();
};
```

and finally for product creation ❶:

```
const createProduct = async (productData, store) => {
    const response = await fetch(`${API.baseUrl}/products`, {
        method: "POST",
        body: JSON.stringify({...productData, ...store})
        //...
    });
    // This should display the new id instead of the old one
    alert(`Product created successfully. ID: ${response.uuid}`) ❶
};
```

Similar changes could be applied throughout the frontend, even though we are covering only four examples here.

Backend

In the backend, products should only have their new identifier and a category field, as shown in the signature of the following Product record:

```
public record Product(UUID uuid, String name, Category category ...) {}
```

Categories should no longer be hardcoded in an enum, and should come from the database instead. This has the pleasant side effect of allowing admins to modify the categories easily in the future, and add or remove categories without performing Shotgun Surgery[1] on the whole codebase.

This means that during product creation, shown in the following code, the old and complex ID generation logic should be replaced with a simple, randomly generated UUID ❶, while the category should be inserted as a foreign key reference to the category table ❷:

Persistence < **API** < UI

```
public Product createProduct(CreateProductPayload createProductPayload) {
    // UUID is randomly generated by the db
    String insert =  "INSERT INTO PRODUCTS" +
        "(SHOP_ID, NAME, CATEGORY_ID) " +
        "VALUES (?, ?, ?) RETURNING *"; ❶

    Integer categoryId = categoryIdFromPayload(
        createProductPayload.category()
    ); ❷


    return jdbcTemplate.queryForObject(
        insert,
        new ProductMapper(),
        createProductPayload.shopId(),
        createProductPayload.name(),
        categoryId
    );
}
```

Persistence

As I mentioned in the previous sections, the persistence layer will contain a new table for categories. A possible implementation is shown in the following code:

Persistence < API < UI

```
groceroo=# \d categories
                    Table "public.categories"
    Column    | Type | Collation | Nullable |       Default
--------------+------+-----------+----------+--------------------
 category_id  | uuid |           | not null | gen_random_uuid()
 name         | text |           | not null |
 ...
```

However, the most disruptive change in the system will be the one on the product table. Its primary key should be replaced with the new UUID ❶, and the table should also contain a foreign key reference to categories ❷:

---

1 Shotgun Surgery is a code smell that refers to when a single change has to be made to many places in the codebase simultaneously. A more detailed explanation is available at *https://oreil.ly/gf8Lv*.

```
groceroo=# \d products
                    Table "public.products"
      Column     | Type | Collation | Nullable |      Default
-----------------+------+-----------+----------+--------------------
 shop_id         | uuid |           | not null |
 name            | text |           |          |
 Product_uuid ❶  | uuid |           | not null | gen_random_uuid()
 category_id     | uuid |           | not null |


Foreign-key constraints:
    "fk_shop" FOREIGN KEY (shop_id) REFERENCES shops(shop_id)
    "products_category_id_fkey" ❷ FOREIGN KEY (category_id) REFERENCES cate-
gories(category_id)
```

Any other table referencing the product table should also be using the UUID as a foreign key ❶. For example, the basket table should look like the following:

```
groceroo=# \d basket
                  Table "public.basket"
    Column    |   Type   | Collation | Nullable | Default
--------------+----------+-----------+----------+---------
 user_id      | uuid     |           | not null |
 quantity     | integer  |           | not null |
 product_uuid | uuid     |           | not null |

Indexes:
    "pkey" PRIMARY KEY, btree (user_id, product_uuid)
Foreign-key constraints:
    "fk_product" FOREIGN KEY (product_uuid) REFERENCES products(product_uuid)❶
    "fk_user" FOREIGN KEY (user_id) REFERENCES users(user_id)
```

As we anticipated in "Current State" on page 242, all database sequences can be
dropped because we don't need to generate the old IDs anymore.

How Do We Get There?

As we discussed in Chapter 3, refactoring live functionality under continuous deployment means we cannot simply go around changing all providers and consumers to
their $N + 1$ version (the one shown in "Target State" on page 250). With no manual
control over when the deployment happens, we risk long periods of incompatibility
in production. Think, for example, of changing just the backend and frontend codebases to use the new ID. The codebase that gets pushed first (and therefore deployed
first) will be incompatible with the other codebase.

That's why, to perform this refactoring safely, we must always keep contracts backward compatible by introducing intermediate increments, which we can deploy

safely. These intermediate steps will ensure that version $N + 1$ of any codebase will remain backward compatible with version N of other codebases in production.

We can achieve this with a pattern that lends itself wonderfully to this type of refactoring, and that I have by now mentioned many times: the expand and contract pattern. If you missed it, now would be a good time to go back to Chapter 3 to have a look at the theory. In the next section, we will put it into practice.

Expand and Contract

Let's see how the expand and contract pattern can be applied to this practical, non-trivial example. Let's zoom into the most pervasive change of this refactoring: shifting the source of truth for the product numbering system. Its current source of truth is in the database: the product ID column within the product table, which should change to a UUID.

We can implement our refactoring with the "alternative field" expansion strategy, specifically by adding an extra database column for the new UUID, coupled with a reference to a proper categories table. I chose this one because it is the most pragmatic for this example, but if you want to have a look at other possible ones, you can refer to Chapter 7.

As is typical of the expand and contract pattern, we can organize the product ID replacement in three logical steps:

1. First, we have the *expand* phase in the provider system (the database), where we need to create a new UUID column alongside the old numerical one. In the same change, we need to also create a new categories table and a reference to it in the product table.

2. Then, in the *migrate* phase, all of the clients (in the backend) using the old ID switch to the new one: the product creation endpoint, product retrieval endpoint, and basket table (which references the old ID with a foreign key). Any code that reads the product should rely on the new category field.

3. Once there are no remaining clients using the old field, we can perform the *contract* phase: delete the numerical ID forever and celebrate a successful migration.

These steps are shown in Figure 9-3.

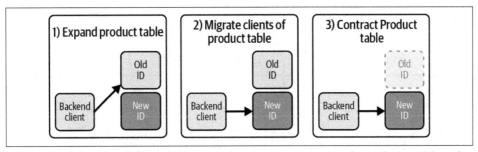

Figure 9-3. A high-level view of the expand and contract pattern for replacing old product IDs

Now that we have more insight into our expansion strategy, we are almost ready to dive into our example again. Before we do that, however, we must tackle another complication.

We are assuming that the clients of the old column can be migrated atomically, in one simple step. In reality, our client (the backend) has another consumer above it: the frontend layer, which also depends on the old product ID. This makes the refactoring a little less trivial, and it gives us an excellent opportunity to showcase how to apply the expand and contract pattern on a system with multiple layers of providers and consumers.

Multiple Layers: Inside Out

In a distributed system with multiple layers of providers and consumers, we must refactor from the inside out: starting from the innermost provider and proceeding in the direction of the outermost consumer. The pattern begins by establishing the expansion path in the innermost provider. This expansion path is then also created in the direct consumers of that provider. This expansion should then proceed outward through each layer's consumers. This process continues until the outermost consumer is reached. Migration has to be done at this level to complete the transition.

In our case, the innermost provider system is our database, and our frontend is our outermost consumer. Therefore, if we want to proceed from the inside out, we have to add the new product ID (expansion path) in two systems before we can migrate: first in the database and then in the backend. Once that is done, the frontend can migrate to the new ID, and we can proceed with the deletion of the old one in the layers below.

You can find a visualization of all the steps in Figure 9-4.

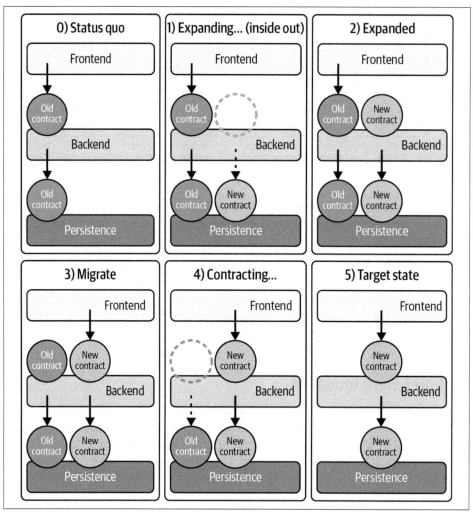

Figure 9-4. The expand and contract pattern on a multilayered application

Let's break down the work shown in Figure 9-4. First, to expand, we need to add the new UUID field in the database layer (step 1). Then, in the backend, the operation that used to support the old ID must be expanded to also accept the new ID (step 2). We are following the dependency order, so all of these can be sent as individual, backward-compatible deployments to production.

Once this is done, we can migrate the frontend (our outermost consumer) to the newly built code path, rendering the old one unused (step 3). Finally, we can go ahead and remove the old code in all the layers (step 4), which takes us to our desired target state (step 5).

This is a very classic web application architecture, but we can work this way regardless of the nature of the infrastructure involved.

We can also think of this as nesting cycles of expand and contract. Notice how we performed an outer cycle of expansion and contraction on the product ID (database layer), which "wrapped" an inner expand and contract cycle for the backend layer. Figure 9-5 is another representation of the same workflow, showcasing this nesting.

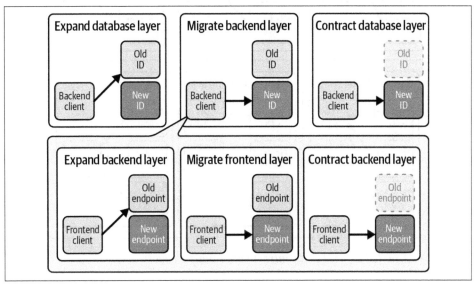

Figure 9-5. A nested expand and contract

However, we're not yet addressing the fact that each layer has *multiple* clients using the old product ID. For instance, the old ID is used by various API endpoints in the backend layer (such as add to basket, get product, and create product) that are in turn accessed from multiple places in the frontend. The product ID is used in almost every feature of the system, after all, not just by one endpoint. Now that we know to proceed from the inside out (or through a nesting expand and contract), how do we also account for this one-to-many relationship between providers and consumers?

To account for the multiple clients (and multiple layers), we simply need to repeat the same steps several times, one for each client of the old ID. In our case, this means addressing each API endpoint in the backend one by one. You can see how in Figure 9-6.

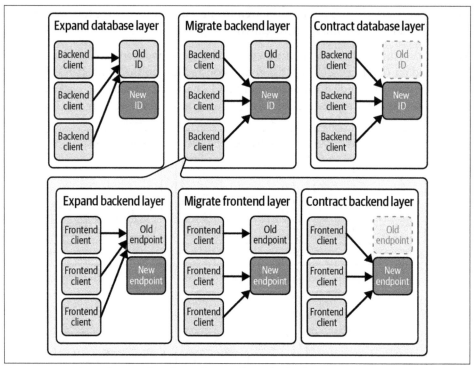

Figure 9-6. A nested expand and contract with multiple clients

After we duplicate the column, we can start migrating clients in the backend layer. The first endpoint must be expanded to support the new ID; then, we can migrate all its clients in the frontend and contract it like before. However, we cannot remove the old database column yet, because it has more endpoints (clients) in the backend using it. We need to proceed in this fashion, endpoint by endpoint, until the old column is unused. The outer expand and contract cycle, in this case, will contain several smaller expand and contract cycles: one for each endpoint that we needed to migrate in the backend layer.

Let's see how we can apply this to the code of the Groceroo platform, deployment by deployment.

Implementing with Expand and Contract

To perform the whole migration of the ID field, we have to start with the outer expand and contract cycle that will duplicate the product ID column in the database layer. Then we can also start addressing its first client: the POST /product endpoint, as shown in Figure 9-7.

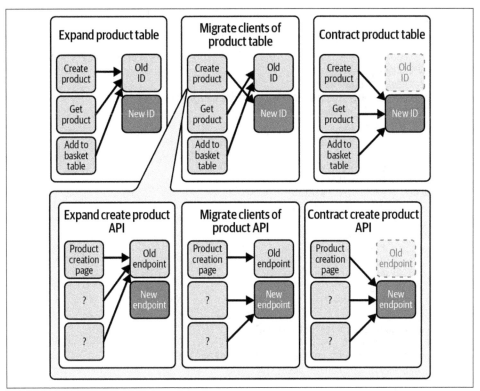

Figure 9-7. The nested expand and contract for the product creation page

After the expansion of the database layer by creating the new UUID, we will zoom in on the POST /product endpoint and perform an "inner" expand and contract cycle between the backend and the frontend. Like we discussed, we are going from the innermost system to the outermost system, building out an alternative code path until the outermost client (the product creation page, in this case) can migrate to it.

Let's take it step by step.

Outer Expand Phase: The Product Table

We will begin with the first step of our refactoring: expanding the product table.

Deployment 1: Expand the product table

First, we need to start the "outer" expand and contract pattern by creating the categories table and our new UUID field, which will live alongside the old one for the duration of the refactoring. We will also go ahead and add the categories table and reference, which are required if we want to stop relying on the old ID later. In the following code, we can see how to achieve this with a database evolution (which could even be split into multiple deployments):

Persistence < API < UI

```
-- new category table
CREATE TABLE CATEGORIES (
    CATEGORY_ID UUID UNIQUE NOT NULL PRIMARY KEY
        DEFAULT gen_random_uuid(),
    NAME TEXT NOT NULL
);

-- seed category table with current categories
INSERT INTO CATEGORIES (name)
    VALUES ('Fruit and vegetables'),
           ('Bathroom products'),
           ('Bakery'),
           ('Deli'),
           ('Fish'),
           ('Meat'),
           ('Prepared foods'),
           ('Pharmacy'),
           ('Frozen food');

-- new product uuid with default value
ALTER TABLE PRODUCTS
    ADD COLUMN PRODUCT_UUID UUID UNIQUE NOT NULL ❶
        DEFAULT gen_random_uuid();

-- new reference to category table (nullable for now)
ALTER TABLE PRODUCTS
    ADD COLUMN CATEGORY_ID UUID ❷
        REFERENCES CATEGORIES(CATEGORY_ID);
```

We are using the "alternative field" expansion strategy. Whenever we are adding a new field to a table that already exists, it should either be set as nullable or have a default. This is to account for populating existing data, but also because after we deploy this change, the current backend code will actively keep writing new entries, and our table needs to keep working in production.

For the product ID, I opted for default values as a strategy ❶: the database layer is perfectly capable of generating random UUIDs, so there's no reason not to let it. Had we accepted NULL values instead, we would have needed to populate missing data later on. In fact, this is the case for our other addition: the category reference in the product table ❷. We can set it to nullable for now, since there is no simple way to calculate a default for new entries. We will fix this with an UPDATE statement to fill in the missing values later on, after the backend starts writing the category IDs in the new inserts.

For simplicity, we won't handle all the nuances of synchronizing data in this chapter. Read Chapter 10 for a more in-depth analysis on data synchronization during expand and contract.

The same table is also subject to read operations. Another key aspect of providing alternative fields is for reads to ensure that existing clients ignore it. This is easily done with our SQL example: we don't have to do anything. Queries have to indicate column names explicitly, which makes our addition perfectly safe. However, what if our product data had been in a NoSQL system, such as a document store? In those cases, clients often consume entries in their entirety, which could lead to problems in deserialization or in the calling systems that will receive unexpected fields. It is always worth double-checking.

We are now done with our expansion. Now that we have created the new ID field, we must migrate all of its clients. This is where our nested expand and contract cycles come in.

Migrating the POST /product Endpoint

The first client using the old ID is the API to create a product, which has the frontend depending on it as well. So, for this endpoint to use the new ID, we need to perform another (nested) expand and contract pattern.

Deployment 2: Expanding the POST /product endpoint

To start the expansion phase, the functionality of POST /product needs to be duplicated: it should be able to generate both the new ID ❶ and the old ID ❷ for new products. The new product ID is generated implicitly because we just added an auto-generated default value in the "outer" expand phase. However, we must also insert the new category reference ❸❹. It is easy to calculate it now that we are in the backend, because we already have the category data from the request payload (before now, it was used to get the right database sequence for the product ID).

We can do all of these changes in the repository layer. Here is the resulting code:

```
                                                      Persistence < API < UI
public Product createProduct(CreateProductPayload createProductPayload) {
    // new id has a default gen_random_uuid()
    String insert =  "INSERT INTO PRODUCTS" +
                     "(PRODUCT_ID ❷, SHOP_ID, NAME, CATEGORY_ID ❸) " +
                     "VALUES (?, ?, ?, ?) RETURNING *"; ❶

    Integer productId = productIdByCategory(createProductPayload.category());
    Integer categoryId = categoryIdFromPayload(
        createProductPayload.category()
    ); ❹
```

```
    return jdbcTemplate.queryForObject(
      insert,
      new ProductMapper(),
      productId,
      createProductPayload.shopId(),
      categoryId
    );
}
```

We must also insert the new category ID in the database. And we need to add the new ID ❶ alongside the old one ❷ in the Product record:

Persistence < API < UI

```
public record Product(Integer id ❷, UUID uuid ❶, String name ...) {
```

as well as in the row mapper that helps retrieve it from the database:

Persistence < API < UI

```
class ProductMapper implements RowMapper<Product> {

    public static final String PRODUCT_ID_OLD_COLUMN = "PRODUCT_ID";
    public static final String PRODUCT_ID_COLUMN = "PRODUCT_UUID";
    public static final String NAME_COLUMN = "NAME";

    @Override
    public Product mapRow(
      ResultSet resultSet,
      int rowNumber
    ) throws SQLException {
        Integer id = resultSet.getInt(PRODUCT_ID_OLD_COLUMN);
        UUID uuid = UUID.fromString(resultSet.getString(PRODUCT_ID_COLUMN));
        String name = resultSet.getString(NAME_COLUMN);

        return new Product(id, uuid, name);
    }
}
```

Finally, we can create the second endpoint ❶ alongside the old one ❷. This new version will return the alternative product ID format, as shown in the following code:

Persistence < API < UI

```
@PostMapping("/products") ❷
@ResponseBody
public Integer createProductOld(@RequestBody CreateProductPayload payload) {
    return repository.createProduct(payload).id();
}

@PostMapping("/v2/products") ❶
@ResponseBody
public UUID createProduct(@RequestBody CreateProductPayload payload) {
    return repository.createProduct(payload).uuid();
}
```

In this expansion, I am following the "duplicate API" strategy with API versioning. The client of the old API is the product creation page, which can now switch to the new one we just created. Let's see how.

Deployment 3: Migrating the POST /product endpoint

We will now migrate the product creation page in the admin interface to the new endpoint. In particular, the frontend reads the return value from the endpoint to show the ID as confirmation to the user. So, migrating it will consist of switching endpoints ❶ and making sure the frontend can read the new format. JavaScript doesn't care about types, so this is pretty straightforward in this case. In the following code for the product creation page, we can see that basically no change is necessary ❷:

Persistence < API < **UI**

```
export const CreateProductPage = () => {
    const store = useContext(StoreContext)

    const createProduct = async (productData, store) => {
        const response = await fetch(`${API.baseUrl}/v2/products` ❶, {
            method: "POST",
            body: JSON.stringify({...productData, ...store})
            //...
        });
        // This displays the UUID now
        alert(`Product created successfully. ID: ${response}`) ❷
    };

    return <>
        <AppHeader/>
        <PageContainer>
            <PageTitle>[Admin] Create product</PageTitle>
            <CreateProductForm onSubmit={(data) => createProduct(data, store)} />
        </PageContainer>;
    </>
}
```

However, if you use a tool such as TypeScript, you might need to update your types to account for the number becoming a string.

Deployment 4: Contracting the POST /product endpoint

Once the frontend has been taken care of, the API can be contracted to return the new ID only instead. As shown in the next snippet, we can just delete the old endpoint:

Persistence < **API** < UI

```
//    @PostMapping("/products") deleted!
//    @ResponseBody
//    public Integer createProductOld(
```

```
//          @RequestBody CreateProductPayload payload
//      ) {
//          return repository.createProduct(payload).id();
//      }

    @PostMapping("/v2/products")
    @ResponseBody
    public UUID createProduct(@RequestBody CreateProductPayload payload) {
        return repository.createProduct(payload).uuid();
    }
```

Now that we have the product creation in place, all new products are getting created with a UUID and a category ID. Before we move on from product creation, however, this could be a good time to ensure that existing data is consistent too. Remember how we left NULLs in the category reference for old products? We can fill in those missing values with an update statement ❶. This means past and future products will be fully populated so that we can start enforcing a NOT NULL constraint too ❷. Here are both statements in a single database evolution (which should be its own separate deployment):

```
UPDATE ❶ products
SET category_id =
 CASE
   WHEN substring(product_id::text from 1 for 1) = '1'
       THEN (SELECT category_id FROM categories WHERE name = 'Fruit and vegeta
bles')
   WHEN substring(product_id::text from 1 for 1) = '2'
       THEN (SELECT category_id FROM categories WHERE name = 'Bathroom prod
ucts')
   WHEN substring(product_id::text from 1 for 1) = '3'
       THEN (SELECT category_id FROM categories WHERE name = 'Bakery')
   WHEN substring(product_id::text from 1 for 1) = '4'
       THEN (SELECT category_id FROM categories WHERE name = 'Deli')
   WHEN substring(product_id::text from 1 for 1) = '5'
       THEN (SELECT category_id FROM categories WHERE name = 'Fish')
   WHEN substring(product_id::text from 1 for 1) = '6'
       THEN (SELECT category_id FROM categories WHERE name = 'Meat')
   WHEN substring(product_id::text from 1 for 1) = '7'
       THEN (SELECT category_id FROM categories WHERE name = 'Prepared foods')
   WHEN substring(product_id::text from 1 for 1) = '8'
       THEN (SELECT category_id FROM categories WHERE name = 'Pharmacy')
   WHEN substring(product_id::text from 1 for 1) = '9'
       THEN (SELECT category_id FROM categories WHERE name = 'Frozen food')
   END;

ALTER TABLE ❷ products ALTER COLUMN category_id SET NOT NULL;
```

The first client of the product table has now been taken care of. Our first nested expand and contract cycle is complete! However, we can't remove the old ID from the table yet, because there are two more clients left in our list. This means we cannot update our repository until then either, and we must keep creating both IDs. Let's address the next client first: the GET /product endpoint.

Migrating the GET /product Endpoint

As shown in Figure 9-8, we can follow a very similar process for the GET product API.

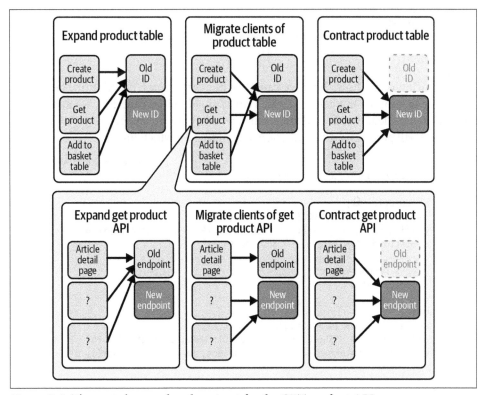

Figure 9-8. The nested expand and contract for the GET product API

Through another nested expand and contract cycle, we will be able to migrate the backend and frontend to retrieve products by their new UUID.

Deployment 5: Expanding the GET /product endpoint

The product retrieval functionality will be duplicated, making products fetchable by the old ID and the new ID.

Not all expansions need to consist of completely new endpoints or fields, as I described in Chapter 7 when listing different expansion strategies. We can mix it up and do something different this time (for illustration purposes), and offer both functionalities within the same endpoint. We can modify the endpoint by allowing the ID parameter to be passed in either format. This is an example of the "generify field type" strategy.

To support this expansion, our endpoint's parameter must change to become more generic, and accept a string type instead of an integer ❶—which could contain the ID in numeric format or in the new UUID format, as shown in the following code:

Persistence < **API** < UI

```
@GetMapping("/products/{id}")
@ResponseBody
public Product getProduct(@PathVariable("id") String id ❶) {
    return repository.getProduct(id);
}
```

The following code shows how we can alter the `getProduct` function in the repository layer to support the generic field. With a small helper function, we analyze the format of the identifier ❶ and determine whether it's an integer or a UUID. The repository will perform a different query depending on which one it is:

Persistence < **API** < UI

```
public Product getProduct(String id) {

    if (isUUID(id) ❶) {
        UUID newFormatId = UUID.fromString(id);
        String select =  "SELECT * FROM PRODUCTS WHERE product_uuid = ?";
        return jdbcTemplate.queryForObject(
          select,
          new ProductMapper(),
          newFormatId
        );
    } else {
        Integer oldFormatId = Integer.parseInt(id);
        String select =  "SELECT * FROM PRODUCTS WHERE product_id = ?";
        return jdbcTemplate.queryForObject(select, new ProductMapper(), oldForma
tId);
    }
}
```

This code is a bit "uglier," but it lets us avoid coming up with awkward endpoint names or API versioning for the sake of temporarily duplicating the functionality. I often use this method because, although the intermediate state looks less than ideal, it is very much throwaway code, whereas less than ideal endpoint names require much more coordination and headache to change. This is an example of the trade-offs to consider with different expansion strategies.

In addition to the ID changes, we should also add the new category field to the product data representation ❶ so that the frontend can read it later:

Persistence < **API** < UI

```
public record Product(
    Integer id,
```

```
        UUID uuid,
        String name,
        Category category ❶
        ...
    ) {
```

Our consumer (the frontend) will now be able to read category data either from the old product identifier or from the product payload.

Deployment 6: Migrating the GET /product endpoint

The only client of the get endpoint in our example is the product detail page, so we just need to migrate the frontend call that fetches the product before rendering the page. It should pass the UUID ❶ instead of the numeric ID. The changes are shown in the following code:

```
                                                    Persistence < API < UI
const getProduct = async (id ❶ /*this should be the uuid now! */ ) => {
    const response = await fetch(`${API.baseUrl}/products/${id}`, {
        method: "GET",
        body: JSON.stringify(product)
        //...
    });
    return response.json();
}
```

We also need to make sure that it renders the category from the product data ❶ instead of relying on the old ID to calculate it:

```
                                                    Persistence < API < UI
return <>
    <AppHeader/>
    <PageContainer>
        <Box className="breadcrumb">
    [City] {store.city} >
    [Store] {store.storeName} >
    [Category] {product.category ❶} >
    {product.name}
        </Box>
```

We can rely on the category data always being present because of the database evolution we performed to fill in past values.

Deployment 7: Contracting the GET /product endpoint

To finish this other expand and contract cycle, we can now contract the backend endpoint to only accept the UUID format.

The controller parameter ❶ can be changed to a UUID type, which is much more specific than just a string, like this:

```
                                                           Persistence < API < UI
@GetMapping("/products/{id}")
@ResponseBody
public Product getProduct(@PathVariable("id") UUID id ❶) {
    return repository.getProduct(id);
}
```

As a consequence, the repository can stop trying to infer the type, as shown here, where we have removed the `if` statement:

```
                                                           Persistence < API < UI
public Product getProduct(UUID id) {
    String select =  "SELECT * FROM PRODUCTS WHERE product_uuid = ?";
    return jdbcTemplate.queryForObject(select, new ProductMapper(), id);
}
```

The code is much cleaner now. After this step, there's only one last client remaining.

Migrating the Basket Table

The last client is a slightly trickier one. Instead of the backend performing direct queries on the table, our last client is another database table. In fact, many other tables (orders, favorites, basket, etc.) could reference the product ID through a foreign key. For this chapter, we will focus on this one.

How to migrate another table might seem puzzling at first, but there is a simple solution. Database references across tables can also be understood as a contract, and by extension a consumer–provider relationship. As we saw in "How Do We Get There?" on page 253, any new layer of provider and consumer can be handled by another layer of the expand and contract pattern, and we can certainly use the same logic here. There is no limit to how many layers of dependencies we can handle. We can just add more nesting.

As you can see in Figure 9-9, we can add two layers of expand and contract instead of one.

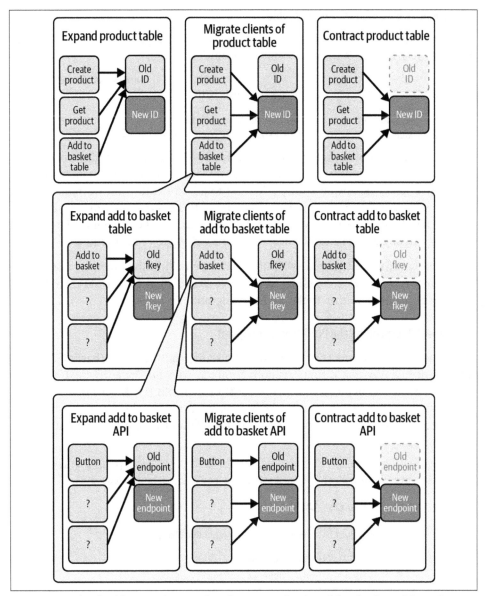

Figure 9-9. The doubly nested expand and contract for the add to basket table and API

Let's go step by step again: we want to migrate the basket table, which is a client of our product table, to the new ID format.

Deployment 8: Expanding the basket table

To migrate the basket table to the new ID, we must first expand it so that it can support both IDs. Let's do it with this database evolution:

Persistence < API < UI

```
ALTER TABLE BASKET ADD COLUMN PRODUCT_UUID UUID;

ALTER TABLE BASKET DROP CONSTRAINT fk_product; ❶
ALTER TABLE BASKET ALTER COLUMN PRODUCT_ID DROP NOT NULL; ❷
```

In this evolution, notice how we don't have a NOT NULL constraint on the new UUID field. We are tolerating absent values, in line with the requirements for the "alternative field" expansion strategy. This is required because the current backend hasn't been updated yet: it will write null values to this column after our deployment. We will handle this the same way we handled NULLs in the category reference: by updating missing entries after the backend starts writing to both columns.

In preparation for the backend switching from one field to the other, we also had to temporarily relax the fk constraints on the table ❶ and allow for the old ID to be nullable too ❷. So let's move on to the backend migration.

Deployment 9: Expanding the POST /basket endpoint

Finally, we can move one layer upward and also expand the POST /basket API. We can code it in a way that it supports both contracts with the "generify field" strategy: adding items to the basket by their new ID ❶ *or* their old ID ❷. This new version is shown in the following code. Just like before, we can offer the functionality in the same endpoint by simply detecting the ID type ❸ and executing different queries accordingly:

Persistence < API < UI

```
public void addToBasket(AddToBasketPayload payload, String productId) {

    if (isUUID(productId) ❸) {

        UUID newProductId = UUID.fromString(productId);

        String insert = "INSERT INTO BASKET AS original " +
                "(product_uuid, user_id, quantity, product_id) " +
                "VALUES (?, ?, ?, ("+
                    "SELECT PRODUCT_ID FROM PRODUCTS " +
                    "WHERE PRODUCT_UUID = ?" ❶ +
                "))" +
                "ON CONFLICT ON CONSTRAINT PKEY DO UPDATE " +
                "SET quantity = original.quantity + excluded.quantity;";

        jdbcTemplate.update(
            insert,
            newProductId,
```

```
            payload.userId(),
            payload.quantity(),
            newProductId);

    } else {
        Integer oldProductId = Integer.parseInt(productId);

        String insert = "INSERT INTO BASKET AS original " +
                        "(product_id, user_id, quantity, product_uuid) " +
                        "VALUES (?, ?, ?, (" +
                            "SELECT PRODUCT_UUID " +
                            "FROM PRODUCTS " +
                            "WHERE PRODUCT_ID = ?" ❷+
                        "))" +
                        "ON CONFLICT ON CONSTRAINT PKEY DO UPDATE " +
                        "SET quantity = " +
                        "original.quantity + excluded.quantity;";

        jdbcTemplate.update(
            insert,
            oldProductId,
            payload.userId(),
            payload.quantity(),
            oldProductId
        );
    }
}
```

Notice how in both inserts, we have to retrieve the value for the missing ID that was not passed (either the old one or the new one) from the product table.

After this deployment is live, we can check that the backend is writing both IDs in the table for all new records. From this point onward, we can deploy a further database evolution to synchronize historical data, as mentioned in the preceding section. For example, the database evolution in the following code will get rid of all existing NULLs:

```
UPDATE BASKET b
SET PRODUCT_UUID = p.PRODUCT_UUID
FROM PRODUCTS p
WHERE b.PRODUCT_ID = p.PRODUCT_ID;
```

Deployment 10: Migrating the POST /basket endpoint

Finally, the frontend "Add to basket" button, which is the only client of this endpoint, can call the backend with the new ID ❶, as shown here:

```
                                            Persistence < API < UI
const addToBasket = async (product) => {

    const response = await fetch(
        `${API.baseUrl}/add-to-basket/${product.uuid}` ❶, {
```

```
        method: "POST",
        body: JSON.stringify(product)
        //...
    });
    return response.json();
};
```

At this point, if we had other endpoints relying on the ID (e.g., one for getting the contents of the basket), we could migrate them to use the new ID too. This is left as an exercise for the reader.

By switching this call to the new ID, we have migrated the very last client of the product table. Now all of the remaining "contract" phases unlock in a cascading fashion, in the backend and in the database layer.

Deployment 11: Contracting the POST /basket endpoint

We can remove the functionality of the POST /basket endpoint that inserts items by their old ID, which is now unused. This greatly simplifies the repository layer we had expanded, as you can see in the following code:

Persistence < **API** < UI

```
public void addToBasket(AddToBasketPayload payload, UUID productId) {
    String insert = "INSERT INTO BASKET AS original " +
            "(product_uuid, user_id, quantity) " +
            "VALUES (?, ?, ?) " +
            "ON CONFLICT ON CONSTRAINT PKEY DO UPDATE " +
            "SET quantity = original.quantity + excluded.quantity;";

    jdbcTemplate.update(insert, productId, payload.userId(), payload.quantity());
}
```

Remember that we had set the old product ID as nullable and removed the fkey constraint, so this doesn't cause the query to fail.

If there is any leftover reference to the old product ID in the backend, it can also be removed in this stage; for example, on the Product record, as shown in the following code:

Persistence < **API** < UI

```
public record Product(UUID uuid, String name ...) {
```

Deployment 12: Contracting the basket table

We can also remove the old product ID field from the basket table ❶ (which is starting to be populated with NULLs anyway), leaving only the reference to the new UUID. While we're at it, we can now reintroduce some stronger constraints ❷. This is all performed by deploying the following database evolution:

Persistence < API < **UI**

```
ALTER TABLE BASKET DROP COLUMN PRODUCT_ID; ❶
```

```
ALTER TABLE BASKET ALTER COLUMN PRODUCT_UUID SET NOT NULL;  ❷
ALTER TABLE BASKET
    ADD CONSTRAINT FK_PRODUCT
    FOREIGN KEY (PRODUCT_UUID)
    REFERENCES PRODUCTS(PRODUCT_UUID);
```

Outer Contract Phase: Cleaning Up the Product Table

Finally, we can bring our outer expand and contract cycle to fruition by removing the old ID in the product table.

Deployment 13: Contracting the product table

Because nothing else references the old ID at this point, it can now be safely removed from the system. We can drop it from its source of truth: the product table. The following database evolution can be sent out as its own deployment:

Persistence < API < UI

```
ALTER TABLE PRODUCTS DROP CONSTRAINT products_pkey;
ALTER TABLE PRODUCTS DROP COLUMN PRODUCT_ID;

ALTER TABLE PRODUCTS ADD CONSTRAINT PKEY PRIMARY KEY (PRODUCT_UUID);
```

We are done! All of our codebases now match the target state.

You might think that this refactoring could have been "easier" by pausing the gate to production, replacing the old product ID everywhere, then doing one big synchronized deployment to production. After all, I just described how this approach requires 13 individual deployments. However, consider this: all deployments we performed contained a trivial amount of code, and every single step has been testable to production individually and been proven to work by the users' continued ability to use the functionality undergoing renovation. The implications of this are not to be underestimated.

On the other hand, a big-bang deployment to production of the "target state" code would have been very risky due to the sheer amount of code that was changed. Can you imagine if there had been an unforeseen error buried in all these lines of code that could have led to data corruption in the most important table of the system? If somebody told me I had to oversee *that* deployment to prod, I would have called a priest first.

Small and incremental deployments also don't prevent other work from going to production while this migration is in progress, because all changes are on the shared codebase at all times. Any new features introduced during this time can be added to temporarily support both IDs. A big-bang replacement would have meant either pausing all other work or operating in such a long-lived branch that "integration hell" would have surely occurred upon merge.

This example was inspired by a real event on one of our projects, so it most definitely is within the realm of challenges that can be faced and overcome by a team using continuous deployment. Overall, this is to show that even the trickiest changes to a distributed system can be broken down, developed incrementally, and deployed continuously in total safety. All it takes is the right mindset, a little bit of planning, and resisting the temptation to dive headfirst in our IDEs and make changes wherever the code leads us.

Summary

In this chapter, we explored a nontrivial example to showcase a framework for changing live features under continuous deployment.

The key to backward-compatible, refactoring-type changes is the expand and contract pattern, which consists of three phases: duplicating the pathway into the functionality of the provider, migrating the consumer so that it uses the alternative path, and cleaning up the unused old code.

When needed, this pattern can be applied to multiple layers of providers and consumers. First, the expand phase must be completed in all providers in an "inside-out" fashion. Then, the migrate phase can begin, starting from the outermost consumer. By following this principle, we can even nest expand and contract cycles in distributed applications with multiple layers of Chapter 8, you saw how we contracts.

One thing we did not cover are special considerations we must take when performing expand and contract on persistence and state storage systems, in order to remove the possibility of data loss. These will be covered in Chapter 10.

Data and Data Loss

In Chapter 9, you saw how to refactor live functionality under continuous deployment. Through the use of the expand and contract pattern, we can plan out our deployments across different codebases in such a way that all changes remain backward compatible. Backward compatibility ensures that all the features relying on the refactoring will keep running flawlessly for users, even though the code itself is still a work in progress. However, this only holds true until our refactoring crosses the contract boundary with a database or any state store. The expand and contract pattern is not enough on its own to safely refactor live databases without loss of service or data.

Let's revisit the example from Chapter 9, where our objective was to switch the product ID referenced in the basket table. In that scenario, we wanted to transition from using one product ID to another. To accomplish this, we implemented a temporary two-column system that allowed both IDs to coexist until all clients fully adopted the new one.

On the surface, this approach may seem foolproof. However, when it comes to databases and continuous deployment, we need to consider that any temporary change we make will impact the flow of data into our databases. This affects what ends up persisted (or more importantly, not persisted) between deployments. That is why we had to introduce an extra data synchronization step (which I will explain in much more detail in this chapter).

This issue isn't exclusive to our previous example; it applies to all situations where we modify the interaction between a persistence layer and the systems that write to it.

The book *Refactoring Databases*[1] thoroughly addresses how to release changes to databases while maintaining backward compatibility. This book remains relevant today as we further the conversation on iterative development, making smaller and smaller changes to production and its underlying database(s). If you're delving into continuous deployment, it's definitely a recommended read.

Nevertheless, and even without a full immersion into database literature, the goal of this chapter is to equip you with some fundamental tools for handling common scenarios that can arise during continuous deployment. I'll continue to rely on our ongoing Groceroo example to illustrate the problem. I'll initially focus on relational databases, which is what Groceroo uses, and at the end of the chapter I'll discuss how to adapt these techniques for NoSQL stores.

Our Task

In Chapter 9, we saw a database refactoring problem with the basket table having to switch its product ID from one format to another. Here, I will introduce a similar, simpler example to demonstrate the issue with databases and incremental changes: renaming a table column.

A new task requires us to do some preparatory refactoring on the users table in our Groceroo system. Product stakeholders want us to persist some new details in the table: in particular, the user's real first name and last name, which will be needed later to fulfill orders and deliveries. Right now, customers have to input information this every time they go through the checkout. Instead, the system should add those fields to the user profiles so that they can be reused for all orders.

The Problem

On our users table, we already have a name field that represents the username the user entered during their registration process, but it doesn't have to be their full, legal name. In fact, it can be anything as long as it is unique in the system. This field is just like any old username: it's used for user registration and login. We *could* simply go ahead and add two new columns, first_name and last_name, but because we already have a column called "name," that would quickly become confusing.

---

1 Scott W. Ambler and Pradmod J. Sadalage, *Refactoring Databases: Evolutionary Database Design* (Boston: Addison-Wesley, 2006).

The Solution

We should change the existing column to "username" first, since that's what it really is. This makes it clearer what the column refers to, and it will save a few "WTFs per minute"[2] when new joiners or existing engineers have a look at the system's internals.

This refactoring, which looks rather innocuous, is actually interesting enough that it will be the focus of the rest of this chapter. Just like in the preceding chapter, we are aiming to deliver it in incremental deployments, with zero disruption of service in production and zero loss of existing data. Let's start by having a look at the current state of the name column and its usages.

Current State

Since we are focusing mainly on the persistence layer, we will only have a look at the database and its primary client: the backend.

Persistence

Here is the name column ❶ in the users table:

Persistence < API < UI

```
groceroo=# \d users;
                Table "public.users"
 Column  | Type | Collation | Nullable |      Default
---------+------+-----------+----------+-------------------
 user_id | uuid |           | not null | gen_random_uuid()
 name ❶  | text |           |          |
 ...
```

Backend

As you can see from the following repository code, the backend performs both read and write operations on name. It is writing to it during user creation ❶ and reading from it during user retrieval ❷. We will focus on these two for our example:

Persistence < **API** < UI

```java
@Repository
public class UserRepository {

  private final JdbcTemplate jdbcTemplate;

  public UserRepository(JdbcTemplate jdbcTemplate) {
    this.jdbcTemplate = jdbcTemplate;
```

---

2 A popular metric for code cleanliness, originally introduced by Thom Holwerda in this cartoon: *https://oreil.ly/w94yE*.

```
  }

  public User create(CreateUserPayload payload) {
    String insert = ❶ "INSERT INTO USERS(NAME) VALUES (?) RETURNING *";

    return jdbcTemplate.queryForObject(insert, new UserMapper(), pay
load.name());
  }

  public User findBy(UUID id) {
    String select = ❷"SELECT NAME, USER_ID FROM USERS WHERE USER_ID = ?";
    return jdbcTemplate.queryForObject(select, new UserMapper(), id);
  }

  private static class UserMapper implements RowMapper<User> {

    public static final String NAME_COLUMN = "NAME";
    public static final String ID_COLUMN = "USER_ID";

    @Override
    public User mapRow(ResultSet resultSet, int rowNumber) throws SQLException {
      UUID uuid = UUID.fromString(resultSet.getString(ID_COLUMN));
      String name = resultSet.getString(NAME_COLUMN);
      return new User(name, uuid);
    }
  }
}
```

Target State

Our target state is also pretty simple this time: we just want the column to go by the new name in all layers.

Persistence

First, we want the actual users table to look like it does in the following declaration. Notice the renaming of the column ❶:

Persistence < API < UI

```
groceroo=# \d users;
                 Table "public.users"
   Column     | Type | Collation | Nullable |      Default
------------+------+-----------+----------+-------------------
 User_id     | uuid |           | not null | gen_random_uuid()
 username ❶  | text |           |          |
```

Backend

In the backend, all operations on the table should also use the new name ❶❷, as shown in the updated repository:

Persistence < **API** < UI

```
@Repository
public class UserRepository {

  private final JdbcTemplate jdbcTemplate;

  public UserRepository(JdbcTemplate jdbcTemplate) {
    this.jdbcTemplate = jdbcTemplate;
  }

  public User create(CreateUserPayload payload) {
    String insert = ❶ "INSERT INTO USERS(USERNAME) VALUES (?) RETURNING *";

    return jdbcTemplate.queryForObject(insert, new UserMapper(), pay
load.name());
  }

  public User findBy(UUID id) {
    String select = ❷ "SELECT USERNAME, USER_ID FROM USERS WHERE USER_ID = ?";
    return jdbcTemplate.queryForObject(select, new UserMapper(), id);
  }


  private static class UserMapper implements RowMapper<User> {

    public static final String USERNAME_COLUMN = "USERNAME";
    public static final String ID_COLUMN = "USER_ID";

    @Override
    public User mapRow(ResultSet resultSet, int rowNumber) throws SQLException {
      UUID uuid = UUID.fromString(resultSet.getString(ID_COLUMN));
      String username = resultSet.getString(USERNAME_COLUMN);
      return new User(username, uuid);
    }
  }

}
```

How Do We Get There?

A database is not often thought of as an independent system, separate from the backend it serves. However, it most definitely is. After all, the backend and the database are two separate executables, most likely running on different machines and usually talking to each other over the network.

This makes it so that refactoring a contract between the two incurs all the complications that we discussed in Chapter 9. We cannot simply bring the database and backend straight to the desired target state and cross our fingers during deployment. So, let's see how we might complete this refactoring in a backward-compatible manner, and how it is different from the other examples presented in Chapter 9.

Failure Mode: Simultaneous Change

More often than not, persistence code (e.g., database evolutions) is kept in the same version control repository as backend code. On top of that, database evolutions are usually applied by the application code itself at startup, as soon as one of the instances with the new version comes alive and detects an out-of-date version of the schema. This further couples the path to production of those two systems, as they go live at more or less the same time.

With such a setup, many teams might be tempted to simply add any database evolution and the code relying on it to the same commit.

In our example, this would mean adding an evolution to rename the column:

Persistence < API < UI

```
ALTER TABLE USERS
    RENAME COLUMN NAME TO USERNAME;
```

and, in the same commit, to also change the repository code to rely on the new name:

Persistence < **API** < UI

```
@Repository
public class UserRepository {

  private final JdbcTemplate jdbcTemplate;

  public UserRepository(JdbcTemplate jdbcTemplate) {
    this.jdbcTemplate = jdbcTemplate;
  }

  public User create(CreateUserPayload payload) {
    String insert = "INSERT INTO USERS(USERNAME) VALUES (?) RETURNING *";

    return jdbcTemplate.queryForObject(insert, new UserMapper(), pay
load.name());
  }
```

These two code changes just happen to be in the same repository, but in reality they will be deployed on two different distributed components. This won't happen simultaneously. In any given deployment, database changes will be deployed in a slightly separate step than the application code. Furthermore, most zero-downtime deployment strategies foresee at least a short window of time where application instances with version N and version $N + 1$ will coexist in production. Zero downtime makes backward compatibility of database changes mandatory, and this change is not backward compatible.

To see the problem in detail, let's have a look at what would happen during a deployment of this change, also illustrated in Figure 10-1.

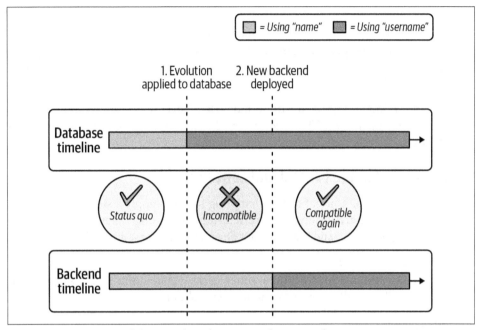

Figure 10-1. Incompatibility window during simultaneous changes

After the database evolutions kick in, at least some of our old application instances will still attempt to write and read using the old format (name) in the database. This will happen until the new version of the backend (relying on username) is fully rolled out to all instances (marked by the second event in the timeline). This situation applies, for example, to rolling deployments and blue/green deployments, or any deployment strategy that guarantees zero downtime by having versions N and $N + 1$ of the application coexist for a period of time. Such a deployment will lead to a brief period of failed requests on version N, and subsequently, data loss.

In particular, this is what will happen to the data:

```
+-----------+
| name      | <- old implementation: backend writes
+-----------+    to "name" column
| alice     |
| bob       |
| shinji    |
+-----------+
| username  | <- database rename applied
```

```
+------------+
| *error!*   | <- some backend instances still trying to write to "name"
| *error!*   |    column
| *error!*   |
| mari       | <- backend update fully applied: all instances writing
| rei        |    to "username" column
...
```

To avoid an incompatibility window or incompatible instances, we can conclude that we should isolate changes belonging to different distributed components in separate deployments and keep them backward compatible. We should follow this rule even when their codebases are versioned together.

To put it more simply, a good rule of thumb is that database evolutions should always be deployed on their own. This also lowers the developers' cognitive load and lets them focus on the schema's backward compatibility.

Failure Mode: Simple Expand and Contract

To solve this scenario, it might also be tempting to try to apply a simple expand and contract pattern. We are dealing with refactoring an existing functionality, after all. We could imagine the expand and contract phases to look something like this:

Expand phase
> Expand our schema by creating another username column. In the same evolution, we will copy all existing data to the new column.

Migration phase
> Migrate all clients to use the new username column.

Contract phase
> Remove the old name column.

We are getting closer to backward compatibility, but we're still not quite there. Using expand and contract in this way will also cause data loss because nothing is being written to the new column between the expand and contract phases, as illustrated in Figure 10-2.

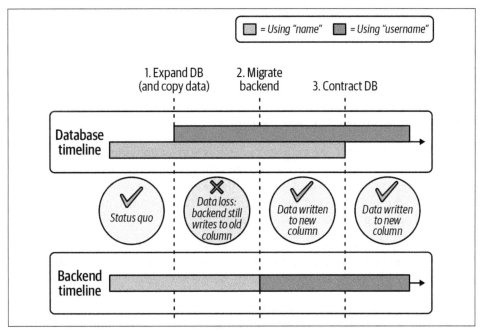

Figure 10-2. Incompatibility window during simple expand and contract

As you can see in Figure 10-2, there will be a gap of data in our new column between the phases. While the new column exists after expansion, nothing is written to it until we deploy our migration phase. When the application starts relying on the new column, it will return empty results or exceptions when retrieving data from that broken time window.

This is what will happen to the table data:

```
+------------+------------+
| name       | username   |
+------------+------------+
| alice      | alice      |   <- expand phase: new column is
| bob        | bob        |      created and existing values are copied
| shinji     | shinji     |
+------------+------------+
| mari       | null       |   <- nothing written to new column between
| rei        | null       |      expand and migrate phases - *data loss!*
+------------+------------+
| null       | gendo      |   <- migration phase: backend starts
| null       | misato     |      using new column
+------------+------------+
             | asuka      |   <- contract phase: old column is removed, backend
             | ritsuko    |      reads and writes from new column
             +------------+
   ...
```

Of course, we could try to avoid this by deploying the backend code for the migrate phase together with the database code for the expand phase, but this just takes us back to the previous scenario: the "simultaneous" change, where we are still introducing a small data-loss window.

So, what do we do?

Solution: Temporary Database Trigger

In *Refactoring Databases*, the authors tackle this sort of scenario, and they suggest relying on a database trigger to address the synchronization between columns and cover the gap. The trigger would augment the existing expand and contract pattern and start synchronizing the old and new columns from the moment the new column is created. Following is an excerpt from Chapter 6 of that book:

> The following code depicts the DDL to rename `Customer.FName` to `Customer.First Name`, creates the `SynchronizeFirstName` trigger that synchronizes the data during the transition period, and removes the original column and trigger after the transition period ends.

```
ALTER TABLE Customer ADD FirstName VARCHAR (40);
COMMENT ON Customer.FirstName 'Renaming of FName column, finaldate =
November 14 2007'

COMMENT ON Customer.FName 'Renamed to FirstName,
dropdate = November 14 2007';

UPDATE Customer SET FirstName = FName;

CREATE OR REPLACE TRIGGER SynchronizeFirstName
BEFORE INSERT OR UPDATE
ON Customer
REFERENCING OLD AS OLD NEW AS NEW
FOR EACH ROW
DECLARE
BEGIN
IF INSERTING THEN
IF :NEW.FirstName IS NULL THEN

:NEW.FirstName := :NEW.FName;
END IF;
IF :NEW.Fname IS NULL THEN
:NEW.FName := :NEW.FirstName;
END IF;
END IF;

IF UPDATING THEN
IF NOT (:NEW.FirstName=:OLD.FirstName) THEN
:NEW.FName:=:NEW.FirstName;
END IF;
IF NOT (:NEW.FName=:OLD.FName) THEN
```

```
  :NEW.FirstName:=:NEW.FName;
  END IF;
  END IF;
  END;
```

This certainly works. As you can see in Figure 10-3, the database trigger takes care of synchronizing the data in the two columns until the backend can step in.

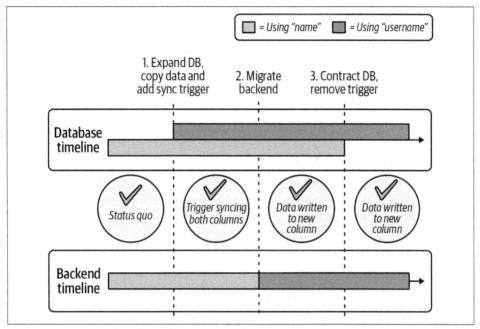

Figure 10-3. Expand and contract with database trigger

This is what will happen to the table data:

```
+------------+------------+
| name       | username   |
+------------+------------+
| alice      | alice      |  <- expand phase: new column is
| bob        | bob        |     created, all existing values are copied
| shinji     | shinji     |     and trigger is added
+------------+------------+
| mari       | mari       |  <- trigger synchronizing columns as backend writes
| rei        | rei        |     to the old one
+------------+------------+
| null       | gendo      |  <- migration phase: backend starts
| null       | misato     |     writing to new column only
+------------+------------+
             | asuka      |  <- contract phase: old column is removed
             | ritsuko    |
             +------------+
  ...
```

However, if you're like me and you're not exactly thrilled to be implementing important logic in SQL (and you just generally shiver at the thought of database triggers), you might find the next two solutions more interesting.

Solution: Double-Write

If we want to avoid database triggers but still want to solve our issue, we can make a different addition to our existing expand and contract pattern: once we have expanded the database column, we must implement a double-writing mechanism for both columns. Once that is in place, we can also synchronize past data so that the new column is fully self-contained. Then, we can finally switch to the new column completely without incurring any data loss (this is the strategy we used with the basket column in the previous chapter).

Following is a step-by-step explanation of this strategy.

Step 1: Expand the database column

We can begin with a first deployment on the database layer, which duplicates the column. All values in the new column are NULL at this point, and both writes and reads are still targeting the old column.

Also, to prepare for the backend to stop writing on the new column, we can relax any NOT NULL constraints on name. These changes are depicted in Figure 10-4.

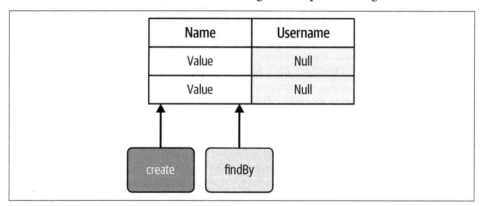

Figure 10-4. The expand step in the double-write strategy

Step 2: Double-write to both columns

Next, we can deploy code on the backend that will write to both columns. New values in username will start getting populated, but old values will remain NULL for now. Any update operations should also reflect on both columns but be tolerant of existing NULLs in the new column (Figure 10-5).

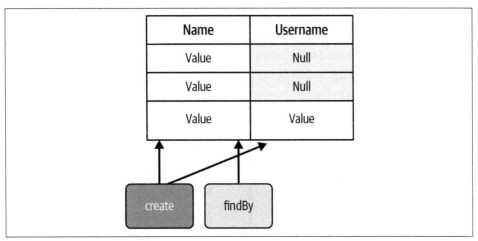

Figure 10-5. The double-write step in the double-write strategy

Step 3: Synchronize the data

Now that new data is being written, we can also migrate previous entries. By deploying a new database evolution, we can synchronize all existing values. This means the new table should not contain any more NULLs (past or future), so we can put stronger constraints on it in the same database evolution (Figure 10-6).

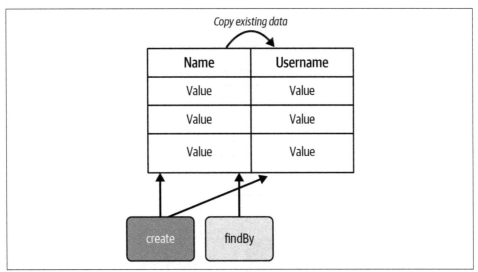

Figure 10-6. The synchronize data step in the double-write strategy

Step 4: Migrate write and read the columns

The new column is kept up-to-date (and is a reliable source of truth for past data as well), so we can start relying on it for both reads and writes.

We can start reading from it and stop writing to the old column. As a consequence, the old column will start getting filled with NULLs (Figure 10-7).

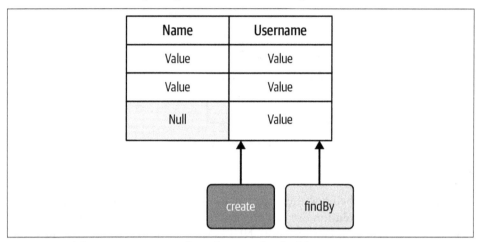

Figure 10-7. The migrate write and read step in the double-write strategy

Step 5: Contract the columns

Finally, we can remove the old column, which is unused (Figure 10-8).

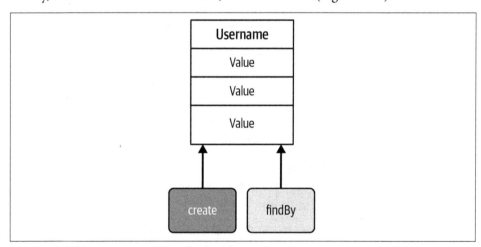

Figure 10-8. The contract step in the double-write strategy

Overall, this process ensures that we are successfully writing new data to both columns before we synchronize past entries, removing the gap we observed in the previous sections. It essentially replaces the update logic of the database trigger with application code, which is more easily testable and observable.

Solution: Double-Read

A similar valid strategy is to implement a double-reading mechanism as a fallback, instead of a double-writing mechanism. We can ensure that the backend tries to read from both columns while it is migrating, essentially using the old column as a fallback. In this manner, we can tolerate NULL values in the new column until we sync all the existing data later on.

Step 1: Expand the database column

Just like before, the expand phase duplicates the column with a database evolution. The new column will be populated with NULLs. We should also prepare the old name column so that we can stop writing to it, removing any NOT NULL or other constraints (Figure 10-9).

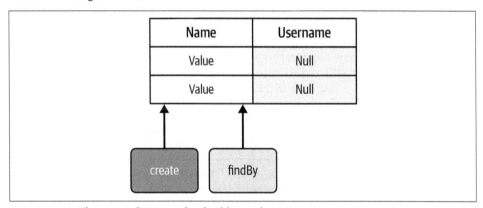

Figure 10-9. The expand step in the double-read strategy

Step 2: Double-read and migrate write to both columns

Next, we can implement a double-read mechanism: existing read operations must use either the new column or the old column interchangeably, keeping the value of whichever is not NULL (Figure 10-10). This allows us to also make the backend start writing to the new column, even in the same deployment. After this change, any value will be in either the new column (new data) or the old column (past data).

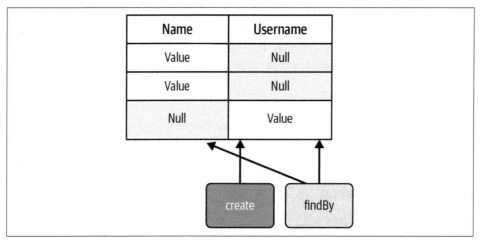

Figure 10-10. The double-read and migrate write step in the double-read strategy

Step 3: Synchronize the data

Now that the new column is the recipient of all new data, we can add a data synchronization step: a database evolution that will copy all past values to the new column. This evolution should not copy any NULLs from the old to the new, of course.

With this change, the new column should not have any more NULLs (past or future), so we can add a NOT NULL constraint to it if necessary (Figure 10-11).

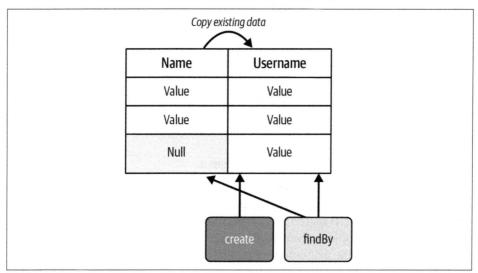

Figure 10-11. The synchronize data step in the double-read strategy

Step 4: Migrate the read

With the new column containing all data, the double-read mechanism has become obsolete. We can migrate the read operations to only rely on `username` (Figure 10-12).

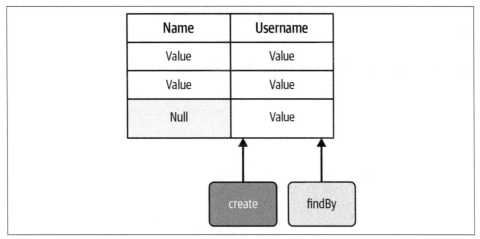

Figure 10-12. The migrate read step in the double-read strategy

Step 5: Contract the old column

Now that the old column is unused, we can once again contract it (Figure 10-13).

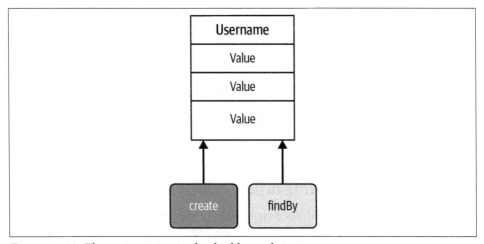

Figure 10-13. The contract step in the double-read strategy

This process, like the previous one, relies on the backend supporting both versions of the column for a time. The main difference is that the duplicated logic affects read operations instead of write operations. These are both augmentations of the traditional expand and contract pattern.

Next, I'll show code examples for how to implement the two alternatives.

Implementing with Double-Write

First, let's have a look at how we can reach the codebase target state with the double-write strategy.

Deployment 1: Expand the Database Column

Let's start with the status quo. We already have production data in our `users` table (simplified here), which of course needs to be supported and preserved throughout:

```
groceroo=# select * from users;
            user_id               | name
----------------------------------+------
 5c176075-fd2c-4e92-9875-4060453de761 | rei
 887677f2-276f-4731-89ab-6acdd3a51bfc | mari
(2 rows)
```

As mentioned, we can proceed with the expansion now. We can add the new `user name` ❶ column. We can also drop the NOT NULL constraint on the old column ❷ so that we can safely stop writing to it later. We can do both in the following evolution:

Persistence < API < UI

```
ALTER TABLE USERS ADD COLUMN USERNAME TEXT; ❶

ALTER TABLE USERS ALTER COLUMN NAME DROP NOT NULL; ❷
```

Immediately after the migration, the situation in the database is that we now have both columns whose usernames are NULL:

```
groceroo=# select * from users;
            user_id               | name  | username
----------------------------------+-------+----------
 5c176075-fd2c-4e92-9875-4060453de761 | rei   |
 887677f2-276f-4731-89ab-6acdd3a51bfc | mari  |
 32717619-cccb-4434-995a-5813aa8557aa | asuka |
(3 rows)
```

Deployment 2: Double-Write to Both Columns

Next, we will implement the double-write behavior on the backend. The repository will write to both the `name` and `username` columns ❶:

Persistence < **API** < UI

```
public User create(CreateUserPayload payload) {
  String insert = "INSERT INTO USERS(NAME, USERNAME)❶ VALUES (?,?) RETURNING
*";
  return jdbcTemplate.queryForObject(insert, new UserMapper(), payload.name(),
payload.name());
}
```

```
public User findBy(UUID id) {
    String query = "SELECT NAME, USER_ID FROM USERS WHERE USER_ID = ?";
    return jdbcTemplate.queryForObject(query, new UserMapper(), id);
}
```

When this code gets deployed to production, the new column will start being populated as well as the old, as you can see from the new record shown in the following example:

```
groceroo=# select * from users;
            user_id                  | name   | username
-------------------------------------+--------+----------
 5c176075-fd2c-4e92-9875-4060453de761 | rei    |
 887677f2-276f-4731-89ab-6acdd3a51bfc | mari   |
 32717619-cccb-4434-995a-5813aa8557aa | asuka  |
 7b18d979-dd4b-4b67-bfb4-ca127275547c | shinji | shinji
(4 rows)
```

However, all previous values are still NULL, which is something we will fix in the next deployment.

Deployment 3: Synchronize the Data

Now that data is being written to username, it's time to synchronize the old values as well ❶, which we can do with the following database evolution, Notice how, in the same database evolution, I have also added a NULL constraint ❷. I was able to do this because, at this stage, we don't expect any NULLs in the column (past or future):

Persistence < API < UI

```
UPDATE USERS SET USERNAME = NAME WHERE USERNAME IS NULL; ❶

ALTER TABLE USERS ALTER COLUMN USERNAME SET NOT NULL; ❷
```

Here is how the data will start looking in production. Both columns continue to be populated with the same data, since the double-write is still in effect:

```
groceroo=# select * from users;
            user_id                  | name   | username
-------------------------------------+--------+----------
 7b18d979-dd4b-4b67-bfb4-ca127275547c | shinji | shinji
 5c176075-fd2c-4e92-9875-4060453de761 | rei    | rei
 887677f2-276f-4731-89ab-6acdd3a51bfc | mari   | mari
 32717619-cccb-4434-995a-5813aa8557aa | asuka  | asuka
(4 rows)
```

Deployment 4: Migrate Write and Read to Both Columns

Finally, we can proceed with the migration phase. Now that both columns have up-to-date data being written to, we can safely switch both reading ❶ and writing ❷ to

---

the new column. The following change takes us to the target state we imagined for our backend:

Persistence < API < UI

```
...

public User create(CreateUserPayload payload) {
    String insert =  "INSERT INTO USERS(USERNAME) ❷ VALUES (?) RETURNING *";
    return jdbcTemplate.queryForObject(insert, new UserMapper(), payload.name());
}

public User findBy(UUID id) {
    String query = "SELECT USERNAME ❶, USER_ID FROM USERS WHERE USER_ID = ?";
    return jdbcTemplate.queryForObject(query, new UserMapper(), id);
}
...
```

Since we are writing to only the new username column, the old name column will start receiving NULL values, as shown in the following code. This doesn't throw an exception, because we had dropped the NOT NULL constraint in the expand phase:

```
groceroo=# select * from users;
               user_id                |  name  | username
--------------------------------------+--------+----------
 7b18d979-dd4b-4b67-bfb4-ca127275547c | shinji | shinji
 5c176075-fd2c-4e92-9875-4060453de761 | rei    | rei
 887677f2-276f-4731-89ab-6acdd3a51bfc | mari   | mari
 32717619-cccb-4434-995a-5813aa8557aa | asuka  | asuka
 be55336e-3e90-4e38-abc4-20a0d07058cb |        | gendo
(5 rows)
```

At this point, we can safely consider the old name column deprecated. All historical data is migrated to the new column, and new data is also just added to it. The old column is unused and will fill up with null values as time goes on. This means we can proceed with the contract phase.

Deployment 5: Contract the Columns

The contract phase is very simple. We just need to deploy an evolution that drops the old column:

Persistence < API < UI

```
ALTER TABLE USERS DROP COLUMN NAME;
```

As you can see in the following code, we have now reached the desired target state for the database schema as well:

```
groceroo=# select * from users;
               user_id                | username
--------------------------------------+----------
 7b18d979-dd4b-4b67-bfb4-ca127275547c | shinji
 5c176075-fd2c-4e92-9875-4060453de761 | rei
```

```
887677f2-276f-4731-89ab-6acdd3a51bfc | mari
32717619-cccb-4434-995a-5813aa8557aa | asuka
be55336e-3e90-4e38-abc4-20a0d07058cb | gendo
45343043-c710-4666-be94-c8ac77ced7d9 | misato
(6 rows)
```

We have successfully refactored our database schema in production with the help of safe continuous deployments—and preserved data integrity throughout.

Implementing with Double-Read

As I explained in "How Do We Get There?" on page 279, we can also implement double-column support in the backend with read operations instead of write operations. Let's see how.

Deployment 1: Expand the Database Column

Just like before, we are starting from an existing table that is very much in use and already contains data:

```
groceroo=# select * from users;
              user_id                 | name
--------------------------------------+------
 5c176075-fd2c-4e92-9875-4060453de761 | rei
 887677f2-276f-4731-89ab-6acdd3a51bfc | mari
(2 rows)
```

Again, just like before, we can add the new username column alongside the old one ❶ and drop the existing NOT NULL constraint on name ❷:

Persistence < API < UI

```
ALTER TABLE USERS ADD COLUMN USERNAME TEXT; ❶

ALTER TABLE USERS ALTER COLUMN NAME DROP NOT NULL; ❷
```

This leaves us with historical data intact in the name column, but only NULL values for username:

```
groceroo=# select * from users;
              user_id                 | name  | username
--------------------------------------+-------+----------
 46803928-1665-4c89-800c-b5d481afa729 | rei   |
 84ad1c4d-7bc6-49ae-86ba-e5ec7220423e | mari  |
 94018957-06cd-4d61-9481-5889e629baff | asuka |
(3 rows)
```

Deployment 2: Double-Read and Migrate Write the Columns

Next, we want to perform the write migration and double-read phase. We can have the backend write to the username column ❶, but try to read from both (prioritizing username) ❷. Following is the repository code to achieve this:

Persistence < **API** < UI

```
...

    public User create(CreateUserPayload payload) {
        String insert = "INSERT INTO USERS(USERNAME) ❶ VALUES (?) RETURNING *";
        return jdbcTemplate.queryForObject(insert, new UserMapper(), pay
load.name());
    }

    public User findBy(UUID id) {
        String query = "SELECT COALESCE(USERNAME, NAME) AS NAME ❷, USER_ID FROM
USERS WHERE USER_ID = ?";
        return jdbcTemplate.queryForObject(query, new UserMapper(), id);
    }

...
```

Here is how the table data will look. While all historical data lives on the old column, all new data lives in the new username column. Either one of them will be NULL, but never both of them:

```
groceroo=# select * from users;
              user_id                 | name  | username
--------------------------------------+-------+----------
 46803928-1665-4c89-800c-b5d481afa729 | rei   |
 84ad1c4d-7bc6-49ae-86ba-e5ec7220423e | mari  |
 94018957-06cd-4d61-9481-5889e629baff | asuka |
 6d2bf0f9-5049-4fbc-9e25-53a45b50609e |       | shinji
(4 rows)
```

The double-read mechanism lets us exploit this fact by using name as a fallback. Next, we need to make the new column self-contained so that we can remove the fallback later.

Deployment 3: Synchronize the Data

Just like before, we can now synchronize older data ❶ and reintroduce a NOT NULL constraint ❷ with this database evolution:

Persistence < API < UI

```
UPDATE USERS SET USERNAME = NAME WHERE USERNAME IS NULL; ❶
ALTER TABLE USERS ALTER COLUMN USERNAME SET NOT NULL; ❷
```

This results in the table looking like this, as old values are carried over to username, but nothing is being written to name anymore:

```
groceroo=# select * from users;
             user_id              | name  | username
----------------------------------+-------+----------
 46803928-1665-4c89-800c-b5d481afa729 | rei   | rei
 84ad1c4d-7bc6-49ae-86ba-e5ec7220423e | mari  | mari
 94018957-06cd-4d61-9481-5889e629baff | asuka | asuka
 6d2bf0f9-5049-4fbc-9e25-53a45b50609e |       | shinji
(4 rows)
```

Deployment 4: Migrate Read the Column

Now that the new column is self-contained, we can rely on it completely for reading, which means we can remove the fallback logic from our repository ❶:

Persistence < API < UI

```
...

  public User create(CreateUserPayload payload) {
    String insert = "INSERT INTO USERS(USERNAME) ❶ VALUES (?) RETURNING *";
    return jdbcTemplate.queryForObject(insert, new UserMapper(), pay
load.name());
  }

  public User findBy(UUID id) {
    String query = "SELECT USERNAME, USER_ID FROM USERS WHERE USER_ID = ?";
    return jdbcTemplate.queryForObject(query, new UserMapper(), id);
  }
...
```

The name column is now unused, and the backend is in its desired target state.

Deployment 5: Contract the Columns

Finally, we can shrink the database schema again, dropping the unused column:

Persistence < API < UI

```
ALTER TABLE USERS DROP COLUMN NAME;
```

This brings our database to the desired target state:

```
groceroo=# select * from users;
             user_id              | username
----------------------------------+----------
 6d2bf0f9-5049-4fbc-9e25-53a45b50609e | shinji
 46803928-1665-4c89-800c-b5d481afa729 | rei
 84ad1c4d-7bc6-49ae-86ba-e5ec7220423e | mari
 94018957-06cd-4d61-9481-5889e629baff | asuka
(4 rows)
```

NoSQL

If your persistence layer is not relational, you might think this chapter did not apply to you. You would be wrong. Even if your database system doesn't enforce a strict schema when writing, it doesn't mean that its clients don't rely on the objects they retrieve being a certain shape (effectively an implicit schema on reading). You should always be careful to keep backward compatibility in your deployments, regardless of the presence of a formal schema.

Even if you are using MongoDB, Redis, DynamoDB, or just plain old files, all of the techniques from this chapter can apply. Executing them, however, might be a little trickier than our example with simple SQL. This is because, while you can implement double writing or double reading in code, most nonrelational databases do not offer batch update or schema evolution tools. Unlike when using a relational database, we can't run an `UPDATE TABLE` and immediately migrate all documents in a MongoDB collection.

Of course, this leaves the problem of how to synchronize old data, especially if we have many records that aren't updated frequently by clients. Here, we have two choices: we can simply keep backward compatibility until all old data is eventually rewritten (or disappears), or we can also implement a background job to perform the migration for all records in our collection.

Migrate on Read

If we can't, or don't want to, update old records, there's an option to let our application code keep doing the heavy lifting of conversion by retaining backward compatibility for a longer period of time.

We can use this approach in two ways.

Migrate on read forever

We can keep old data as it is and let the code convert it at read time indefinitely. This is not ideal, but it is sometimes inevitable when our data store is immutable by design. This means that if we refactor our code data structures multiple times, we might have to keep many versions of our migrate-on-read logic.

Although this strategy might discourage us from refactoring our database often, there are ways that it can be made more tolerable. For example, some years ago I had the good fortune to work on a system with a by-the-book implementation of Command Query Responsibility Segregation (CQRS) and event sourcing. This meant that the event store was append-only, and there was no way to alter old records. This was for good reason: as the system was used by the country's treasury, it needed to be completely auditable and maintain a spotless record of all the transactions that flowed through it.

However, the team still wanted to change the shape of the event classes in the codebase, whose names and fields mapped closely to the event payloads. Such a tight coupling between data and application code meant that it was really hard to refactor, even when we needed to amend the domain language. Even renaming a simple field was complicated and required deserialization tricks, especially if it was renamed more than once. As you can imagine, more complex refactorings were completely out of the question.

This prompted us to implement a permanent migrate-on-read system. The system altered the shape of the events right after reading their raw payload from the database, but *before* they got converted into our domain objects. We started to store each event document with a version in it, with no version implying version = 0. Each new refactoring would cause a version bump and required the creation of an "event upgrader" function whose job was to convert any event of a given version $N - 1$ to version N. Once all the upgrader functions had been applied in sequence, the event's payload could be used to instantiate its class with the latest code.

This might seem like a lot of overhead (and it was!), but this mechanism was confined to a small area of the codebase, and it gave us the crucial freedom to refactor our classes while still keeping the system compliant to strong auditability requirements. In short: not all is lost if you cannot touch existing data.

Migrate on read and convert on write

Fortunately, most systems don't have such strict requirements on data changes. When we *are* allowed to actually make updates, we can simply change write operations so that they create or update records to the new format. This means that both data shapes in the database will coexist until the old data fades away and all records are completely rewritten. Of course, until that moment, the application code needs to be able to read from both.

For example, I have used this approach in a product data ingestion system that was in charge of consuming product data from an XML feed and then writing it to storage. Whenever we had to make changes to the "schema" in our own storage, we would make the application read both formats first. Then, we could deploy code that updated the writes to the new format.

This system refreshed the full product catalog from scratch every night, so we could simply clean up the backward-compatible code the day after, when the old data had already disappeared.

I find that this approach is ideal for such a scenario: where "old data" is short-lived, or has an expiration date after which it becomes irrelevant.

Custom Batch Update

If we want all data to match the new shape as quickly as possible, we can also add a background job that takes care of updating all the old records. Its execution should always follow the deployment that makes the code write in the new format, to prevent data in the deprecated shape from being accidentally written *after* the migration. Such a background job is necessary for applications in which old data does not expire. At least, that is if we want to clean up our backward-compatible code at some point.

In the same product-data ingestion system from the preceding section, for example, we also maintained collections with data that was not "copied over" from someone else's feed, and for which our service was the source of truth (i.e., older data couldn't be erased). This meant that we had to adopt this strategy for those other collections, effectively mixing approaches. This can be a common occurrence if you use NoSQL for a variety of data coming from different sources.

Conclusion on NoSQL

Overall, even if migrating data with NoSQL databases is trickier, it doesn't mean that NoSQL databases discourage refactoring. In fact, it might be quite the opposite. For example, the fallback mechanisms I described throughout this chapter are easier to manage in NoSQL than with a traditional relational database. Double-write is easy because there is no write schema to update first: the backend can just start writing whatever it wants, whenever it wants. Double-read can be easier too because queries themselves don't need to specify column names, and you can handle the fallback entirely in code.

With NoSQL, once you have figured out your relevant data migration mechanism(s), you can apply any of the techniques from this chapter without worrying about updating an explicit schema.

Summary

In this chapter, I explained how databases and persistence layers in general are affected by automated deployments to production. When refactoring, we might need to change the contract of a persistence layer, which requires special consideration as any temporary incompatibility might cause data loss.

First, you learned some strategies that don't work: changing evolutions and backend simultaneously, and applying a "traditional" expand and contract pattern. Then, we explored the strategies that *do* work: database triggers, and supporting multiple versions of the schema on the consumer side as well as the provider side. In particular, the latter can be achieved with two techniques that augment expand and contract: double writes or double reads to the persistence layer.

Zooming in on the implementation of these two strategies, you saw how they allow us to incrementally change the persistence layer in production without risking data loss. Being comfortable with applying this thought process is one of the key aspects of practicing continuous deployment safely. These strategies can also be applied to NoSQL types of storage, with the caveat that there needs to be an alternative data synchronization mechanism.

After Development

Part IV explores the post-development activities that bring the process of continuous deployment to fruition. It explains how to safely conduct exploratory testing in production, and discusses release and A/B testing strategies.

CHAPTER 11

Testing in Production

In this chapter, I'll talk about the benefits of testing in production, which is the environment we share with our users. I'll cover why it is worthwhile and how to do it safely.

When we test in production, we still hide prerelease features from users until we are ready to reveal them, but we segregate the behavior using logic built into our application instead of via separate deployments. You're already familiar with the techniques around feature flagging that we use to disable unfinished features. In previous chapters, I also mentioned how most feature flag frameworks allow for sophisticated toggle ON strategies. Some of those strategies are particularly interesting because they allow developers, QA engineers, and selected stakeholders to peek under a toggle to verify the feature. That's what we will cover in this chapter.

In particular, we'll look at the most common activation strategies we can leverage to perform exploratory testing, and the trade-offs between them (have another look at Chapters 3 and 8 if you want to refresh your knowledge on feature toggles in general). We'll also cover how to manage test data, debugging, and other challenges. This lets us build our confidence that the features work like they should in the most authentic context possible: production.

Overall, testing features in production is not just *possible* for continuous deployment teams: it should be part of their routine. Production exploratory tests should at the very least be done in addition to the preproduction tests we are all used to—and if they are good enough, a team might choose to *exclusively* test in production. If you want to know what that looks like, keep reading.

Why You Should Test in Production

Overall, exploratory testing directly in production provides much better insights into how software behaves in the real world and helps uncover issues that are simply not reproducible in preproduction. Seeing features work in production gives greater confidence to stakeholders and developers alike, lowering the decision barrier for releases and leading to much quicker experimentation.

I will now expand upon the ways in which production testing is more accurate than preproduction testing.

In both theory and practice, production environments are the most reliable way to confidently test production conditions. In theory, even the most well-maintained staging environment suffers from limitations in how closely its configuration, data, traffic, and software reproduce in production. In practice, a well-maintained staging environment is also a rarity in and of itself, due to the difficulty in coordinating shared environments across multiple teams (and the high engineering cost in doing so). The following subsections detail some common ways that testing in production offers more reliable conditions for establishing trust in an upcoming release.

Data Volume Accuracy

The size of data in databases, filesystems, caches, queues, or any state storage engine in production is not comparable to that in preproduction. Preproduction storage usually contains only whatever sample data is used for manual testing, or it contains seed data for automated tests, which is trivial in volume.

This difference means that we might discover nonperformant database queries, evolutions, or updates only when they are applied to production. Also, code that manipulates data collections resulting from those queries can suffer from similar issues. It is not possible to know whether it will be performant with large inputs until it is actually executed in that scenario.

All of these issues only become visible when the code runs on realistic and much bigger data sets.

Think, for example, of a report functionality that has to process large amounts of data and condense it into a nicely formatted *.csv* or *.pdf* file. It might run just fine in preproduction, only for us to discover that the report generation takes ages in production. The worst part is that this will only be discovered upon release.

If we tested that functionality in production instead (under a feature toggle), we would spot the performance problem much earlier, and we would have plenty of time to pivot. For example, we could introduce performance optimizations such as additional indexes or even let our product owner know that they should rethink the flow of the feature so that the report is provided asynchronously.

Some engineers might be tempted to solve this data volume mismatch by generating randomized filler data. This is still not ideal, because the frequency of certain values in a big data set (such as names or products) is another factor that can affect performance; for example, when caching or indexing. This approach is also vulnerable to another type of issue, which I will explain in the next section.

Data Shape Accuracy

Real, user-generated data is often well outside of what we can predict and generate when we think of a feature from the happy path perspective. Even the most creative QA engineers can have blind spots, and if a user can enter weird enough inputs to break a feature, they will.

Historical data lingering in production is an even more annoying issue. Like a diamond, user input is (usually) forever. Despite regulation by frameworks such as GDPR, most data is never deleted once it gets stored, and it will be hoarded in our systems for years. However, data is always subjected to the natural forces of our product evolving around it: the codebase storing it changes, it gets lugged from one system to another, and as a result, it is often tweaked or migrated to different formats along the way. Often, all of these accumulated changes leave older data in funny shapes that become archeological oddities only found in production.

Our code being incompatible with unexpected data, whether old or new, might cause unforeseen bugs to features that seemed to work fine with only the optimistic data set we created in preproduction.

For example, on one of the systems my team and I worked with, we had a problem with datetime precisions. It started like many problems start for software teams: at some unspecified point in our codebase's past, someone (maybe us?) had changed the date library. While the old library used to generate datetimes with second-level precision, the new one would generate them in milliseconds. Because of this, we ended up with products that had two slightly different date formats in the database. However, our system was accidentally smart enough to read both correctly, so this issue went unnoticed for a long time—long enough that the entire team had a chance to forget about the library change.

The slightly different formats were never a problem in production, until they were. A long while later, we introduced another system that had to consume product data from the original system. It turned out that this new system was *not* smart enough to handle both formats automagically. After testing it in preproduction, however, everything seemed fine: that is because we were generating new test data with the (reasonable) assumption that everything would follow the current date format. Obviously, shortly after release, the feature started failing in production, seemingly randomly. It was only upon taking a closer look that we noticed it was only failing when encountering products that were older than a year or so.

This could have been completely prevented if we had tested in production instead. If we had, we could have easily migrated the historical data to match, or we could have changed the code to handle both formats before the release.

Realistic Request Patterns

Speaking of user behavior, sometimes users break features by generating requests in patterns that we might not expect.

Think, for example, of users hitting their browser back button at a *very* inconvenient time while in the middle of a flow. Or, in the case of the report generation example from "Data Volume Accuracy" on page 306, users might be tempted to mash the report button if they perceive a delay, which can cause an accidental denial of service if the report is very resource intensive. Since this can only happen in production, where the report is bound to be slower, testing the functionality there can surface the issue earlier. Once it becomes evident, it can be handled, for example, by altering the UX to limit concurrent reports per user, or by disabling the button temporarily.

This type of problem can also be caught through A/B testing and canary releases, which I'll describe in the next chapter.

Realistic Incoming Traffic Volume

Preproduction machines receive hardly any traffic under normal circumstances. Thoroughly load-testing every change going through the pipeline is not really an economically viable or time-sensitive option either. Because of this, each change being tested in preproduction might hide performance issues, memory leaks, or any other type of resource exhaustion defect. In addition, even the best load tests usually don't replicate fully realistic traffic patterns: production is a unique blend of specific traffic curves throughout the day, the number of reads versus writes, the delay between specific requests, and so on and so on.

If we have our feature under a toggle, we can test its performance in production through a canary deployment, through shadow traffic, or by releasing it to a small section of users.

Realistic Outgoing Traffic Volume

In addition to realistic incoming traffic to the application, we must also consider realistic outgoing traffic *from* the application.

When our system relies on any downstream system to fulfill its contract, there will be a tight coupling between incoming requests and outgoing requests. These outgoing requests can affect the number of open network sockets/open files, application-facing connection pools, cache behavior…which can all cause problems when the application is faced with some realistic load coming from users. On top of that, most of the aspects affected by outgoing traffic are likely to be configured differently in production in the first place.

Realistic Size and Number of Servers

Preproduction environments are almost always smaller than production environments in terms of number of machines or containers, as the very low incoming traffic keeps scaling activity quiet. This can hide bugs that only show up when more than one instance is running (think of different instances competing for external resources, or code accidentally relying on the user hitting the same instance for consecutive requests).

If we wanted to fix this issue, we *could* configure staging so that it always runs with roughly the same number of machines. But then we would need to explain to our stakeholders why their cloud provider bills have doubled. It is much easier to test in production directly.

While replicating horizontal scaling is at least somewhat achievable, this is often not the case with vertical scaling (i.e., the size of the machines themselves). If you have to deal with actual servers or virtual machines, it is especially common for preproduction infrastructure to be a low-powered version of the real thing. Instances, in addition to being fewer in number, are likely to have fewer resources, such as memory and CPU cores, making it hard to tell whether our code can make the most out of a powerful server. For example, if we test on production instances, we might find that we can parallelize some tasks differently to make the most out of a high number of CPUs. With more memory per instance, we might also find out that we can make application caching policies more aggressive.

Realistic Application Configuration

Application configuration can differ between production and preproduction in many ways. For example, there can be variations in database configurations, including connection strings, credentials, and settings around connection pools. External service configurations such as third-party services, authentication, and access privileges may differ too. While preproduction environments use sandbox or stub APIs, the production environment connects to the actual third-party services, which might not respect exactly the same contract. Authentication settings, thread pool size, internal URLs, caching policies...any line in our application config that differs between production and preproduction is a potential minefield of surprises when releasing.

Realistic Network Configuration

Any infrastructure in preproduction will likely be accessible only from within the organization, making the network setup look very different. The first obvious difference is the presence of authentication or IP-based restrictions. Having far fewer users in staging also means that content delivery networks (CDNs) or proxy services such as Cloudflare and Akamai might be absent or configured very differently. Their caching policies might be set up differently too: caching heavily in production to protect the origin servers but not caching at all in preproduction to allow for easier testing. This introduces yet another surprising difference between environments that is often forgotten.

Different rules might also apply to outbound requests. Think, for example, of corporate proxies allow-listing only certain domains. These network differences can show up in unexpected ways when we connect our applications to other services in the outside world.

In one of my teams, a task once remained blocked on our board for a month because of a restrictive network configuration that was present in production only. This was blocking our app from talking to a specific third-party system. Fortunately, we were deploying and testing in production frequently, which allowed us to discover the issue during development. Because of this, we were able to parallelize other work while the issue was fixed by the appropriate team. If we had not deployed anything, or if we had not tested in production until the very end, things would have looked pretty bad for our release deadline.

Real Version of Other Teams' Services

We don't have many guarantees about how other teams' preproduction applications are managed: how similarly they are configured to the real thing, what test data they have been seeded with, and whether their deployed version corresponds to the live one during our testing. The big assumption made by each team testing service integration in preproduction is that they are verifying version $N + 1$ of their service against version N of all other services, where N is the current production version. But if all teams make that same assumption, then the preproduction integration starts to look more like a cluster of $N + 1$ versions talking to each other, with no guarantee of what will happen once one of them is released.

And things are hardly that simple. As teams accumulate different changes, some services will be at their $N + 2$ or $N + 10$ version, or they could have even been reverted back to $N - 1$, all of which could change at any moment, before or after our testing. Overall, the only way we can guarantee the integration with the live version of surrounding services is by checking and monitoring the integration in production itself.

Real Version of Third-Party Services

If we have few guarantees about other teams' test environments, we have even fewer guarantees with sandboxes provided by third-party vendors, which is often all we can use in preproduction. There is additional communication overhead whenever we need to figure out if their preproduction will behave similarly to the production at all.

Testing these interactions in production is far more reliable, but the logistics of it can get a bit tricky. There need to be strong agreements on how to perform manual tests in prod, especially when the third-party system deals with sensitive or monetary transactions. Using test data incorrectly might lead to costly or awkward mistakes here. However, the criticality of these exchanges between systems is a reason in and of itself to make the extra effort and arrange for safe test data in production. If a mistake in one or two test transactions can be costly and awkward, a mistake with thousands of real transactions (caused by inaccurate pre-prod testing) can be very much worse. Testing in production guarantees that our system integration is sound in the environment that gives us the highest level of confidence.

Lower Cost

Load-testing in preproduction is a widely adopted practice by teams wanting to make sure their features are sound performance-wise. However, besides the high likelihood of being inaccurate, it can also get very expensive very quickly if done often, due to having to scale up extra resources. We can reduce the need for load testing (and also our cloud provider bills) by verifying our new features respond well to traffic with shadow traffic and/or canary releases instead. One of the companies I worked with also ran (gentler) load tests directly in production, to motivate the engineering teams to take scalability seriously.

Another cost factor being reduced is engineering cost, which is often orders of magnitude higher than infrastructure cost. The amount of engineering time needed to arrange for a realistic preproduction environment is high, and we can diminish it by testing most features directly in production instead.

Better Data Hygiene

Last but not least, wanting to have the "perfect" staging environment sometimes leads teams—either by accident or on purpose—to copy production data or traffic into their preproduction infrastructure. Even when this data can be somehow anonymized, this is a very risky practice and can lead to serious security incidents. It's also easy to slip into accidental noncompliance with regulations such as GDPR and CCPA. Furthermore, data anonymization can degrade testing accuracy even further.

To make things worse, staging storage is often configured with less-strict access restrictions than production. This not only increases the risk of exposing data, but it also introduces another way production can fail when staging works. We can avoid this by having another way to prove that features won't break once they are faced with real user data: seeing if they fail where the real user data lives in the first place.

How to Test in Production

We spent the first part of this chapter talking about the "why" of testing in production. Now let's talk about the "how."

I mentioned feature toggles a lot so far, and it is indeed feature toggles that are the main enablers of this practice. The way the simplest toggle works is with two states: the feature is ON for everyone or OFF for everyone. However, the majority of feature toggle frameworks have evolved well past those two simple states, and they now allow for much more sophistication. This is especially useful for exploratory testing. In the next section, I will talk about a few solutions that I use very often, and I will provide examples that will be based once again on our Groceroo application.

Feature Toggle Activation Strategies

The ideal feature flag configuration strategy for manual testing must respect just two criteria:

Precision
> It allows intentional targeting of specific users or requests (this excludes, for example, configurations such as traffic percentage, random assignment to A/B groups, and broad categories of users).

Ease of use
> This is not just for developers, but also for less technical stakeholders who might be interested in seeing the feature (i.e., our poor product owner shouldn't have to learn to use the terminal if they want to see the feature working).

There are many feature flag solutions out there, and there's a wide spectrum between completely managed feature flags as a service and custom-built solutions that you can implement from scratch. We can't possibly cover all of them or all of their unique features. That is why, for our examples, I will talk about configuration strategies in the abstract rather than refer to one specific tool. The rest of this section is meant to give you a broad idea of what is possible. You should check your framework to see if any other options are available in addition to (or instead of) what is covered here. Go ahead and be creative, as long as it respects those two criteria.

Now let's dive into our example. We will once again have a look at the first user story of our "last-minute items" carousel feature, which I described in detail in Chapter 6. Here is a refresher of the new feature we want to add:

Summary

As a user

I want to see a selection of last-minute possible purchases before I complete my order

So that I can quickly add anything I might have forgotten

Acceptance criteria

Given I have items in the basket

And the current shop has last-minute purchases configured

When I go to checkout

Then I should see a carousel with some last-minute purchases for the current shop

Given I have items in the basket

And the current shop does not have any last-minute purchases configured

When I go to checkout

Then I should see the normal checkout page without any extra carousel

Figure 11-1 is a mock-up of the carousel we want to show on our checkout page.

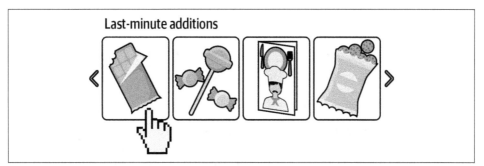

Figure 11-1. The "last-minute items" mock-up

Figure 11-2 shows the current status quo of the page in production.

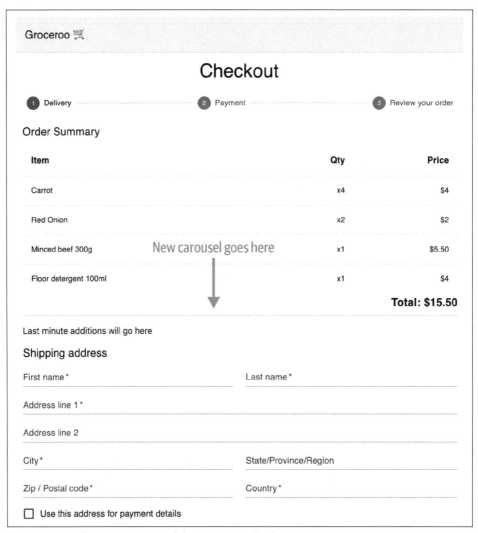

Figure 11-2. The current state of the Groceroo checkout page

As I mentioned, we want to test out this new feature in production without disturbing users. We are going to leverage different feature toggle configurations (mostly evaluated on the server side) so that the carousel is visible to us only while testing and the rest of the users keep seeing the "status quo" page. In these examples, we will rely on the feature toggle I showed in Chapter 8.

Query parameters

One of the most straightforward ways to do exploratory testing with a feature toggle is to use a query parameter to control its ON/OFF status. When the query parameter is present and set to the correct value, the state of the toggle will be ON only for that particular request, as shown in Figure 11-3.

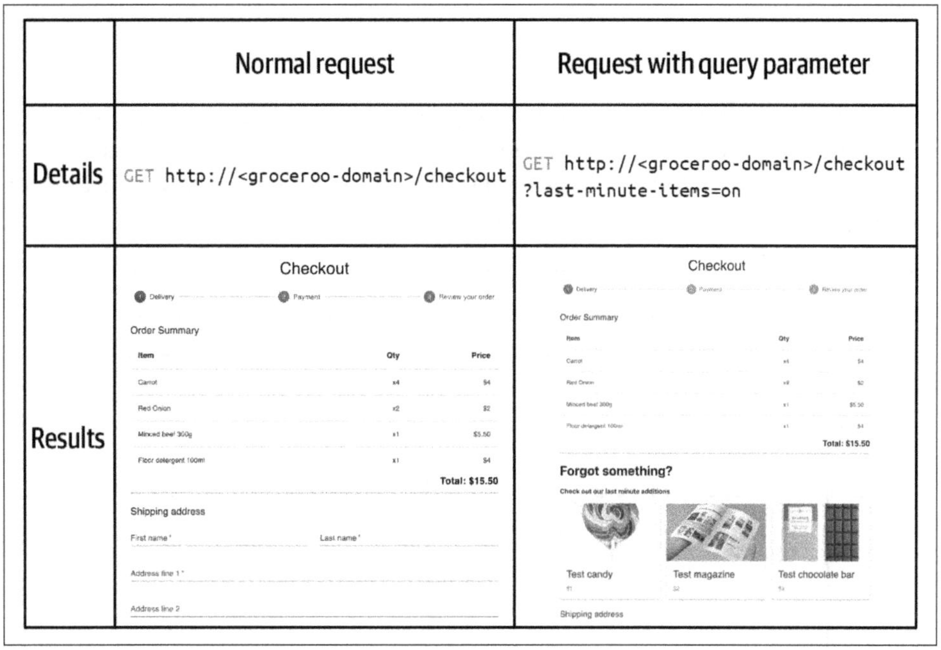

	Normal request	Request with query parameter
Details	`GET http://<groceroo-domain>/checkout`	`GET http://<groceroo-domain>/checkout ?last-minute-items=on`
Results		

Figure 11-3. A feature flag with a query parameter

Where to use. This strategy is very versatile, and in particular it is great for feature flags that operate on pages of applications rendered on the server side, where the query parameter will be evaluated once and then used throughout the backend and frontend code.

Single-page applications (SPAs) can also make use of query parameters, but ensuring that they stay confined to a specific "page" or route might get a bit awkward depending on your strategy for manipulating URLs within the SPA context.

Query parameters for feature flag values can also be used with pure API endpoints. However, while it's technically possible to use them, query params can feel unnatural when dealing with any HTTP verb other than GET. If we are adding a flag to a POST, PATCH, PUT, or DELETE endpoint, it could be better to see if we can control the activation status through a header or through the payload instead, provided it doesn't disturb serialization and deserialization.

When to use. Manipulating query params offers control and granularity, and all the convenience of a URL bar that sits right at the top of everyone's browser window. However, it can also become inconvenient if the feature we are building affects a user flow that consists of many requests in sequence. For example, it would quickly become annoying to test a multistep checkout flow like this, where every step is on a different URL.

Request headers

Custom headers are another powerful toggle activation strategy and one that I personally use very often. We can use headers in two ways: a single header that controls all feature flags (the X-Toggles code in Figure 11-4), or a different custom header for each toggle (X-Toggle-last-minute-items).

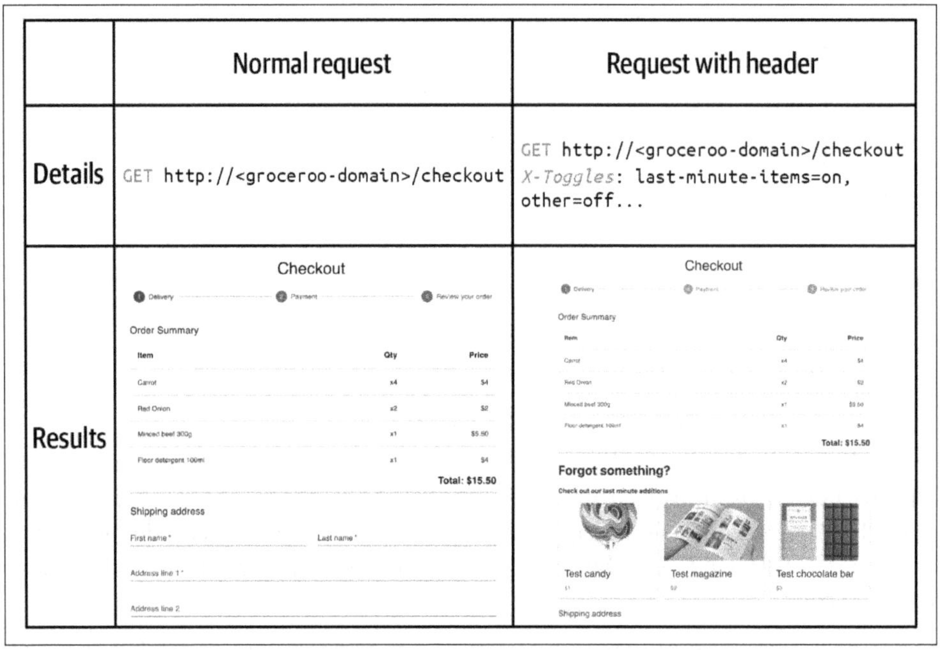

Figure 11-4. A feature flag with a custom header

Where to use. This strategy works really well for applications rendered on the server side, as well as pure HTTP APIs. However, it cannot be evaluated easily within static websites and/or apps rendered only on the client side. Their files are often statically served, so there won't be an easy option to add logic that interprets request headers. On the browser side, it's not possible to read the headers of the request that originated the current page.

When to use. Using custom headers, like query parameters, affects a toggle's state on a per-request basis, so they might be inconvenient for long user flows composed of many requests. However, unlike query parameters, there are many browser extensions that make it really easy to add custom headers to all requests indiscriminately (or even by domain). This means that testing long user flows with this strategy can be much more convenient than manipulating URLs, as one simply turns custom headers on and off as needed.

In my experience, these browser extensions are easy to use by even nontechnical folks, which is why they were a favorite strategy in my teams.

Cookies

Storing feature toggle activation in cookies can be thought of as a subset of the "headers" strategy. After all, cookies are just headers themselves. Once again, the activation happens on a per-request basis, but browsers' cookie management offers a layer of sophistication that makes them especially convenient for exploratory testing.

Just like before, we can have a specific cookie to store all toggle states, as shown in Figure 11-5, or even one cookie per toggle.

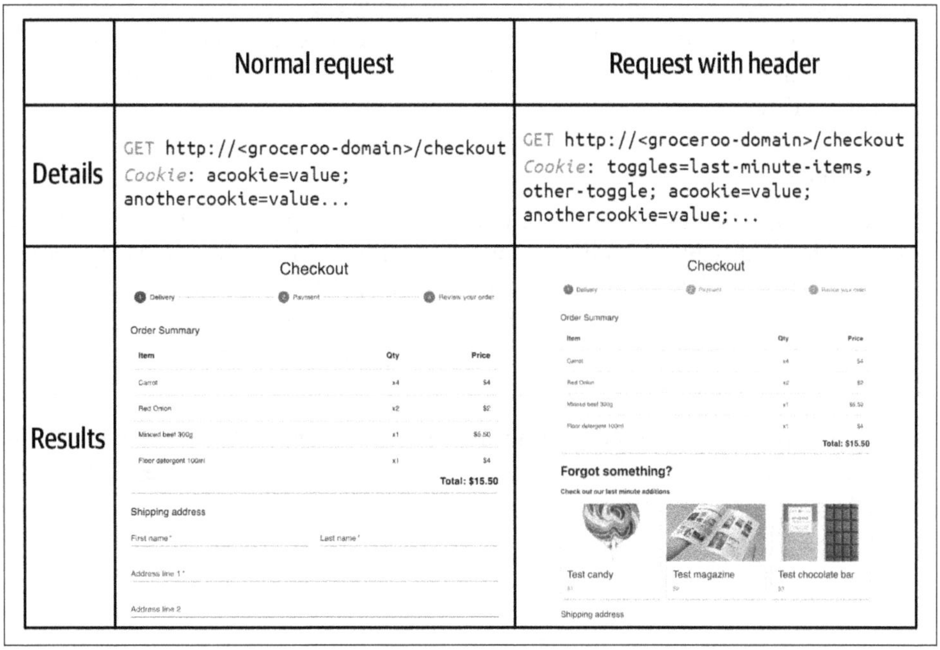

	Normal request	Request with header

Details	`GET http://<groceroo-domain>/checkout`
	`Cookie: acookie=value;`
	`anothercookie=value...`
		`GET http://<groceroo-domain>/checkout`
		`Cookie: toggles=last-minute-items,`
		`other-toggle; acookie=value;`
		`anothercookie=value;...`

Results		

Figure 11-5. A feature flag with a cookie

Where to use. Although cookies are just another header implementation-wise, they also come with perks due to the special treatment they receive from browsers. This special treatment enables several things. First and foremost is the evaluation on the browser side, because they are easily accessible via JavaScript. In addition, browsers store the cookie state in between page loads, as opposed to the headers, which will be simply forgotten. This means it is possible to set them once and then use them indefinitely (or at least until we clear the browser's data).

Another advantage of cookies is that they are managed completely by the browser. As a result, we can easily set them in our dev tools tab, and they are already domain specific. Therefore, we can go without the extra browser extensions (and fiddling with domains) that are needed for the request headers strategy.

One use case where I would discourage the use of cookies is pure HTTP APIs. Cookies are a browser-related concept, and it might be counterintuitive to read a cookie if we don't expect our application to be called from one.

When to use.   Cookies can be even more convenient than headers for long user flows. Instead of having to install custom extensions, browsers already natively offer ways to manipulate cookies that nondevelopers can easily use.

Due to their tendency to "stick around" for multiple requests, however, I would not recommend using cookies at all if it is important that the `toggle=on` value is sent only for the granularity of one request. Setting and unsetting cookies all the time can get repetitive and annoying.

User identifier

The last strategy I want to showcase is one that does not operate by the granularity of a request, but rather by all requests sent by the same application user. Many feature toggle frameworks allow developers to integrate their application's concept of what a "user" is, and when that is done, they enable toggle activation for a selected group. We might be able to specify users by their ID, username, email address, or any other attribute that uniquely identifies them.

In the context of the request, nothing in particular changes. Users authenticate as usual, and the application will decide if they are allowed to see the toggle, as shown in Figure 11-6.

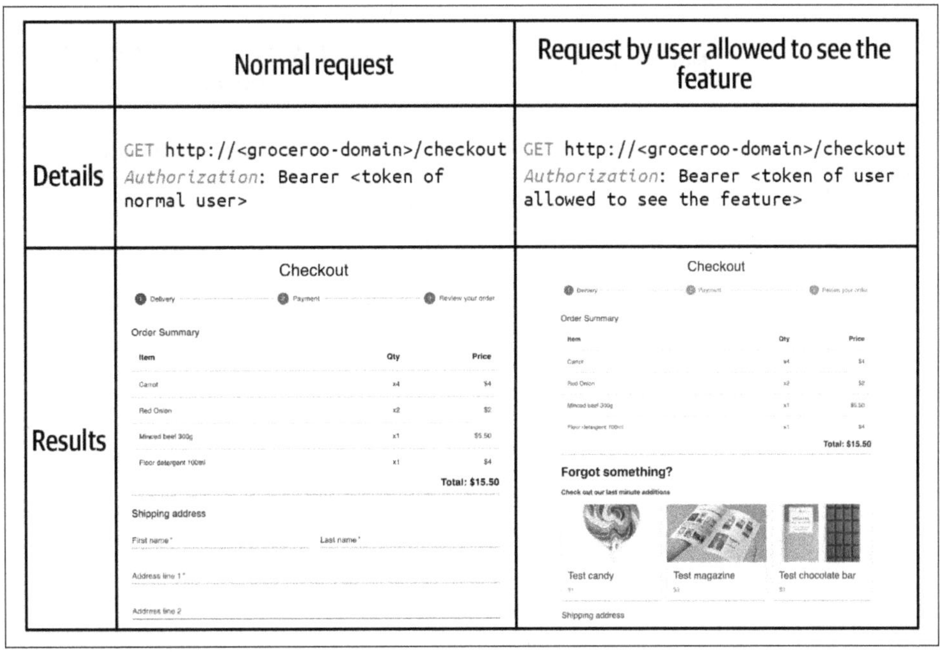

	Normal request	Request by user allowed to see the feature
Details	GET http://<groceroo-domain>/checkout Authorization: Bearer <token of normal user>	GET http://<groceroo-domain>/checkout Authorization: Bearer <token of user allowed to see the feature>
Results		

Figure 11-6. A feature flag with a user identifier

Where to use. This strategy can be used in any application where there is a meaningful concept of "user" and "log in."

When to use. This is an especially helpful strategy because it allows us to immediately allow-list users, such as our product owners and QAs, to see the feature without having them fiddle with individual requests or browser sessions. However, it has an important limitation: it can only be applied to systems where there is a strong concept of user identity.

User roles

Users are a standard and widespread concept supported by many applications, but your application may have other domain concepts to which we can attach prerelease behavior. For example, perhaps your application groups users into "roles," one of which could be flagged as having access to prerelease features (e.g., "admins" or "testers").

Just like with the previous strategy, users authenticate as usual, and the application will determine whether they belong to a group that is allowed to see the toggle (Figure 11-7).

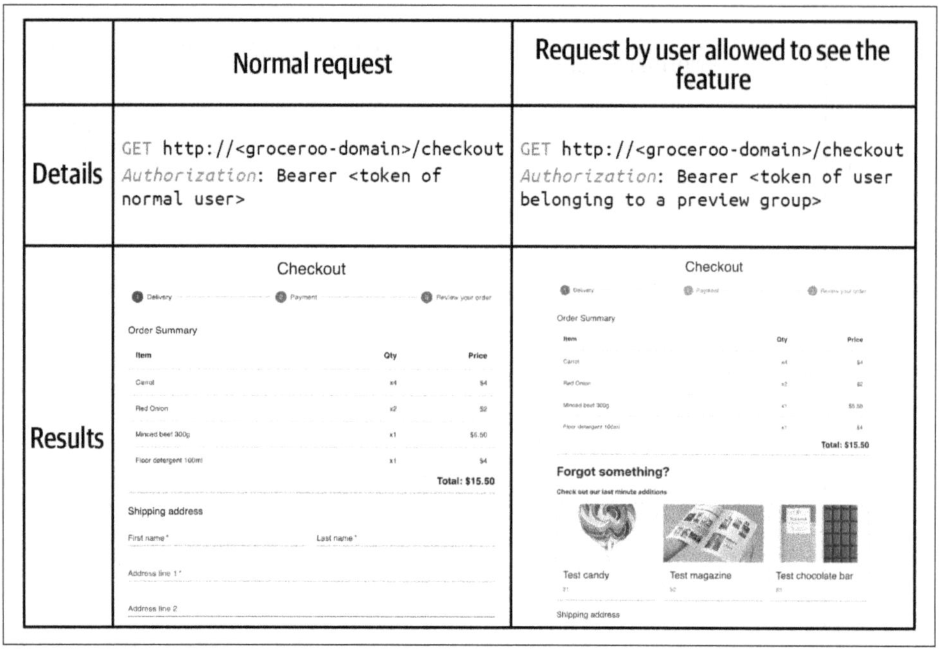

	Normal request	Request by user allowed to see the feature
Details	`GET` `http://<groceroo-domain>/checkout` `Authorization`: `Bearer <token of normal user>`	`GET` `http://<groceroo-domain>/checkout` `Authorization`: `Bearer <token of user belonging to a preview group>`
Results	Checkout ... Order Summary ... Total: $15.50 ... Shipping address ...	Checkout ... Order Summary ... Total: $15.50 ... Forgot something? Test candy ... Test magazine ... Test chocolate bar ...

Figure 11-7. A feature flag with a user role

Where to use. This strategy can be used whenever your application has a convenient domain concept that can be used to segregate behavior.

When to use. This is best used in applications where different features are available to different users as a matter of the requirements and business logic of the application itself. That way, you can reuse these configuration mechanisms for testing in production and expose prerelease functionality in a way that's natural to users of the application.

Challenges

In this section, I will cover some of the challenges that teams might encounter while switching their manual testing environment to production, along with some mitigations.

Managing test data

Unfortunately, not all features can be tested in production with the existing data already present in the system. Some features can only be verified by adding test-only data. Any production test can be roughly classified into two clusters: the kind that requires tinkering with data and the kind that doesn't.

Performing exploratory testing on features in the first cluster means altering or creating data with data that will impact other users or requests; for example, adding fake products with a new attribute we want to test or performing fake orders to trigger the checkout flow. This is not a problem when we are doing our exploratory testing in preproduction, but it can quickly become one when switching to production, where real users could stumble upon our experiments or our application needs to deal with monetary transactions.

Feature flags on their own are not enough to support this kind of production testing. It is imperative to also implement a test data strategy to ensure that test items are kept separate from real, user-generated data, both in reading and in writing.

This might seem like a daunting task. Allowing test data to exist in production can be scary because making mistakes in this area can result in awkward situations where fake (aka synthetic) transactions get mixed up with real ones. However, this is a reason in and of itself to make the extra effort and arrange for a framework to create safe test data in production. After all, if a mistake in one or two test transactions can be embarrassing, it means that the area is critical enough that we can't afford to potentially overlook bugs, which can affect thousands of *real* transactions.

Hiding test data. I have heard some colorful stories about hiding test data from users. For example, in a company where listings were searched by their location, developers were geotagging "test-only" listings so that they only showed up in an uninhabited island in the Pacific Ocean, where no user was likely to go look for them. Although this was clearly a stroke of genius, there are more sustainable ways to hide test data that don't run the risk of exposing unnecessary information to users who are bored enough to look for it.

The simplest approach I have witnessed has been to mark test data or transactions with a "test-only" flag. This way, it can be safely filtered out unless some specific conditions are true. The conditions under which test data can be shown in read-only operations can be managed the same way feature toggle activation is: for example, by adding special headers or query parameters to a request, or by enabling it for certain "superusers" only. In fact, test data being visible or invisible can be implemented as a feature flag in the first place, albeit a more permanent one.

Writing data can follow a very similar approach. Test-only data can be generated by hand (e.g., by seeding through database evolutions), or under very specific conditions such as a special header being sent or a form field being ticked. For example, one of our clients had a test production user who was allowed to make orders that bypassed the payment process. All of the orders generated with that user were promptly ignored by the system, and this allowed developers to perform plenty of production tests on post-checkout user flows, such as their "order confirmation" page and email. The test-only payment method for that user was even named "deduction from wages" ;). On other projects, colleagues saw magic credit card numbers that would trigger specific error cases with the payment. Whatever the strategy, I strongly recommend allowing test data writing for sensitive transactions. Even if you don't want to test in production, this can be useful for any environment.

When data is not visible throughout the system by default, another viable strategy is to create "test-only" groups of data that can be toggled on and off all at once.

Preventing test data leakages. With test data, one caveat to be aware of is what happens when our system exchanges data with others in our production network. We certainly don't want test items to leak to downstream systems that don't have any awareness of the fact that they should be hidden. If we are providers of an API, we might need to choose between different policies for test data:

- Test data is only local to our system, used for our own testing, and is never returned to consumers of our APIs.
- Allow consumers to optionally request test data by setting a specific flag, and let them take responsibility for handling it appropriately.
- Always return test data alongside real data, appropriately flagged. This is the option that requires the most communication, as the existence of test data becomes part of the contract and should always be managed by all consumers.

Wanting to keep things simple and isolate changes might tempt us to default to option 1, or maybe option 2. However, I encourage you to consider implementing option 3 instead.

One of the most powerful testing setups I have seen was in a company where the team managing product data *always* returned test items. All dependent teams were aware of this, and they all took the responsibility for managing and filtering it. This brought extra work and extra communication overhead, but it also gave a framework to all teams to adapt their consumers when data needed to change shape or new features were released. The product data team would provide examples of "test products" in advance, and everyone had a chance to update their system to reflect the new features, testing them in production for themselves.

Debugging frontend code

Debugging frontend JavaScript code that runs in the browser, especially in a production environment, presents distinct challenges compared to preproduction.

In production builds, JavaScript code undergoes thorough minification and optimization, altering variable and function names to shrink the bundle size. This makes the code nearly impossible to read and debug, even when testing a feature under toggle.

With the addition of transpilation, as for JSX and TypeScript, most modern frontend code is completely unrecognizable once it is packaged for users.

In preproduction environments, this issue is typically addressed by publishing source maps. *Source maps* are files that provide a mapping between the original, human-readable source code and the optimized, minified code that's actually executed by the browser. In particular, they allow the browser's developer tools to trace obfuscated code lines back to the original lines so that you can view source and set debugging breakpoints against a readable version of the code. This unlocks a much improved debugging experience, as engineers can use most of the browser's tools as if they were pointing to the original source code.

However, most teams these days exclude source maps from production for "security" purposes. Source maps expose the original, unminified code, which might contain sensitive information or proprietary logic, which many companies feel poses a risk. Therefore, omitting source maps in production has become a standard practice.

The case for source maps in production. In my opinion, the practice of excluding source maps from production should be challenged. Not only can they greatly help with production manual testing and debugging, but I find that "security by obscurity"[1] is not a reliable method of keeping information safe, nor is it a helpful mindset about security.

After all, even horribly obfuscated JavaScript code can be reverse-engineered, given enough patience and tooling. If it can be done for the code of the original Game Boy Pokémon games, it can definitely be done for any old website. If some logic in that code really represents a sensitive trade secret, it had best be moved to the backend, where it can be safely hidden away from curious eyes.

On a sort-of-ethical standpoint, one could even argue that the JavaScript code in question executes on the users' devices, not on servers owned by the company. Therefore, any user should be freely given access to a plain and legible version of it. This keeps companies accountable, and the internet an overall nicer place.

In conclusion, I warmly recommend enabling source maps in production. They only take an extra few seconds of build time, and they incur no performance penalty for normal users (they are only downloaded when opening the browser's developer tools). In return, they make frontend production code friendlier to developers and end users alike.

---

1 Security by obscurity is the reliance on secrecy as the main method of providing security to a system or component.

Where that is not possible, there are still possible workarounds: for example, hosting the source map files in separate production infrastructure that is IP restricted, or requiring special authentication headers.

Life After Staging

Performing production testing with feature toggles means that the time-consuming endeavor to build near-perfect, ever-so-complicated staging environments can finally diminish, or even become obsolete.

At the beginning of this chapter, I mentioned how teams might stop relying on staging completely when their production testing is good enough. Now that we have seen some techniques to get us to that "good enough" benchmark, let's see what life for those teams can look like.

Without reliance on staging, developers, QAs, and product owners can focus their testing in the same environment: production. Developers can use it to check how their in-progress code is evolving, QAs can later step in to verify the feature matches the acceptance criteria, the whole team can use it for important demos, and product owners can use it to sign features off for release. This means that different pre-prod environments won't be coupled to the team's delivery process anymore, and there won't be any confusion as to what is deployed and where, or even as to which feature toggles are active or inactive in which environment. This change to the team's workflow is summarized in Figure 11-8.

Preproduction infrastructure can be kept to the sensible minimum that is required by automated tests, so they can verify changes on infrastructure and integration. For example, this could include spinning up the application and the immediate surrounding infrastructure that it requires...but not attempting to connect staging to every third-party service, make it match the size of production, or fill it with "production-like" data. Staging doesn't need to be an overly engineered behemoth that integrates with anything and everything.

As a result, teams doing continuous deployment can have increasingly lightweight preproduction environments—and fewer of them. Some teams take yet another step and do away with preproduction infra altogether, only leveraging contract testing and stub containers to simulate the context surrounding their running application. By getting rid of staging, you get back a huge amount of time you can invest in alternative confidence measures. This could be seen as quite a radical approach, but I believe not needing to rely on preproduction at all is a worthwhile goal for any team, whether it decides to actually go a step further and physically remove the infrastructure or not. I believe continuous deployment gives us the perfect opportunity to rethink the usefulness of clunky staging environments, even though they have been an ever-present fixture in the industry.

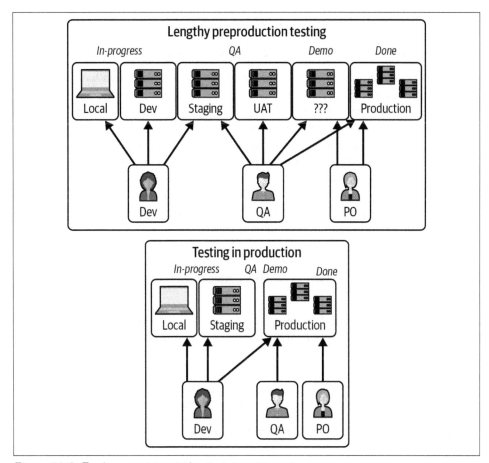

Figure 11-8. Environments mapping to team processes

Here, I will point you to one of the case studies in Part V: the company ClimatePartner, whose developers have decided to go without staging environments for most of their systems. Not only does this choice encourage good practices to test in production and reduce the company's costs, but it also helps reduce its carbon footprint (which is very much in line with its culture).

When writing this chapter, I was reminded of an old joke that I've heard often in programming forums. It goes like this:

> Everybody has a test environment. Some people are lucky enough to have a separate production environment.

This joke is a bit ancient: it seems to come from a time when it wasn't common to have thorough tests, and businesses weren't always willing to invest in preproduction infrastructure. Back then, defects could go to production unchecked and would possibly be hotfixed on the running servers directly. However, things have come a long way in most companies since then. Nowadays, extensive automated test suites are quite common, as are very elaborate preproduction setups.

Just like code, sometimes processes start overly simple too, and then have to grow to be quite complex before they can be made simple again. Except in the end, their simplicity is intentional and designed instead of a sign of immaturity. I feel like this is what is happening with software quality assurance. Testing in production used to be a half-serious joke because it was often the only way to do any testing whatsoever. Then, in the past few decades, companies built complicated preproduction systems and entire QA departments to make up for it. However, practices and techniques have now evolved even beyond that. Testing directly in production is no longer a sign of unprofessionalism and sloppiness. Rather, it can be a sign of a very mature engineering team. This evolution can be seen in Figure 11-9.

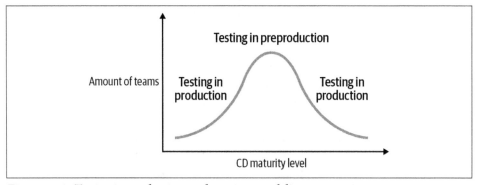

Figure 11-9. Testing in production and continuous delivery maturity

Of course, if your team is testing in production, *you* have to be the judge of whether that is because you are on the right side or the left side of the curve in the figure. This is an easy judgment to make if you work in a big enterprise that used to have a complicated preproduction environment and then invested in more modern testing approaches. However, if your company is a new startup that adopted this practice from day zero, then you might want to double-check that you have the adequate technical baseline to consider yourself among the top performers of continuous delivery. You can refer back to Chapter 4 for this.

A lot of safety practices need to be mature enough to allow a team to test in production almost exclusively. Because of this, I like to think of it as a guiding light and a finish line in the continuous delivery journey of my teams. In the context of continuous deployment, this is how I would amend that joke I heard:

> Everybody has a production environment. Some teams are disciplined enough to not need a separate testing environment.

It may not be funny anymore, but at least it is up-to-date.

Summary

In this chapter, I talked about the ins and outs of performing exploratory testing in production.

Regardless of the investment in preproduction environments, they will never be able to accurately replicate production conditions. This makes production testing much preferable to preproduction testing. Manual exploratory testing in the final environment can increase our confidence, cost less money, and keep user data more secure.

Frameworks that implement runtime feature flags allow us to enable features for very specific requests or very specific users. This allows developers, QA engineers, and product owners to take a sneak peek at the functionality in production before a release, but also during development. This strategy can be complemented by using specifically flagged test data in production, which will be hidden from normal users and only show up during testing.

In the next chapter, we will take a look at what happens *after* exploratory testing in production. When our features are demonstrably complete, functional, and performant, we need to actually release them to users.

CHAPTER 12
Releasing

Congratulations! You've made it to the final chapter of this step-by-step journey to production with continuous deployment. In the preceding chapters, I described a workflow for building, testing, and of course *deploying* software continuously. Now it's time to turn our attention to *releasing* it.

As I explained in Chapter 3, continuous deployment enforces a distinction between deployments and releases. Deployments are routine technical events that happen multiple times a day, driven by engineering needs. Most importantly, they are executed without affecting unsuspecting users in production. Releases, on the other hand, are free to adopt a cadence of their own, independent of that of deployments; they exist purely as a business event and are driven by product needs. While the majority of this book focused on engineering and therefore deployments, it is only fair that we end the book by giving some thought to the product side.

After all, the ultimate goal of building software should be to *definitely affect* users in production, which is only possible with well-thought-out and well-planned releases. Otherwise, we might as well not have bothered with continuous deployment at all. Releasing is not just another step in the value stream of code. It is the only moment when any activity around building software can finally come to fruition. Because of its importance, we should execute this step carefully and methodically, leveraging engineering tools to extract as much feedback as our users will give us.

In particular, I will focus on two techniques that have been key for my teams to unlock rapid and meaningful feedback: canary releases and A/B testing. These techniques, both made possible by feature flagging, empower us to roll out software with confidence, minimize risk, and gather data about feature performance. And by performance, I don't (just) mean how quickly our application can serve a response. I mean its performance from the point of view of engagement, conversion rates, and overall user happiness.

Like I did earlier in this book, I will start with antipatterns of the past to talk through the motivations behind the best practices of today.

Antipattern: Big Bang Releases

When code deployments and releases were synonymous, new features had only two states: either they were present in production or they weren't. Deploying all code that had accumulated for a given feature implied a big bang release of that feature to all users.

From an engineering perspective, most of us already have an intuitive feeling for why big bang releases are a bad idea. We know how they increase the risk that uncaught bugs will affect the entire user base at once, and we know how they produce sudden influxes of traffic that our infrastructure might not withstand. However, something that some engineers might not have an intuitive understanding of is how they also complicate the data-gathering process, making life more difficult for data analysts and product owners.

Comparing Before Versus After States

With a big bang release process, the only data available about a feature's performance is a "before versus after"' comparison. Such a comparison is susceptible to pollution from all sorts of uncontrollable variables that affect engagement in different ways from one week to the next. Here are some examples:

Seasonal patterns
Seasonal patterns can be described as predictable changes in user behavior throughout the year. For example, it is not uncommon for retail companies to release shiny new features ahead of high-visibility events such as Black Friday and the December holidays. If engagement and conversions increase, the release might even be considered a great success. However, it is debatable how much of that success can be attributed to the feature itself versus the different nature of user traffic during that particular period.

Singular events
Beyond predictable seasonal events (which we are at least able to control for) lies the realm of real-world randomness; that is, nonseasonal and unpredictable occurrences that can also trigger significant changes in user behavior. We can cluster these into two groups:

Changes outside the organization
These can be world events such as the COVID-19 pandemic and geopolitical events, but also something mundane such as the new PlayStation N being released.

Changes within the organization
> Examples here include marketing campaigns, popular products getting added to the stock, popular products no longer being out of stock…or even simple miscommunication between departments leading to public-facing activities that influence users to behave differently.

Multiple changes
> When several releases are happening in close succession (perhaps managed by different teams), it becomes hard to tell which release is driving changes in engagement, traffic, conversions, and so on. This is especially true for features affecting the same user flow.

Competitor activity
> No product lives in isolation, and most are situated in a market full of competitors. What happens with competitor products is completely out of the purview of what we can influence, and yet it can affect the behavior of our own users either positively or negatively. With rival platforms also adding features, taking features out, or changing their pricing, attributing causality to one particular release becomes even more complex.

With all these variables at play in a "before versus after" scenario, it becomes nearly impossible to make confident cause-and-effect claims about a new feature. Unsurprisingly, this hinders the decision-making process around the product, making it hard to judge the performance of past iterations or predict the success of new ones.

Comparing Simultaneous States

All polluting variables mentioned in the previous section had one thing in common: they change over time and mostly unpredictably. The solution to collecting more meaningful feedback during a release is therefore to remove time as a factor and to compare users' behavior around the feature *simultaneously* rather than *sequentially*. This allows a much cleaner comparison, as all the variables are equal between the control and test groups.

By using partial instead of big-bang releases, we can navigate the complex process of gathering feedback with much more grace and precision.

Antipattern: Partial Releases Through Partial Deployments

In Chapter 4, I explained how deployment strategies are sometimes used as a QA tool. This is done with manual intervention during a deployment, to allow for manual testing on the part of infrastructure where version $N + 1$ has been rolled out (e.g.,

QAing on the blue stack in a blue/green deployment). We already covered why this is an antipattern, especially with continuous deployment.

During my work, I have also seen how this strategy is sometimes used to perform partial releases. This is how it goes: version $N + 1$ of the application (with the feature) is deployed to only some instances, and user behavior is compared against instances with version N (without the feature). Once the feature has been proven, version $N + 1$ is rolled out to 100% of the production stack. This also applies to systems with multiple copies of their production infrastructure in several locations, where new deployments are tried by users in one location before being manually rolled out to the rest.

This workflow can allow for simultaneous comparison of different versions. However, as I mentioned in Chapter 4, it is incompatible with the practice of continuous deployment (and it is a significant step back in the practice of continuous delivery, in my opinion). This is because it couples product feedback with the technical life cycle of code, introducing a clunky process for rolling out new changes. Think, for example, of rolling out a version $N + 2$ with an urgent bug fix in this workflow, while a comparison is already running between versions N and $N + 1$. In short, "partial" deployments like this act as a manual gate to production for code changes.

This kind of gate to production, which is product based, can be even more troublesome than a typical manual QA gate, which is technical in nature. This is because its opening and closing is not even fully owned by the engineering team. Instead, it involves different stakeholders such as product owners, who are concerned with the timing of releases and might not be aware of the technical difficulties of maintaining a partially deployed state. This can make completing deployments really clunky, because it couples infrastructure rollouts with product experimentation.

By now, you have seen how deployments are inadequate as a feature experimentation tool, whether data collection happens in a "before versus after" fashion or in a "parallel" fashion by deploying to only parts of the infrastructure. So, what should we use instead?

Using Feature Flags for Releases

We should manage feature releases with a mechanism that is much smarter and more expressive than code deployments: runtime feature flags.

Until now, we have seen the benefits of feature flags mostly from an engineering perspective: letting us decouple deployments from releases, hiding work in progress, and testing in production. However, where most feature flag frameworks really shine is their granular control over the release process, allowing us to split the traffic exposed to a feature and therefore unlocking the power of simultaneous comparison without compromising the flow of code to production.

By now, it should be pretty evident that runtime feature flags are my overwhelming recommendation for managing new features at all stages of their life cycle. I already explained how to configure them for development and production testing, so now I'm going to show you how to integrate them in your infrastructure in a way that supports all kinds of releases.

Coordinating Feature Flag Releases in Distributed Systems

Most interesting systems nowadays are not monolithic: they are split into (micro)services. As a consequence of that, interesting features within those interesting systems can span more than one service at the same time, leading to feature flags that also span more than one service.

When feature flags are used to hide and test work in progress, each team can manage its own flag state independently of other teams. It is of no concern if the flag is ON in one system and OFF in another during testing—the overall feature is still hidden from users, after all. But when we release, the flag state must be synchronized across all the systems involved so that we can achieve a consistent user experience. The question that follows is: how can we coordinate feature releases across different services?

Consider the architecture shown in Figure 12-1.

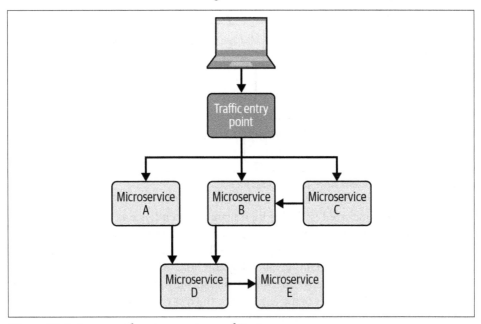

Figure 12-1. An example microservices architecture

If we have a feature spanning systems A, B, and D, we must find some way for those services to know which requests are supposed to show the new feature and which ones shouldn't. There are several different ways to store the state for feature flags. The first we will discuss is the simplest: where each application holds its own flag state.

Antipattern: Independent Flag State for Each Service

As shown in Figure 12-2, each application can independently hold the same toggle, which is technically the simplest solution and requires the least coordination across teams.

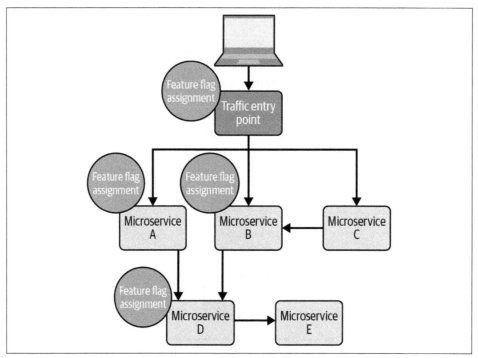

Figure 12-2. Independent flags for each service

However, the debt incurred with this high team independence is paid later, when it's time to release a feature spanning multiple systems. In that case, a big coordination effort is needed so that the flag state (ON or OFF) changes in all those systems simultaneously. Also, there are many invalid flag combinations that create opportunities for error. If the release of the feature is partial (e.g., only 30% of traffic), it is very difficult to guarantee that a user being assigned to the test group in system A will also be assigned to the test group in systems B and D.

It follows that, while this setup is simple to manage (and often occurs organically in organizations that start to adopt feature flags one team at a time), it needs some refinement when releases start spanning multiple services. To avoid too much coordination at release time, we can coordinate flags at implementation time instead.

Propagating Flag State Down the Call Chain

One way to coordinate feature flag implementation is to agree on a way to propagate flag state across different services. As shown in Figure 12-3, the flag state is held by only one system, usually the one closest to the users. Once the user is assigned to the test group or control group, that information is propagated by all the downstream systems in the following requests.

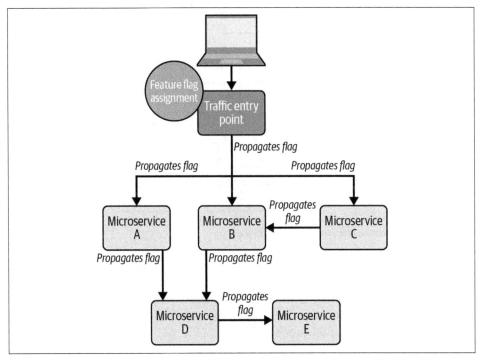

Figure 12-3. Propagating flag state down the call chain

With this approach, all systems will correctly see whichever group the request has been assigned to and will not need to perform any more assignment decisions. For example, the flag state might be included in a custom header or in part of the URL. The way in which each service receives the flag needs to be agreed upon, of course, which is a coordination cost that must be paid up front.

Another coordination cost with this setup is that when a team wants to change a flag value, it must change it in the traffic entry point system, so the team needs to have some knowledge of how it works.

Centralized Feature Flag State

Another way to coordinate systems around flag states is not through propagation, but through centralization. In Figure 12-4, you can see how a centralized feature flag service can be implemented to hold the flag state for all services and can be queried independently by any system that is interested in the state of the flag.

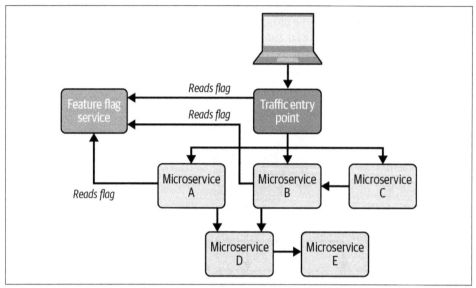

Figure 12-4. A centralized feature flag service

This approach is very flexible because only the systems interested in the state of the flag need the knowledge of how to query the service. However, it also incurs a high cost: the flag system must be created and maintained, which is what makes feature flags as a service such an attractive proposition to many companies (e.g., through tools such as Optimizely and LaunchDarkly).

Another aspect to consider is that there is definitely a performance penalty in repeating the same flag request multiple times along the call chain. This is why it is not uncommon to see a mixed setup with both centralization and propagation, where only some systems make calls to the service and propagate the state to other systems that depend on it.

Now that you have seen where we can store and propagate the feature flag state, let's consider how to configure it beyond a simple ON or OFF at release time: in particular, how to leverage this infrastructure to partially expose the traffic to new features.

Canary Releases

Canary releases, inspired by the canaries used in coal mines as an early warning system,[1] offer a phased approach to exposing changes at runtime. They work by selectively revealing a feature to a chosen group of users before letting it be seen by the whole audience. Just like the proverbial canary in the coal mine, these early adopters provide precious feedback, allowing teams to address any problems that weren't caught by automated and/or exploratory testing. The types of issues caught by canary releases are usually very interesting. They often go beyond simple bugs and logical flaws in implementation and can range from performance issues to data consistency issues—anything that can only be revealed by unleashing a sizable portion of real user traffic on a brand-new feature.

Canary releases are useful beyond risk mitigation, however. They allow us to compare our user sample's behavior with the rest of our user base, as they are engaging with our product simultaneously, with the only different variable being the feature itself. This means that even when the functionality is perfectly developed, performing a canary release is not a waste in engineering efforts: quite the opposite. It provides an opportunity to gather early user feedback and make data-driven decisions, letting us know whether the feature was well thought out in the first place.

In the following subsections, I will describe several strategies we can use for selecting a relevant representative group of users in a canary release with feature flags. All feature flag frameworks are different, so once again, this is only meant to give you a broad idea of what is possible, rather than representing all the possible ways in which a runtime flag can be configured for a canary release.

By Traffic Percentage

With a canary release by traffic percentage, the feature will be enabled for a randomized group of users representing a subset of the total group. For instance, if the initial release percentage is set to 5%, only 5% of the user base will experience the new feature, while the remaining 95% continue to use the stable version.

With this strategy, it is common to start from a small group (a single-digit percentage) and progressively ramp up the traffic seeing the new feature over the course of a few hours, as in Figure 12-5. After each increment of traffic, the team can keep a close eye on dashboards and other monitoring tools to ensure that the service is handling the ramp-up smoothly.

---

1 Canaries used to be employed in coal mines to detect the presence of carbon monoxide. The canaries' rapid breathing, small size, and high metabolism led them to succumb well before the miners did, thereby giving the miners time to act.

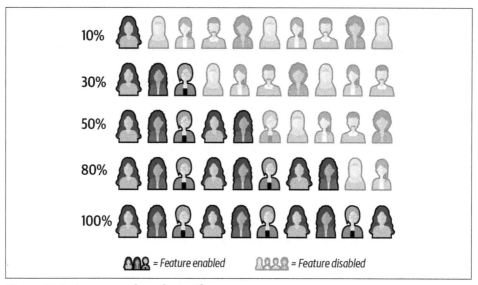

Figure 12-5. A canary release by traffic percentage

Although the requests are chosen randomly at first, you should make sure to employ cookies and other mechanisms to "remember" which group users were assigned to. This prevents the same user being exposed to different versions of the product in the same session, which would quickly get confusing and degrade their experience.

This is the most straightforward strategy for canary-releasing a new feature, and it's the one I have personally been using the most often by virtue of its simplicity.

By Device

Canary releases by device involve gradually rolling out new features to specific device types or platforms, such as desktop, mobile web, iOS, or Android. This strategy allows us to assess the impact of changes on different devices before releasing them to the entire user base.

For example, we can enable a feature flag for desktop users while keeping it disabled for mobile web, iOS, and Android users initially (Figure 12-6). This is especially useful when we want to closely monitor for device-specific issues one device type at a time.

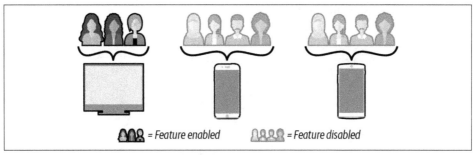

Figure 12-6. A canary release by device

This strategy is simple to implement when we are talking about a mobile web ecosystem, where there will be a shared codebase and a single flag. However, it requires more coordination when dealing with separate apps for each device. When maintaining a separate executable for each device, we can coordinate them in two ways: with one toggle for each device/platform or with a single backend-controlled toggle.

Per-device toggle

In a toggle-per-device scenario, every frontend of the application will have its own independently controlled flag. This is a very simple strategy, but it also means littering different codebases with the same toggle code and therefore spending more coordination effort during release and cleanup.

Backend-controlled toggle

A backend-controlled toggle, on the other hand, is a bit more complex to implement: all devices will need to perform a backend call to retrieve the state of the toggle before deciding whether to show the feature or not (which also incurs a performance penalty). The backend, in turn, has to evaluate whether the toggle should be ON or OFF for each call. It can do so by considering the device type (e.g., by interpreting a User-Agent header, or through other custom identifying information sent by the application itself). This strategy requires more up-front engineering investment, but it pays off later with centralized control over the release process and a simpler cleanup phase.

By Country

A canary release by country involves enabling or disabling a feature based on a user's geographical location. This type of release is useful for companies operating in multiple markets: each country has unique characteristics or user behaviors, sometimes making it necessary to gather market-specific feedback.

Also, realistically, some markets are more financially important than others. A canary release by country can leverage that fact to allow using noncore, lower-risk markets as early beta testers.

You can see an example in Figure 12-7.

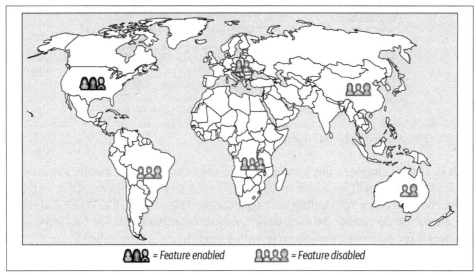

Figure 12-7. A canary release that uses US and Canada markets as beta testers

Enabling features by country can be achieved through many different approaches, some of them provided by most feature flag frameworks and others relying heavily on the system's infrastructure. Here are a few examples:

Geolocation data
 Where available, geolocation data allows us to identify the country or region with a good degree of accuracy.

IP address
 Although it is less precise than geolocation data, we can also use a device's IP address to restrict feature availability. The advantage of this method is that the IP is guaranteed to be present for all requests.

Domain
 Some larger companies will own and use different top-level domains (TLDs) for different markets, such as *.fr*, *.it*, *.eu*, and *.es*. The requested domain can be used as a basis for serving different versions of the website, even if the infrastructure serving traffic behind all domains is the same.

Locale
 Even when multimarket companies only operate with one generic TLD, such as *.com*, there is most likely an internationalization framework built into the platform so that the language and content for each region can be customized. We can leverage that information to identify which market users come from, which in

most cases we can find in the request URL (e.g., *my-website.com/FR-fr/some-page*) or headers.

By User Segment

Perhaps the most sophisticated approach, canaries by user segment allow releasing to specific, application-dependent segments within the overall user base. This approach allows us to assess the reception of features among groups with different behaviors.

By integrating the feature flag system with the application's definition of "user," developers can selectively enable or disable a feature based on domain-specific criteria. For instance, they could target specific user segments defined by subscription tiers, such as free users, basic plan users, and premium plan users, as shown in Figure 12-8. This can be especially helpful if, for example, the subscription tier model includes early access to features among the advertised perks.

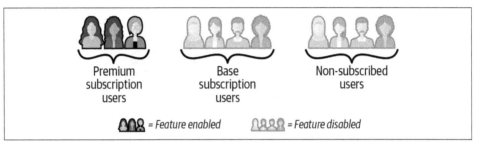

Figure 12-8. A canary release by user segment

Following are some examples of the many interesting user segments for canary releases that can vary based on the application:

Roles
Such as administrators, managers, and regular users. These usually have different levels of engagement with the platform.

Demographics
Such as age, gender, and occupation.

Behavior or engagement based
Such as frequent purchasers, new users, and dormant users.

Feedback contributors
Users who actively provide feedback or participate in beta-testing programs. Canary releases for this segment can involve early access to new features, allowing them to provide feedback and potentially reshape the final version.

"Friends and family"

Users who are employees of the company or who have a family member who works there. Such users could be among the first beta testers.

A/B Testing

A/B testing offers a more data-driven approach to releasing changes. This different way of managing releases allows us to evaluate and compare different variations of our software by exposing them to distinct user groups. It works by randomly assigning users to either the control group (A), which experiences the existing version of the software, or the experiment group (B), which uses the new version. Just like the "traffic percentage" strategy of canary releases, users are assigned randomly to either group A or group B. The size of group B is determined by examining the minimum amount of traffic necessary to generate meaningful data. An example is shown in Figure 12-9.

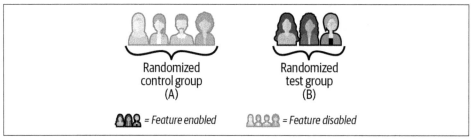

Figure 12-9. A/B testing groups

By collecting and comparing data from both groups, a team can accurately measure the impact of its changes and make better-informed decisions about whether a feature is there to stay. Statistical rigor plays a fundamental role here, ensuring that conclusions are based not on random fluctuations but on statistically significant differences.

Analytics

While the impact of canary releases is mostly evaluated through application monitoring and observability tools, in my experience A/B testing is where page analytics tools really get a chance to shine in our delivery workflow.

The two complement each other in any type of release, but it is even more imperative that we have a good analytics setup if we want to perform insightful A/B testing. Observability tools gather logs, metrics, and traces to gain insights into the *internal* workings and behavior of a system. Analytics, on the other hand, have a stronger focus on the *external* behavior of the system as experienced by our users, which more closely serves the primary purpose of product experimentation. Analytics tools offer comprehensive user behavior analysis, such as session duration, page views, click heatmaps, and funnel analysis. We should use such insights to assess the impact of different variations on user engagement.

While observability may also provide some level of insight into user behavior, its focus is on system-level insights rather than granular user behavior analysis. In addition, most analytics tools also provide either built-in statistical analysis capabilities themselves or integrations with tools that do. This helps a great deal when determining whether observed differences in A/B groups are statistically significant.

As engineers, we need to enable data analyst roles in (or outside) our teams to meaningfully compare different variations within analytics tools. Therefore, we need to ensure that our analytics tracking and event data is kept up-to-date, and we need to enrich it with A/B test assignment information. This can be achieved by sending custom data or by utilizing built-in features for tracking experiments.

Experiment Best Practices

This is a book written by a software engineer for other software engineers, so I consider it out of scope to explain all the ways we arrange for the perfect A/B test or how to actually analyze results. However, I still want to give you an overview of some of the A/B testing practices I have encountered with clients so that you know what to expect from an engineering perspective. Most of all, I will focus on how those practices impact the software delivery life cycle.

Test one variable at a time

Introducing changes atomically is crucial if we want to be accurate when determining their impact. If you modify multiple visible behaviors simultaneously, it can become difficult to disentangle their effects. The effects of multiple changes on user behavior could interact, overlap, or even cancel each other out, leading to ambiguous results. For example, if you modify both the text of a button and its location on the page, it becomes challenging to determine which change was responsible for any observed impact. Therefore, you should expect A/B tests to be planned in a way that covers a small surface area.

Avoid test parallelism

For the same reasons we should only test one variable at a time within an A/B test, we should also take care to only conduct one test at a time (at least in the same area of the application). If multiple tests are conducted in parallel, there will be a combinatorial explosion of versions of the platform that our users could end up seeing, which makes analyzing data difficult and potentially misleading.

Have a sufficient sample size

Depending on your traffic volume, A/B tests may need to run for days or weeks to offer statistically sound insights. You can get an idea of exactly how much time could be needed by using a sample size calculator (*https://oreil.ly/Nna_3*) to reliably determine how many data points you need in order to test a certain effect. Tools like these help data analysts avoid reaching rash conclusions on the basis of underpowered experiments, or having an experiment last longer than is necessary. Overall, you should expect a meaningful A/B test to last at least a few days, and you should plan your workflow accordingly as a team.

Schedule Delivery Around Experiments

In the preceding section, we saw how A/B tests need to be granular, be isolated, and run for a long time (from an engineering perspective). In addition, we have limited opportunities for running them at the same time (see "Multivariate tests" on page 346), especially when they affect components on the same page. Companies can address this issue by coordinating around a centralized A/B testing calendar and ensuring that every team is aware of which experiments are coming up. After all, we don't want our team to finish building a feature, only to have to wait three months before it is able to A/B-test it with real user traffic.

The consequences of not doing this planning effectively can be serious for the technical health of the codebase: as more and more features can get built but not enabled, the release risk for each one will increase as the codebase keeps changing behind the toggle. Feature toggles also won't get cleaned up in a reasonable time frame, which can lead to an explosion of toggle combinations that make the code hard to reason about and even harder to test.

This confusion also happens at the product and human levels. Too many experiments-in-waiting lead to interference between tests and unclear organizational priorities. Whenever you can, pursue each experiment quickly, cleanly, and wholeheartedly so that you can learn its lessons before moving on to the next experiment.

Types of A/B Tests

Now that we have covered the best practices around A/B testing, we can go into a little more detail regarding the different types of A/B tests we might encounter in the wild. Let's start with the simplest.

Tests with two variants

An A/B test with two variants is the simplest approach, and the one we have considered to be the "default" so far. It involves presenting only two versions of the experience to the user. These versions are similar, except for one variation within them that might affect the user's behavior.

However, there are also more specialized A/B tests that offer interesting capabilities for optimizing different aspects of a product. These types of A/B tests go beyond a simple comparison between two almost-identical variations and provide insights into more complex scenarios. Two such approaches that are widely utilized are multivariate testing and split testing. Let's start with the latter.

Split or redirect tests

A split test is a special kind of A/B test where, instead of experiencing a change in part of the page between variants, users get sent down entirely different flows, as shown in Figure 12-10. Teams can use this strategy when the new version of the page differs enough from the original that A/B-testing every single component or toggling every element on the page would be impractical. For example, this can be used when changing an entire user flow (such as a checkout flow) or redesigning an entire page and its content.

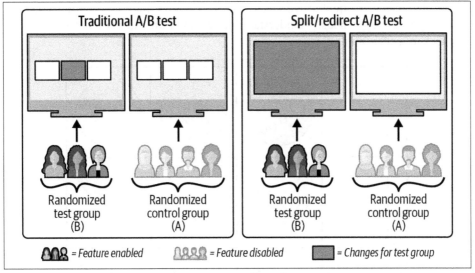

Figure 12-10. A traditional A/B test versus a split/redirect A/B test

Technically, doing a split test is most easily achieved by sending users to different URLs, depending on the version they should be seeing. We can do this by altering the entry point to the user flow (e.g., a link in a button) or by adding HTTP redirects. However, we can also use other strategies independent of the URL, such as changing routing rules in a reverse proxy behind the scenes. Whatever strategy we employ, we should ensure that the logic for these behaviors is controllable by the same type of toggle we would use for a standard A/B test, which gives us runtime control and painless rollbacks.

Multivariate tests

Multivariate testing is a variant of A/B testing that allows you to simultaneously test multiple variations of different elements or features on a web page, instead of just a status quo and a test variation. In multivariate testing, you can test combinations of small changes to determine which combination performs best. Instead of comparing entire variations against each other, it focuses on measuring the impact of individual elements. This specific subtype of A/B test is most useful to gauge how text and visual elements on a page work together.

Full factorial. The most common way to do multivariate testing is with a full-factorial approach. Full-factorial multivariate testing involves testing all possible combinations of variables across equal portions of website traffic. For example, if you have two variants of one element on the page and three variants of another, there will be six unique combinations to test (Figure 12-11). Each of these combinations will be configured to receive an equal distribution of approximately 16.66% of traffic. This way, we can gain a comprehensive understanding of how different variables interact and impact user engagement.

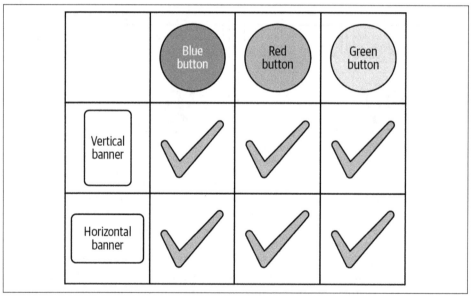

Figure 12-11. A multivariate full-factorial A/B test

Fractional factorial. Fractional-factorial multivariate testing is an alternative to full-factorial testing in which only a subset or fraction of the possible combinations of variables is tested with your website traffic (Figure 12-12). Unlike full-factorial testing, not all combinations are evaluated directly. Instead, statistical techniques are used to infer the performance of the untested combinations based on the results of the tested combinations. This approach, while offering less precision, requires less traffic because fewer combinations are tested.

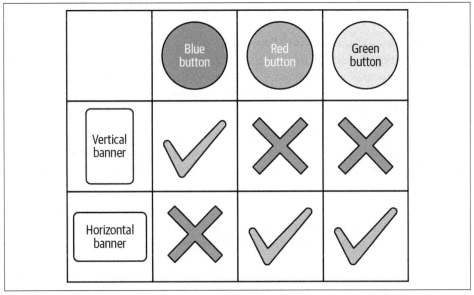

Figure 12-12. A multivariate fractional-factorial A/B test

The implementation of a multivariate-style test can be much trickier than a traditional A/B test with only two variations. Most feature flag frameworks deal with *boolean* flags that are either ON or OFF for each request, as opposed to A or B or C. That is because feature flags emerged first as an engineering de-risking strategy rather than as a product experimentation tool. In my experience, few feature flag platforms and frameworks support multivariate-style flags nowadays (LaunchDarkly (*https:// oreil.ly/Ef1TT*) being one of the exceptions). In the past, when one of our teams needed to run a test with three different variations, we had to code this behavior from scratch to support switching between the three states.

While implementation of multivariate testing can be just as clunky for many teams that are used to simpler testing strategies, it remains an incredibly powerful tool for quicker experimentation. Most importantly, it alleviates the need for lengthy consecutive A/B tests that can hold up the release schedule for weeks and weeks. I look forward to seeing more and more feature flag frameworks supporting multiple variations. I hope this will be a small next step in the direction of product experimentation vocabulary seeping into engineering tools.

Do You Need a Canary Release or an A/B Test?

At this point, you might be wondering what is the difference between A/B testing and canary releases. After all, both of them expose the new feature to a subset of users with the purpose of getting early feedback. They are also implemented in similar ways, especially if we look at the traffic percentage strategy of canary releases versus A/B tests.

In my view, the crucial distinction between them is the *intent* of the practice: that is, de-risking releases (canary releases) versus product experimentation (A/B testing). In short, canary releases are designed to tell you if there is an unexpected issue with your release. A/B tests, on the other hand, are designed to tell you if your hypothesis about user behavior is correct.

The primary focus of canary releases is to expose changes to a gradually increasing audience for risk mitigation purposes. This has the ultimate goal of rolling the feature out to 100% of the user base, once it has been proven that there are no regressions or negative impacts.

A/B testing, on the other hand, focuses on conducting a more rigorous comparison among different variations, aiming to prove the feature's worthiness with statistical significance. It is performed with the goal of gaining a greater understanding of our users' preferences, which is a more involved and often lengthier process. It often involves weeks of data gathering, requires data analyst roles to distill insights from it, and necessitates company-wide coordination to ensure that different A/B tests are not interfering with each other.

As a result of thorough A/B testing, a new feature or initiative might be dropped altogether and not simply "fixed until it works," as is usually the case with a canary release.

Both A/B testing and canary releases have their own advantages and use cases, but together they form a powerful toolkit for managing releases. For example, one might choose a simpler canary release process where they have extremely high confidence that the feature will stay in production (perhaps it was explicitly requested by a customer, it is mandated by law, or it is a migration from a legacy system to a new one). If, on the other hand, our product team is betting on a shiny and courageous new idea, more rigorous validation with A/B testing could be the more appropriate tool. As always, it is up to us as engineers to ensure that we present all the tools available to our stakeholders so that they can make better-informed decisions.

Summary

In this chapter, we explored feature toggles as a tool to perform canary releases and A/B testing, which allows teams to improve their precision around product experimentation.

Canary releases help de-risk the launch of new features by gradually exposing them to a subset of users, monitoring their impact, and mitigating any potential issues. They can be configured by request percentage, by device, by location, and even by custom user segments (depending on how we want to pilot our features in low-risk groups).

A/B testing, on the other hand, is a practice mostly focused on product experimentation that helps us compare different variations (usually the status quo versus the new feature) and measure their impact on the key engagement metrics that matter to the product. It is also possible to run special types of A/B tests: split/redirect tests to compare entire pages or user flows, or multivariate tests to find the most effective combination of multiple variables at once.

By leveraging both of these techniques at the right times, organizations can minimize risks associated with feature releases and, most importantly, gather information for more data for data-driven decision making, which leads to better product performance. I hope that this chapter showed you why a powerful feature toggle framework is worth the investment and how valuable it can be to involve the product function in its configuration.

This reflection concludes our overall journey on implementing continuous deployment, starting from feature slicing and ending up here: in front of our users. Indeed, this final step is the most important because it is where all the engineering practices we explored in the preceding chapters will finally pay off and will show our stakeholders why the investment was worth the effort. It is imperative to let our business take advantage of continuous deployment's speed and flexibility if we want to implement this engineering practice to its full potential.

Conclusion and Next Steps

This book took you on the full journey of continuous deployment. After a theoretical introduction in Part I, we dove into the software delivery life cycle in Part II, where we discussed how to prepare a sturdy and production-ready backlog, split features with the flexibility of granular deployments in mind, and make every increment production ready from its inception. This was followed by Part III, where we dove even deeper, exploring the code itself and talking about breaking down user stories into small and immediate deployments to production—without disrupting our users and with backward compatibility kept in complex distributed systems. Finally, in Part IV, you learned how to put this knowledge into practice by using exploratory testing in production and releasing changes gradually and safely, which unlocks data-driven product experimentation.

Throughout the book, we explored the benefits and challenges of continuous deployment and the mindset shift required to embrace this practice fully. I hope you learned something new when reading this book because I certainly learned a lot while writing it.

In Part V, I have included some case studies from companies practicing continuous deployment "in the wild." Continuous delivery has become a well-loved practice for the engineers I interviewed, enabling them to deliver high-quality software at an unprecedented pace. By automating every step of code's path to production, their teams can now iterate, respond to user feedback, and deliver value to customers with as much speed and efficiency as is technically possible. So, if you can spare some extra time, don't stop reading just yet: their concrete experience is definitely worth learning about, probably even more so than the theory and examples I provided so far.

As I hand over the metaphorical pen to the other industry experts and let them do the rest of the writing for me, I want to express my heartfelt gratitude to all the readers who have stuck with me this far (and even the ones who didn't!). I want to especially wish good luck to those who are considering including continuous deployment in their portfolio of engineering practices. I wish you a journey full of successes and, more importantly, learning. The landscape of software development is an ever-changing one, and I look forward to hearing your feedback and experiences on how continuous deployment might reshape software development in your organizations.

I leave you with a quotation from Kent Beck:

> My goal in laying out the project style was to take everything I knew to be valuable about software engineering and turn the dials to 10. [...] It took experience to find out that what I thought was 10 on the dial was actually only 8 or 6.[1]

---

1 Kent Beck, with Cynthia Andres, *Extreme Programming Explained: Embrace Change, Second Edition* (Boston: Addison-Wesley, 2004).

PART V
Case Studies

Part V features a collection of case studies written by industry professionals who have hands-on experience with continuous deployment. You will learn about their companies' journey toward continuous deployment, the challenges they overcame, the quality gates they implemented, and how they structured their software's path to production.

Case Study: AutoScout24

To kickstart our case studies section, Simon Mittermüller and Thiago Vacare will tell us about the adoption of continuous deployment at AutoScout24, a European online car marketplace. Simon joined AutoScout24 in 2016. As a principal software engineer, he is a key contributor to the strategic direction of Product Engineering, driving technical decisions and cross-team efforts. Part of his role is to ensure a balance between rapid progress and the reliability and quality of AutoScout24. Thiago has been at AutoScout24 since 2020. As a platform engineer, he designs, builds, and maintains infrastructure and frameworks to support and abstract software applications and services from developer teams. He has worked in different platform teams, managing a Kubernetes cluster with more than 400 microservices, developing Accelerate metrics to enhance product delivery and continuous integration/continuous delivery (CI/CD), migrating platforms to AWS, and managing incidents. In this case study, you can read about their experience with continuous deployment.

AutoScout24's Context

AutoScout24 is the largest pan-European online car market, with over 30 million users per month and more than 43,000 dealer partners. It offers a comprehensive platform for buying and selling cars online, including used and new cars, motorcycles, caravans, and transporters. The platform provides features such as smart search, financing, price and car evaluation, and a secure environment through dealer ratings provided by its users.

As a comprehensive mobility marketplace, AutoScout24 specifically invests in growth areas such as digital retail, leasing, car subscriptions, electric mobility, and online car purchasing. With AutoScout24 smyle, users are able to complete the entire purchase of vehicles online. Leasing specialist LeasingMarkt.de joined the AutoScout24 group in 2020, and B2B auction platform AUTOproff joined in 2022. Together, these marketplaces significantly drive forward the digitalization of the European car trade.

AutoScout24 has around 800 employees across 19 locations in Europe. Our engineering org comprises over 200 developers working with 2,000+ GitHub repositories and 1,000+ services. More than 1,500 pipelines ensure that our software is built and shipped to production with an average deployment time of 6 minutes and a build time averaging 15 minutes. We handle around 74,000 pipeline jobs each month, reflecting our capability to effectively manage extensive and frequent deployments in a high-demand technical environment.

Our Platform Engineering group creates internal products to simplify tasks for product engineering teams. The group's goal is to enable product engineers to focus on enhancing the company's product instead of dealing with infrastructure complexities. Platform Engineering builds and manages robust, scalable, and efficient platforms that automate infrastructure tasks, ensure reliability and security, and provide insights and observability to systems.

To achieve this goal, Platform Engineering develops internal products that cover different aspects of software development and infrastructure management. These include tools for software delivery, computing, observability, infrastructure as code (IaC), AWS management, project templates, messaging, and incident management. We use different technologies, such as Python, Golang, TypeScript, and Bash, and IaC tools such as AWS CDK, AWS CloudFormation, and Terraform, to automate and manage cloud infrastructure.

The Product Engineering teams are the driving force behind all customer-centric products. The teams are responsible for the development and maintenance of frontends, backends, databases, and other infrastructure components such as queues. They are standing on the shoulders of giants: AWS and our Platform Engineering group. They leverage a microservices architecture based on Java and TypeScript. Services communicate via REST or GraphQL, fostering rapid and independent product evolution.

Adoption of Continuous Deployment at AutoScout24

In 2014, our organization had three environments: a production environment, a reference environment (that was intended to be a "scaled down" clone of production to run the tests against, but it ended up with a mix of different database or service versions), and a dev environment (that was always broken). We used TeamCity as a CI/CD tool, but most pipelines had manual approval steps, such as to promote the "build" from ref to prod. We had a big, shared Oracle database where all services were integrated. We had a backup data center that was not working. Some changes to our products required downtime. We had to over-provision our resources to the maximum because they did not scale. We had a dedicated QA team to test all changes in the ref environment, and then in the production environment again. These and many other issues made us radically change how we thought about software delivery.

We then started a cultural shift from monolithic applications in the data center to autoscaling microservices in the cloud ("cloud-native," AWS) and autonomous teams in an Agile setup. We adopted a trunk-based development approach, using blue/green deployments and feature toggles to make our deployments safer and more reliable. The new microservices were automatically deployed to production from day one.

Overcoming Organizational Obstacles

There are always challenges when implementing standards, mainly because not everyone will understand the reasons behind them at first. People tend to think "things just work, so why change it?" However, we can show that our processes can be even better, and with the right approach, we can overcome these challenges.

We took the following steps:

- We started by promoting a culture of learning with all teams so that we could adapt and evolve the standards if needed.

- We encouraged open communication and feedback channels. We established clear communication channels and collaboration frameworks between teams, especially across Platform Engineering and Product Engineering. This is part of the onboarding process for new joiners so that everyone knows where to go to ask questions, give feedback, and subscribe to announcements of new feature releases and system downtimes.

- We fostered a culture of shared responsibility where everyone understands their role in the development process. We have cross-functional teams consisting of members from different departments who work together toward the same goal.

- We followed the "You build it, you run it" principle. The developers are responsible for creating tests, shipping the product, and ensuring that everything is working as expected. However, if something goes wrong, we run blameless incident processes and reviews because no one should feel bad for making mistakes. We want to learn from failures while encouraging people to try new things. We empowered development teams with the necessary tools and training to take ownership of the code they produce. We fostered a culture of accountability where teams take pride in delivering high-quality software.

- We led by example, showcasing the benefits of continuous deployment through successful pilot projects or case studies. We have multiple integration tests, unit tests on every deployment, and nightly integration tests that run more complex tests to ensure that everything works as expected in our Platform Engineering products. This gives us high confidence when we need to make changes to our products, which also boosts our confidence in them and gives an excellent example to Product Engineering teams that use them.

- We built confidence in deployments by starting with small, incremental changes. We implemented automated testing and quality assurance processes to catch errors early in the development cycle. We gradually increased the frequency and scope of deployments as confidence grew. We ensured that platform teams provided the necessary infrastructure and tools to support CI/CD while development teams focused on delivering features and improvements.

- We acquired a few companies over time. Such events are a good opportunity to brush up on our processes for these acquired companies. We learned that assessing acquired companies' existing processes and technologies is crucial to identifying gaps or opportunities for alignment. One good example was that one of the acquired companies used GitHub actions for its CI/CD, and that was something we wanted to try or start implementing in AutoScout24 for some time. So, we used the opportunity to learn from that company and incorporate some of its feedback. Finally, we didn't start empty-handed when we started using GitHub actions in AutoScout24. We provided training and support to integrate the new teams into the continuous deployment workflow. We fostered a culture of collaboration and knowledge sharing between teams from different organizational backgrounds.

In all cases, it's essential to approach the transition to continuous deployment with patience, persistence, and a focus on continuous improvement. Addressing organizational obstacles systematically and involving key stakeholders in the process can pave the way for the successful adoption of continuous deployment within your organization.

Overcoming Technical Obstacles

During our journey toward continuous deployment, we faced several obstacles of a technical nature as well.

First, we wanted to reduce our blast radius and followed the principle of least privilege, limiting the access to data, resources, and applications to authorized users or roles only. For example, we use secret management tools to securely store sensitive information outside of the codebases. We also implement a range of security measures that run as part of the pipelines, such as vulnerability scans, dependency checks, and secure configuration management. We keep our dependencies and libraries up-to-date with semiautomatic updates.

We shifted our focus from optimizing mean time between failures toward mean time to recover. A critical capability for this is to have fast deployments to allow "fix forward." It takes continuous effort to identify and eliminate bottlenecks in this process. We try to parallelize tasks in the pipelines, cache dependencies, optimize build scripts, and use lightweight containers. We also want to be notified quickly if things go south. Hence, we invested in having excellent observability and prompt alerting.

Finally, we invest in comprehensive automated testing, including unit tests and integration tests, to ensure that the code is bug-free and ready to be deployed throughout the day without any fear of breaking anything in production.

AutoScout24's Implementation of Continuous Deployment

At AutoScout24, the decision to use a pull request (PR) is up to the individual teams or depends on the criticality of the service being developed. The teams rely heavily on feature toggles to push to production code that is not yet fully finished, well understood, or tested. This approach allows for frequent pushes to production, keeping changes small and manageable. It also enables developers and product managers to test changes in the production environment and receive early feedback. By using feature toggles, the teams can safely and efficiently iterate on their code, improving the overall development process. Some teams deploy several times a day.

The journey of code from development to production involves several steps. First, the developer builds the feature locally and runs the test suite with mocked or Dockerized production dependencies. Then, the service can be started locally, with Dockerized dependencies or by calling other services in the production environment (if feasible). The developer then pushes the branch to GitHub and creates a PR, which triggers the CI pipeline to run test suites and other quality checks. After the PR is reviewed and merged, the CI/CD pipeline kicks off the build, tests, and integration tests. Subsequently, the pipeline automatically deploys the service to production via AWS CloudFormation (using CDK).

Some steps, such as heavy integration tests with Dockerized environments, and normal unit tests, can be executed in parallel. Smoke tests or UI tests are executed on the production service, and finally the pipeline sends success metrics to Datadog and Slack. In rare cases, we even duplicate the infrastructure (e.g., the service, or even the database) to reduce the impact of a failed upgrade (such as a major upgrade of an Elasticsearch cluster version or other RDS database configuration).

How AutoScout24 Makes Continuous Deployment Safe

Following are some of the main practices that act as quality gates in the path to production at AutoScout24.

Code review process

At AutoScout24, the code review process varies depending on the criticality of the service and the team responsible for its development. Several patterns and processes are used to ensure that code is thoroughly reviewed before being deployed to production:

Classic PR review

One common approach is the classic PR review, where developers submit their code changes for review by their peers. This process allows for constructive feedback and helps to catch potential issues before the code is merged.

Pair programming

Another approach is pair programming, where two developers work together on the same code, continuously reviewing each other's work in real time. This approach promotes knowledge sharing and helps to improve code quality.

Straight to the main branch

In some cases, code changes may be pushed straight to the main branch, behind a feature toggle. This approach allows for rapid deployment of new features, with the review taking place after the feature is finished and before it is released to users (by switching the toggle ON).

Overall, the code review process at AutoScout24 is flexible and adaptable, allowing teams to choose the approach that works best for them and their specific needs.

Test automation

Test automation is an essential part of the software development process, allowing our teams to verify the functionality of their code quickly and reliably. At Auto-Scout24, several types of automated tests are used to ensure the quality of the codebase. These include unit tests, which test individual components in isolation, and integration tests, which test the interactions between components. These tests are typically executed as part of the continuous integration process, with each code change triggering a new build and test run.

We try to "integrate in production," meaning that some of our tests may call production systems as part of the test execution. This couples our CI/CD to the availability of the dependencies. We mitigate this by allowing ourselves to skip these tests in such cases. Whether we can follow that approach highly depends on the industry and business domain (e.g., GDPR requirements might rule out some of the patterns to test in production).

We also run smoke tests after the deployment on the production systems to test the most critical paths of that service. To some extent, we run end-to-end user journey tests on a regular basis to understand whether complex business flows that involve many services (even external ones) are correct. Of course, every team can run any other kind of test; for example, load tests or testing disaster recovery procedures.

Additionally, we use AWS CDK as the standard for IaC, and we provide opinionated templates to the developers. These templates also include some test suites that demonstrate how to test the IaC layer to reduce "bugs" on the infrastructure level. We ensure that the CDK test changes are precisely what we validate and change to ensure that everything runs smoothly.

Zero-downtime deployments

Our main platform solution to run production services is Infinity, a custom compute solution based on Kubernetes using AWS EKS and AWS CloudFormation custom resources. Infinity runs more than 1,000 pods across different business areas, with services deployed 100 times almost daily. For deployment, we use the rolling update strategy in Kubernetes with an unavailability of 0% and a max surge of 25% by default.

Let's say we have two replicas of a service X in Kubernetes. When we have a new deployment, the service can increase to 25% above its initially defined value and 0% below its desired value, which causes us to have a minimum number of replicas during deployment ready to receive requests. Before terminating old pods, Kubernetes performs health checks on the new pods to ensure that they are ready to serve traffic. This prevents any downtime or disruption caused by deploying pods that are not yet operational.

Observability

Observability is a crucial part of understanding and managing the behavior of our production systems. We use observability tools such as metrics, traces, alerts, logs, dashboards, and SLOs with Datadog as our observability platform, which eliminates the need to manage infrastructure and offers easy integration into other systems.

Following a culture of transparency, we allow the teams to see cross-service metrics, which helps them debug issues more quickly and build helpful dashboards. We have implemented SLO best practices and provided modules for teams to create their own SLO dashboards. In addition, we have mapped our critical user journey so that all critical services have proper SLOs and alarms, and we also educate teams with SLO best practices courses. At a higher level, we also have key performance indicators (KPIs) to understand when and how our changes affect the business.

How AutoScout24 Supports Junior Engineers

We encourage new joiners to have a chance to deploy to a production system early on, even as part of the onboarding journey. This helps increase their confidence in the delivery process and in the services they work with. We do a lot of pair programming, and we gradually increase the complexity of tasks for juniors while relying on the confidence in our test suites and deployment practices. We have heavily invested in high-quality onboarding materials (e.g., recorded videos of walk-throughs, examples, and links to our reference docs), which we continuously improve as we go.

Case Study: OTTO

For our second case study, we will look at continuous deployment at OTTO. Tom Vollerthun is an executive professional software developer (although he isn't entirely convinced job titles are helpful, he remarks), and he has been working at OTTO as a software engineer and technical team lead for over 10 years. Here is Tom's overview of OTTO's approach to continuous deployment.

OTTO's Context

OTTO is one of the biggest European retailers and ecommerce shops. At the time of writing this, it has over 6,100 employees, 14.5 million products (~26 million variations), and 20,000 brands from over 5,000 partners. The platform itself receives up to 6 million qualified visits per day and up to 10 orders per second.

OTTO's engineers are organized into 60 autonomous Agile teams working on the Otto.de website, with several more in backend or IT departments. Collectively, they achieve more than 60 deployments to production per day through continuous deployment.

Within OTTO, I have recently changed to the team that's responsible for making product data available to external marketing partners like Google Shopping, Twitch, and Facebook as well as price comparison portals like Billiger.de. The product data is filtered and converted according to the adjustable configuration of business departments, exported into over 70 formats, and updated several hundred times per day. My most recent previous teams were responsible for personalized recommendations within the shop as well as a real-time bidding system for sponsored products.

Adoption of Continuous Deployment at OTTO

We started on the road to continuous deployment in 2011, when OTTO's Lhotse Project was set up to replace the existing Intershop Software with a shop that's built in-house, using Agile processes such as Scrum.

Continuous deployment was never a goal in itself, but only a means to achieve an overarching goal: when a new feature is created, it will be of value to the company only if it has an impact on customers. The long-winded QA processes and deployment cycles of several months that were common at the time weren't helpful. Instead, changes should create value quickly while keeping the risks controllable, so automation and test suites are a core necessity, even when things inevitably break. We learned that reducing the mean time to delivery (MTTD) is more important than increasing the mean time between failures (MTTF).

Besides the main goal of creating value without undue delay, we saw several nice side effects of continuous deployments:

- Changes to live systems are small, so the potential impact can be identified quickly.

- It decouples the technical deployment (code changes have arrived in the live environment) from business deployments/releases (the changes are active and can have an impact on customers) through toggles, so changes can be activated during business hours when the whole team is available to monitor the impact.

- The use of toggles means that changes can be deactivated just as quickly, and gradual rollouts or A/B tests can be performed with relative ease. This enables us to validate the impact of the changes with actual data instead of a gut feeling.

- Trunk-based development with toggles reduces the risk of big merges and allows, for example, code refactorings to benefit the whole development team quickly. The risk of long-lived feature branches (big change sets that are difficult to merge, roll out, or revert) is mitigated.

- Comprehensive test suites prevent breaking valuable features while still allowing the quick deployment of bug fixes.

Working with Organizational Barriers

Since the OTTO company has a long tradition and was an early adopter of technology in general, waterfall processes with its infamously elaborate QA phases and long deployment cycles were well established when our department decided to change pace and embrace Agile development and deployment strategies. So, one of the main challenges was a cultural change for the management to trust the development teams to forgo all these manual QA tests and still develop stable software of the highest quality.

Naturally, the instinct was to place a manual QA between the test systems and the live environment. The consequences were natural and apparently commonplace as well: the QA team was held responsible for all bugs in the live system, so it was reluctant to quickly release changes, which resulted in frustration of the development teams and their stakeholders because features weren't released with the velocity that was possible and that they expected.

Having to take responsibility for changes the QA team itself had little impact on had several consequences, but probably most impactful was the decision to allow only a single deployment at a time. It's a reasonable decision given the circumstances, because the team members felt that only in that way could a deployment be correlated with a change in shop behavior. The result was a shared deployment pipeline for all teams that paused the deployments of all teams while one team's deployment was under way. The resulting friction, especially if a deployment had to be rolled back, was immense.

I deeply believe that these kinds of organizational challenges can't be tackled with a single measure, because the underlying conflict between the QA and development teams had its basis in a lack of influence on, or even just oversight over, systems that people felt responsible for. Naturally, it took some time and several attempts, but in my personal opinion, the integration of QA people into the development teams was a key change: instead of being relegated to the very end of a long process, QA people could work with their development teams and stakeholders from the first moments a new feature was planned. They could advise the teams on best testing practices, manual tests could be automated by the team's developers, and tests that were previously duplicated between the QA team and development team could be removed. Instead of being responsible for systems they had little or no influence on, the responsibility was shared within the team, relieving the QA people from the unwanted role of a delayer.

I am convinced that the much closer relationship between developers and QA, sometimes resulting in QA becoming full stack developers in their teams, resulted in more trust in the quality of the team's work on the one hand and better and more meaningful test suites on the other. This in turn allowed everyone to let go of overengineered and flaky processes, resulting in less friction and frustration and ultimately much better performance.

Here's a diagram of the count of weekly deployments in 2014–2015:

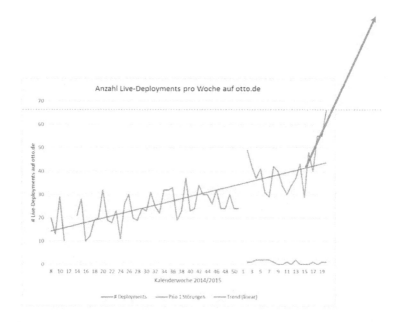

As you can see, a fundamental change took place in early 2015: not only did the number of live deployments start to skyrocket, but the number of live incidents didn't significantly change at the same time. The deep integration of QA into teams is still a recommended best practice in our department, and the number of live deployments has only gone up since then. Because we don't rely on a shared pipeline anymore (teams often run their own continuous integration [CI] server or use GitHub actions for deployments), getting the numbers is much more difficult these days, but the last time I checked we were at around 100 live deployments per day.

Working with Technical Barriers

When starting with continuous deployment, apart from the organizational obstacles of establishing trust in Agile processes, we also encountered several technical hurdles. When we started our journey, the concept of consumer-driven contract tests as described by Martin Fowler in 2006 wasn't new, but despite the value and safety they provide, they weren't a well-established practice in the industry.

Consequently, our first attempts at using them were quite naïve. Starting with JAR files that should be run in the pipelines of service providers, we quickly discovered that major changes of Java versions can break tests as well. Later, teams started creating some services in Node.js, and the availability of a Java runtime couldn't be relied upon.

Some tests required the service providers to have a headless browser available on their build server, and again, version changes would break tests.

It took several years and a migration to AWS before we found a reliable and resilient mechanism for triggering and running CDC tests without undue overhead for the teams of service providers: a network call to a rest endpoint of the consumer will run their test (e.g., as a lambda), and the return code informs about the success or failure of the test.

OTTO's Implementation of Continuous Deployment

It's important to point out that at OTTO, teams define their own deployment processes depending on their needs. A team that is responsible for the checkout will probably need different tests to feel safe compared to a team that's handling the advertisements.

Every commit that passes the fully automatic pipeline will be deployed to the live system, so the number of times that happens depends on the time between commits. We encourage developers to commit very often, which might be as often as "every few minutes up to a half hour" or only once a day. At one point, we experimented with automatic pushes so that if all tests on the developer machine were successful, the change was immediately pushed by a script. But due to the poor comment messages and hardly any advantages to manual pushes, it never gained traction. It is very unusual for an unfinished feature to remain unpushed on the developer's machine until the next working day, especially since parents of young children (and not only them) enjoy the freedom to remain absent on very short notice. If it can't be helped at all, it has been known that a change is pushed into a branch instead of main, but since that counteracts most of the advantages of continuous deployment, it's very rare indeed.

OTTO's Path to Production

It bears repeating that teams at OTTO enjoy a wide area of autonomy, so the path to production can differ vastly between teams. Using our sponsored products (advertisement) system as an example, a frontend change would see these steps:

The change is committed on the developer's machine. The toggle is disabled by default, but tests for both states are in place. If all unit, component, and integration tests of the suite are green, it's pushed to the GitHub repository. Since the change is made in a repository that contains frontend code, there will be tests for the JavaScript code as well.

The change triggers a pipeline that will compile the code, verify code style compliance, and find low-hanging fruit with static code analysis. We have found that the number of false positives that are highlighted by these tools (e.g., Findbugs or

Cobertura) have improved over the years, but to avoid blindness to permanently red pipeline steps, these tools need to be carefully configured. Some teams found these necessary configurations to be so time-consuming that they decided to forgo static code analysis completely and focus on other ways to keep code quality at a high level.

The same development test suite with all unit, component, and integration tests is executed by the build server, and given all tests were successful, a Docker image with the compiled artifact is created and pushed into the team's Docker repository.

After the deployment of the new Docker image into a nonlive environment, the running server can be inspected with more tests. Depending on the type of microservice that's under test, that can include visual regression tests with JLineUp or the Galen Framework, functional frontend tests with Selenium, or CDC tests for changes to an API that other teams are depending on. In our case, JLineUp will create a screenshot of a testing page before the changes are deployed as well as after the deployment. Since the feature toggle adding the CSS class is disabled, there will be no visible changes and the test is successful.

Depending on the team's needs, the change might be deployed to other intermediate environments, but in this case there is no further deployment to QA or pre-live environments.

So now the change is verified as good, and it can be deployed into the live environment. Again, the toggle is disabled by default, there's no impact on users of the page, and the technical deployment (bringing the code into the live system) is finished.

A smoke test checks that the integration into Otto.de is working as expected. Since these tests are volatile by nature (many integrating teams, network instability, etc.), many teams will automatically repeat a failing smoke test. They might even schedule them to run continuously, effectively making this a monitoring of their live system.

The business deployment/release (making the change visible to our users) consists of activating the feature toggle, and it can take place at any time the product owner is available: usually accompanied by a developer, they activate the toggle in the test environment and verify that the change to the button color is indeed correct.

Depending on the feature, the toggle's activation strategy in the live environment can be quite complex, including gradual rollouts (active for a percentage of requests) or even an onsite experiment that will expose some users to the change over several weeks so that the impact on the click or order behavior can be closely monitored. For the sake of simplicity of this example, the feature toggle in the live environment is just activated by a developer, and now the feature is live and ready to be cleaned up.

Since the feature toggle is now permanently active and the product owner doesn't plan to revert the button to the old color anytime soon, the feature toggle is removed, and the pipeline will run again.

How OTTO Makes Continuous Deployment Safe

The realization that we will never be able to prevent bugs completely, no matter how elaborate the test suite or QA process is, has shifted our focus from bug prevention to the ability of fast rollout for bug fixes (MTBF/MTTR). Many teams find that prioritizing a green pipeline is valuable. It not only keeps the door open to quickly deploy eventually necessary bug fixes, but also keeps the team's focus on the most important gateway to bring fixes for inevitably occurring bugs to the live system.

That said, of course there's a huge zoo of practices and mindsets that help reduce the risk of bugs happening in the first place or limiting their impact should they occur.

Team culture

Since our teams are set up as feature teams with a long-term responsibility for their part of Otto.de, they develop a keen feeling of product responsibility. While at times short-lived project teams are established, they are never building systems for the website, but mostly tooling for business departments or content for a one-time marketing measure.

The independence and autonomy of teams is an important value in our department, so teams are encouraged to avoid interrupting the work of other teams with bugs.

Resilience patterns

We use resilience patterns such as circuit breakers, aggressive timeouts, and graceful degradation, and we avoid intersystem communication during a user request, all of which results in a website that's still usable even if some systems aren't behaving as they should.

Test automation

Most importantly, we enjoy the freedom to invest a lot of time into automation and test coverage so that we don't need to feel uncomfortable or at risk with immediate, unsupervised deployments. Automation of everything (from tests, pipelines and deployments, over infrastructure, and database allocation, to the setup of a developer's machine) is an investment that pays many times over for long-lived teams.

When writing tests, we always try to keep the test pyramid in mind so that we're testing the smallest amount of code possible, usually through unit tests—lots of unit tests. They are so fast that it's almost impossible to have too many. They truly are the foundation of the test pyramid, and the safety they provide in fully automated, unsupervised deployments is hard to overstate.

The interaction between several small units within a Spring context is tested with component tests, and integration tests handle database, filesystem, or cloud operations. These tests can usually be executed on every developer's machine, and they will be executed in the first step of the deployment pipeline. Failing them in the pipeline, however, is frowned upon because failures are so easily avoided by running them locally before pushing.

API requests are often mocked away to reduce the dependencies to external systems; they are usually tested with CDC tests when the external system is deployed. If that's not possible (e.g., because the external system isn't able to execute a CDC test), the team might create a fake service to verify the requests and responses.

JavaScript tests verify the correctness of frontend code: unit tests for business logic and integration tests for the interaction with browser APIs or backend systems. Visual regression tests with screenshots (JLineUp, Cypress) or layout descriptions (Galen Framework) ensure that the result still looks like it should. And after a deployment, smoke tests verify that the feature's integration into the larger context still works. Sometimes these are expanded into regular running monitoring tests.

Deployment strategy

Our initial strategy, almost a decade ago, was blue/green deployments, where all servers were duplicated, and half of them were always kept on standby so that a change could be deployed to the inactive half before switching over. After the introduction of MESOS, and especially after our migration to AWS, the inactive servers didn't need to remain in place between deployments, so we didn't incur the cost of keeping duplicate servers.

Nowadays, however, most teams are using the rolling deployment feature of AWS's CloudFormation to replace only a percentage of the running servers at a time. Of course, that practice requires a very close focus on database changes; one of the many reasons why relational databases with strict schemas aren't very common at OTTO. But even changes to NoSQL databases might require several deployments with backward-compatible code so that the change can be performed safely and in a controlled manner.

The four-eyes principle

Most teams are practicing pair or mob programming to not only facilitate knowledge sharing, but also encourage best coding practices through the (at least) four-eyes principle. That said, this has long since been a huge topic of discussion at OTTO, so it's not surprising to see the whole gamut of strategies in our department. I will share only my opinion here.

I'm a strong proponent of pair programming, although it can admittedly incur quite some mental overhead for the pairs. For example, people have different needs for breaks or reading documentation. Furthermore, communicating with another developer about code the whole day can be very draining. The upside, however, is usually much-improved code quality, better and more meaningful tests, fewer bugs or copy/paste errors, and the ability to continue development even if other team members aren't available due to meetings, illness, or moving to another team.

I found mob programming to be even more efficient for knowledge transfer in teams, but the other advantages of pair programming (improved code quality, better and more meaningful tests, fewer bugs and copy/paste errors) don't scale equally. Since the cost of mental overhead and the necessity of strong moderation can make mob programming quite tedious indeed, I recommend it only for specific phases; for example, when a team explores new technologies or business cases. Much more than pairing, mobbing sessions should be well prepared so that, for example, participants don't first need to read some documentation before being able to participate, or to ensure that everyone can feel like an active member of the discussion.

While I have worked in teams that prefer code reviews, their biggest weakness in my experience is their much-reduced velocity: code reviews are easily perceived as an interruption of the task a developer is working on, so the review is either cursory or overly strict in retaliation.

Small refactorings to the code that would've been simple for a pair (like renaming things or extracting methods) now need the reviewer to explain the requested change in writing, the original developer to read that and implement the change, and the need to create another pull request, which might or might not meet the reviewer's expectation. It's not rare to see such a review cycle take several days before a feature can move on, or in the other extreme, to forgo these change requests completely because the overhead appears unreasonable compared to the improvement in code quality.

How OTTO Supports Junior Engineers with Continuous Deployment

Junior engineers are treated exactly like all other developers in the team, because they work responsibly and to the best of their knowledge. Often, pair programming with other team members will result in a steep learning curve for them, and before long they are as focused on quality and delivery of value as everyone else.

Of course, nobody is perfect and mistakes happen, but that is true for more experienced colleagues as well: being well-rested and hydrated, taking breaks from the demanding task of crafting complex business requirements into code, and looking after one another are important steps to create healthy and high-performing teams, but sooner or later someone will make a mistake. And no matter how long-winded or detailed a QA phase is for any given change, bugs will still find their way to our users, so the safety these slow processes provide is only superficial.

Since mistakes and bugs are inevitable anyway, it's a good thing that we are focusing on optimizing the mean time to recovery: errors can't be very complex, because the deployed changes are small, and they can be quickly mitigated by deactivating a toggle or deploying a bug fix or a revert commit.

There are a lot of reasons for errors: people can be tired because their child is sick, they can be distracted while looking forward to a holiday, or they could in fact be inexperienced. In general, these errors won't find their way to the live system in the first place. Our comprehensive test suites will usually find these software misbehaviors and end with a red pipeline instead of a bug in our live environment. The few cases where a truly simple mistake (because, let's be honest, that's what junior engineers might create) isn't detected by the pipeline is a good opportunity to improve the test suite instead of allowing fear or distrust to slow the team down.

Of course, focusing on fast recovery doesn't mean error prevention is completely irrelevant. But our processes and pipelines are streamlined to deliver value quickly instead of deliberately slowing down deployments in order to gain superficial safety.

Links and Resources

You can find a lot of information about our processes and insights in our tech blog: *https://oreil.ly/K0Co5*.

For additional information:

- Fast-feedback cycle: *https://oreil.ly/_colu*
- Process automation: *https://oreil.ly/BhOA1*
- Visual regression tests with JLineUp: *https://oreil.ly/q1dWP*
- CDCs: *https://oreil.ly/Ly98O*
- Feature toggles: *https://oreil.ly/PBIEJ*

Case Study: N26

For our third case study, we will look at continuous deployment at N26. Alberto Ramírez Fernández is a principal engineer in the N26 Platform Engineering group, and he has kindly offered to explain how N26 approaches continuous deployments to production. Before he switched to the principal engineer role, he worked within the continuous integration/continuous delivery (CI/CD) group (within the internal Platform Engineering domain), which maintains the tools that allow every engineer at N26 to build and deliver software.

N26's Context

Today N26 is one of the fastest-growing digital banks in the world. As a fully licensed German bank built on the latest technology, N26 makes banking faster, easier, and more trustworthy. Founded in 2013, N26 has welcomed more than 8 million customers in 24 markets to date. As of 2024, N26 employs a diverse team of more than 1,500 people from over 80 nations.

Adoption of Continuous Deployment at N26

Continuous deployment was adopted around 2016 as part of the transition from a monolithic architecture to a service-oriented one. On the one hand, the monolithic application kept using a release train where the team had to manually promote changes following two weeks of testing them. On the other hand, new services came with changes in processes and practices, with continuous deployment being one of them. As more services popped up, better tooling and automation were required. Therefore, tooling to enhance automated end-to-end (E2E) testing in the distributed environment, CI/CD shared libraries, and much more made the transition easier. Adopting continuous deployment along with other practices (and investing in internal tooling to support them) proved to be the right thing to do, as a constellation of new services showed up in the following years.

Currently, continuous deployment is the standard at N26. Teams are used to it and they complement it with good observability, testing strategies, and other practices such as CI and code reviews. It is also documented as part of the onboarding process so that new joiners get used to it quite quickly and in a safe way, enabling them to contribute with small code changes and bring them into production without any big risks for customers.

As N26 is a digital bank that is 100% online, technology and best practices are quite important for us, and continuous deployment makes it possible to move quickly and detect potential issues earlier. As our internal team structures are optimized for autonomy and delivery speed, building incrementally and deploying software continuously allows us to iterate and learn more quickly.

Working Within Industry Regulations

Banking is a highly regulated industry, and N26 operates with a full German banking license. Understanding what is important for our customers when it comes to security, compliance, privacy, and availability is key to understanding the high level of requirements within the banking industry.

This is a huge topic and is difficult to summarize, but in a nutshell, to make continuous deployment work within our context we focus on the following topics:

Multiple lines of defense
> For example, we use peer reviews to ensure that the code that gets integrated into the main branch is validated and matches expectations.

Traceability
> For us, it is imperative to keep a record of what goes live. In this regard, keeping track of every version released and the process it went through, test suites executed, authors, reviewers, and product request that triggered it is mandatory.

Well-defined and automated processes
> We cannot make continuous deployment work without defining all the change management processes and automating them as much as possible. In this regard, we found Dave Farley's post about continuous compliance (*https://oreil.ly/ WRavx*) quite inspiring. Nowadays, we have automated compliance checks that act as gates before going live, and we have further iterations planned for this.

Working with Technical Barriers

Recently we adopted the Declarative GitOps paradigm to deploy services into Kubernetes (using ArgoCD). We wanted to have a declarative configuration per application, collocated either within the service's repository or in a repository sidecar (both of which have been trending in the past few years).

Whenever we merge code into the main branch, run the CI and compliance checks, and publish an artifact into the repository, one of the processes needs to bump the version to be released (i.e., a commit hash) into the application configuration manifest. This way, the Kubernetes reconciliation mechanism ensures that the service is always running the version that is declared in the manifest.

We encountered a big challenge here: this component would have push permissions over all the repositories onboarded into the platform and would be able to force-push into the main branch, bypassing the four-eyes principle that is important to us. One can agree that if this component is automated, was audited, and was developed using internal practices, it would be safe to use, and that is true. However, to eliminate the low but existing risk of a malicious actor obtaining access to the component, we implemented a single repository holding all the application configurations (more than 200 at the time of writing this). This is not the more scalable solution, nor is the developer experience the best, but we managed to limit the attack surface as, again, security is of utmost importance to us.

N26's Implementation of Continuous Deployment

Everything starts with a ticket, as all the changes into production must be correlated to a ticket that describes the purpose (business, product, tech, etc.) of the change. Every team has its own way of working, but trunk-based development with short-lived feature branches (*https://oreil.ly/W64Sn*) is by far the most adopted collaboration model at N26.

With a local branch, we often code and run tests locally to validate that everything is correct. Every small iteration gets committed, and when we have the feature ready, we open a pull request (PR). Teams have a strong commitment to review PRs as soon as possible so as not to temporarily block peers. When doing pair programming, the PR usually gets approved by the peer instantaneously. However, we still need to go through the PR (not committing straight to the main branch) to ensure a compliant review of the change. The PR also contains a set of gates (which depend on the nature of the repository), to ensure applicable compliance checks, automated test suites, and quality and security assurance checks.

When the PR is approved, the author merges it and the code gets integrated into the main branch. At this point, the CI/CD pipeline gets triggered, some of the checks that ran previously in the PR along with some others run in the main branch, and the outcome is an artifact (usually a container image) that gets stored in our internal Artifact Registry. When the artifact is ready, the continuous deployment pipeline starts, which brings the artifact through the multiple environments and runs database migrations and other automated checks (E2E tests, security tests, health checks) before promoting it to the next environment and up to the production environment.

For bigger features, we may need to split the work into smaller iterations, delivering them one by one to production (through the process just defined). Sometimes, along with CI and CD, we also use feature flags to decouple delivery from the release. This process also follows the four-eyes principle, as multiple lines of defense are needed when changing the live environment.

All these steps are fully automated and are described as code (following all the same change management processes). They run automatically based on some events that trigger them (PR opened, push to the main branch, artifact is ready, etc.) and take between 20 and 40 minutes end to end (based on how big the testing suites are) for the majority of the services and a few hours for other, bigger repositories that use other branching and collaboration models.

How N26 Makes Continuous Deployment Safe

Engineers at N26 use multiple patterns and techniques at different stages and levels to make it safer to go to production. I described some of them already: the four-eyes principle, where a review from a peer is mandatory; automated compliance and security checks; automated test suites and quality assurance; automatic promotion over multiple environments if the changes fulfill some requirements; using feature flags to turn new features on and off; and A/B testing to test them.

Other patterns may be in networking levels, such as access control lists or circuit breakers to prevent issues introduced in new code from having a massive impact in the whole infrastructure. This way, the blast radius would get reduced too.

Last but not least, securing the supply chain is a topic we continuously review and assess, and we may implement additional new patterns and techniques this year.

Test automation

I am a big supporter of the testing pyramid. Therefore, the vast majority of my tests are unit tests.

Usually I test from the outside in, focusing on the public API of the subject under test and replacing collaborators with fakes or mocks or in-memory/Noop implementations, but this depends on the layer and the use case (I am also a big promoter of ports and adapters). Usually, for application services under test, I may provide either a mock or a fake; for domain services, I may replace collaborators with a fake or an in-memory/Noop implementation. But for domain models or root aggregates, I may not replace any of the collaborators, as my understanding of those is that they should be treated as black boxes.

On the other hand, I usually test the infrastructure layer using integration testing; for example, integration with the database (using the repository pattern), REST APIs, messaging producers/consumers, and so on. With integration tests, we use a local containerized version of the infrastructure layer (database, mock server, etc.) and test that the repository/service behaves as expected.

On top of unit and integration tests, we might have a few component tests to check the happy path. We would do this if, for instance, we think about the microservices architecture just spinning up the service under test with all the upstream and downstream dependencies mocked, and testing the happy path as a black box. This is not common, and therefore we may have a couple of component tests as well.

All the tests described so far (unit, integration, and component) should be able to run fast locally. They should also run during PRs and integration within the main branch (I did not refer to this as CI intentionally, as I know this is a big topic, but internally we call these "CI checks").

Finally, we also have E2E tests. At N26, for years we have had a strong culture of testing our system end to end, even though it is quite complex given the nature of our distributed architecture. This is because our understanding of providing proof of testing of the customer's end-to-end features in an environment should be as similar to the production environment as possible as we go through describing scenarios, running the E2E tests for all those scenarios, and keeping the record (for future traceability) of the test execution. In a highly regulated environment, this is important.

Deployment strategy

The runtime platform we invest in the most nowadays is Kubernetes, which has a huge adoption at N26. We mostly use ArgoCD and Argo Workflows to deploy services into Kubernetes. The declarative GitOps pattern fits really well within our regulated environment, as it helps us keep track not only of the source code but also of the application's configuration in multiple environments. Furthermore, with Argo Workflows we can define more complex pipelines with multiple gates and promotions that fit the requirements of the majority of our teams.

Moreover, as N26's tech stack is heterogeneous, there are other systems that either do not run on Kubernetes or are still in the transition phase from the previous runtime platform to the new one based on Kubernetes and Argo. In both use cases, we use a kind of blue/green deployment on EC2 instances on AWS (spot instances along with on-demand ones based on certain internal rules), with the application running as a Docker container in most cases.

Depending on the nature of the software to be released (microservices, web, or mobile application), the test suite is different and may have its own particularities, but in general, E2E testing always runs in the staging environment before going to production.

Four-eyes principle

We require the four-eyes principle for changes to promote them into the cloud. We have a strong policy regarding this topic, as per regulation, we need to ensure that no arbitrary changes are made to production.

We use PRs to provide proof of peer review. Mob programming and pair programming are also encouraged and many teams do them, which makes the PR approval process faster because the code was reviewed live. However, the PRs along with an explicit approval are mandatory for better tracking.

It is worth adding that in the case of an incident, engineers who are on call may break the glass[1] as we prioritize the stability of the system for our customers. However, these events trigger some sort of alert for later review by another peer along with the security team.

Observability

We implement observability differently depending on the nature of the application. For example, mobile applications may structure their observability around the number of sessions without fatal errors or traces, while web applications may value the errors in the browser and the performance metrics more.

Furthermore, backend services may use a combination of metrics, traces, and logs, and most of them use standard monitors and dashboards that the observability team provides out of the box as part of the platform and that teams can adapt to their needs. Monitors around the number of errors or high latency are quite common, but because the monitors based on key performance indicator (KPI) metrics are the most useful for the majority of the teams, most recently we have been moving more and more toward service-level objectives using those KPIs as base indicators.

Last but not least, it is worth noting that monitoring and alerting are usually defined as code along with each backend repository so that we can keep track of all the changes, reproduce and rebuild the monitors and dashboards in case of disaster, and bring them into multiple environments if needed.

How N26 Supports Junior Engineers

When a junior engineer joins N26, they go through the regular onboarding process, from the more general overview sessions to the ones driven by their teams. These sessions make sure they understand the internal ways of working, our processes and practices, and our tooling and internal platform. Additionally, they get assigned a buddy who helps them during the first few months for a better ramp-up.

---

1 That is, escalate privileges to gain access to production.

As soon as they start working in a team, junior engineers may require a bit more follow-up from more senior or lead engineers so that they get used to the code, the team's routines, the documentation, and so on. However, from the very beginning of their journey in the team (second or third week), junior engineers can (and are encouraged to) bring changes into production without any additional requirement, since the change management process is well-defined, all the steps are automated, and we have a variety of safety nets, lines of defense, and monitoring in place. Therefore, they can start contributing as soon as they feel comfortable to do so.

Links and Resources

- *https://medium.com/insiden26*
- *https://n26.com/en/careers*

Case Study: ClimatePartner

For our next case study, Ilias Bartolini will describe continuous deployment at ClimatePartner. Ilias is a team lead working across two teams in the Emission Reductions and Authorization & Identity Management domains. His role is a combination of people management, technical leadership, and delivery support.

ClimatePartner's Context

ClimatePartner supports companies on their journey toward net zero. For around 20 years, the organization has been developing solutions that enable its clients to make voluntary climate action commitments combining software, consulting, and reduction solutions. ClimatePartner's industry-specific solutions cover the entire process, from calculating carbon footprints to setting reduction targets and implementing reduction measures. ClimatePartner also supports companies in financing global and regional climate projects and providing detailed and transparent communication on their climate action commitments. This includes labeling solutions that confirm the comprehensive and strategic approach of a company's voluntary climate action measures.

With around 500 employees in 12 offices, ClimatePartner supports more than 6,000 clients from over 60 countries. We have a product engineering department of approximately 50 people in six teams divided across three different locations.

ClimatePartner digital products are very diverse in nature. I worked across two teams: Emission Reductions and Authorization & Identity Management, where we primarily build tools aimed at our B2B customers. Typical users of our applications are sustainability managers or our internal sustainability specialists. The results of the core tools, such as footprint calculation, are also integrated in transparency pages that are instead a public view aimed at general consumers.

On top of the core tools, we offer API integration solutions and have more strict availability requirements. Our applications are composed of approximately 25 independently deployable units, and each team supports on average four or five services.

Adoption of Continuous Deployment at ClimatePartner

At the beginning of 2020, ClimatePartner went through a period of rapid growth. At that time, we introduced a new tech stack and adopted a service-oriented architecture to split our monolith and enable more autonomous teams. Continuous deployment became the de facto standard of the new technology stack based on the previous experiences of our team leads at that time. Some of the legacy services have also been migrated to this style of development.

People in our organization embraced the change quickly. A certain level of support and knowledge was needed from experienced folks and the platform team, but once the first continuous deployment pipelines were set up, everyone embraced it. The only open challenge has been in transitioning our original monolith, which as of today still has a different deployment process. Autonomy was left to the team to keep the process it found more suitable within its context.

ClimatePartner's Implementation of Continuous Deployment

Our tasks and stories are typically small: each pair may deploy two or three times per day on average before they are complete. Bigger or more complex stories may get deployed more than 10 times before being completed.

Typically an engineer in their daily activities commits and pushes their code directly on the main branch. On every push, a GitHub action pipeline executes the build, test, and packaging automation steps on the main branch. All of these run in isolation, without integration with other services that are typically stubbed. If tests are successful, a new container image is created and versioning is attached to the application by simply using the last git commit SHA. After the container is successfully created, the following steps involve automatically deploying the new image on our existing production infrastructure.

We practice infrastructure as code (IaC) using Terraform in our pipelines, while the build, test, packaging, and deployment of the application are part of the primary application deployment pipeline.

The other parts of the infrastructure (e.g., application cluster setup, domains, database) are on the same repository but are applied in a separate GitHub action pipeline that has a "plan" step executed on every push but that can be reviewed, triggered manually, and have its changes applied when needed.

In parallel to the production deployment, we have actions that execute other non-blocking steps such as static code analysis and code coverage checks using Sonar.

How ClimatePartner Makes Continuous Deployment Safe

There are three primary elements of the safety net for engineers:

- Good test automation coverage
- Good system observability with production alerts for all the main "golden signals" of monitoring
- Confidence that in case of application errors, we can revert our changes within a few minutes

Test automation

As part of our teams' practices, we assume most of the time that every change has been test-driven and has good test coverage at the unit and service levels.

Our test pyramid focuses more on the intermediate levels, and we simulate browser-based interactions for the frontends. Most services are tested in isolation during our pipeline build, and all dependencies are stubbed based on the agreed contract.

The services are integrated directly in production, and therefore we rely more on good observability and a fast response time to catch service integration errors. Some services and teams have adopted consumer-driven contract (CDC) testing, but our experience has received mixed feedback in this regard.

Zero downtime

The majority of our systems run in AWS with ECS and Fargate. We deploy new versions by doing a rolling upgrade of the application containers to the new version.

Feature toggles

We have different types of toggles in our systems. First, we have feature toggles typically used by the product engineering teams to hide work in progress on new features. Second, we have service toggles that are used to customize which application modules are available to our customers. We use these both for access management and to incrementally release new modules to certain customer accounts.

Observability

In our default platform and tech stack, we require Datadog integ8ration for all our services. All services come with predefined dashboards that include monitoring the "golden" signals and comprehensive tracking for our frontend applications. Our primary concern is to alert on application errors. In our context, performance and scale are typically not a primary concern, but we still have alerts based on user behaviors.

Four-eyes principle

We don't have a formal code review process. Instead, we primarily encourage pair programming, and we practice trunk-based development pushing directly to main. Only on rare occasions do we organize ensemble programming sessions, or we create ad hoc branches if needed.

Testing in production

Part of our continuous deployment philosophy has also included the idea to embrace "test in production" techniques. Most of our systems do not have a staging environment but only production, which also has a good side effect of reducing our cloud usage bills and carbon footprint. The primary expectation is for different teams to try to integrate directly in production.

The nature of our system is such that application accounts need to have strong data separation requirements. We take advantage of this to keep demo and test data in separate application accounts directly in production and also mark them programmatically as test accounts. When this is not possible, we isolate test data by adding a test property or test attribute on the root entities of our domain model. Our test data in production is typically never shown, and there are hardcoded rules to exclude it in a few places; for example, a user can see test data only when they are logged in to test accounts.

This approach has become a challenge when integrating with third-party systems such as CRM and ERP tools that have different environments and release cycles. For these integrations, we resorted to mirroring their setup by adding a staging environment. But differently from traditional deployment processes, our deployment to staging is nonblocking for going to production. Our staging and production environments are deployed in parallel in our pipelines.

While building REST API integration with other applications, we also often practice expand and contract techniques to evolve our API contracts.

How ClimatePartner Supports Junior Engineers with Continuous Deployment

Continuous deployment is usually very easily embraced by junior engineers. Onboarding of junior engineers still goes through certain phases: starting only on one codebase, and selecting simpler tasks that we label "good for onboarding."

Pair programming allows for a faster learning and onboarding experience compared to a process based on pull requests. New engineers have reported that the faster feedback of continuous deployment allowed them to learn more quickly.

At the same time, some new engineers reported feeling more apprehensive when initially pushing code directly to production. In the first two to three months, we make sure there is always a person available to pair with junior team members for small changes. Overall, we believe that continuous deployment needs to be adopted in an environment that is based on psychological safety and trust.

Case Study: Motability Operations

For our next case study, Julian Austin and Lloyd Jones will describe the practice of continuous deployment at the UK company Motability Operations. As head of software engineering and Agile transformation at Motability Operations, Julian has played a pivotal role in leading the adoption of continuous deployment throughout the organization, preparing a cultural baseline for its success. Lloyd has co-championed this effort and will share his experience working "on the ground" as an Agile and software engineering team lead, where he looks after all engineering practices required to perform continuous deployment effectively.

Motability Operations' Context

Motability Operations is the company behind the UK Motability car, powered wheelchair, and scooter, and we help over 690,000 people with disabilities and their families get on the road.

For over 40 years, our affordable, accessible Motability Scheme service has helped to keep millions of customers mobile. Our aim is to meet our customers' different disability needs by providing a wide range of affordable vehicles. Today, over 710,000 people with disabilities and their families benefit from the worry-free mobility available through the Scheme. Our customers can lease cars, wheelchair accessible vehicles (WAVs), scooters, and powered wheelchairs. All our cars come with insurance, maintenance, breakdown assistance, and a mileage allowance of 60,000 miles.

MO's turnover is £4.7 billion, and we made profits in 2022 of £923 million, all of which was reinvested back into the Scheme for the benefit of our disabled customers.

Software engineering teams build and *run* all the bespoke software used across the enterprise. The teams have removed close to 95% of their legacy software and replaced it with a cloud-first microservices and micro-UI architecture. This includes our Digital Customer software that is used to onboard new customers onto the

Scheme, to apply for a renewal vehicle at the end of the lease, or to update personal details and preferences.

We also build and run the software that is responsible for efficiently managing the return and sale of over 200,000 end-of-lease vehicles annually, driving a multibillion-pound revenue stream, as described in a recent blog post (*https://oreil.ly/L9EfC*).

Adoption of Continuous Deployment at Motability Operations

We started talking about continuous deployment in 2018. We were embarking on a digital transformation initially, and we sent a small team on a residency to Red Hat Labs.

Working with Organizational Barriers

We found some organizational obstacles to the adoption of continuous deployment at first, including pushback from our Business Risk department, various security concerns, fear of the unknown, and a lack of automation. We also had separate pipelines for non-prod and prod environments. Here is how we worked to address these obstacles:

Julian: I sat down with the Business Risk department in July 2023 to review the risk controls for Software Engineering. As part of that meeting, I took them through the concept of continuous deployment. Their immediate view was that this greatly increased the risk of failure with software deployments. However, once I explained in detail what we were doing and how we were doing it, along with the benefits of continuous deployment, they accepted that this technique and the way we planned to implement it would actually reduce the risk. Continuous deployment is now recorded as a *risk mitigation* control for reducing the risk of failure with software releases. It is no longer thought of as a risk.

Lloyd: I spent a lot of time with our Change and Release management team. They come from a world of legacy infrastructure, physical hardware, and scheduled ITIL-style[1] release processes. Most of my time was spent educating them on the theory of continuous deployment and the fact that it reduces risk, enables agility, and enhances the ability to resolve issues quickly. I worked with them and our developer experience team to design a self-documenting continuous deployment pipeline that ensures visibility of changes that are happening.

---

1 ITIL stands for Information Technology Infrastructure Library.

Working with technical barriers

We also had some technical barriers, mainly due to separate Jenkins instances for production, preproduction, and non-prod deployments. This made it challenging to manage a unified view of the entire pipeline. To solve this, we initially implemented a Jenkins instance in a management cluster that would simply orchestrate calls to the other Jenkins pipelines. We then iterated to remove the dependencies on the individual Jenkins instances.

Our other technical challenge was coupled with the preceding issue but ended up being fairly straightforward: implementing ArgoCD as our tool for the GitOps process. As is usually the case with any new tool, there were some small teething pains.

Motability Operations' Implementation of Continuous Deployment

Following is an example of our standard path to production at Motability Operations. However, teams have the flexibility to enable, disable, and customize most of these steps, so there might be some variations from team to team. For example, we haven't quite got SonarQube working with multimodule projects yet, so this stage is skipped for the handful of multimodule projects we have:

- An engineer pushes a change to a source repo (we currently use Bitbucket).
- A webhook triggers a pipeline execution in Jenkins.
- We unit-test, build, push to SonarQube, and do a Snyk scan. Some of these steps will fail the execution and others will not.
- We package the application into a "final" image version.
- The image is promoted to our non-prod Nexus repository.
- Jenkins pushes to a GitOps mono-repo (we have one per tenant in our cloud infra). This defines the state (version, config, etc.) for the first non-prod environment.
- ArgoCD picks up the change to the GitOps repo and triggers OpenShift to begin the rollout.
- Pods scale down and are upgraded in a blue/green manner.
- Additional journey automation tests may be run.
- Steps 6 through 9 may repeat for one or two additional non-prod environments.
- An image is promoted to the prod Nexus repository.
- Jenkins commits to the GitOps repo defining the state for the pre-prod environment.

- Steps 7 through 9 happen as before, although testing will be different.
- We repeat steps 12 and 13 for production.
- There may be a feature flag to enable in LaunchDarkly. This is contextual to the team and its work at the time.

Behind the scenes, Jenkins also does a few interesting tasks that make our tools a little bit better to use:

- It maintains the original Jira ticket with build and deployment information.
- It tells Bitbucket about the build and deployment.
- It keeps a database record of the service, what team "owns it," where the repo is, what the latest version is, who changed it last, and when it was last deployed.
- A release note Jira ticket is created and linked to the database record of the service, the commit, the GitOps commit, and the original Jira ticket.
- The release note is updated per environment and closed by Jenkins once prod deployment has happened.

During the implementation of a single task or user story, this path to production is generally triggered end to end from 5 to 25 times. This is dependent on the component and on the maturity of the team maintaining it. We want to reduce the total number of non-prods to one, but we are not there just yet and different teams have slightly different numbers. However, flexibility was one of the aims when we started this journey.

How Motability Makes Continuous Deployment Safe

At Motability, we employ several practices and tools to ensure the safety of continuous automated deployments.

Test automation

We have automated tests, from unit- to UI-based journey tests. Our test pyramid is still too fat in the middle, which results in some fragility of testing, but this has improved massively since we introduced continuous deployment.

There are also some synthetic monitoring tests that run against production using Dynatrace.

Zero-downtime deployments

We achieve zero downtime through the use of blue/green deployments in our environments, with Jenkins and ArgoCD orchestrating our continuous integration/

continuous delivery (CI/CD) pipelines. For our infrastructure, we use RedHat, Openshift, and Kubernetes, all on top of AWS.

Continuous code reviews

We mostly pair-program in our software engineering teams, where numbers don't allow us to use informal code reviews or pull requests as required. Generally we have a "two pairs of eyes on everything" rule.

Observability

We are still maturing in the area of observability, but we have some tools of choice: mostly Dynatrace, Opsgenie, and Splunk. We are pretty well covered in terms of surfacing errors to the right team and responding to them.

Recently, a group kicked off an SRE initiative to better understand our capabilities and weaknesses. I think where we need more work is understanding things like suitable service-level objectives (SLOs) and monitoring of trends over time.

Feature flags

Feature flags via LaunchDarkly have replaced our internally built tools. Blue/green and, more recently, canary releases are being used.

Encouraging contributions

We have a DevX team that acts as the custodian of the Path to Prod library. This team actively supports it and continues to add features, as well as educating others. It also encourages and welcomes contributions from others.

How Motability Operations Supports Teams

Motability aims to support engineers who might not be familiar with continuous deployment at different stages of their journey within the company.

Junior engineers

We support junior engineers by pairing them heavily, and rotating whom they pair with. This ensures exposure to a range of engineering experience. We encourage juniors to get involved with the whole development life cycle and continuous deployment as soon as possible.

Hiring

We look to hire passionate and engaged engineers. We don't expect to hire people who have all the skills we need. This includes continuous deployment experience, as so few companies are consistently working this way at the moment. Many have the vision of full continuous deployment, but few, it seems, have managed to achieve it. [Valentina's note: hopefully this book will help!]

Onboarding

We support new engineers to upskill in any gaps they have. This is primarily done through pair-programming support and the fact that we have a DevX enablement team that has automated and ready-made templates to ease the adoption of continuous deployment.

We have a Path to Prod library that has the effect of abstracting a lot of the detail away from engineers. It has commoditized continuous deployment for our teams. Anyone can use it as is and get a consistent experience from it. If their use case is atypical, or if they are just interested, then they can dive into the details and customize. The best ideas get baked back into the core library for others to use.

Case Study: REA Group

For our next case study, Alison Rosewarne will walk us through the adoption of continuous deployment at REA Group. Alison is the executive manager of Architecture and Tech L&D at REA.

REA's Context

REA Group is an ASX-listed digital business specializing in property and one of Australia's startup success stories. We're using technology to change the way the world experiences property. Through our digital platforms, we provide access to the largest and most engaged audience of property seekers, deliver superior customer value, and offer comprehensive insights into Australia's housing market.

At the time of writing, REA Group is an ASX Top 20–listed company with a market capitalization of $23.81 billion. REA employs over 3,000 people across Australia and India. Around 1,000 of our 1,600 Australia-based employees are dedicated to functions supporting delivery of digital products.

I maintain the architecture function at REA as well as learning and development supporting our technology community. Our architecture function helps bring our tech strategy to life through enabling processes (such as our tech decision-making and system health frameworks), contribution to strategic initiatives, and ownership of our overall architecture practice. Our Tech L&D function is part of a broader learning function and offers a combination of social learning support, self-service learning resources, and dedicated training events.

In previous roles at REA, I have owned a variety of systems including the web home page of Realestate.com.au, which sustains an average load of 1,000 to 2,000 requests per minute (RPMs).

Adoption of Continuous Deployment at REA

REA is traditionally an early adopter of industry trends and new technology. In 2010, we were already using continuous integration (CI) and test automation to increase quality. In 2012, the company experimented successfully with deployment automation, and multiple greenfield initiatives were being deployed on demand via automated build steps. These builds were the envy of other teams that still coordinated fortnightly release programs following lengthy documents. These initiatives aimed to decrease the ceremony and risk around large deployments and release value more regularly to real users.

In 2013, REA quickly moved to experimentation with continuous deployment, aiming to continue learning, entrench the mindset shift, and release features more often. Our cloud adoption was well underway, and we found DevOps techniques very complementary. This became the preferred way of working by 2014, and incrementally rolled into more critical and core systems.

From this point forward, continuous delivery (CD) was our default way of working, with continuous deployment preferred. This included automated build, test, and deployment pipelines along with monitoring and simple rollback approaches.

Regardless of deployment approach, we always keep our main branch in a deployable state and make use of feature toggles and dark code to allow on-demand releases and continuation of work. These changes took place at a time when we were migrating from the data center to the cloud as well as shifting to "You build it, you run it" for all teams, providing an opportunity to upskill and deploy more often and more safely.

In 2021, we formalized our views by including "Deploy continuously" in our refreshed architectural principles. This principle states:

> Creating short feedback loops is a critical component of building agile software. Minimizing the time between starting work on a change and having it live in production reduces built up risk, minimizes codebase contention, and brings forward learning opportunities. We are only able to fully validate ideas by getting them into the hands of real customers—short feedback loops are a key enabler for this. These short feedback loops support our ability to respond quickly to new feature requests, bug fixes, and security updates.

We codified this principle into our system health framework, REA's way to articulate our expectations of our software and assess progress toward improvement goals. CD, supported by fully scripted build steps and an effective suite of tests, is the baseline expectation. In addition, in 2022 we started tracking adoption of continuous deployment as well, with this criterion part of our highest expectations of engineering excellence. Over 80% of our fleet is continuously deployed today.

Overcoming organizational barriers

In hindsight, the early experimentation by cross-functional teams was a key ingredient to continued adoption. Our QAs were part of this team, as were our product managers. Involving our QAs up front allowed them to codesign and coach us through the transition to shift-left our quality thinking, where everyone needs to consider quality earlier in the process. They helped us consider more scenarios during kickoffs and write more comprehensive automated tests. Even teams without dedicated QA people benefited from these lessons and adopted continuous deployment keenly.

Involving our product managers meant they could lead our Go-To-Market team through the change and help support any production issues, as they were committed to the value enabled in the end.

Different teams have different cultures, and there was hesitancy around removing that "safety net" of a separate QA stage, which allowed developers to offload some of the responsibility of ensuring working code in production to another role. Consistent positive messaging of "let's give this a try" as well as emphasis on the benefits for developers that their work would be live, useful, and appreciated sooner worked well.

To effectively manage production issues, the team applied our "no blame" approach to post-incident reviews, where they adapted and shared what they had learned with interested onlookers. The early experimentation helped identify what was needed to get started and demonstrated the value in a tangible way. This certainly showed when critical vulnerabilities were detected in common frameworks. The continuous deployment teams were patched and done within a day, while others took weeks if not longer.

Overcoming technical barriers

A lot of the technical obstacles we faced related to the technology available in a pre-DevOps world. Most of our deployments were conducted by humans following standard operating procedure (SOP) documents with a lot of assumed knowledge. We had excellent monitoring and good infrastructure as code (IaC) practices, but there was often "ClickOps" glue and many environments were treated as "cattle, not pets." We had to take a parallel approach, experimenting and validating technology with our greenfield systems while also uplifting our existing systems.

We paired developers with operations team members to conduct deploys, improving our documentation along the way and establishing the path for automation. We shifted our IaC from centralized repositories to live right alongside the system's code (or at least closer to it) and scripted deployment steps so that config changes could also trigger releases. It took a lot of experimenting to land on a CI server that worked for everyone (we tried Hudson, Jenkins, Go, and Bamboo before landing on BuildKite).

It took a serious incident, where we lost all of our build pipelines, to really learn that build pipeline config was as important as infrastructure config and should be managed the same way.

We also needed new patterns to provide access control and security around deployment orchestration. Keys needed to be encrypted before storage in version control, and decrypted on demand within production. All of this configuration, automation, and logging certainly increased audit visibility and made incident response a lot faster.

Achieving zero-downtime deployment has led us to build in-house tooling for this capability. We've also rethought our approach to deploying and serving commonly cached assets, such as CSS and JavaScript.

Over time, our reliance on other environments (such as staging) decreased. Production was such a continually evolving target that we needed more emphasis on backward compatibility with our APIs. The Pact (*https://oreil.ly/soOHY*) consumer-driven contract testing tool was created at this time to help manage this challenge. Today, many teams only spin up pre-prod or staging environments on demand for activities such as load testing. Instead, they rely on their machines, CI, and production.

Some challenges were clear when white-boarding the desired state and planning a thin slice or minimum viable product (MVP); others were unexpected bumps or brick walls we encountered along the way. Like any Agile team, we adapted and learned and kept our sense of humor.

REA's Implementation of Continuous Deployment

Deployment frequency of code changes for a single task or user story is highly dependent on the team's ways of working, including how small it slices its cards, its comfort with continuous deployment, whether the work is in a system it owns (or in another team's system), and other factors.

Generally, new code is rolled into production at least once, and we would prefer to break cards into the smallest slice that delivers value and can be released, rather than having very long-running cards that are incrementally released throughout development. We develop on short-lived branches and create pull requests (PRs) for work. Once a PR has been merged, the build is triggered.

The first stage of the build provides verification of the change. We have a number of build steps, usually executed in parallel to check the change. This includes scanning for security vulnerabilities, linting, and static analysis; executing automated tests; and configuration validation. Usually the build artifact (i.e., Docker container) is built and published in parallel as well, to reduce overall build time.

Next, some of our builds perform a canary deployment to production. These builds either will release the change to a subset of production traffic or will be dark-launched in production to enable further automated testing.

Next, the change is released to production via internal tooling, providing a zero-downtime release with a red/black approach. The new service needs to respond to a health check before it is brought into service. REA utilizes caching extensively, supporting high traffic volumes; therefore, it can be hours before some changes are visible. The vast majority, however, are released within minutes.

From this point on, we rely on monitoring and alerting to detect any issues. Humans are on call and will be paged if an issue is detected; they can then judge whether a release rollback is required or something else is at play. Rollback might involve triggering the build on a previously "known good" version, issuing a git revert to cause a new deployment to production, or manually redeploying a previous version.

Our mobile codebases, generally following a weekly release train, also embrace these practices to realize the value within this ecosystem as well. We continuously deploy builds to an internal app library that is then distributed to test devices, ensuring that each change is in the hands of real users in a short time frame.

How REA Makes Continuous Deployment Safe

The REA team uses many patterns and techniques to enable safe and frequent releases.

Assuming a solid foundation of a shift-left quality mindset, no-blame incident response, and automation, we then look to specifics. Feature toggles are the most common enabler for continuous deployment and can be scoped as small as one card or as large as a small initiative. Internal platforms we have created to accelerate web, native, and data processing all include feature toggling capability.

For larger initiatives, dark launching is fairly common and useful to experience continuous deployment without impacting end users or to line up with a larger Go-To-Market (GTM) campaign.

For APIs, we implement a variety of approaches depending on the API consumers. Generally, maintaining backward compatibility for very long periods provides the least disruption. API versioning and expand and contract are useful techniques where you have a high degree of influence over both API consumers and API providers (or a strong desire and ability to manage such changes).

We have an internal catalog of systems and observability tools to understand API consumers where we do need to manage migrations or deprecations. Occasionally, we've maintained facades allowing API clients to remain unaware of re-platforms behind the scenes. For partner APIs or those powering mobile platforms, again backward compatibility and monitoring consumption patterns help manage the long tail of usage.

Test automation

Our test automation approach is based on Mike Cohn's test pyramid in that we value a large number of isolated and therefore fast tests, and then have fewer and fewer tests that integrate and execute more slowly. It is rare for automated tests to require dependent systems to be running for verification, preferring consumer contract testing for such scenarios.

Zero-downtime deployments

For the most part, our deployments are red/black (synonymous with blue/green) these days. This means new component versions are deployed in production and then brought into service (to receive production traffic) once they self-report as healthy.

We've built internal tools to orchestrate these deployments: one specifically for serverless workloads and another for long-running workloads. Our compute generally leverages Amazon ECS with EC2 or Fargate, and we're experimenting with Kubernetes.

Code reviews

We use a variety of mechanisms for code review. Our sensible default for development is pair programming, and occasionally mob programming, although this is rarer and often a learning tool. Code that is ready for production is bundled into a PR.

Each PR triggers a build that performs the verification steps; this allows the reviewer to focus on the actual delta. The PR is reviewed and approved by a separate individual (or pair), focusing on the design and consistency within the overall codebase. The code author(s) would then merge the PR triggering the production deployment.

Observability

Observability of our environments is based on logging, metrics, and transaction request tracing.

All system components produce logs (e.g., access logs, application logs), and these are centrally aggregated for convenience. Retention windows and archiving strategies are necessary for high-volume systems as well as paying careful attention to log contents, ensuring that they support debugging without being too verbose.

Sensible defaults for default metrics are built into our deployment tooling, which may then be customized. Response time, SSL certifications, and error rates are part of these defaults, with CPU utilization typically the driver for autoscaling. Custom metrics may be built for key user journey outcomes and monitored via preset thresholds or anomaly detection.

Transaction IDs are applied to requests to support tracing. Centrally aggregated logs can be queried by these IDs to understand system correlation.

We've experimented with synthetic monitoring but have generally found that usage is high and consistent enough without needing to simulate user operations.

Excessive error rates or response times most frequently trigger alerting and human response. Deeper insights into root causes generally come from analyzing logs or digging into data from our application performance monitoring (APM) tools.

How REA Supports Junior Engineers with Continuous Deployment

Our technical onboarding, which every role goes through (not just juniors), covers the what, why, and how of continuous deployment. This gives everyone a common understanding of the approach and value, while also showing the safety that has been built into the system and our culture.

Junior engineers, like all staff, have access to their manager, learning support, and career pathways. Our teams are usually designed with a range of experience levels, with a focus on pairing, to support learning on the job.

We also run Entry to REA programs, supporting diverse cohorts of new joiners to REA. This includes our graduate program, for recent university graduates, and our Springboard to Tech program, for females who are switching careers or returning after a break, with a focus on technical up-skilling. In 2023, we piloted our first Women in Systems Engineering internship program in partnership with Grad Girls. These programs allow for more facilitated learning that is built into the program structure, a series of rotations with our teams to provide a variety of learning experiences, and an ongoing program mentor.

Case Study: Maze

For our next case study, we'll look at Maze, a user research company that began its journey with continuous deployment during its startup phase. Atte Huhtakangas (engineering manager) and Maarten Ackermans (staff engineer) will walk us through their journey with the practice.

Maze's Context

Maze is a user research platform that makes products work for people. Maze empowers companies to build the right products more quickly by making user insights available at the speed of product development. Built for ease of use, Maze allows researchers, designers, and product managers to collect and share user insights when they're needed most, putting them at the center of every decision.

We have around 100 employees, 35 of whom are spread over seven teams in engineering.

We are members of the Developer Experience team and part of the Platform department. Our primary responsibility is to maintain Maze's code repositories, developer tooling, and the continuous integration/continuous delivery (CI/CD) pipeline. By doing so, we aim to improve our developers' experience and productivity, ensuring that they have the necessary tools and resources to deliver high-quality products.

Adoption of Continuous Deployment at Maze

For years, we considered continuous deployment the holy grail, which we would achieve "someday." However, we never quite seemed able to prioritize the work needed to get there. The deployment pipeline worked well enough for our needs at the time.

The transition to continuous deployment was not without its challenges. The first cracks in our deployment pipeline started appearing when we moved our code into a monorepo while our team multiplied. Each release included increasingly more pull requests (PRs) and took more manual effort to prepare, test, and deploy. We struggled with this workflow for over a year. Eventually, we switched from a Gitflow workflow to a trunk-based git workflow. This new workflow followed continuous delivery, automatically preparing each commit to the trunk branch as a release. However, the last step was still manual: it was up to an individual developer to press the deployment button, once all build and test checks had passed, to deploy the release to production. Our release frequency increased significantly, from once or twice a week to a few times daily.

Continuous deployment was still our end goal; unfortunately, the next problem to solve seemed to be a greater obstacle because of the limitations of our CI/CD platform provider. However, the benefits of continuous deployment were too significant to ignore. One missing feature, in particular, was non-negotiable for continuous deployment to become a reality: we needed a sequential build and deployment queue for each releasable commit on our trunk branch. Therefore, we had to look at other CI/CD platforms. One RFC document and several proofs of concept later, we concluded that GitHub Actions was the way forward, as it promised everything we needed for continuous deployment. The following quarter, we completed the implementation and switched our monorepo deployments to the new GitHub Actions pipeline. We had finally achieved continuous deployment.

Overcoming Organizational Challenges

The biggest cultural obstacle to overcome in our move toward automated deployments was the need for more confidence in our tests. Those fears were not entirely unfounded; we needed better testing coverage in some parts of the product. We were also unsuccessful in dealing with flaky acceptance tests, the leading cause of instability in our deployment pipeline. As we scaled the company and the product, it became clear that manual testing was no longer feasible, forcing us to rely on automation. Only with time did our fears start to disappear. Our move to the trunk-based git workflow we mentioned earlier helped: more automatically tested deployments gave us the confidence we needed. However, people needed more time to be ready to rely on automated deployments. For that to happen, we needed to prove our deployment pipeline was stable before we could justify removing the manual trigger from our deployments.

As we committed to migrating to the new CI/CD platform, we recognized the need to involve the wider Engineering department in addressing the test coverage and stability issues. We worked together until the test coverage and stability were solid. This collaborative effort allowed us to implement continuous deployment on the new platform. We started with our two staging environments, parallel to the old pipeline still deploying to production, to confirm everything was working as intended. Once we were confident, we also switched deployments on for the production environment, keeping the old deployment pipeline "shadow-building" each commit as backup, just in case we needed to revert to it quickly.

As additional safeguards, we created CI workflows that anyone could trigger on demand. These workflows played a crucial role in creating peace of mind by providing a safety net in case of any issues. One of these workflows allows us to deploy any given commit to a single service, and another workflow makes it easy to roll the whole product back to a previous release, which is particularly useful during an incident.

Overcoming Technical Challenges

Our main technical difficulty was handling deployments with the many packages in our monorepo. We programmatically determine which packages have changed since the last release and only build and deploy those. This change detection works with dependencies too: if a shared library changes that multiple services depend on, we rebuild and deploy all those services. End-to-end tests are also tricky: we run the changed services locally in CI containers and create a mesh with other shared services in one of our staging environments. This meshed approach has some downsides, mainly because tests in other feature branches with active work in progress also use this staging environment. Ideally, we would spin up short-lived, isolated environments for every release, but that is a problem for another day.

Maze's Implementation of Continuous Deployment

We encourage developers to create small and incremental PRs, preferably stacking PRs on each other, to keep changes easily reviewable and reduce risk in deployments. One method we use to avoid large PRs is to use feature flags to merge unfinished features to production so that they can be tested internally and rolled out progressively to users.

In particular, engineers create a branch for every task they work on. Usually, an engineer opens a draft PR shortly after they push their branch to GitHub. Each commit starts the PR CI pipeline, which reports as "PR checks" on whether there are any issues: failing tests, static analysis errors, and so on. Once the PR author is confident about the changes, they move the PR status from "draft" to "open." Team members of the author and code owners for that package are then notified by GitHub and requested to review the PR.

When the PR has at least one approval and is passing PR checks, the author merges the PR, which gets placed in the merge queue. This merge queue ensures that no conflicting changes have merged to the trunk branch between the last CI run on the PR and the merge. This merge queue runs additional CI checks. It is possible to queue multiple PRs in the merge queue, which runs CI checks for each. After the merge queue CI checks have passed, GitHub squash-merges the PR to the trunk branch, which could be batched with up to five PRs in a single commit (assuming their checks have also passed). If one of the checks fails for a PR in the merge queue, the PR is rejected from the merge queue and resets to being "open," requiring additional review. GitHub then automatically rebases the other PRs in the merge queue so that they no longer have the rejected PR in their history and restarts the CI checks.

Every commit on the trunk branch triggers a new release in CI. A queue exists for these releases too, as only one release can run simultaneously. A release builds and deploys changed services to the staging environments first, where it runs acceptance tests. If they pass, it continues by deploying those services to production. At the start of a release, it acquires a lock that it only unlocks again after the release successfully deploys to production. This lock ensures that any engineer can manually restart the release if it fails. It also prevents new, queued releases from running if the current release is incomplete.

How Maze Makes Continuous Deployment Safe

We can safely deploy API changes by avoiding breaking changes in the same release. Instead, we mark API endpoints as deprecated and generate API schemas based on the existing endpoints. These generated schemas help detect breaking changes automatically and make changes to API endpoints more visible in PR reviews. After clients no longer use these deprecated API endpoints, a cleanup PR removes them.

Our test automation comprises unit, integration, and end-to-end tests run per package. We also have acceptance tests that span all services and test the product as a whole.

Unit tests are of the smallest form, testing single functions, classes, or frontend components. Integration tests encompass logic within a single domain, such as creating a user and verifying the data exists using an in-memory representation of our database or writing a comment and testing that the frontend application state has been updated. End-to-end tests are service endpoint tests from the perspective of other services communicating with that service. Acceptance tests are browser tests that test the product from a user's perspective.

For each PR commit, CI builds run the unit, integration, and end-to-end tests for each changed package. Acceptance tests are independent of changed packages, and CI always runs these tests for each PR commit to ensure maximum confidence.

The merge queue only runs unit and integration tests.

We deploy the changed services to our staging environments for a release and only run the acceptance tests. These must pass for the release to deploy the changed services to production.

In our deployment pipeline, we build and push all Docker artifacts to AWS ECR, reusing the same artifact for all environments according to the 12-factor app methodology. After that, we deploy to Kubernetes with ArgoCD using a rolling update strategy. Additionally, we use the Serverless framework to deploy AWS lambda functions, which are direct deployments.

We work with PRs, requiring at least one review to review all the changes. Pair and mob programming are encouraged, although this is optional, and some teams do these more than others.

We use Datadog to monitor our production services. We utilize synthetic monitoring, Datadog Watchdog, and APM/RUM error tracking to detect issues and declare incidents. Most importantly, all telemetry includes the deployed version. This version annotation allows us to correlate any problems with a specific release.

How Maze Supports Junior Engineers with Continuous Deployment

We have written documentation about our release process covering our continuous deployment process. This documentation is part of the onboarding materials all new engineers read. Continuous deployment allows engineers to focus on development instead of how our deployments work technically, because the deployment pipeline is entirely automated after merging the PR. Finally, our team is always available in Slack to answer all engineers' questions.

Case Study: TravelPerk

For our last case study, we will learn about continuous deployment in the context of a rapidly growing startup: TravelPerk. Javier Tejero (director of architecture) and Roberto Mosca (principal software engineer) will share details about TravelPerk's continuous deployment culture, which started early and grew alongside the company. Both of them work in the Foundations team, which is the team responsible for the overall platform and infrastructure of the company.

TravelPerk's Context

TravelPerk is a hyper-growth business travel management platform. The platform aims to innovate business travel with an end-to-end solution that gives travelers freedom while providing their companies with more control. The company is headquartered in Barcelona, with business hubs in London; Birmingham, England; Edinburgh; Berlin; Chicago; Boston; and Miami.

TravelPerk today is valued at over $1.4 billion, following a recent additional $104 million raised through a D1 extension investment round in January 2024, backed by new investor SoftBank Vision Fund 2 and existing investors Kinnevik and Felix Capital. With this funding infusion, TravelPerk will increase investment into its platform, enhancing the customer experience through new inventory capabilities and launching new business travel services, as well as expanding product automation through AI.

The company has around 1,200 employees, including over 350 of what we call "builders," incorporating roles such as engineering, product, data design, and security.

TravelPerk customers access the core business offering through three client apps: a web application, and mobile apps for iOS and Android. These client apps are powered by a constellation of backend services, including the main monolith and a few dozen microservices. All these services process millions of requests a day. In our engineering department, we have a strong sense of ownership, which is summarized by the motto "You build it, you own it." Each squad owns and runs its own services and applications. For the two monoliths that we have, frontend and backend, ownership is split between the different teams, and we make sure every line of code is owned by someone. This means that each team is responsible for the deployment of its own services/apps. The team takes care of its own infrastructure and the health of the continuous integration/continuous delivery (CI/CD) pipelines it owns.

Adoption of Continuous Deployment at TravelPerk

In the early stages of our startup, circa 2017, we made the strategic decision to implement continuous deployment to our production environment as we transitioned from Heroku to AWS. This pivotal move was guided by our desire to significantly enhance our adaptability and responsiveness to changes, and to foster a culture of rapid innovation. We believe that many players at that time were captivated by the "Move fast and break things" philosophy, which underscored the importance of speed and flexibility in the development processes. To ensure a seamless and safe transition to continuous deployment, we invested heavily in automated testing.

During the switch to continuous deployment, we didn't find strong organizational barriers. The CTO and the VP were behind the decisions and pushed for us to move to AWS and adopt it. At the time, we were a small team of engineers with no dedicated QA department. It was just natural that every feature we implemented would be covered by automated tests and also thoroughly manually tested before deployment to production. Direct automatic deployment on merge to the main branch was a natural choice in that environment, and adopting it so early allowed us to evolve our continuous deployment practices organically as we grew.

Ensuring the platform's reliability and stability was our priority when making the switch to continuous deployment. To prevent deployed changes from disrupting the application's functionality, it was essential to test these changes comprehensively and neutrally within the pipeline. With an extensive suite of unit and integration tests already in place, we opted to integrate end-to-end (E2E) tests to safeguard critical user workflows. Consequently, we developed a series of E2E tests designed to provide optimal coverage of the application's features.

TravelPerk's Implementation of Continuous Deployment

The granularity of the work required to implement a new feature strongly depends on the size of the task. Sometimes it only takes a commit, and sometimes development can last for a longer period and amount to dozens of pull requests (PRs). In the latter case, work in progress is hidden behind feature flags or other types of switches that we can enable per user or per account/company. We have a flexible feature flag implementation that allows us to enable a feature flag for individual users, groups of users, a specific percentage of users, or entire companies (users belong to companies or accounts). For each PR that is merged, our path to production is triggered end to end.

The path to production for each increment has changed over time, and it depends on the size of the project on which the developer is working.

Smaller projects/repositories reflect the way we have been implementing continuous deployment since the beginning. The developer commits a change to a branch in Git-Hub and opens a PR. The PR will be reviewed by peers within the developer's squad, and from other squads (depending on the type of expertise required to properly review the code). Opening the PR and updating the branch triggers a CI pipeline that usually runs the build step (to make sure the code can be built), several checks (e.g., linting, type checking, dependency checking, format checking, security checking), and all automated unit tests. Once the PR is approved and the corresponding CI build is green, the developer can merge the PR to main. Merging to main triggers the CD pipeline, which usually reruns all the checks run in the PR plus the deployment steps to all our environments in parallel: nonproduction and production alike (we have several production and nonproduction environments that are always deployed to at the same time, so they all run the same code). Once the deployment step has been completed, the change will be visible in all our environments, including production, of course.

However, we also have projects where continuous deployment is not suitable, such as our monoliths. There, the volume of PRs merged to the main branch is significantly higher, and running the CD pipeline for every commit can be problematic. In those cases, the process is more complex and involves a merge queue, to make sure the change is safe when combined with other PRs, and a scheduled deployment process that runs every 20 minutes and deploys all changes merged since the last successful deployment. Each merge to the main branch triggers a build that produces a deployment artifact. The scheduled deployment process checks for the most recent artifact and deploys it to our environments.

We make our artifacts immutable and customize each environment through configuration. For our web application, we are also in the process of creating a release manager that provides better observability on all deployments and allows for quick automatic rollback of failed deployments.

How TravelPerk Makes Continuous Deployment Safe

Within TravelPerk, we use a number of techniques to guarantee no regressions with continuous deployment, such as feature flags, API versioning, the expand and contract pattern, and observability.

Hiding with work in progress

Feature flags allow us to test features internally and with smaller groups of users before they are released more broadly. We use API versioning in case of breaking changes, but we prefer to implement changes in a backward-compatible way by replacing or making fields redundant before we remove them.

Code reviews

Code review is done through PR reviews with a set of review policies. All files in all repositories are attributed to the squad that owns them, thanks to a CODEOWNERS file. When a PR changes a file owned by a certain squad, we recommend getting reviews from that squad. In some repositories and for sensitive changes (e.g., payments domain), we enforce reviews by the owners of the file. For the rest, we invest in maintaining a culture of engineering excellence, promoting best practices through automated linting and static analysis of code, and offering continuous training in our engineering department around every sort of technical topic. We have extensive internal documentation on guidelines and best practices that we adopt, and we run guilds to share knowledge and continuously review our practices.

Automated tests

We use several levels of testing: unit tests, integration tests, E2E tests, and contract tests. On our design system project, we also have visual regression tests. Since our migration to micro frontends, we have introduced integration testing, which checks the interoperability of changes in a micro frontend with all the other micro frontends. These tests use stubbing of backend requests to make them faster and more stable and contract tests to ensure the reliability of the stubs used in the tests.

On top of that, we also run security analysis on the code to ensure its safety. All tests are executed in our CI/CD pipelines at different levels: unit and integration tests are always run (in PRs and after merging to the main branch). Other, more expensive tests, such as E2E tests, are only run in the merge queue before merging to the main branch. Synthetic tests are implemented in AWS CloudWatch and run directly against our production environment.

Zero downtime

For backend services, we deploy most of the code to ECS, which has a blue/green deployment to guarantee zero downtime. We have some mechanisms in place to ensure that the database layer is compatible with the latest code release, and we only perform database migrations that are backward compatible (e.g., destructive operations might be applied once the running code does not depend on them). We also apply continuous deployment to services running on AWS Lambda.

Our frontend assets are deployed on S3 and distributed through our CDN. There, we use versioning to keep track of the current release and allow for quick rollback. We are in the process of creating a release management system that would allow canary releases of our frontend assets, better observability of our deployments, and automated rollback of problematic releases, thanks to the integration with our synthetic tests.

Observability

Despite all of this, there is the occasional possibility that a regression ends up in the production environment. In that case, we rely on a comprehensive set of monitors, which allow us to detect problems in production as soon as possible. We also rely on synthetic tests in AWS CloudWatch running every minute for early problem detection.

Observability is key to our strategy, and we strive to create effective, actionable metrics throughout the platform.

We have more than 1,000 monitors covering known and unexpected sources of errors, such as HTTP errors, slow endpoints, slow queries, queue congestion, and database resources, connected to our incident management process to ensure prompt intervention and recovery. We have been investing in response times through the monitoring of service-level objectives (SLOs) at several levels, from low-level response time of single endpoints to high-level metrics on user workflows. This allows us to receive quick feedback when a change leads to a degradation in the performance of an endpoint or the execution of a workflow and the possibility of a quick intervention to fix it. As we mentioned before, we also use synthetic tests on our production environment to quickly identify and solve problems that made their way to production.

How TravelPerk Onboards Engineers to Continuous Deployment

Our engineering onboarding process ensures that our developers can start contributing code in a matter of days. As such, developers can very quickly see their contribution go live in our production environment.

Continuous deployment is such an integral part of our engineering culture that it is treated as a default. New joiners are supported by their assigned engineer buddies and team members in adopting our deployment practices with confidence. At the same time, we make sure that guidelines and guardrails are in place to confidently embrace such practices and act as owners for any code/feature a developer contributes.

Index

About the Author

Valentina Servile is lead software developer at Thoughtworks based in Bangkok, working with and advising multiple clients on continuous deployment in distributed systems. She has worked in several cross-functional teams dealing with big distributed systems and microservices, continuous delivery practices, and evolutionary architectures in a variety of tech stacks.

As well as writing code, she enjoys mentoring her colleagues and helping Thoughtworks advise their clients on how to improve their software delivery practices in order to release safely and often—and enable their businesses to respond to change.

Colophon

The animal on the cover of *Continuous Deployment* is a northern fulmar (*Fulmarus glacialis*), also known as an Arctic fulmar. It is a seabird native to the subarctic regions of the northern Pacific and Atlantic Oceans. Though superficially similar to gulls, they are in fact more closely related to petrels and albatrosses. Northern fulmars vary in color from mostly white with gray wings to uniformly gray. They have hooked beaks with two nasal tubes along the top edge.

Northern fulmars have a wingspan of up to 44 inches and can reach 18 inches in length. They are long-lived birds, regularly reaching up to 30 years in the wild, and they typically do not begin breeding until they are 8 to 10 years old. Northern fulmars are opportunistic feeders, eating a variety of marine life as well as carrion and refuse, and they can dive up to 10 feet underwater to catch fish. They have been known to travel up to 600 miles round trip to find food for their young. As a defense against intruders or predators, northern fulmars can spit a foul-smelling oil from their stomachs for several yards.

The northern fulmar is considered a species of least concern. Many of the animals on O'Reilly covers are endangered; all of them are important to the world.

The cover illustration is by Karen Montgomery, based on an antique line engraving from *Animate Creation*. The series design is by Edie Freedman, Ellie Volckhausen, and Karen Montgomery. The cover fonts are Gilroy Semibold and Guardian Sans. The text font is Adobe Minion Pro; the heading font is Adobe Myriad Condensed; and the code font is Dalton Maag's Ubuntu Mono.

O'REILLY®

Learn from experts.
Become one yourself.

Books | Live online courses
Instant answers | Virtual events
Videos | Interactive learning

Get started at oreilly.com.

Milton Keynes UK
Ingram Content Group UK Ltd.
UKHW011501030924
447785UK00002B/9